THE GOLDEN BOUGH

A STUDY IN MAGIC AND RELIGION

THIRD EDITION

PART VII

BALDER THE BEAUTIFUL

VOL. I

MACMILLAN AND CO., Limited
LONDON · BOMBAY · CALCUTTA · MADRAS
MELBOURNE

THE MACMILLAN COMPANY
NEW YORK · BOSTON · CHICAGO
DALLAS · ATLANTA · SAN FRANCISCO

THE MACMILLAN COMPANY
OF CANADA, LIMITED
TORONTO

BALDER
THE BEAUTIFUL

THE FIRE-FESTIVALS OF EUROPE
AND THE DOCTRINE OF THE EXTERNAL SOUL

BY

Sir JAMES GEORGE FRAZER

Hon. D.C.L., Oxford; Hon. LL.D., Glasgow;
Hon. Litt.D., Durham;
Fellow of Trinity College, Cambridge.

IN TWO VOLUMES

VOL. I

NEW YORK
THE MACMILLAN COMPANY
1935

COPYRIGHT

PREFACE

In this concluding part of *The Golden Bough* I have discussed the problem which gives its title to the whole work. If I am right, the Golden Bough over which the King of the Wood, Diana's priest at Aricia, kept watch and ward was no other than a branch of mistletoe growing on an oak within the sacred grove; and as the plucking of the bough was a necessary prelude to the slaughter of the priest, I have been led to institute a parallel between the King of the Wood at Nemi and the Norse god Balder, who was worshipped in a sacred grove beside the beautiful Sogne fiord of Norway and was said to have perished by a stroke of mistletoe, which alone of all things on earth or in heaven could wound him. On the theory here suggested both Balder and the King of the Wood personified in a sense the sacred oak of our Aryan forefathers, and both had deposited their lives or souls for safety in the parasite which sometimes, though rarely, is found growing on an oak and by the very rarity of its appearance excites the wonder and stimulates the devotion of ignorant men. Though I am now less than ever disposed to lay weight on the analogy between the Italian priest and the Norse god, I have allowed it to stand because it furnishes me with a pretext for discussing not only the general question of the external soul in popular superstition, but also the fire-festivals of Europe, since fire played a part both in the myth of Balder and in the ritual of the Arician grove. Thus Balder the

v

Beautiful in my hands is little more than a stalking-horse to carry two heavy pack-loads of facts. And what is true of Balder applies equally to the priest of Nemi himself, the nominal hero of the long tragedy of human folly and suffering which has unrolled itself before the readers of these volumes, and on which the curtain is now about to fall. He, too, for all the quaint garb he wears and the gravity with which he stalks across the stage, is merely a puppet, and it is time to unmask him before laying him up in the box.

To drop metaphor, while nominally investigating a particular problem of ancient mythology, I have really been discussing questions of more general interest which concern the gradual evolution of human thought from savagery to civilization. The enquiry is beset with diffi-culties of many kinds, for the record of man's mental development is even more imperfect than the record of his physical development, and it is harder to read, not only by reason of the incomparably more subtle and complex nature of the subject, but because the reader's eyes are apt to be dimmed by thick mists of passion and prejudice, which cloud in a far less degree the fields of comparative anatomy and geology. My contribution to the history of the human mind consists of little more than a rough and purely pro-visional classification of facts gathered almost entirely from printed sources. If there is one general conclusion which seems to emerge from the mass of particulars, I venture to think that it is the essential similarity in the working of the less developed human mind among all races, which corre-sponds to the essential similarity in their bodily frame revealed by comparative anatomy. But while this general mental similarity may, I believe, be taken as established, we must always be on our guard against tracing to it a multi-tude of particular resemblances which may be and often are due to simple diffusion, since nothing is more certain than that the various races of men have borrowed from each other many of their arts and crafts, their ideas, customs, and institutions. To sift out the elements of culture which a race has independently evolved and to distinguish them accurately from those which it has derived from other races is a task of extreme difficulty and delicacy, which promises to occupy students of man for a long time to come ; indeed so complex are the facts and so imperfect in most cases is the historical record that it may be doubted whether in regard to many of the lower races we shall ever arrive at more than probable conjectures.

Since the last edition of *The Golden Bough* was published some thirteen years ago, I have seen reason to change my views on several matters discussed in this concluding part of the work, and though I have called attention to these changes in the text, it may be well for the sake of clearness to recapitulate them here.

In the first place, the arguments of Dr. Edward Westermarck have satisfied me that the solar theory of the European fire-festivals, which I accepted from W. Mannhardt, is very slightly, if at all, supported by the evidence and is probably erroneous. The true explanation of the festivals I now believe to be the one advocated by Dr. Westermarck himself, namely that they are purificatory in intention, the fire being designed not, as I formerly held, to reinforce the sun's light and heat by sympathetic magic, but merely to burn or repel the noxious things, whether conceived as material or spiritual, which threaten the life of man, of animals, and of plants. This aspect of the fire-festivals had not wholly escaped me in former editions ; I pointed it out explicitly, but, biassed perhaps by the great authority of Mannhardt, I treated it as secondary and subordinate instead of primary and dominant. Out of deference to Mannhardt, for whose work I entertain the highest respect, and because the evidence for the purificatory theory of the fires is perhaps not quite conclusive, I have in this edition repeated and even reinforced the arguments for the solar theory of the festivals, so that the reader may see for himself what can be said on both sides of the question and may draw his own conclusion ; but for my part I cannot but think that the arguments for the purificatory theory far outweigh the arguments for the solar theory. Dr. Westermarck based his criticisms largely on his own observations of the Moham-medan fire-festivals of Morocco, which present a remarkable resemblance to those of Christian Europe, though there seems no reason to assume that herein Africa has borrowed from Europe or Europe from Africa. So far as Europe is concerned, the evidence tends strongly to shew that the grand evil which the festivals aimed at combating was witchcraft, and that they were conceived to attain their end by actually burning the witches, whether visible or invisible, in the flames. If that was so, the wide prevalence and the immense popularity of the fire-festivals provides us with a measure for estimating the extent of the hold which the belief in witchcraft had on the European mind before the rise of Christianity or rather of rationalism ; for Christianity, both Catholic and Protestant, accepted the old belief and enforced it in the old way by the faggot and the stake. It was not until human reason at last awoke after the long slumber of the Middle Ages that this dreadful obsession gradually passed away like a dark cloud from the intel-lectual horizon of Europe.

Yet we should deceive ourselves if we imagined that the belief in witchcraft is even now dead in the mass of the people ; on the contrary there is ample evidence to shew that it only hibernates under the chilling influence of rationalism, and that it would start into active life if that influence were ever seriously relaxed. The truth seems to be that to this day the peasant remains a pagan and savage at heart ; his civilization is merely a thin veneer which the hard knocks of life soon abrade, exposing the solid core of paganism and savagery below. The danger created by a bottomless layer of ignorance and superstition under the crust of civilized society is lessened, not only by the natural torpidity and inertia of the bucolic mind, but also by the progressive decrease of the rural as compared with the urban population in modern states ; for I believe it will be found that the artisans who congregate in towns are far less retentive of primitive modes of thought than their rustic brethren. In every age cities have been the centres and as it were the lighthouses from which ideas radiate into the surrounding darkness, kindled by the friction of mind with mind in the crowded haunts of men ; and it is natural that at these beacons of intellectual light all should partake in some measure of the general illumination. No doubt the mental ferment and unrest of great cities have their dark as well as their bright side ; but among the evils to be apprehended from them the chances of a pagan revival need hardly be reckoned.

Another point on which I have changed my mind is the nature of the great Aryan god whom the Romans called Jupiter and the Greeks Zeus. Whereas I formerly argued that he was primarily a personification of the sacred oak and only in the second place a personification of the thundering sky, I now invert the order of his divine functions and believe that he was a sky-god before he came to be associated with the oak. In fact, I revert to the traditional view of Jupiter, recant my heresy, and am gathered like a lost sheep into the fold of mythological orthodoxy. The good shepherd who has brought me back is my friend Mr. W. Warde Fowler. He has removed the stone over which I stumbled in the wilderness by explaining in a simple and natural way how a god of the thundering sky might easily come to be afterwards associated with the oak. The explanation turns on the great frequency with which, as statistics prove, the oak is struck by lightning beyond any other tree of the wood in Europe. To our rude forefathers, who dwelt in the gloomy depths of the primaeval forest, it might well seem that the riven and blackened oaks must indeed be favourites of the sky-god, who so often descended on them from the murky cloud in a flash of lightning and a crash of thunder.

This change of view as to the great Aryan god necessarily affects my interpretation of the King of the Wood, the priest of Diana at Aricia, if I may take that discarded puppet out of the box again for a moment. On my theory the priest represented Jupiter in the flesh, and accordingly, if Jupiter was primarily a sky-god, his priest cannot have been a mere incarnation of the sacred oak, but must, like the deity whose commission he bore, have been invested in the imagination of his worshippers with the power of overcasting the heaven with clouds and eliciting storms of thunder and rain from the celestial vault. The attribution of weather-making powers to kings or priests is very common in primitive society, and is indeed one of the principal levers by which such personages raise themselves to a position of superiority above their fellows. There is therefore no improbability in the supposition that as a representative of Jupiter the priest of Diana enjoyed this reputation, though positive evidence of it appears to be lacking.

Lastly, in the present edition I have shewn some grounds for thinking that the Golden Bough itself, or in common parlance the mistletoe on the oak, was supposed to have dropped from the sky upon the tree in a flash of lightning and therefore to contain within itself the seed of celestial fire, a sort of smouldering thunderbolt. This view of the priest and of the bough which he guarded at the peril of his life has the advantage of accounting for the importance which the sanctuary at Nemi acquired and the treasure which it amassed through the offerings of the faithful; for the shrine would seem to have been to ancient what Loreto has been to modern Italy, a place of pilgrimage, where princes and nobles as well as commoners poured wealth into the coffers of Diana in her green recess among the Alban hills, just as in modern times kings and queens vied with each other in enriching the black Virgin who from her Holy House on the hillside at Loreto looks out on the blue Adriatic and the purple Apennines. Such pious prodigality becomes more intelligible if the greatest of the gods was indeed believed to dwell in human shape with his wife among the woods of Nemi.

These are the principal points on which I have altered my opinion since the last edition of my book was published. The mere admission of such changes may suffice to indicate the doubt and uncertainty which attend enquiries of this nature. The whole fabric of ancient mythology is so foreign to our modern ways of thought, and the evidence concerning it is for the most part so fragmentary, obscure, and conflicting that in our attempts to piece together and interpret it we can hardly hope to reach conclusions that will completely satisfy either ourselves or others. In this as in other branches of study it is the fate of theories to be washed away like children's castles of sand by the rising tide of knowledge, and I am not so presumptuous as to expect or desire for mine an exemption from the common lot. I hold them all very lightly and have used them chiefly as convenient pegs on which to hang my collections of facts. For I believe that, while theories are transitory, a record of facts has a permanent value, and that as a chronicle of ancient customs and beliefs my book may retain its utility when my theories are as obsolete as the customs and beliefs themselves deserve to be.

I cannot dismiss without some natural regret a task which has occupied and amused me at intervals for many years. But the regret is tempered by thankfulness and hope. I am thankful that I have been able to conclude at least one chapter of the work I projected a long time ago. I am hopeful that I may not now be taking a final leave of my indulgent readers, but that, as I am sensible of little abatement in my bodily strength and of none in my ardour for study, they will bear with me yet a while if I should attempt to entertain them with fresh subjects of laughter and tears drawn from the comedy and the tragedy of man's endless quest after happiness and truth.

J. G. FRAZER.

CAMBRIDGE, *17th October* 1913.

CONTENTS

Chapter V.—The Interpretation of the Fire-Festivals . . . Pp. 328-346

CHAPTER I

BETWEEN HEAVEN AND EARTH

§ 1. *Not to touch the Earth*

WE have travelled far since we turned our backs on Nemi and set forth in quest of the secret of the Golden Bough. With the present volume we enter on the last stage of our long journey. The reader who has had the patience to follow the enquiry thus far may remember that at the outset two questions were proposed for answer : Why had the priest of Aricia to slay his predecessor ? And why, before doing so, had he to pluck the Golden Bough ?[1] Of these two questions the first has now been answered. The priest of Aricia, if I am right, was one of those sacred kings or human divinities on whose life the welfare of the community and even the course of nature in general are believed to be intimately dependent. It does not appear that the subjects or worshippers of such a spiritual potentate form to themselves any very clear notion of the exact relationship in which they stand to him ; probably their ideas on the point are vague and fluctuating, and we should err if we attempted to define the relationship with logical precision. All that the people know, or rather imagine, is that somehow they themselves, their cattle, and their crops are mysteriously bound up with their divine king, so that according as he is well or ill the community is healthy or sickly, the flocks and herds thrive or languish with disease, and the fields yield an abundant or a scanty harvest. The worst evil which they can conceive of is the natural death of their ruler, whether he succumb to

The priest of Aricia and the Golden Bough.

[1] *The Magic Art and the Evolution of Kings,* i. 44.

sickness or old age, for in the opinion of his followers such a death would entail the most disastrous consequences on themselves and their possessions ; fatal epidemics would sweep away man and beast, the earth would refuse her increase, nay the very frame of nature itself might be dissolved.   To guard against these catastrophes it is necessary to put the king to death while he is still in the full bloom of his divine manhood, in order that his sacred life, transmitted in unabated force to his successor, may renew its youth, and thus by successive transmissions through a perpetual line of vigorous incarnations may remain eternally fresh and young, a pledge and security that men and animals shall in like manner renew their youth by a perpetual succession of generations, and that seedtime and harvest, and summer and winter, and rain and sunshine shall never fail.   That, if my conjecture is right, was why the priest of Aricia, the King of the Wood at Nemi, had regularly to perish by the sword of his successor.

What was the Golden Bough ?   But we have still to ask, What was the Golden Bough ? and why had each candidate for the Arician priesthood to pluck it before he could slay the priest ?   These questions I will now try to answer.

Sacred kings and priests forbidden to touch the ground with their feet.   It will be well to begin by noticing two of those rules or taboos by which, as we have seen, the life of divine kings or priests is regulated.   The first of the rules to which I desire to call the reader's attention is that the divine personage may not touch the ground with his foot.   This rule was observed by the supreme pontiff of the Zapotecs in Mexico ; he profaned his sanctity if he so much as touched the ground with his foot.[1]   Montezuma, emperor of Mexico, never set foot on the ground ; he was always carried on the shoulders of noblemen, and if he lighted anywhere they laid rich tapestry for him to walk upon.[2]   For the Mikado of Japan to touch the ground with his foot was a shameful

---

[1] H. H. Bancroft, *Native Races of the Pacific States* (London, 1875–1876), ii. 142 ; Brasseur de Bourbourg, *Histoire des Nations civilisées du Mexique et de l'Amérique-Centrale* (Paris, 1857–1859), iii. 29.

[2] *Manuscrit Ramirez, Histoire de*

l'origine des Indiens, publié par D. Charnay (Paris, 1903), p. 108 ; J. de Acosta, *The Natural and Moral History of the Indies,* bk. vii. chap. 22, vol. ii. p. 505 of E. Grimston's translation, edited by (Sir) Clements R. Markham (Hakluyt Society, London, 1880).

degradation ; indeed, in the sixteenth century, it was
enough to deprive him of his office.   Outside his palace he
was carried on men's shoulders ; within it he walked on
exquisitely wrought mats.[1]   The king and queen of Tahiti
might not touch the ground anywhere but within their
hereditary domains ; for the ground on which they trod
became sacred.   In travelling from place to place they were
carried on the shoulders of sacred men.   They were always
accompanied by several pairs of these sanctified attendants ;
and when it became necessary to change their bearers, the
king and queen vaulted on to the shoulders of their new
bearers without letting their feet touch the ground.[2]   It was
an evil omen if the king of Dosuma touched the ground,
and he had to perform an expiatory ceremony.[3]   Within
his palace the king of Persia walked on carpets on which
no one else might tread ; outside of it he was never seen on
foot but only in a chariot or on horseback.[4]   In old days
the king of Siam never set foot upon the earth, but was
carried on a throne of gold from place to place.[5]   Formerly
neither the kings of Uganda, nor their mothers, nor their
queens might walk on foot outside of the spacious enclosures
in which they lived.   Whenever they went forth they were
carried on the shoulders of men of the Buffalo clan, several
of whom accompanied any of these royal personages on a
journey and took it in turn to bear the burden.   The king
sat astride the bearer's neck with a leg over each shoulder
and his feet tucked under the bearer's arms.   When one of
these royal carriers grew tired he shot the king on to the
shoulders of a second man without allowing the royal feet
to touch the ground.   In this way they went at a great
pace and travelled long distances in a day, when the king
was on a journey.   The bearers had a special hut in the

[1] *Memorials of the Empire of Japon
in the XVI. and XVII. Centuries,*
edited by T. Rundall (Hakluyt Society,
London, 1850), pp. 14, 141 ; B.
Varenius, *Descriptio regni Japoniae
et Siam* (Cambridge, 1673), p. 11 ;
Caron, "Account of Japan," in John
Pinkerton's *Voyages and Travels*
(London, 1808–1814), vii. 613 ;
Kaempfer, "History of Japan," in
id. vii. 716.

[2] W. Ellis, *Polynesian Researches,*
Second Edition (London, 1832–1836),
iii. 102 *sq.* ; Captain James Wilson,
*Missionary Voyage to the Southern
Pacific Ocean* (London, 1799), p. 329.

[3] A. Bastian, *Der Mensch in der
Geschichte* (Leipsic, 1860), iii. 81.

[4] Athenaeus, xii. 8, p. 514 C.

[5] *The Voiages and Travels of John
Struys* (London, 1684), p. 30.

king's enclosure in order to be at hand the moment they were wanted.[1]   Among the Bakuba or rather Bushongo, a nation in the southern region of the Congo, down to a few years ago persons of the royal blood were forbidden to touch the ground ; they must sit on a hide, a chair, or the back of a slave, who crouched on hands and feet ; their feet rested on the feet of others.   When they travelled they were carried on the backs of men ; but the king journeyed in a litter supported on shafts.[2]   Among the Ibo people about Awka, in Southern Nigeria, the priest of the Earth has to observe many taboos ; for example, he may not see a corpse, and if he meets one on the road he must hide his eyes with his wristlet.   He must abstain from many foods, such as eggs, birds of all sorts, mutton, dog, bush-buck, and so forth.   He may neither wear nor touch a mask, and no masked man may enter his house.   If a dog enters his house, it is killed and thrown out.   As priest of the Earth he may not sit on the bare ground, nor eat things that have fallen on the ground, nor may earth be thrown at him.[3] According to ancient Brahmanic ritual a king at his in-auguration trod on a tiger's skin and a golden plate ; he was shod with shoes of boar's skin, and so long as he lived thereafter he might not stand on the earth with his bare feet.[4]

Certain persons on certain occasions forbidden to touch the ground with their feet.

But besides persons who are permanently sacred or tabooed and are therefore permanently forbidden to touch the ground with their feet, there are others who enjoy the character of sanctity or taboo only on certain occasions, and to whom accordingly the prohibition in question only applies at the definite seasons during which they exhale the odour of sanctity.   Thus among the Kayans or Bahaus of Central

---

[1] Rev. J. Roscoe, " Further Notes on the Manners and Customs of the Baganda," *Journal of the Anthropological Institute*, xxxii. (1902) pp. 62, 67 ; *id.*, *The Baganda* (London, 1911), pp. 154 *sq.*   Compare L. Decle, *Three Years in Savage Africa* (London, 1898), p. 445 note : " Before horses had been introduced into Uganda the king and his mother never walked, but always went about perched astride the shoulders of a slave—a most ludicrous sight.   In this way they often travelled hundreds of miles."   The use both of horses and of chariots by royal personages may often have been intended to prevent their sacred feet from touching the ground.

[2] E. Torday et T. A. Joyce, *Les Bushongo* (Brussels, 1910), p. 61.

[3] Northcote W. Thomas, *Anthropological Report on the Ibo-speaking Peoples of Nigeria* (London, 1913), i. 57 *sq.*

[4] *Satapatha Brâhmana*, translated by Julius Eggeling, Part iii. (Oxford, 1894) pp. 81, 91, 92, 102, 128 *sq.* (*Sacred Books of the East*, vol. xli.).

Borneo, while the priestesses are engaged in the performance
of certain rites they may not step on the ground, and boards
are laid for them to tread on.[1]   At a funeral ceremony
observed by night among the Michemis, a Tibetan tribe
near the northern frontier of Assam, a priest fantastically
bedecked with tiger's teeth, many-coloured plumes, bells, and
shells, executed a wild dance for the purpose of exorcising
the evil spirits ; then all fires were extinguished and a new
light was struck by a man suspended by his feet from a
beam in the ceiling ; " he did not touch the ground," we are
told, " in order to indicate that the light came from heaven."[2]
Again, newly born infants are strongly tabooed ; accordingly
in Loango they are not allowed to touch the earth.[3]   Among
the Iluvans of Malabar the bridegroom on his wedding-day
is bathed by seven young men and then carried or walks
on planks from the bathing-place to the marriage booth ; he
may not touch the ground with his feet.[4]   With the Dyaks
of Landak and Tajan, two districts of Dutch Borneo, it is a
custom that for a certain time after marriage neither bride
nor bridegroom may tread on the earth.[5]   Warriors, again,
on the war-path are surrounded, so to say, by an atmosphere
of taboo ; hence some Indians of North America might not
sit on the bare ground the whole time they were out on a
warlike expedition.[6]   In Laos the hunting of elephants
gives rise to many taboos ; one of them is that the chief
hunter may not touch the earth with his foot.   Accordingly,
when he alights from his elephant, the others spread a
carpet of leaves for him to step upon.[7]   German wiseacres
recommended that when witches were led to the block or
the stake, they should not be allowed to touch the bare

---

[1] A. W. Nieuwenhuis, *Quer durch
Borneo* (Leyden, 1904–1907), i. 172.

[2] Letter of Missionary Krick, in
Annales de la Propagation de la Foi,
xxvi. (1854) pp. 86-88.

[3] Pechuel-Loesche, "Indiscretes aus
Loango," *Zeitschrift für Ethnologie*,
x. (1878) pp. 29 *sq.*

[4] Edgar Thurston, *Ethnographic
Notes in Southern India* (Madras,
1906), p. 70.

[5] M. C. Schadee, " Het familieleven
en familierecht der Dajaks van Landak

en Tajan," *Bijdragen tot de Taal-
Land- en Volkenkunde van Nederlandsch-Indië*, lxiii. (1910) p. 433.

[6] James Adair, *History of the
American Indians* (London, 1775),
p. 382 ; *Narrative of the Captivity
and Adventures of John Tanner*
(London, 1830), p. 123.   As to the
taboos to which warriors are subject
see *Taboo and the Perils of the Soul*,
pp. 157 *sqq.*

[7] Étienne Aymonier, *Notes sur le
Laos* (Saigon, 1885). p. 26.

earth, and a reason suggested for the rule was that if they touched the earth they might make themselves invisible and so escape. The sagacious author of *The Striped-petticoat Philosophy* in the eighteenth century ridicules the idea as mere silly talk. He admits, indeed, that the women were conveyed to the place of execution in carts ; but he denies that there is any deep significance in the cart, and he is prepared to maintain this view by a chemical analysis of the timber of which the cart was built. To clinch his argument he appeals to plain matter of fact and his own personal experience. Not a single instance, he assures us with apparent satisfaction, can be produced of a witch who escaped the axe or the fire in this fashion. " I have myself," says he, " in my youth seen divers witches burned, some at Arnstadt, some at Ilmenau, some at Schwenda, a noble village between Arnstadt and Ilmenau, and some of them were pardoned and beheaded before being burned. They were laid on the earth in the place of execution and beheaded like any other poor sinner ; whereas if they could have escaped by touching the earth, not one of them would have failed to do so." [1]

Sacred or tabooed persons apparently thought to be charged with a mysterious virtue like a fluid, which will run to waste or explode if it touches the ground.

Apparently holiness, magical virtue, taboo, or whatever we may call that mysterious quality which is supposed to pervade sacred or tabooed persons, is conceived by the primitive philosopher as a physical substance or fluid, with which the sacred man is charged just as a Leyden jar is charged with electricity ; and exactly as the electricity in the jar can be discharged by contact with a good conductor, so the holiness or magical virtue in the man can be discharged and drained away by contact with the earth, which on this theory serves as an excellent conductor for the magical fluid. Hence in order to preserve the charge from running to waste, the sacred or tabooed personage must be carefully prevented from touching the ground ; in electrical language he must be insulated, if he is not to be emptied of the precious substance or fluid with which he, as a vial, is filled to the brim. And in many cases apparently the insulation of the tabooed person is recommended as a precaution not merely for his own sake but for the sake of others ; for

[1] *Die gestriegelte Rockenphilosophie*[5] (Chemnitz, 1759), pp. 586 *sqq.*

since the virtue of holiness or taboo is, so to say, a powerful explosive which the smallest touch may detonate, it is necessary in the interest of the general safety to keep it within narrow bounds, lest breaking out it should blast, blight, and destroy whatever it comes into contact with.

But things as well as persons are often charged with the mysterious quality of holiness or taboo ; hence it frequently becomes necessary for similar reasons to guard them also from coming into contact with the ground, lest they should in like manner be drained of their valuable properties and be reduced to mere commonplace material objects, empty husks from which the good grain has been eliminated. Thus, for example, the most sacred object of the Arunta tribe in Central Australia is, or rather used to be, a pole about twenty feet high, which is completely smeared with human blood, crowned with an imitation of a human head, and set up on the ground where the final initiatory ceremonies of young men are performed. A young gum-tree is chosen to form the pole, and it must be cut down and transported in such a way that it does not touch the earth till it is erected in its place on the holy ground. Apparently the pole represents some famous ancestor of the olden time.[1]

Things as well as persons can be charged with the mysterious quality of holiness or taboo; and when so charged they must be kept from contact with the ground.

Again, at a great dancing festival celebrated by the natives of Bartle Bay, in British New Guinea, a wild mango tree plays a prominent part. The tree must be self-sown, that is, really wild and so young that it has never flowered. It is chosen in the jungle some five or six weeks before the festival, and a circle is cleared round its trunk. From that time the master of the ceremonies and some eight to twenty other men, who have aided him in choosing the tree and in clearing the jungle, become strictly holy or tabooed. They sleep by themselves in a house into which no one else may intrude : they may not wash or drink water, nor even allow it accidentally to touch their bodies : they are forbidden to eat boiled food and the fruit of mango trees : they may drink only the milk of a young coco-nut which has been baked, and they may eat certain fruits and vegetables, such as paw-

Festival of the wild mango tree in British New Guinea.

---

[1] Baldwin Spencer and F. J. Gillen, *Native Tribes of Central Australia* (London, 1899), pp. 364, 370 *sqq.*, 629 ; *id., Across Australia* (London, 1912), ii. 280, 285 *sq.*

paws (*Carica papaya*) and sugar-cane, but only on condition that they have been baked.   All refuse of their food is kept in baskets in their sleeping-house and may not be removed from it till the festival is over.   At the time when the men begin to observe these rules of abstinence, some six to ten women, members of the same clan as the master of the ceremonies, enter on a like period of mortification, avoiding the company of the other sex, and refraining from water, all boiled food, and the fruit of the mango tree.   These fasting men and women are the principal dancers at the festival. The dancing takes place on a special platform in a temporary village which has been erected for the purpose.   When the platform is about to be set up, the fasting men rub the stepping posts and then suck their hands for the purpose of extracting the ghost of any dead man that might chance to be in the post and might be injured by the weight of the platform pressing down on him.   Having carefully extracted these poor souls, the men carry them away tenderly and set them free in the forest or the long grass.

The wild mango tree not allowed to touch the ground.   On the day before the festival one of the fasting men cuts down the chosen mango tree in the jungle with a stone adze, which is never afterwards put to any other use; an iron tool may not be used for the purpose, though iron tools are now common enough in the district.   In cutting down the mango they place nets on the ground to catch any leaves or twigs that might fall from the tree as it is being felled, and they surround the trunk with new mats to receive the chips which fly out under the adze of the woodman ; for the chips may not drop on the earth.   Once the tree is down, it is carried to the centre of the temporary village, the greatest care being taken to prevent it from coming into contact with the ground.   But when it is brought into the village, the houses are connected with the top of the mango by means of long vines decorated with streamers.   In the afternoon the fasting men and women begin to dance, the men bedizened with gay feathers, armlets, streamers, and anklets, the women flaunting in parti-coloured petticoats and sprigs of croton leaves, which wave from their waistbands as they dance.   The dancing stops at sundown, and when the full moon rises over the shoulder of the

eastern hill (for the date of the festival seems to be determined with reference to the time of the moon), two chiefs
mount the gables of two houses on the eastern side of the
square, and, their dusky figures standing sharply out against
the moonlight, pray to the evil spirits to go away and not
to hurt the people.   Next morning pigs are killed by being
speared as slowly as possible in order that they may squeal
loud and long ; for the people believe that the mango trees
hear the squealing, and are pleased at the sound, and bear
plenty of fruit, whereas if they heard no squeals they would
bear no fruit.   However, the trees have to content themselves with the squeals ; the flesh of the pigs is eaten by the
people.   This ends the festival.

Next day the mango is taken down from the platform,   Final dis-
wrapt in new mats, and carried by the fasting men to their   position of
the wild
sleeping house, where it is hung from the roof.   But after   mango tree
an interval, it may be of many months, the tree is brought
forth again.   As to the reason for its reappearance in public
opinions are divided ; but some say that the tree itself orders
the master of the ceremonies to bring it forth, appearing to
him in his dreams and saying, " Let me smell the smoking
fat of pigs.   So will your pigs be healthy and your crops
will grow."   Be that as it may, out it comes, conducted by
the fasting men in their dancing costume ; and with it come
in the solemn procession all the pots, spoons, cups and so
forth used by the fasting men during their period of holiness
or taboo, also all the refuse of their food which has been
collected for months, and all the fallen leaves and chips of
the mango in their bundles of mats.   These holy relics are
carried in front and the mango tree itself brings up the rear
of the procession.   While these sacred objects are being
handed out of the house, the men who are present rush up,
wipe off the hallowed dust which has accumulated on them,
and smear it over their own bodies, no doubt in order to
steep themselves in their blessed influence.   Thus the tree
is carried as before to the centre of the temporary village,
care being again taken not to let it touch the ground.   Then
one of the fasting men takes from a basket a number of
young green mangoes, cuts them in pieces, and places them
with his own hands in the mouths of his fellows, the other

fasting men, who chew the pieces small and turning round spit the morsels in the direction of the setting sun, in order that "the sun should carry the mango bits over the whole country and everyone should know." A portion of the mango tree is then broken off and in the evening it is burnt along with the bundles of leaves, chips, and refuse of food, which have been stored up. What remains of the tree is taken to the house of the master of the ceremonies and hung over the fire-place ; it will be brought out again at intervals and burned bit by bit, till all is consumed, whereupon a new mango will be cut down and treated in like manner. The ashes of the holy fire on each occasion are gathered by the people and preserved in the house of the master of the ceremonies.[1]

The ceremony apparently intended to fertilize the mango trees.

The meaning of these ceremonies is not explained by the authorities who describe them ; but we may conjecture that they are intended to fertilize the mango trees and cause them to bear a good crop of fruit. The central feature of the whole ritual is a wild mango tree, so young that it has never flowered : the men who cut it down, carry it into the village, and dance at the festival, are forbidden to eat mangoes : pigs are killed in order that their dying squeals may move the mango trees to bear fruit : at the end of the ceremonies pieces of young green mangoes are solemnly placed in the mouths of the fasting men and are by them spurted out towards the setting sun in order that the luminary may carry the fragments to every part of the country ; and finally when after a longer or shorter interval the tree is wholly consumed, its place is supplied by another. All these circumstances are explained simply and naturally by the supposition that the young mango tree is taken as a representative of mangoes generally, that the dances are intended to quicken it, and that it is preserved, like a May-pole of old in England, as a sort of general fund of vegetable life, till the fund being exhausted by the destruction of the tree it is renewed by the importation of a fresh young tree from the forest. We can therefore understand why, as a storehouse of vital energy, the tree should be carefully kept from

[1] C. G. Seligmann, M.D., *The Melanesians of British New Guinea* (Cambridge, 1910), pp. 589-599.

contact with the ground, lest the pent-up and concentrated energy should escape and dribbling away into the earth be dissipated to no purpose.

To take other instances of what we may call the con- Sacred
servation of energy in magic or religion by insulating sacred objects
bodies from the ground, the natives of New Britain have a of various
secret society called the Duk-duk, the members of which allowed to
masquerade in petticoats of leaves and tall headdresses of ground.
wickerwork shaped like candle extinguishers, which descend to the shoulders of the wearers, completely concealing their faces. Thus disguised they dance about to the awe and terror, real or assumed, of the women and uninitiated, who take, or pretend to take, them for spirits. When lads are being initiated into the secrets of this august society, the adepts cut down some very large and heavy bamboos, one for each lad, and the novices carry them, carefully wrapt up in leaves, to the sacred ground, where they arrive very tired and weary, for they may not let the bamboos touch the ground nor the sun shine on them. Outside the fence of the enclosure every lad deposits his bamboo on a couple of forked sticks and covers it up with nut leaves.[1] Among the Carrier Indians of North-Western America, who burned their dead, the ashes of a chief used to be placed in a box and set on the top of a pole beside his hut : the box was never allowed to touch the ground.[2] In the Omaha tribe of North American Indians the sacred clam shell of the Elk clan was wrapt up from sight in a mat, placed on a stand, and never suffered to come in contact with the earth.[3] The Cherokees and kindred Indian tribes of the United States used to have certain sacred boxes or arks, which they regularly took with them to war. Such a holy ark consisted of a square wooden box, which contained " certain consecrated vessels made by beloved superannuated women, and of such various antiquated forms, as would have puzzled Adam to have given significant names to each." The

[1] George Brown, D.D., *Melanesians and Polynesians* (London, 1910), pp. 60 *sq.*, 64. As to the Duk-duk society, see below, vol. ii. pp. 246 *sq.*
[2] John Keast Lord, *The Naturalist in Vancouver Island and British Columbia* (London, 1866), ii. 237.

[3] Edwin James, *Account of an Expedition from Pittsburgh to the Rocky Mountains* (London, 1823), ii. 47 ; Rev. J. Owen Dorsey, " Omaha Sociology," *Third Annual Report of the Bureau of Ethnology* (Washington, 1884), p. 226.

leader of a war party and his attendant bore the ark by
turns, but they never set it on the ground nor would they
themselves sit on the bare earth while they were carrying it
against the enemy. Where stones were plentiful they rested
the ark on them ; but where no stones were to be found,
they deposited it on short logs. " The Indian ark is deemed
so sacred and dangerous to be touched, either by their own
sanctified warriors, or the spoiling enemy, that they durst
not touch it upon any account. It is not to be meddled
with by any, except the war chieftain and his waiter, under
the penalty of incurring great evil. Nor would the most
inveterate enemy touch it in the woods, for the very same
reason." After their return home they used to hang the
ark on the leader's red-painted war pole.[1] At Sipi, near
Simla, in Northern India, an annual fair is held, at which
men purchase wives. A square box with a domed top
figures prominently at the fair. It is fixed on two poles to
be carried on men's shoulders, and long heavily-plaited petticoats hang from it nearly to the ground. Three sides of
the box are adorned with the head and shoulders of a
female figure and the fourth side with a black yak's tail.
Four men bear the poles, each carrying an axe in his right
hand. They dance round, with a swinging rhythmical step,
to the music of drums and a pipe. The dance goes on for
hours and is thought to avert ill-luck from the fair. It is
said that the box is brought to Simla from a place sixty
miles off by relays of men, who may not stop nor set the
box on the ground the whole way.[2] In Scotland, when
water was carried from sacred wells to sick people, the
water-vessel might not touch the earth.[3] In some parts of
Aberdeenshire the last bunch of standing corn, which is
commonly viewed as very sacred, being the last refuge of
the corn-spirit retreating before the reapers, is not suffered
to touch the ground ; the master or " gueedman " sits down
and receives each handful of corn as it is cut on his lap.[4]

[1] James Adair, *History of the American Indians* (London, 1775), pp. 161-
163.
[2] (Sir) Henry Babington Smith, in
Folk-lore, v. (1894) p. 340.
[3] Miss C. F. Gordon Cumming, *In
the Hebrides* (London, 1883), p. 211.
[4] W. Gregor, " Quelques coutumes
du Nord-est du Comté d'Aberdeen,"
Revue des Traditions populaires, iii.
(1888) p. 485 B. Compare *Spirits of
the Corn and of the Wild*, i. 158 *sq.*

Again, sacred food may not under certain circumstances be brought into contact with the earth. Some of the aborigines of Victoria used to regard the fat of the emu as sacred, believing that it had once been the fat of the black man. In taking it from the bird or giving it to another they handled it reverently. Any one who threw away the fat or flesh of the emu was held accursed. "The late Mr. Thomas observed on one occasion, at Nerre-nerre-Warreen, a remarkable exhibition of the effects of this superstition. An aboriginal child—one attending the school —having eaten some part of the flesh of an emu, threw away the skin. The skin fell to the ground, and this being observed by his parents, they showed by their gestures every token of horror. They looked upon their child as one utterly lost. His desecration of the bird was regarded as a sin for which there was no atonement." [1] The Roumanians of Transylvania believe that "every fresh-baked loaf of wheaten bread is sacred, and should a piece inadvertently fall to the ground, it is hastily picked up, carefully wiped and kissed, and if soiled, thrown into the fire—partly as an offering to the dead, and partly because it were a heavy sin to throw away or tread upon any particle of it." [2] At certain festivals in south-eastern Borneo the food which is consumed in the common house may not touch the ground ; hence, a little before the festivals take place, foot-bridges made of thin poles are constructed from the private dwellings to the common house. [3] When Hall was living with the Esquimaux and grew tired of eating walrus, one of the women brought the head and neck of a reindeer for him to eat. This venison had to be completely wrapt up before it was brought into the house, and once in the house it could only be placed on the platform which served as a bed. "To have placed it on the floor or on the platform behind the fire-lamp, among the walrus, musk-ox, and polar-bear meat which occupy a goodly portion of both of these places, would have horrified the whole town, as, according to the actual

---

[1] R. Brough Smyth, *Aborigines of Victoria* (Melbourne and London, 1878), i. 450.

[2] E. Gerard, *The Land beyond the Forest* (Edinburgh and London, 1888),

ii. 7.

[3] F. Grabowsky, "Der Distrikt Dusson Timor in Südost-Borneo und seine Bewohner," *Das Ausland*, 1884, No. 24, p. 470.

belief of the Innuits, not another walrus could be secured this year, and there would ever be trouble in catching any more."[1]　But in this case the real scruple appears to have been felt not so much at placing the venison on the ground as at bringing it into contact with walrus meat.[2]

Magical implements and remedies thought to lose their virtue by contact with the ground.

Sometimes magical implements and remedies are supposed to lose their virtue by contact with the ground, the volatile essence with which they are impregnated being no doubt drained off into the earth.　Thus in the Boulia district of Queensland the magical bone, which the native sorcerer points at his victim as a means of killing him, is never by any chance allowed to touch the earth.[3]　The wives of rajahs in Macassar, a district of southern Celebes, pride themselves on their luxuriant tresses and are at great pains to oil and preserve them.　Should the hair begin to grow thin, the lady resorts to many devices to stay the ravages of time ; among other things she applies to her locks a fat extracted from crocodiles and venomous snakes. The unguent is believed to be very efficacious, but during its application the woman's feet may not come into contact with the ground, or all the benefit of the nostrum would be lost.[4] Some people in antiquity believed that a woman in hard labour would be delivered if a spear, which had been wrenched from a man's body without touching the ground, were thrown over the house where the sufferer lay.　Again, according to certain ancient writers, arrows which had been extracted from a body without coming into contact with the earth and laid under sleepers, acted as a love-charm.[5]　Among the peasantry of the north-east of Scotland the prehistoric

---

[1] *Narrative of the Second Arctic Expedition made by Charles F. Hall*, edited by Prof. J. E. Nourse (Washington, 1879), pp. 110 *sq.*

[2] See *Taboo and Perils of the Soul*, pp. 207 *sqq.*

[3] Walter E. Roth, *Ethnological Studies among the North-West-Central Queensland Aborigines* (Brisbane and London, 1897), p. 156, § 265.　The custom of killing a man by pointing a bone or stick at him, while the sorcerer utters appropriate curses, is common among the tribes of Central Australia ; but amongst them there seems to be

no objection to place the bone or stick on the ground ; on the contrary, an Arunta wizard inserts the bone or stick in the ground while he invokes death and destruction on his enemy.　See Baldwin Spencer and F. J. Gillen, *Native Tribes of Central Australia* (London, 1899), pp. 534 *sqq.* ; *id.*, *Northern Tribes of Central Australia* (London, 1904), pp. 455 *sqq.*

[4] Hugh Low, *Sarawak* (London, 1848), pp. 145 *sq.*

[5] Pliny, *Naturalis Historia*, xxviii. 33 *sq.*

weapons called celts went by the name of "thunderbolts" and were coveted as the sure bringers of success, always provided that they were not allowed to fall to the ground.[1]

In ancient Gaul certain glass or paste beads attained great celebrity as amulets under the name of serpents' eggs; it was believed that serpents, coiling together in a wriggling, writhing mass, generated them from their slaver and shot them into the air from their hissing jaws. If a man was bold and dexterous enough to catch one of these eggs in his cloak before it touched the ground, he rode off on horseback with it at full speed, pursued by the whole pack of serpents, till he was saved by the interposition of a river, which the snakes could not pass. The proof of the egg being genuine was that if it were thrown into a stream it would float up against the current, even though it were hooped in gold. The Druids held these beads in high esteem; according to them, the precious objects could only be obtained on a certain day of the moon, and the peculiar virtue that resided in them was to secure success in law suits and free access to kings. Pliny knew of a Gaulish knight who was executed by the emperor Claudius for wearing one of these amulets.[2] Under the name of Snake Stones (*glain neidr*) or Adder Stones the beads are still known in those parts of our own country where the Celtic population has lingered, with its immemorial superstitions, down to the present or recent times; and the old story of the origin of the beads from the slaver of serpents was believed by the modern peasantry of Cornwall, Wales, and Scotland as by the Druids of ancient Gaul. In Cornwall the time when the serpents united to fashion the beads was commonly said to be at or about Midsummer Eve; in Wales it was usually thought to be spring, especially the Eve of May Day, and even within recent years persons in the Principality have affirmed that they witnessed the great

Serpents eggs or Snake Stones.

---

[1] Rev. Walter Gregor, *Notes on the Folk-lore of the North-East of Scotland* (London, 1881), p. 184. As to the superstitions attaching to stone arrow-heads and axeheads (celts), commonly known as "thunderbolts," in the British Islands, see W. W. Skeat, "Snake-stones and Stone Thunderbolts," *Folk-lore*, xxiii. (1912) pp. 60 *sqq.*; and as to such superstitions in general, see Chr. Blinkenberg, *The Thunderweapon in Religion and Folklore* (Cambridge, 1911).

[2] Pliny, *Naturalis Historia*, xxix. 52-54.

vernal congress of the snakes and saw the magic stone in
the midst of the froth.   The Welsh peasants believe the
beads to possess medicinal virtues of many sorts and to be
particularly efficacious for all maladies of the eyes.   In Wales
and Ireland the beads sometimes went by the name of the
Magician's or Druid's Glass (*Gleini na Droedh* and *Glaine
nan Druidhe*).   Specimens of them may be seen in museums ;
some have been found in British barrows.   They are of
glass of various colours, green, blue, pink, red, brown, and so
forth, some plain and some ribbed.   Some are streaked with
brilliant hues.   The beads are perforated, and in the Highlands of Scotland the hole is explained by saying that when
the bead has just been conflated by the serpents jointly, one
of the reptiles sticks his tail through the still viscous glass.
An Englishman who visited Scotland in 1699 found many
of these beads in use throughout the country.   They were
hung from children's necks to protect them from whooping
cough and other ailments.   Snake Stones were, moreover, a
charm to ensure prosperity in general and to repel evil
spirits.   When one of these priceless treasures was not on
active service, the owner kept it in an iron box to guard it
against fairies, who, as is well known, cannot abide iron.[1]

[1] W. Borlase, *Antiquities, Historical and Monumental, of the County
of Cornwall* (London, 1769), pp. 142
sq.; J. Brand, *Popular Antiquities of
Great Britain* (London, 1882–1883),
i. 322 ; J. G. Dalyell, *Darker Superstitions of Scotland* (Edinburgh, 1834),
pp. 140 *sq.* ; Daniel Wilson, *The
Archaeology and Prehistoric Annals
of Scotland* (Edinburgh, 1851), pp.
303 *sqq.*; Lieut.-Col. Forbes Leslie,
*The Early Races of Scotland and their
Monuments* (Edinburgh, 1866), i. 75
sqq. ; J. G. Campbell, *Witchcraft and
Second Sight in the Highlands and
Islands of Scotland* (Glasgow, 1902),
pp. 84-88 ; Marie Trevelyan, *Folk-lore
and Folk-stories of Wales* (London,
1909), pp. 170 *sq.*; J. C. Davies,
Folk-lore of West and Mid-Wales
(Aberystwyth, 1911), p. 76.   Compare W. W. Skeat, "Snakestones and
Stone Thunderbolts," *Folk-lore*, xxiii.
(1912) pp. 45 *sqq.*   The superstition
is described as follows by Edward
Lhwyd in a letter quoted by W.
Borlase (*op. cit.* p. 142) : " In most
parts of Wales, and throughout all
Scotland, and in Cornwall, we find it
a common opinion of the vulgar, that
about Midsummer-Eve (though in the
time they do not all agree) it is usual
for snakes to meet in companies ; and
that, by joining heads together, and
hissing, a kind of bubble is formed,
which the rest, by continual hissing,
blow on till it passes quite through the
body, and then it immediately hardens,
and resembles a glass-ring, which whoever finds (as some old women and
children are persuaded) shall prosper
in all his undertakings.   The rings
thus generated, are called *Gleineu
Nadroeth* ; in English, Snake-stones.
They are small glass amulets, commonly about half as wide as our finger-
rings, but much thicker, of a green
colour usually, though sometimes blue,
and waved with red and white."

Pliny mentions several medicinal plants, which, if they
were to retain their healing virtue, ought not to be allowed
to touch the earth.[1]   The curious medical treatise of
Marcellus, a native of Bordeaux in the fourth century of our
era, abounds with prescriptions of this sort ; and we can
well believe the writer when he assures us that he borrowed
many of his quaint remedies from the lips of common folk
and peasants rather than from the books of the learned.[2]
Thus he tells us that certain white stones found in the
stomachs of young swallows assuage the most persistent
headache, always provided that their virtue be not impaired
by contact with the ground.[3]   Another of his cures for the
same malady is a wreath of fleabane placed on the head,
but it must not touch the earth.[4]   On the same condition a
decoction of the root of elecampane in wine kills worms ; a
fern, found growing on a tree, relieves the stomach-ache ; and
the pastern-bone of a hare is an infallible remedy for colic,
provided, first, it be found in the dung of a wolf, second,
that it does not touch the ground, and, third, that it is not
touched by a woman.[5]   Another cure for colic is effected by
certain hocus-pocus with a scrap of wool from the forehead
of a first-born lamb, if only the lamb, instead of being
allowed to fall to the ground, has been caught by hand as it
dropped from its dam.[6]   In Andjra, a district of Morocco,
the people attribute many magical virtues to rain-water
which has fallen on the twenty-seventh day of April, Old
Style ; accordingly they collect it and use it for a variety of
purposes.   Mixed with tar and sprinkled on the door-posts
it prevents snakes and scorpions from entering the house :
sprinkled on heaps of threshed corn it protects them from
the evil eye : mixed with an egg, henna, and seeds of cress
it is an invaluable medicine for sick cows : poured over a

*Medicinal
plants,
water, etc.,
not allowed
to touch
the earth.*

[1] Pliny, *Naturalis Historia*, xxiv.
12 and 68, xxv. 171.

[2] Marcellus, *De medicamentis*, ed.
G. Helmreich (Leipsic, 1889), preface,
p. i. : " *Nec solum veteres medicinae
artis auctores Latino dumtaxat sermone
perscriptos . . . lectione scrutatus sum,
sed etiam ab agrestibus et plebeis remedia
fortuita atque simplicia, quae experi-
mentis probaverant didici.*"   As to
Marcellus and his work, see Jacob

Grimm, " Ueber Marcellus Burdiga-
lensis," *Abhandlungen der königlichen
Akademie der Wissenschaft zu Berlin*,
1847, pp. 429-460 ; *id.*, " Ueber die
Marcellischen Formeln," *ibid.*, 1855,
pp. 50-68.

[3] Marcellus, *De medicamentis*, i. 68.

[4] Marcellus, *op. cit.* i. 76.

[5] Marcellus, *op. cit.* xxviii. 28 and
71, xxix. 35.

[6] Marcellus, *op. cit.* xxix. 51.

plate, on which a passage of the Koran has been written, it strengthens the memory of schoolboys who drink it ; and if you mix it with cowdung and red earth and paint rings with the mixture round the trunks of your fig-trees at sunset on Midsummer Day, you may depend on it that the trees will bear an excellent crop and will not shed their fruit untimely on the ground. But in order to preserve these remarkable properties it is absolutely essential that the water should on no account be allowed to touch the ground ; some say too that it should not be exposed to the sun nor breathed upon by anybody.[1] Again, the Moors ascribe great magical efficacy to what they call " the sultan of the oleander," which is a stalk of oleander with a cluster of four pairs of leaves springing from it. They think that the magical virtue is greatest if the stalk has been cut immediately before midsummer. But when the plant is brought into the house, the branches may not touch the ground, lest they should lose their marvellous qualities.[2] In the olden days, before a Lithuanian or Prussian farmer went forth to plough for the first time in spring, he called in a wizard to perform a certain ceremony for the good of the crops. The sage seized a mug of beer with his teeth, quaffed the liquor, and then tossed the mug over his head. This signified that the corn in that year should grow taller than a man. But the mug might not fall to the ground ; it had to be caught by somebody stationed at the wizard's back, for if it fell to the ground the consequence naturally would be that the corn also would be laid low on the earth.[3]

§ 2. *Not to see the Sun*

The second rule to be here noted is that the sun may not shine upon the divine person. This rule was observed

[1] Edward Westermarck, " Midsummer Customs in Morocco," *Folklore*, xvi. (1905) pp. 32 *sq.*; *id.*, *Ceremonies and Beliefs connected with Agriculture, certain Dates of the Solar Year, and the Weather in Morocco* (Helsingfors, 1913), pp. 75 *sq.*

[2] E. Westermarck, " Midsummer Customs in Morocco," *Folk-lore*, xvi.

(1905) p. 35 ; *id.*, *Ceremonies and Beliefs connected with Agriculture, certain Dates of the Solar Year, and the Weather in Morocco* (Helsingfors, 1913), pp. 88 *sq.*

[3] Matthäus Prätorius, *Deliciae Prussicae*, herausgegeben von Dr. W. Pierson (Berlin, 1871), p. 54.

both by the Mikado and by the pontiff of the Zapotecs.
The latter " was looked upon as a god whom the earth was
not worthy to hold, nor the sun to shine upon." [1]   The
Japanese would not allow that the Mikado should expose
his sacred person to the open air, and the sun was not
thought worthy to shine on his head.[2]   The Indians of
Granada, in South America, " kept those who were to be
rulers or commanders, whether men or women, locked up
for several years when they were children, some of them
seven years, and this so close that they were not to see the
sun, for if they should happen to see it they forfeited their
lordship, eating certain sorts of food appointed ; and those
who were their keepers at certain times went into their retreat or prison and scourged them severely." [3]   Thus, for
example, the heir to the throne of Bogota, who was not
the son but the sister's son of the king, had to undergo a
rigorous training from his infancy : he lived in complete
retirement in a temple, where he might not see the sun nor
eat salt nor converse with a woman : he was surrounded by
guards who observed his conduct and noted all his actions :
if he broke a single one of the rules laid down for him, he
was deemed infamous and forfeited all his rights to the
throne.[4]   So, too, the heir to the kingdom of Sogamoso,
before succeeding to the crown, had to fast for seven years
in the temple, being shut up in the dark and not allowed to
see the sun or light.[5]   The prince who was to become Inca
of Peru had to fast for a month without seeing light.[6]   On

[1] H. H. Bancroft, *Native Races of the
Pacific States* (London, 1875–1876),
ii. 142 ; Brasseur de Bourbourg, *Histoire des Nations civilisées du Mexique
et de l'Amérique Centrale* (Paris, 1857–
1859), iii. 29.

[2] Kaempfer, " History of Japan," in
J. Pinkerton's *Voyages and Travels*,
vii. 717 ; Caron, " Account of Japan,"
ibid. vii. 613 ; B. Varenius, *Descriptio
regni Japoniae et Siam* (Cambridge,
1673), p. 11 : " *Radiis solis caput nun-
quam illustrabatur : in apertum aërem
non procedebat.*"

[3] A. de Herrera, *General History of
the vast Continent and Islands of
America*, trans. by Capt. John Stevens
(London, 1725–1726), v. 88.

[4] H. Ternaux-Compans, *Essai sur
l'ancien Cundinamarca* (Paris, N.D.),
p. 56 ; Theodor Waitz, *Anthropologie
der Naturvölker*, iv. (Leipsic, 1864)
p. 359.

[5] Alonzo de Zurita, " Rapport sur
les differentes classes de chefs de la
Nouvelle - Espagne," p. 30, in H.
Ternaux-Compans's *Voyages, Relations
et Mémoires originaux, pour servir à
l'Histoire de la Découverte de l'Amérique*
(Paris, 1840) ; Th. Waitz, *l.c.* ; A.
Bastian, *Die Culturländer des alten
Amerika* (Berlin, 1878), ii. 204.

[6] Cieza de Leon, *Second Part of the
Chronicle of Peru* (Hakluyt Society,
London, 1883), p. 18.

the day when a Brahman student of the Veda took a bath, to signify that the time of his studentship was at an end, he entered a cow-shed before sunrise, hung over the door a skin with the hair inside, and sat there; on that day the sun should not shine upon him.[1]

Tabooed persons not allowed to see the sun.

Again, women after childbirth and their offspring are more or less tabooed all the world over; hence in Corea the rays of the sun are rigidly excluded from both mother and child for a period of twenty-one or a hundred days, according to their rank, after the birth has taken place.[2] Among some of the tribes on the north-west coast of New Guinea a woman may not leave the house for months after childbirth. When she does go out, she must cover her head with a hood or mat; for if the sun were to shine upon her, it is thought that one of her male relations would die.[3] Again, mourners are everywhere taboo; accordingly in mourning the Ainos of Japan wear peculiar caps in order that the sun may not shine upon their heads.[4] During a solemn fast of three days the Indians of Costa Rica eat no salt, speak as little as possible, light no fires, and stay strictly indoors, or if they go out during the day they carefully cover themselves from the light of the sun, believing that exposure to the sun's rays would turn them black.[5]

Certain persons forbidden to see fire.

On Yule Night it has been customary in parts of Sweden from time immemorial to go on pilgrimage, whereby people learn many secret things and know what is to happen in the coming year. As a preparation for this pilgrimage, "some secrete themselves for three days previously in a dark cellar, so as to be shut out altogether from the light of

[1] *The Grihya Sûtras*, translated by H. Oldenberg, Part ii. (Oxford, 1892) pp. 165, 275 (*Sacred Books of the East*, vol. xxx.). Umbrellas appear to have been sometimes used in ritual for the purpose of preventing the sunlight from falling on sacred persons or things. See W. Caland, *Altindisches Zauberritual* (Amsterdam, 1900), p. 110 note [12]. At an Athenian festival called Scira the priestess of Athena, the priest of Poseidon, and the priest of the Sun walked from the Acropolis under the shade of a huge white umbrella which was borne over their heads by the Eteobutads. See Har-

pocration and Suidas, *s.v.* Σκίρον; Scholiast on Aristophanes, *Eccles.* 18.

[2] Mrs. Bishop, *Korea and her Neighbours* (London, 1898), ii. 248.

[3] J. L. van Hasselt, "Eenige aanteekeningen aangaande de bewoners der N. Westkust van Nieuw Guinea," *Tijdschrift voor Indische Taal- Land-en Volkenkunde*, xxxi. (1886) p. 587.

[4] A. Bastian, *Die Völker des östlichen Asien*, v. (Jena, 1869) p. 366.

[5] W. M. Gabb, "On the Indian Tribes and Languages of Costa Rica," *Proceedings of the American Philosophical Society held at Philadelphia*, xiv. (Philadelphia, 1876), p. 510.

heaven.   Others retire at an early hour of the preceding morning to some out-of-the-way place, such as a hay-loft, where they bury themselves in the hay, that they may neither see nor hear any living creature ; and here they remain, in silence and fasting, until after sundown ; whilst there are those who think it sufficient if they rigidly abstain from food on the day before commencing their wanderings. During this period of probation a man ought not to see fire, but should this have happened, he must strike a light with flint and steel, whereby the evil that would otherwise have ensued will be obviated." [1]   During the sixteen days that a Pima Indian is undergoing purification for killing an Apache he may not see a blazing fire. [2]

Acarnanian peasants tell of a handsome prince called Sunless, who would die if he saw the sun.   So he lived in an underground palace on the site of the ancient Oeniadae, but at night he came forth and crossed the river to visit a famous enchantress who dwelt in a castle on the further bank.   She was loth to part with him every night long before the sun was up, and as he turned a deaf ear to all her entreaties to linger, she hit upon the device of cutting the throats of all the cocks in the neighbourhood.   So the prince, whose ear had learned to expect the shrill clarion of the birds as the signal of the growing light, tarried too long, and hardly had he reached the ford when the sun rose over the Aetolian mountains, and its fatal beams fell on him before he could regain his dark abode. [3]

The story of Prince Sunless.

[1] L. Lloyd, *Peasant Life in Sweden* (London, 1870), p. 194.

[2] H. H. Bancroft, *Native Races of the Pacific States*, i. 553.   See *Taboo*

and the Perils of the Soul, p. 182.

[3] L. Heuzey, *Le Mont Olympe et l'Acarnanie* (Paris, 1860), pp. 458 *sq.*

CHAPTER II

THE SECLUSION OF GIRLS AT PUBERTY

§ 1. *Seclusion of Girls at Puberty in Africa*

Girls at
puberty
forbidden
to touch
the ground
and to see
the sun.

NOW it is remarkable that the foregoing two rules—not to touch the ground and not to see the sun—are observed either separately or conjointly by girls at puberty in many parts of the world. Thus amongst the negroes of Loango girls at puberty are confined in separate huts, and they may not touch the ground with any part of their bare body.[1] Among the Zulus and kindred tribes of South Africa, when the first signs of puberty shew themselves " while a girl is walking, gathering wood, or working in the field, she runs to the river and hides herself among the reeds for the day, so as not to be seen by men. She covers her head carefully with her blanket that the sun may not shine on it and shrivel her up into a withered skeleton, as would result from exposure to the sun's beams. After dark she returns to her home and is secluded " in a hut for some time.[2] During her seclusion, which lasts for about a fortnight, neither she nor the girls who wait upon her may drink any milk, lest the cattle should die. And should she be overtaken by the first flow while she is in the fields, she must, after hiding in the bush, scrupulously avoid all pathways in returning home.[3] A

---

[1] Pechuel-Loesche, " Indiscretes aus Loango," *Zeitschrift für Ethnologie*, x. (1878) p. 23.

[2] Rev. J. Macdonald, " Manners, Customs, Superstitions, and Religions of South African Tribes," *Journal of the Anthropological Institute*, xx. (1891) p. 118.

[3] Dudley Kidd, *The Essential Kafir* (London, 1904), p. 209. The prohibition to drink milk under such circumstances is also mentioned, though without the reason for it, by L. Alberti (*De Kaffers aan de Zuidkust van Afrika*, Amsterdam, 1810, p. 79), George Thompson (*Travels and Adventures in Southern Africa*, London, 1827, ii. 354 *sq.*), and Mr. Warner (in Col.

reason for this avoidance is assigned by the A-Kamba of British East Africa, whose girls under similar circumstances observe the same rule. "A girl's first menstruation is a very critical period of her life according to A-Kamba beliefs. If this condition appears when she is away from the village, say at work in the fields, she returns at once to her village, but is careful to walk through the grass and not on a path, for if she followed a path and a stranger accidentally trod on a spot of blood and then cohabited with a member of the opposite sex before the girl was better again, it is believed that she would never bear a child." She remains at home till the symptoms have ceased, and during this time she may be fed by none but her mother. When the flux is over, her father and mother are bound to cohabit with each other, else it is believed that the girl would be barren all her life.[1] Similarly, among the Baganda, when a girl menstruated for the first time she was secluded and not allowed to handle food ; and at the end of her seclusion the kinsman with whom she was staying (for among the Baganda young people did not reside with their parents) was obliged to jump over his wife, which with the Baganda is regarded as equivalent to having intercourse with her. Should the girl happen to be living near her parents at the moment when she attained to puberty, she was expected on her recovery to inform them of the fact, whereupon her father jumped over her mother. Were this custom omitted, the Baganda, like the A-Kamba, thought that the girl would never have children or that they would die in infancy.[2] Thus the pretence of sexual intercourse between the parents or other relatives of

---

Maclean's *Compendium of Kafir Laws and Customs*, Cape Town, 1866, p. 98). As to the reason for the prohibition, see below, p. 80.

[1] C. W. Hobley, *Ethnology of A-Kamba and other East African Tribes* (Cambridge, 1910), p. 65.

[2] Rev. J. Roscoe, *The Baganda* (London, 1911), p. 80. As to the interpretation which the Baganda put on the act of jumping or stepping over a woman, see *id.*, pp. 48, 357 note [1]. Apparently some of the Lower Congo people interpret the act similarly. See

J. H. Weeks, "Notes on some Customs of the Lower Congo People," *Folk-lore*, xix. (1908) p. 431. Among the Baganda the separation of children from their parents took place after weaning ; girls usually went to live either with an elder married brother or (if there was none such) with one of their father's brothers ; boys in like manner went to live with one of their father's brothers. See J. Roscoe, *op. cit.* p. 74. As to the prohibition to touch food with the hands, see *Taboo and the Perils of the Soul*, pp. 138 *sqq.*, 146 *sqq.*, etc.

the girl was a magical ceremony to ensure her fertility. It
is significant that among the Baganda the first menstruation
was often called a marriage, and the girl was spoken of as
a bride.[1] These terms so applied point to a belief like that
of the Siamese, that a girl's first menstruation results from
her defloration by one of a host of aerial spirits, and that the
wound thus inflicted is repeated afterwards every month by
the same ghostly agency.[2] For a like reason, probably, the
Baganda imagine that a woman who does not menstruate
exerts a malign influence on gardens and makes them
barren[3] if she works in them. For not being herself
fertilized by a spirit, how can she fertilize the garden?

Seclusion
of girls at
puberty
among the
tribes of
the Tan-
ganyika
plateau.
Among the Amambwe, Winamwanga, Alungu, and
other tribes of the great plateau to the west of Lake
Tanganyika, " when a young girl knows that she has attained
puberty, she forthwith leaves her mother's hut, and hides
herself in the long grass near the village, covering her face
with a cloth and weeping bitterly. Towards sunset one of
the older women—who, as directress of the ceremonies, is
called *nachimbusa*—follows her, places a cooking-pot by the
cross-roads, and boils therein a concoction of various herbs,
with which she anoints the neophyte. At nightfall the girl
is carried on the old woman's back to her mother's hut.
When the customary period of a few days has elapsed, she
is allowed to cook again, after first whitewashing the floor of
the hut. But, by the following month, the preparations for
her initiation are complete. The novice must remain in her
hut throughout the whole period of initiation, and is carefully
guarded by the old women, who accompany her whenever
she leaves her quarters, veiling her head with a native cloth.
The ceremonies last for at least one month." During this
period of seclusion, drumming and songs are kept up within
the mother's hut by the village women, and no male, except,
it is said, the father of twins, is allowed to enter. The
directress of the rites and the older women instruct the

[1] Rev. J. Roscoe, *The Baganda*,
p. 80.
[2] De la Loubere, *Du royaume de
Siam* (Amsterdam, 1691), i. 203. In
Travancore it is believed that women
at puberty and after childbirth are
peculiarly liable to be attacked by
demons. See S. Mateer, *The Land of
Charity* (London, 1871), p. 208.

[3] Rev. J. Roscoe, *The Baganda*,
p. 80.

young girl as to the elementary facts of life, the duties of
marriage, and the rules of conduct, decorum, and hospitality
to be observed by a married woman.   Amongst other things
the damsel must submit to a series of tests such as leaping
over fences, thrusting her head into a collar made of thorns,
and so on.   The lessons which she receives are illustrated
by mud figures of animals and of the common objects of
domestic life.   Moreover, the directress of studies em-
bellishes the walls of the hut with rude pictures, each with
its special significance and song, which must be understood
and learned by the girl.[1]   In the foregoing account the
rule that a damsel at puberty may neither see the sun nor
touch the ground seems implied by the statement that
on the first discovery of her condition she hides in long
grass and is carried home after sunset on the back of an
old woman.

Among the Nyanja-speaking tribes of Central Angoniland, in British Central Africa, when a young girl finds that
she has become a woman, she stands silent by the pathway
leading to the village, her face wrapt in her calico.   An old
woman, finding her there, takes her off to a stream to bathe ;
after that the girl is secluded for six days in the old woman's
hut.   She eats her porridge out of an old basket and her
relish, in which no salt is put, from a potsherd.   The basket
is afterwards thrown away.   On the seventh day the aged
matrons gather together, go with the girl to a stream, and
throw her into the water.   In returning they sing songs, and
the old woman, who directs the proceedings, carries the
maiden on her back.   Then they spread a mat and fetch
her husband and set the two down on the mat and shave
his head.   When it is dark, the old women escort the girl to
her husband's hut.   There the *ndiwo* relish is cooking on the
fire.   During the night the woman rises and puts some salt
in the pot.   Next morning, before dawn, while all is dark
and the villagers have not yet opened their doors, the young
married woman goes off and gives some of the relish to her
mother and to the old woman who was mistress of the
ceremony.   This relish she sets down at the doors of their

Seclusion of girls at puberty among the tribes of British Central Africa.

---

[1] C. Gouldsbury and H. Sheane, *The Great Plateau of Northern Nigeria*
(London, 1911), pp. 158-160.

houses and goes away. And in the morning, when the sun has risen and all is light in the village, the two women open their doors, and there they find the relish with the salt in it ; and they take of it and rub it on their feet and under their arm-pits ; and if there are little children in the house, they eat of it. And if the young wife has a kinsman who is absent from the village, some of the relish is put on a splinter of bamboo and kept against his return, that when he comes he, too, may rub his feet with it. But if the woman finds that her husband is impotent, she does not rise betimes and go out in the dark to lay the relish at the doors of her mother and the old woman. And in the morning, when the sun is up and all the village is light, the old women open their doors, and see no relish there, and they know what has happened, and so they go wilily to work. For they persuade the husband to consult the diviner that he may discover how to cure his impotence ; and while he is closeted with the wizard, they fetch another man, who finishes the ceremony with the young wife, in order that the relish may be given out and that people may rub their feet with it. But if it happens that when a girl comes to maturity she is not yet betrothed to any man, and therefore has no husband to go to, the matrons tell her that she must go to a lover instead. And this is the custom which they call *chigango*. So in the evening she takes her cooking pot and relish and hies away to the quarters of the young bachelors, and they very civilly sleep somewhere else that night. And in the morning the girl goes back to the *kuka* hut.[1]

Abstinence from salt associated with a rule of chastity in many tribes.

From the foregoing account it appears that among these tribes no sooner has a girl attained to womanhood than she is expected and indeed required to give proof of her newly acquired powers by cohabiting with a man, whether her husband or another. And the abstinence from salt during the girl's seclusion is all the more remarkable because as soon as the seclusion is over she has to use salt for a particular purpose, to which the people evidently attach very great importance, since in the event of her husband proving impotent she is even compelled, apparently, to commit

[1] R. Sutherland Rattray, *Some Folk-lore Stories and Songs in Chinyanja* (London, 1907), pp. 102-105.

adultery in order that the salted relish may be given out as usual.   In this connexion it deserves to be noted that among the Wagogo of German East Africa women at their monthly periods may not sleep with their husbands and may not put salt in food.[1]   A similar rule is observed by the Nyanja-speaking tribes of Central Angoniland, with whose puberty customs we are here concerned.   Among them, we are told, " some superstition exists with regard to the use of salt.   A woman during her monthly sickness must on no account put salt into any food she is cooking, lest she give her husband or children a disease called *tsempo (chitsoko soko)*, but calls a child to put it in, or, as the song goes, ' *Natira mchere ni bondo chifukwa n'kupanda mwana*,' and pours in the salt by placing it on her knee, because there is no child handy. Should a party of villagers have gone to make salt, all sexual intercourse is forbidden among the people of the village, until the people who have gone to make the salt (from grass) return.   When they do come back, they must make their entry into the village at night, and no one must see them. Then one of the elders of the village sleeps with his wife. She then cooks some relish, into which she puts some of the salt.   This relish is handed round to the people who went to make the salt, who rub it on their feet and under their armpits." [2]   Hence it would seem that in the mind of these people abstinence from salt is somehow associated with the idea of chastity.   The same association meets us in the customs of many peoples in various parts of the world.   For example, ancient Hindoo ritual prescribed that for three nights after a husband had brought his bride home, the two should sleep on the ground, remain chaste, and eat no salt.[3] Among the Baganda, when a man was making a net, he had to refrain from eating salt and meat and from living with his wife ; these restrictions he observed until the net took its first catch of fish.   Similarly, so long as a fisherman's nets or traps were in the water, he must live apart from his wife, and neither he nor she nor their children might eat salt or

[1] Rev. H. Cole, "Notes on the Wagogo of German East Africa," *Journal of the Anthropological Institute*, xxxii. (1902) pp. 309 *sq.*

[2] R. Sutherland Rattray, *op. cit.*

pp. 191 *sq.*

[3] *The Grihya Sutras*, translated by H. Oldenberg, Part i. p. 357, Part ii. p. 267 (*Sacred Books of the East*, vols, xxix., xxx.).

meat.[1] Evidence of the same sort could be multiplied,[2] but without going into it further we may say that for some reason which is not obvious to us primitive man connects salt with the intercourse of the sexes and therefore forbids the use of that condiment in a variety of circumstances in which he deems continence necessary or desirable. As there is nothing which the savage regards as a greater bar between the sexes than the state of menstruation, he naturally prohibits the use of salt to women and girls at their monthly periods.

Seclusion of girls at puberty among the tribes about Lake Nyassa and on the Zambesi.

With the Awa-nkonde, a tribe at the northern end of Lake Nyassa, it is a rule that after her first menstruation a girl must be kept apart, with a few companions of her own sex, in a darkened house. The floor is covered with dry banana leaves, but no fire may be lit in the house, which is called "the house of the Awasungu," that is, "of maidens who have no hearts."[3] When a girl reaches puberty, the Wafiomi of Eastern Africa hold a festival at which they make a noise with a peculiar kind of rattle. After that the girl remains for a year in the large common hut (*tembe*), where she occupies a special compartment screened off from the men's quarters. She may not cut her hair or touch food, but is fed by other women. At night, however, she quits the hut and dances with young men.[4] Among the Barotse or Marotse of the upper Zambesi, "when a girl arrives at the age of puberty she is sent into the fields, where a hut is constructed far from the village. There, with two or three companions, she spends a month, returning home late and starting before dawn in order not to be seen by the men. The women of the village visit her, bringing food and honey, and singing and dancing to amuse her. At the end of a month her husband comes and fetches her. It is only after this ceremony that women have the right to smear themselves with ochre."[5] We may suspect that the chief reason why

[1] Rev. J. Roscoe, *The Baganda* (London, 1911), pp. 393 *sq.*, compare pp. 396, 398.

[2] See *Totemism and Exogamy*, iv. 224 *sqq.*

[3] Sir Harry H. Johnston, *British Central Africa* (London, 1897), p. 411.

[4] Oscar Baumann, *Durch Massai-land zur Nilquelle* (Berlin, 1894), p. 178.

[5] Lionel Decle, *Three Years in Savage Africa* (London, 1898), p. 78. Compare E. Jacottet, *Études sur les Langues du Haut-Zambèze*, Trcisième Partie (Paris, 1901), pp. 174 *sq.* (as to the A-Louyi).

the girl during her seclusion may visit her home only by
night is a fear, not so much lest she should be seen by men,
as that she might be seen by the sun.   Among the Wafiomi,
as we have just learned, the young woman in similar circumstances is even free to dance with men, provided always that
the dance is danced at night.   The ceremonies among the
Barotse or Marotse are somewhat more elaborate for a girl of
the royal family.   She is shut up for three months in a place
which is kept secret from the public ; only the women of her
family know where it is.   There she sits alone in the darkness of the hut, waited on by female slaves, who are strictly
forbidden to speak and may communicate with her and with
each other only by signs.   During all this time, though she
does nothing, she eats much, and when at last she comes forth,
her appearance is quite changed, so fat has she grown.   She
is then led by night to the river and bathed in presence of
all the women of the village.   Next day she flaunts before
the public in her gayest attire, her head bedecked with
ornaments and her face mottled with red paint.   So everybody knows what has happened.[1]

Among the northern clans of the Thonga tribe, in
South-Eastern Africa, about Delagoa Bay, when a girl
thinks that the time of her nubility is near, she chooses
an adoptive mother, perhaps in a neighbouring village.
When the symptoms appear, she flies away from her own
village and repairs to that of her adopted mother " to weep
near her."   After that she is secluded with several other girls
in the same condition for a month.   They are shut up in a
hut, and whenever they come outside they must wear a dirty
greasy cloth over their faces as a veil.   Every morning they
are led to a pool and plunged in the water up to their necks.
Initiated girls or women accompany them, singing obscene
songs and driving away with sticks any man who meets them ;
for no man may see a girl during this time of seclusion.   If
he saw her, it is said that he would be struck blind.   On
their return from the river, the girls are again imprisoned
in the hut, where they remain wet and shivering, for they
may not go near the fire to warm themselves.   During
their seclusion they listen to lascivious songs sung by

Seclusion
of girls at
puberty
among the
Thonga of
Delagoa
Bay.

[1] E. Béguin, *Les Ma-rotsé* (Lausanne and Fontaines, 1903), p. 113.

grown women and are instructed in sexual matters. At
the end of the month the adoptive mother brings the
girl home to her true mother and presents her with a pot
of beer.[1]

Seclusion
of girls at
puberty
among the
Caffre
tribes of
South
Africa.
Among the Caffre tribes of South Africa the period of a
girl's seclusion at puberty varies with the rank of her father.
If he is a rich man, it may last twelve days ; if he is a chief,
it may last twenty-four days.[2]   And when it is over, the girl
rubs herself over with red earth, and strews finely powdered
red earth on the ground, before she leaves the hut where she
has been shut up.   Finally, though she was forbidden to drink
milk all the days of her separation, she washes out her mouth
with milk, and is from that moment regarded as a full-grown
woman.[3]   Afterwards, in the dusk of the evening, she carries
away all the objects with which she came into contact in the
hut during her seclusion and buries them secretly in a
sequestered spot.[4]   When the girl is a chief's daughter the
ceremonies at her liberation from the hut are more elaborate
than usual.   She is led forth from the hut by a son of her
father's councillor, who, wearing the wings of a blue crane, the
badge of bravery, on his head, escorts her to the cattle kraal,
where cows are slaughtered and dancing takes place.   Large
skins full of milk are sent to the spot from neighbouring
villages ; and after the dances are over the girl drinks milk
for the first time since the day she entered into retreat.   But
the first mouthful is drunk by the girl's aunt or other female
relative who had charge of her during her seclusion ; and a
little of it is poured on the fire-place.[5]   Amongst the Zulus,
when the girl was a princess royal, the end of her time of
separation was celebrated by a sort of saturnalia : law and
order were for the time being in abeyance : every man,
woman, and child might appropriate any article of property :
the king abstained from interfering ; and if during this reign
of misrule he was robbed of anything he valued he could only

[1] Henri A. Junod, *The Life of a
South African Tribe* (Neuchatel,
1912- 1913), i. 178 *sq.*

[2] G. McCall Theal, *Kaffir Folk-lore*
(London, 1886), p. 218.

[3] L. Alberti, *De Kaffers aan de
Zuidkust van Afrika* (Amsterdam,
1810), pp. 79 *sq.* ; H. Lichtenstein,

Reisen im südlichen Africa (Berlin,
1811–1812), i. 428.

[4] Gustav Fritsch, *Die Eingeborenen
Süd-Afrika's* (Breslau, 1872), p. 112.
This statement applies especially to the
Ama-Xosa.

[5] G. McCall Theal, *Kaffir Folk-
lore*, p. 218.

recover it by paying a fine.[1]   Among the Basutos, when girls
at puberty are bathed as usual by the matrons in a river,
they are hidden separately in the turns and bends of the
stream, and told to cover their heads, as they will be visited
by a large serpent.   Their limbs are then plastered with clay,
little masks of straw are put on their faces, and thus arrayed
they daily follow each other in procession, singing melancholy
airs, to the fields, there to learn the labours of husbandry in
which a great part of their adult life will be passed.[2]   We
may suppose, though we are not told, that the straw masks
which they wear in these processions are intended to hide
their faces from the gaze of men and the rays of the sun.

Among the tribes in the lower valley of the Congo, such as
the Bavili, when a girl arrives at puberty, she has to pass two
or three months in seclusion in a small hut built for the purpose.   The hair of her head is shaved off, and every day the
whole of her body is smeared with a red paint (*takulla*) made
from a powdered wood mixed with water.   Some of her
companions reside in the hut with her and prepare the paint
for her use.   A woman is appointed to take charge of the
hut and to keep off intruders.   At the end of her confinement she is taken to water by the women of her family and
bathed ; the paint is rubbed off her body, her arms and legs
are loaded with brass rings, and she is led in solemn procession
under an umbrella to her husband's house.   If these ceremonies were not performed, the people believe that the girl
would be barren or would give birth to monsters, that the
rain would cease to fall, the earth to bear fruit, and the fishing
to be successful.[3]   Such serious importance do these savages

---

[1] Rev. Canon Henry Callaway, *Nursery Tales, Traditions, and Histories of the Zulus* (Natal and London, 1868), p. 182, note [20]. From one of the Zulu texts which the author edits and translates (p. 189) we may infer that during the period of her seclusion a Zulu girl may not light a fire. Compare above, p. 28.

[2] E. Casalis, *The Basutos* (London, 1861), p. 268.

[3] J. Merolla, "Voyage to Congo," in J. Pinkerton's *Voyages and Travels* (London, 1808–1814), xvi. 238 ; Father Campana, "Congo ; Mission

Catholique de Landana," *Les Missions Catholiques*, xxvii. (1895) p. 161 ; R. E. Dennett, *At the Back of the Black Man's Mind* (London, 1906), pp. 69 *sq.* According to Merolla, it is thought that if girls did not go through these ceremonies, they would " never be fit for procreation." The other consequences supposed to flow from the omission of the rites are mentioned by Father Campana. From Mr. Dennett's account (*op. cit.* pp. 53, 67-71) we gather that drought and famine are thought to result from the intercourse of a man with a girl who has not yet

ascribe to the performance of rites which to us seem so childish.

§ 2. Seclusion of Girls at Puberty in New Ireland, New Guinea, and Indonesia

Seclusion of girls at puberty in New Ireland.

In New Ireland girls are confined for four or five years in small cages, being kept in the dark and not allowed to set foot on the ground. The custom has been thus described by an eye-witness. " I heard from a teacher about some strange custom connected with some of the young girls here, so I asked the chief to take me to the house where they were. The house was about twenty-five feet in length, and stood in a reed and bamboo enclosure, across the entrance to which a bundle of dried grass was suspended to show that it was strictly ' *tabu*.' Inside the house were three conical structures about seven or eight feet in height, and about ten or twelve feet in circumference at the bottom, and for about four feet from the ground, at which point they tapered off to a point at the top. These cages were made of the broad leaves of the pandanus-tree, sewn quite close together so that no light and little or no air could enter. On one side of each is an opening which is closed by a double door of plaited cocoa-nut tree and pandanus-tree leaves. About three feet from the ground there is a stage of bamboos which forms the floor. In each of these cages we were told there was a young woman confined, each of whom had to remain for at least four or five years, without ever being allowed to go outside the house. I could scarcely credit the story when I heard it ; the whole thing seemed too horrible to be true. I spoke to the chief, and told him that I wished to see the inside of the cages, and also to see the girls that I might make them a present of a few beads. He told me that it was ' *tabu*,' forbidden for any men but their own relations to look at them ; but I suppose the promised beads

---

passed through the " paint-house," as the hut is called where the young women live in seclusion. According to O. Dapper, the women of Loango paint themselves red on every recurrence of their monthly sickness ; also they tie a cord tightly round their heads and take care neither to touch their husband's food nor to appear before him (*Description de l'Afrique*, Amsterdam, 1686, p. 326).

acted as an inducement, and so he sent away for some old
lady who had charge, and who alone is allowed to open the
doors.   While we were waiting we could hear the girls talking to the chief in a querulous way as if objecting to something or expressing their fears.   The old woman came at
length and certainly she did not seem a very pleasant jailor
or guardian ; nor did she seem to favour the request of the
chief to allow us to see the girls, as she regarded us with
anything but pleasant looks.   However, she had to undo the
door when the chief told her to do so, and then the girls peeped
out at us, and, when told to do so, they held out their hands
for the beads.   I, however, purposely sat at some distance away
and merely held out the beads to them, as I wished to draw
them quite outside, that I might inspect the inside of the cages.
This desire of mine gave rise to another difficulty, as these
girls were not allowed to put their feet to the ground all the
time they were confined in these places.   However, they
wished to get the beads, and so the old lady had to go outside and collect a lot of pieces of wood and bamboo, which
she placed on the ground, and then going to one of the girls,
she helped her down and held her hand as she stepped from
one piece of wood to another until she came near enough to
get the beads I held out to her.   I then went to inspect the
inside of the cage out of which she had come, but could
scarcely put my head inside of it, the atmosphere was so hot
and stifling.   It was clean and contained nothing but a few
short lengths of bamboo for holding water.   There was only
room for the girl to sit or lie down in a crouched position
on the bamboo platform, and when the doors are shut it must
be nearly or quite dark inside.   The girls are never allowed
to come out except once a day to bathe in a dish or wooden
bowl placed close to each cage.   They say that they per-
spire profusely.   They are placed in these stifling cages
when quite young, and must remain there until they are
young women, when they are taken out and have each a
great marriage feast provided for them.   One of them was
about fourteen or fifteen years old, and the chief told us
that she had been there for five years, but would soon be
taken out now.   The other two were about eight and ten
years old, and they have to stay there for several years

longer." [1]　A more recent observer has described the custom as it is observed on the western coast of New Ireland.　He says : "A *buck* is the name of a little house, not larger than an ordinary hen-coop, in which a little girl is shut up, sometimes for weeks only, and at other times for months. . . . Briefly stated, the custom is this.　Girls, on attaining puberty or betrothal, are enclosed in one of these little coops for a considerable time.　They must remain there night and day. We saw two of these girls in two coops ; the girls were not more than ten years old, still they were lying in a doubled-up position, as their little houses would not admit of them lying in any other way.　These two coops were inside a large house ; but the chief, in consideration of a present of a couple of tomahawks, ordered the ends to be torn out of the house to admit the light, so that we might photograph the *buck*.　The occupant was allowed to put her face through an opening to be photographed, in consideration of another present." [2]　As a consequence of their long enforced idleness in the shade the girls grow fat and their dusky complexion bleaches to a more pallid hue.　Both their corpulence and their pallor are regarded as beauties.[3]

---

[1] The Rev. G. Brown, quoted by the Rev. B. Danks, "Marriage Customs of the New Britain Group," *Journal of the Anthropological Institute*, xviii. (1889) pp. 284 *sq.* ; *id.*, *Melanesians and Polynesians* (London, 1910), pp. 105-107. Compare *id.*, "Notes on the Duke of York Group, New Britain, and New Ireland," *Journal of the Royal Geographical Society*, xlvii. (1877) pp. 142 *sq.* ; A. Hahl, "Das mittlere Neumecklenburg," *Globus*, xci. (1907) p. 313. Wilfred Powell's description of the New Ireland custom is similar (*Wanderings in a Wild Country*, London, 1883, p. 249). According to him, the girls wear wreaths of scented herbs round the waist and neck ; an old woman or a little child occupies the lower floor of the cage ; and the confinement lasts only a month. Probably the long period mentioned by Dr. Brown is that prescribed for chiefs' daughters. Poor people could not afford to keep their children so long idle. This distinction is sometimes expressly stated.　See above, p. 30.　Among the Goajiras of Colombia rich people keep their daughters shut up in separate huts at puberty for periods varying from one to four years, but poor people cannot afford to do so for more than a fortnight or a month.　See F. A. Simons, "An Exploration of the Goajira Peninsula," *Proceedings of the Royal Geographical Society*, N.S., vii. (1885) p. 791.　In Fiji, brides who were being tattooed were kept from the sun (Thomas Williams, *Fiji and the Fijians*, Second Edition, London, 1860, i. 170).　This was perhaps a modification of the Melanesian custom of secluding girls at puberty.　The reason mentioned by Mr. Williams, "to improve her complexion," can hardly have been the original one.

[2] Rev. R. H. Rickard, quoted by Dr. George Brown, *Melanesians and Polynesians*, pp. 107 *sq.* His observations were made in 1892.

[3] R. Parkinson, *Dreissig Jahre in der Südsee* (Stuttgart, 1907), p. 272.

In Kabadi, a district of British New Guinea, " daughters of chiefs, when they are about twelve or thirteen years of age, are kept indoors for two or three years, never being allowed, under any pretence, to descend from the house, and the house is so shaded that the sun cannot shine on them." [1] Among the Yabim and Bukaua, two neighbouring and kindred tribes on the coast of German New Guinea, a girl at puberty is secluded for some five or six weeks in an inner part of the house ; but she may not sit on the floor, lest her uncleanness should cleave to it, so a log of wood is placed for her to squat on.   Moreover, she may not touch the ground with her feet ; hence if she is obliged to quit the house for a short time, she is muffled up in mats and walks on two halves of a coconut shell, which are fastened like sandals to her feet by creeping plants.   During her seclusion she is in charge of her aunts or other female relatives.   At the end of the time she bathes, her person is loaded with ornaments, her face is grotesquely painted with red stripes on a white ground, and thus adorned she is brought forth in public to be admired by everybody.   She is now marriageable.[2]   Among the Ot Danoms of Borneo girls at the age of eight or ten years are shut up in a little room or cell of the house, and cut off from all intercourse with the world for a long time.   The cell, like the rest of the house, is raised on piles above the ground, and is lit by a single small window opening on a lonely place, so that the girl is in almost total darkness. She may not leave the room on any pretext whatever, not even for the most necessary purposes.   None of her family may see her all the time she is shut up, but a single slave woman is appointed to wait on her.   During her lonely confinement, which often lasts seven years, the girl occupies herself in weaving mats or with other handiwork.   Her bodily growth is stunted by the long want of exercise, and

Seclusion of girls at puberty in New Guinea and Borneo.

The natives told Mr. Parkinson that the confinement of the girls lasts from twelve to twenty months.   The length of it may have been reduced since Dr. George Brown described the custom in 1876.

[1] J. Chalmers and W. Wyatt Gill, *Work and Adventure in New Guinea*

(London, 1885), p. 159.

[2] H. Zahn and S. Lehner, in R. Neuhauss's *Deutsch Neu-Guinea* (Berlin, 1911), iii. 298, 418-420.   The customs of the two tribes seem to be in substantial agreement, and the accounts of them supplement each other.   The description of the Bukaua practice is the fuller.

when, on attaining womanhood, she is brought out, her complexion is pale and wax-like.   She is now shewn the sun, the earth, the water, the trees, and the flowers, as if she were newly born.   Then a great feast is made, a slave is killed, and the girl is smeared with his blood.[1]   In Ceram girls at puberty were formerly shut up by themselves in a hut which was kept dark.[2]   In Yap, one of the Caroline Islands, should a girl be overtaken by her first menstruation on the public road, she may not sit down on the earth, but must beg for a coco-nut shell to put under her.   She is shut up for several days in a small hut at a distance from her parents' house, and afterwards she is bound to sleep for a hundred days in one of the special houses which are provided for the use of menstruous women.[3]

Seclusion of girls at puberty in Ceram and Yap.

§ 3.   *Seclusion of Girls at Puberty in the Torres Straits Islands and Northern Australia*

Seclusion of girls at puberty in Mabuiag, Torres Straits.

In the island of Mabuiag, Torres Straits, when the signs of puberty appear on a girl, a circle of bushes is made in a dark corner of the house.   Here, decked with shoulder-belts, armlets, leglets just below the knees, and anklets, wearing a chaplet on her head, and shell ornaments in her ears, on her chest, and on her back, she squats in the midst of the bushes, which are piled so high round about her that only her head is visible.   In this state of seclusion she must remain for three months.   All this time the sun may not shine upon her, but at night she is allowed to slip out of the hut, and the bushes that hedge her in are then changed.   She may not feed herself or handle food, but is fed by one or two old women, her maternal aunts, who are especially appointed to look after her.   One of these women cooks food for her at a special fire in the forest.   The girl is forbidden to eat turtle or

[1] C. A. L. M. Schwaner, *Borneo, Beschrijving van het stroomgebied van den Barito* (Amsterdam, 1853–1854), ii. 77 *sq.*; W. F. A. Zimmermann, *Die Inseln des Indischen und Stillen Meeres* (Berlin, 1864–1865), ii. 632 *sq.*; Otto Finsch, *Neu Guinea und seine Bewohner* (Bremen, 1865), pp. 116 *sq.*

[2] J. G. F. Riedel, *De sluik- en kroesharige rassen tusschen Selebes en Papua* (The Hague, 1886), p. 138.
[3] A. Senfft, "Ethnographische Beiträge über die Karolineninsel Yap," *Petermanns Mitteilungen*, xlix. (1903) p. 53; *id.*, "Die Rechtssitten der Jap-Eingeborenen," *Globus*, xci. (1907) pp. 142 *sq.*

turtle eggs during the season when the turtles are breeding ;
but no vegetable food is refused her.   No man, not even her
own father, may come into the house while her seclusion
lasts ; for if her father saw her at this time he would certainly
have bad luck in his fishing, and would probably smash his
canoe the very next time he went out in it.   At the end of
the three months she is carried down to a fresh-water creek
by her attendants, hanging on to their shoulders in such a
way that her feet do not touch the ground, while the women
of the tribe form a ring round her, and thus escort her to
the beach.   Arrived at the shore, she is stripped of her ornaments, and the bearers stagger with her into the creek, where
they immerse her, and all the other women join in splashing
water over both the girl and her bearers.   When they come
out of the water one of the two attendants makes a heap of
grass for her charge to squat upon.   The other runs to the
reef, catches a small crab, tears off its claws, and hastens
back with them to the creek.   Here in the meantime a fire
has been kindled, and the claws are roasted at it.   The girl
is then fed by her attendants with the roasted claws.   After
that she is freshly decorated, and the whole party marches
back to the village in a single rank, the girl walking in the
centre between her two old aunts, who hold her by the
wrists.   The husbands of her aunts now receive her and lead
her into the house of one of them, where all partake of food,
and the girl is allowed once more to feed herself in the usual
manner.   A dance follows, in which the girl takes a prominent part, dancing between the husbands of the two aunts
who had charge of her in her retirement.[1]

Among the Yaraikanna tribe of Cape York Peninsula, in
Northern Queensland, a girl at puberty is said to live by herself for a month or six weeks ; no man may see her, though
any woman may.   She stays in a hut or shelter specially
made for her, on the floor of which she lies supine.   She
may not see the sun, and towards sunset she must keep
her eyes shut until the sun has gone down, otherwise it is
thought that her nose will be diseased.   During her seclusion

Seclusion of girls at puberty in Northern Australia.

[1] Dr. C. G. Seligmann, in *Journal of the Anthropological Institute*, xxix. (1899) pp. 212 *sq.* ; *id.*, in *Reports of* the *Cambridge Anthropological Expedition to Torres Straits*, v. (Cambridge, 1904) pp. 203 *sq.*

she may eat nothing that lives in salt water, or a snake would kill her. An old woman waits upon her and supplies her with roots, yams, and water.[1] Some tribes are wont to bury their girls at such seasons more or less deeply in the ground, perhaps in order to hide them from the light of the sun. Thus the Larrakeeyah tribe in the northern territory of South Australia used to cover a girl up with dirt for three days at her first monthly period.[2] In similar circumstances the Otati tribe, on the east coast of the Cape York Peninsula, make an excavation in the ground, where the girl squats. A bower is then built over the hole, and sand is thrown on the young woman till she is covered up to the hips. In this condition she remains for the first day, but comes out at night. So long as the period lasts, she stays in the bower during the day-time, but is not again covered with sand. Afterwards her body is painted red and white from the head to the hips, and she returns to the camp, where she squats first on the right side, then on the left side, and then on the lap of her future husband, who has been previously selected for her.[3] Among the natives of the Pennefather River, in the Cape York Peninsula, Queensland, when a girl menstruates for the first time, her mother takes her away from the camp to some secluded spot, where she digs a circular hole in the sandy soil under the shade of a tree. In this hole the girl squats with crossed legs and is covered with sand from the waist downwards. A digging-stick is planted firmly in the sand on each side of her, and the place is surrounded by a fence of bushes except in front, where her mother kindles a fire. Here the girl stays all day, sitting with her arms crossed and the palms of her hands resting on the sand. She may not move her arms except to take food from her mother or to scratch herself; and in scratching herself she may not touch herself with her own hands, but must use for the purpose a splinter of wood, which, when it is not in use, is stuck in her hair. She may speak to nobody but her mother; indeed nobody else would

[1] Dr. C. G. Seligmann, in *Reports of the Cambridge Expedition to Torres Straits*, v. (Cambridge, 1904) p. 205.
[2] L. Crauford, in *Journal of the* *Anthropological Institute*, xxiv. (1895) p. 181.
[3] Dr. C. G. Seligmann, *op. cit.* v. 206.

think of coming near her. At evening she lays hold of the
two digging-sticks and by their help frees herself from the
superincumbent weight of sand and returns to the camp.
Next morning she is again buried in the sand under the
shade of the tree and remains there again till evening.
This she does daily for five days. On her return at
evening on the fifth day her mother decorates her with a
waist-band, a forehead-band, and a necklet of pearl-shell,
ties green parrot feathers round her arms and wrists and
across her chest, and smears her body, back and front, from
the waist upwards with blotches of red, white, and yellow
paint. She has in like manner to be buried in the sand at
her second and third menstruations, but at the fourth she is
allowed to remain in camp, only signifying her condition by
wearing a basket of empty shells on her back.[1] Among the
Kia blacks of the Proserpine River, on the east coast of
Queensland, a girl at puberty has to sit or lie down in a
shallow pit away from the camp ; a rough hut of bushes is
erected over her to protect her from the inclemency of the
weather. There she stays for about a week, waited on by
her mother and sister, the only persons to whom she may
speak. She is allowed to drink water, but may not touch
it with her hands ; and she may scratch herself a little with
a mussel-shell. This seclusion is repeated at her second
and third monthly periods, but when the third is over she
is brought to her husband bedecked with savage finery.
Eagle-hawk or cockatoo feathers are stuck in her hair : a
shell hangs over her forehead : grass bugles encircle her
neck and an apron of opossum skin her waist : strings are
tied to her arms and wrists ; and her whole body is mottled
with patterns drawn in red, white, and yellow pigments and
charcoal.[2]

Among the Uiyumkwi tribe in Red Island the girl
lies at full length in a shallow trench dug in the foreshore,
and sand is lightly thrown over her legs and body up
to the breasts, which appear not to be covered. A rough
shelter of boughs is then built over her, and thus she

Seclusion of girls at puberty in the islands of Torres Straits.

---

[1] Walter E. Roth, *North Queens-*
land Ethnography, Bulletin No. 5,
Superstition, Magic, and Medicine
(Brisbane, 1903), pp. 24 *sq.*

[2] Walter E. Roth, *op. cit.* p. 25.

remains lying for a few hours. Then she and her attendant go into the bush and look for food, which they cook at a fire close to the shelter. They sleep under the boughs, the girl remaining secluded from the camp but apparently not being again buried. At the end of the symptoms she stands over hot stones and water is poured over her, till, trickling from her body on the stones, it is converted into steam and envelops her in a cloud of vapour. Then she is painted with red and white stripes and returns to the camp. If her future husband has already been chosen, she goes to him and they eat some food together, which the girl has previously brought from the bush.[1] In Prince of Wales Island, Torres Strait, the treatment of the patient is similar, but lasts for about two months. During the day she lies covered up with sand in a shallow hole on the beach, over which a hut is built. At night she may get out of the hole, but she may not leave the hut. Her paternal aunt looks after her, and both of them must abstain from eating turtle, dugong, and the heads of fish. Were they to eat the heads of fish no more fish would be caught. During the time of the girl's seclusion, the aunt who waits upon her has the right to enter any house and take from it anything she likes without payment, provided she does so before the sun rises. When the time of her retirement has come to an end, the girl bathes in the sea while the morning star is rising, and after performing various other ceremonies is readmitted to society.[2] In Saibai, another island of Torres Straits, at her first monthly sickness a girl lives secluded in the forest for about a fortnight, during which no man may see her ; even the women who have spoken to her in the forest must wash in salt water before they speak to a man. Two girls wait upon and feed the damsel, putting the food into her mouth,

---

[1] Dr. C. G. Seligmann, in *Reports of the Cambridge Anthropological Expedition to Torres Straits*, v. (Cambridge, 1904), p. 205.

[2] From notes kindly sent me by Dr. C. G. Seligmann. The practice of burying a girl at puberty was observed also by some Indian tribes of California, but apparently rather for the purpose of producing a sweat than for the sake of concealment. The treatment lasted only twenty-four hours, during which the patient was removed from the ground and washed three or four times, to be afterwards reimbedded. Dancing was kept up the whole time by the women. See H. R. Schoolcraft, *Indian Tribes of the United States* (Philadelphia, 1853-1856), v. 215.

for she is not allowed to touch it with her own hands.   Nor may she eat dugong and turtle.   At the end of a fortnight the girl and her attendants bathe in salt water while the tide is running out.   Afterwards they are clean, may again speak to men without ceremony, and move freely about the village.   In Yam and Tutu a girl at puberty retires for a month to the forest, where no man nor even her own mother may look upon her.   She is waited on by women who stand to her in a certain relationship (*mowai*), apparently her paternal aunts.   She is blackened all over with charcoal and wears a long petticoat reaching below her knees.   During her seclusion the married women of the village often assemble in the forest and dance, and the girl's aunts relieve the tedium of the proceedings by thrashing her from time to time as a useful preparation for matrimony.   At the end of a month the whole party go into the sea, and the charcoal is washed off the girl.   After that she is decorated, her body blackened again, her hair reddened with ochre, and in the evening she is brought back to her father's house, where she is received with weeping and lamentation because she has been so long away.[1]

§ 4.   *Seclusion of Girls at Puberty among the Indians of North America*

Among the Indians of California a girl at her first menstruation "was thought to be possessed of a particular degree of supernatural power, and this was not always regarded as entirely defiling or malevolent.   Often, however, there was a strong feeling of the power of evil inherent in her condition.   Not only was she secluded from her family and the community, but an attempt was made to seclude the world from her.   One of the injunctions most strongly laid upon her was not to look about her.   She kept her head bowed and was forbidden to see the world and the sun.   Some tribes covered her with a blanket.   Many of the customs in this connection resembled those of the North Pacific Coast most strongly, such as the prohibition to the girl to touch or scratch her head with her hand, a special implement being furnished her for the purpose.   Sometimes

[1] Dr. C. G. Seligmann, in *Reports of the Cambridge Anthropological Expedition to Torres Straits*, v. 201 *sq.*

she could eat only when fed and in other cases fasted
altogether. Some form of public ceremony, often accompanied by a dance and sometimes by a form of ordeal for
the girl, was practised nearly everywhere. Such ceremonies
were well developed in Southern California, where a number
of actions symbolical of the girl's maturity and subsequent
life were performed." [1] Thus among the Maidu Indians of
California a girl at puberty remained shut up in a small
separate hut. For five days she might not eat flesh or fish
nor feed herself, but was fed by her mother or other old
woman. She had a basket, plate, and cup for her own use,
and a stick with which to scratch her head, for she might
not scratch it with her fingers. At the end of five days she
took a warm bath and, while she still remained in the hut
and plied the scratching-stick on her head, was privileged to
feed herself with her own hands. After five days more she
bathed in the river, after which her parents gave a great
feast in her honour. At the feast the girl was dressed in
her best, and anybody might ask her parents for anything
he pleased, and they had to give it, even if it was the hand
of their daughter in marriage. During the period of her
seclusion in the hut the girl was allowed to go by night to
her parents' house and listen to songs sung by her friends
and relations, who assembled for the purpose. Among the
songs were some that related to the different roots and seeds
which in these tribes it is the business of women to gather
for food. While the singers sang, she sat by herself in a
corner of the house muffled up completely in mats and skins ;
no man or boy might come near her. [2] Among the Hupa,
another Indian tribe of California, when a girl had reached
maturity her male relatives danced all night for nine successive nights, while the girl remained apart, eating no meat
and blindfolded. But on the tenth night she entered the
house and took part in the last dance. [3] Among the Wintun,

[1] A. L. Kroeber, " The Religion of
the Indians of California," *University
of California Publications in American
Archaeology and Ethnology*, vol. iv.
No. 6 (September, 1907), p. 324.

[2] Roland B. Dixon, " The Northern
Maidu," *Bulletin of the American
Museum of Natural History*, vol. xvii.
Part iii. (May 1905) pp. 232 *sq.*,
compare pp. 233-238.

[3] Stephen Powers, *Tribes of California* (Washington, 1877), p. 85
(*Contributions to North American Ethnology*, vol. iii.).

another Californian tribe, a girl at puberty was banished from
the camp and lived alone in a distant booth, fasting rigidly
from animal food ; it was death to any person to touch or
even approach her.[1]

In the interior of Washington State, about Colville, " the
customs of the Indians, in relation to the treatment of
females, are singular.   On the first appearance of the menses,
they are furnished with provisions, and sent into the woods,
to remain concealed for two days ; for they have a superstition, that if a man should be seen or met with during that
time, death will be the consequence.   At the end of the
second day, the woman is permitted to return to the lodge,
when she is placed in a hut just large enough for her to lie
in at full length, in which she is compelled to remain for
twenty days, cut off from all communication with her friends,
and is obliged to hide her face at the appearance of a man.
Provisions are supplied her daily.   After this, she is required
to perform repeated ablutions, before she can resume her
place in the family.   At every return, the women go into
seclusion for two or more days." [2]   Among the Chinook
Indians who inhabited the coast of Washington State, from
Shoalwater Bay as far as Grey's Harbour, when a chief's
daughter attained to puberty, she was hidden for five days
from the view of the people ; she might not look at them
nor at the sky, nor might she pick berries.   It was believed
that if she were to look at the sky, the weather would be
bad ; that if she picked berries, it would rain ; and that when
she hung her towel of cedar-bark on a spruce-tree, the tree
withered up at once.   She went out of the house by a
separate door and bathed in a creek far from the village.
She fasted for some days, and for many days more she
might not eat fresh food.[3]

Amongst the Aht or Nootka Indians of Vancouver
Island, when girls reach puberty they are placed in a sort
of gallery in the house " and are there surrounded com-

Marginal notes:

Seclusion of girls at puberty among the Indians of Washington State.

Seclusion of girls at puberty among the Nootka Indians of Vancouver Island.

[1] Stephen Powers, *op. cit.* p. 235.
[2] Charles Wilkes, *Narrative of the United States Exploring Expedition*, New Edition (New York, 1851), iv. 456.
[3] Franz Boas, *Chinook Texts* (Wash-

ington, 1894), pp. 246 *sq.*   The account, taken down from the lips of a Chinook Indian, is not perfectly clear ; some of the restrictions were prolonged after the girl's second monthly period.

pletely with mats, so that neither the sun nor any fire can be seen. In this cage they remain for several days. Water is given them, but no food. The longer a girl remains in this retirement the greater honour is it to the parents ; but she is disgraced for life if it is known that she has seen fire or the sun during this initiatory ordeal."[1] Pictures of the mythical thunder-bird are painted on the screens behind which she hides. During her seclusion she may neither move nor lie down, but must always sit in a squatting posture. She may not touch her hair with her hands, but is allowed to scratch her head with a comb or a piece of bone provided for the purpose. To scratch her body is also forbidden, as it is believed that every scratch would leave a scar. For eight months after reaching maturity she may not eat any fresh food, particularly salmon ; moreover, she must eat by herself, and use a cup and dish of her own.[2]

Seclusion of girls at puberty among the Haida Indians of the Queen Charlotte Islands. Among the Haida Indians of the Queen Charlotte Islands girls at puberty were secluded behind screens in the house for about twenty days. In some parts of the islands separate fires were provided for the girls, and they went out and in by a separate door at the back of the house. If a girl at such a time was obliged to go out by the front door, all the weapons, gambling-sticks, medicine, and other articles had to be removed from the house till her return, for otherwise it was thought that they would be unlucky ; and if there was a good hunter in the house, he also had to go out at the same time on pain of losing his good luck if he remained. During several months or even half a year the girl was bound to wear a peculiar cloak or hood made of cedar-bark, nearly conical in shape and reaching

---

[1] G. M. Sproat, *Scenes and Studies of Savage Life* (London, 1868), pp. 93 *sq.*

[2] Franz Boas, in *Sixth Report on the North-Western Tribes of Canada*, pp. 40-42 (separate reprint from the *Report of the British Association for the Advancement of Science*, Leeds meeting, 1890). The rule not to lie down is observed also during their seclusion at puberty by Tsimshian girls, who always sit propped up between boxes and mats ; their heads are covered with

small mats, and they may not look at men nor at fresh salmon and olachen. See Franz Boas, in *Fifth Report on the North-Western Tribes of Canada*, p. 41 (separate reprint from the *Report of the British Association for the Advancement of Science*, Newcastle-upon-Tyne meeting, 1889) ; G. M. Dawson, *Report on the Queen Charlotte Islands, 1878* (Montreal, 1880), pp. 130 B *sq.* Some divine kings are not allowed to lie down. See *Taboo and the Perils of the Soul*, p. 5.

down below the breast, but open before the face. After the
twenty days were over the girl took a bath ; none of the
water might be spilled, it had all to be taken back to the
woods, else the girl would not live long.   On the west coast
of the islands the damsel might eat nothing but black cod
for four years ; for the people believed that other kinds of
fish would become scarce if she partook of them.   At Kloo
the young woman at such times was forbidden to look at
the sea, and for forty days she might not gaze at the fire ;
for a whole year she might not walk on the beach below
high-water mark, because then the tide would come in,
covering part of the food supply, and there would be bad
weather.   For five years she might not eat salmon, or the
fish would be scarce ; and when her family went to a salmon-
creek, she landed from the canoe at the mouth of the creek
and came to the smoke-house from behind ; for were she to
see a salmon leap, all the salmon might leave the creek.
Among the Haidas of Masset it was believed that if the
girl looked at the sky, the weather would be bad, and that
if she stepped over a salmon-creek, all the salmon would
disappear.[1]

Amongst the Tlingit (Thlinkeet) or Kolosh Indians of
Alaska, when a girl shewed signs of womanhood she used to
be confined to a little hut or cage, which was completely
blocked up with the exception of a small air-hole.   In this
dark and filthy abode she had to remain a year, without fire,
exercise, or associates.   Only her mother and a female slave
might supply her with nourishment.   Her food was put in
at the little window ; she had to drink out of the wing-bone
of a white-headed eagle.   The time of her seclusion was
afterwards reduced in some places to six or three months or
even less.   She had to wear a sort of hat with long flaps,

Seclusion
of girls at
puberty
among the
Tlingit
Indians of
Alaska.

---

[1] George M. Dawson, *Report on the
Queen Charlotte Islands, 1878* (Montreal, 1880), p. 130 B ; J. R. Swanton, *Contributions to the Ethnology of
the Haida* (Leyden and New York,
1905), pp. 48-50 (*The Jesup North
Pacific Expedition, Memoir of the
American Museum of Natural History*,
New York).   Speaking of the customs
observed at Kloo, where the girls had
to abstain from salmon for five years,
Mr. Swanton says (p. 49) : "When
five years had passed, the girl came
out, and could do as she pleased."
This seems to imply that the girl was
secluded in the house for five years.
We have seen (above, p. 32) that
in New Ireland the girls used sometimes to be secluded for the same
period.

that her gaze might not pollute the sky ; for she was thought unfit for the sun to shine upon, and it was imagined that her look would destroy the luck of a hunter, fisher, or gambler, turn things to stone, and do other mischief. At the end of her confinement her old clothes were burnt, new ones were made, and a feast was given, at which a slit was cut in her under lip parallel to the mouth, and a piece of wood or shell was inserted to keep the aperture open.[1]

Seclusion of girls at puberty among the Tsetsaut and Bella Coola Indians of British Columbia.
In the Tsetsaut tribe of British Columbia a girl at puberty wears a large hat of skin which comes down over her face and screens it from the sun. It is believed that if she were to expose her face to the sun or to the sky, rain would fall. The hat protects her face also against the fire, which ought not to strike her skin ; to shield her hands she wears mittens. In her mouth she carries the tooth of an animal to prevent her own teeth from becoming hollow. For a whole year she may not see blood unless her face is blackened ; otherwise she would grow blind. For two years she wears the hat and lives in a hut by herself, although she is allowed to see other people. At the end of two years a man takes the hat from her head and throws it away.[2] In the Bilqula or Bella Coola tribe of British Columbia, when a girl attains puberty she must stay in the shed which serves as her bedroom, where she has a separate fireplace. She is not allowed to descend to the main part of the house, and may not sit by the fire of the family. For four days she is

---

[1] G. H. von Langsdorff, *Reise um die Welt* (Frankfort, 1812), ii. 114 *sq.* ; H. J. Holmberg, "Ethnographische Skizzen über die Völker des Russischen Amerika," *Acta Societatis Scientiarum Fennicae*, iv. (Helsingfors, 1856) pp. 319 *sq.* ; T. de Pauly, *Description Ethnographique des Peuples de la Russie* (St. Petersburg, 1862), *Peuples de l'Amérique Russe*, p. 13 ; A. Erman, "Ethnographische Wahrnehmungen und Erfahrungen an den Küsten des Berings-Meeres," *Zeitschrift für Ethnologie*, ii. (1870) pp. 318 *sq.* ; H. H. Bancroft, *Native Races of the Pacific States* (London, 1875–1876), i. 110 *sq.* ; Rev. Sheldon Jackson, "Alaska and its Inhabitants," *The American Antiquarian*,

ii. (Chicago, 1879–1880) pp. 111 *sq.* ; A. Woldt, *Captain Jacobsen's Reise an der Nordwestküste Americas, 1881-1883* (Leipsic, 1884), p. 393 ; Aurel Krause, *Die Tlinkit-Indianer* (Jena, 1885), pp. 217 *sq.* ; W. M. Grant, in *Journal of American Folk-lore*, i. (1888) p. 169 ; John R. Swanton, "Social Conditions, Beliefs, and Linguistic Relationship of the Tlingit Indians," *Twenty-sixth Annual Report of the Bureau of American Ethnology* (Washington, 1908), p. 428.

[2] Franz Boas, in *Tenth Report of the Committee on the North-Western Tribes of Canada*, p. 45 (separate reprint from the *Report of the British Association for the Advancement of Science*, Ipswich meeting, 1895).

bound to remain motionless in a sitting posture. She fasts during the day, but is allowed a little food and drink very early in the morning. After the four days' seclusion she may leave her room, but only through a separate opening cut in the floor, for the houses are raised on piles. She may not yet come into the chief room. In leaving the house she wears a large hat which protects her face against the rays of the sun. It is believed that if the sun were to shine on her face her eyes would suffer. She may pick berries on the hills, but may not come near the river or sea for a whole year. Were she to eat fresh salmon she would lose her senses, or her mouth would be changed into a long beak.[1]

Among the Tinneh Indians about Stuart Lake, Babine Lake, and Fraser Lake in British Columbia " girls verging on maturity, that is when their breasts begin to form, take swans' feathers mixed with human hair and plait bands, which they tie round their wrists and ankles to secure long life. At this time they are careful that the dishes out of which they eat, are used by no other person, and wholly devoted to their own use ; during this period they eat nothing but dog fish, and starvation *only* will drive them to eat either fresh fish or meat. When their first periodical sickness comes on, they are fed by their mothers or nearest female relation by *themselves*, and on no account will they touch their food with their own hands. They are at this time also careful not to touch their heads with their hands, and keep a small stick to scratch their heads with. They remain outside the lodge, all the time they are in this state, in a hut made for the purpose. During all this period they wear a skull-cap made of skin to fit very tight ; this is never taken off until their first monthly sickness ceases ; they also wear a strip of black paint about one inch wide across their eyes, and wear a fringe of shells, bones, etc., hanging down from their foreheads to below their eyes ; and this is never taken off

Seclusion of girls at puberty among the Tinneh Indians of British Columbia.

---

[1] Franz Boas, in *Fifth Report of the Committee on the North-Western Tribes of Canada*, p. 42 (separate reprint from the *Report of the British Association for the Advancement of Science*, New- castle-upon-Tyne meeting, 1889) ; *id.*, in *Seventh Report*, etc., p. 12 (separate reprint from the *Report of the British Association for the Advancement of Science*, Cardiff meeting, 1891).

till the second monthly period arrives and ceases, when the nearest male relative makes a feast ; after which she is considered a fully matured woman ; but she has to refrain from eating anything fresh for one year after her first monthly sickness ; she may however eat partridge, but it must be cooked in the crop of the bird to render it harmless. I would have thought it impossible to perform this feat had I not seen it done. The crop is blown out, and a small bent willow put round the mouth ; it is then filled with water, and the meat being first minced up, put in also, then put on the fire and boiled till cooked. Their reason for hanging fringes before their eyes, is to hinder any bad medicine man from harming them during this critical period : they are very careful not to drink whilst facing a medicine man, and do so only when their backs are turned to him. All these habits are left off when the girl is a recognised woman, with the exception of their going out of the lodge and remaining in a hut, every time their periodical sickness comes on. This is a rigidly observed law with both single and married women." [1]

Seclusion of girls at puberty among the Tinneh Indians of Alaska.

Among the Hareskin Tinneh a girl at puberty was secluded for five days in a hut made specially for the purpose ; she might only drink out of a tube made from a swan's bone, and for a month she might not break a hare's bones, nor taste blood, nor eat the heart or fat of animals, nor birds' eggs.[2] Among the Tinneh Indians of the middle Yukon valley, in Alaska, the period of the girl's seclusion lasts exactly a lunar month ; for the day of the moon on which the symptoms first occur is noted, and she is sequestered until the same day of the next moon. If the season is winter, a corner of the house is curtained off for her use by a blanket or a sheet of canvas ; if it is summer, a small tent is erected for her near the common one. Here she lives and sleeps. She wears a long robe and a large

---

[1] "Customs of the New Caledonian women belonging to the Nancaushy Tine, or Stuart's Lake Indians, Natotin Tine, or Babine's and Nantley Tine, or Fraser Lake Tribes," from information supplied by Gavin Hamilton, chief factor of the Hudson's Bay Company's service, who has been for many years among these Indians, both he and his wife speaking their languages fluently (communicated by Dr. John Rae), *Journal of the Anthropological Institute*, vii. (1878) pp. 206 *sq.*

[2] Émile Petitot, *Traditions Indiennes du Canada Nord-ouest* (Paris, 1886), pp. 257 *sq.*

hood, which she must pull down over her eyes whenever she leaves the hut, and she must keep it down till she returns. She may not speak to a man nor see his face, much less touch his clothes or anything that belongs to him ; for if she did so, though no harm would come to her, he would grow unmanly. She has her own dishes for eating out of and may use no other ; at Kaltag she must suck the water through a swan's bone without applying her lips to the cup. She may eat no fresh meat or fish except the flesh of the porcupine. She may not undress, but sleeps with all her clothes on, even her mittens. In her socks she wears, next to the skin, the horny soles cut from the feet of a porcupine, in order that for the rest of her life her shoes may never wear out. Round her waist she wears a cord to which are tied the heads of femurs of a porcupine ; because of all animals known to the Tinneh the porcupine suffers least in parturition, it simply drops its young and continues to walk or skip about as if nothing had happened. Hence it is easy to see that a girl who wears these portions of a porcupine about her waist, will be delivered just as easily as the animal. To make quite sure of this, if anybody happens to kill a porcupine big with young while the girl is under-going her period of separation, the foetus is given to her, and she lets it slide down between her shirt and her body so as to fall on the ground like an infant.[1] Here the imitation of childbirth is a piece of homoeopathic or imitative magic designed to facilitate the effect which it simulates.[2]

Among the Thompson Indians of British Columbia, when a girl attained puberty, she was at once separated from all the people. A conical hut of fir branches and bark was erected at some little distance from the other houses, and in it the girl had to squat on her heels during the day. Often a deep circular hole was dug in the hut and the girl squatted in the hole, with her head projecting above the surface of the ground. She might quit the hut for various purposes in the early morning, but had always to be back at sunrise. On the first appearance of the symptoms her face was

Seclusion of girls at puberty among the Thompson Indians of British Columbia.

---

[1] Fr. Julius Jetté, S.J., "On the Superstitions of the Ten'a Indians," *Anthropos*, vi. (1911) pp. 700-702.

[2] Compare *The Magic Art and the Evolution of Kings*, i. 70 *sqq.*

Seclusion
of girls at
puberty
among the
Thompson
Indians of
British
Columbia.
painted red all over, and the paint was renewed every
morning during her term of seclusion. A heavy blanket
swathed her body from top to toe, and during the first four
days she wore a conical cap made of small fir branches,
which reached below the breast but left an opening for the
face. In her hair was fastened an implement made of deer-
bone with which she scratched herself. For the first four
days she might neither wash nor eat, but a little water was
given her in a birch-bark cup painted red, and she sucked
up the liquid through a tube made out of the leg of a crane,
a swan, or a goose, for her lips might not touch the surface
of the water. After the four days she was allowed, during
the rest of the period of isolation, to eat, to wash, to lie
down, to comb her hair, and to drink of streams and springs.
But in drinking at these sources she had still to use her
tube, otherwise the spring would dry up. While her
seclusion lasted she performed by night various ceremonies,
which were supposed to exert a beneficial influence on her
future life. For example, she ran as fast as she could,
praying at the same time to the Earth or Nature that she
might be fleet of foot and tireless of limb. She dug trenches,
in order that in after life she might be able to dig well and
to work hard. These and other ceremonies she repeated for
four nights or mornings in succession, four times each morning,
and each time she supplicated the Dawn of the Day. Among
the Lower Thompson Indians she carried a staff for one
night ; and when the day was breaking she leaned the staff
against the stump of a tree and prayed to the Dawn that
she might be blessed with a good husband, who was sym-
bolized by the staff. She also wandered some nights to
lonely parts of the mountains, where she would dance, im-
ploring the spirits to pity and protect her during her future
life ; then, the dance and prayer over, she would lie down on
the spot and fall asleep. Again, she carried four stones in
her bosom to a spring, where she spat upon the stones and
threw them one after the other into the water, praying that
all disease might leave her, as these stones did. Also she
ran four times in the early morning with two small stones
in her bosom ; and as she ran the stones slipped down
between her bare body and her clothes and fell to the

ground.   At the same time she prayed to the Dawn that when she should be with child, she might be delivered as easily as she was delivered of these stones.   But whatever exercises she performed or prayers she offered on the lonely mountains during the hours of darkness or while the morning light was growing in the east, she must always be back in her little hut before the sun rose.   There she often passed the tedious hours away picking the needles, one by one, from the cones on two large branches of fir, which hung from the roof of her hut on purpose to provide her with occupation.   And as she picked she prayed to the fir-branch that she might never be lazy, but always quick and active at work.   During her seclusion, too, she had to make miniatures of all the articles that Indian women make, or used to make, such as baskets, mats, ropes, and thread. This she did in order that afterwards she might be able to make the real things properly.   Four large fir-branches also were placed in front of the hut, so that when she went out or in, she had to step over them.   The branches were renewed every morning and the old ones thrown away into the water, while the girl prayed, " May I never bewitch any man, nor my fellow-women !   May it never happen ! "   The first four times that she went out and in, she prayed to the fir-branches, saying, "'If ever I step into trouble or difficulties or step unknowingly inside the magical spell of some person, may you help me, O Fir-branches, with your power ! " Every day she painted her face afresh, and she wore strings of parts of deer-hoofs round her ankles and knees, and tied to her waistband on either side, which rattled when she walked or ran.   Even the shape of the hut in which she lived was adapted to her future rather than to her present needs and wishes.   If she wished to be tall, the hut was tall ; if she wished to be short, it was low, sometimes so low that there was not room in it for her to stand erect, and she would lay the palm of her hand on the top of her head and pray to the Dawn that she might grow no taller.   Her seclusion lasted four months.   The Indians say that long ago it extended over a year, and that fourteen days elapsed before the girl was permitted to wash for the first time. The dress which she wore during her time of separation was afterwards taken to the top of a hill and burned, and the rest of her clothes were hung up on trees.[1]

Among the Lillooet Indians of British Columbia, neighbours of the Thompsons, the customs observed by girls at puberty were similar. The damsels were secluded for a period of not less than one year nor more than four years, according to their own inclination and the wishes of their parents. Among the Upper Lillooets the hut in which the girl lodged was made of bushy fir-trees set up like a conical tent, the inner branches being lopped off, while the outer branches were closely interwoven and padded to form a roof. Every month or half-month the hut was shifted to another site or a new one erected. By day the girl sat in the hut ; for the first month she squatted in a hole dug in the middle of it ; and she passed the time making miniature baskets of birch-bark and other things, praying that she might be able to make the real things well in after years. At the dusk of the evening she left the hut and wandered about all night, but she returned before the sun rose. Before she quitted the hut at nightfall to roam abroad, she painted her face red and put on a mask of fir-branches, and in her hand, as she walked, she carried a basket-rattle to frighten ghosts and guard herself from evil. Among the Lower Lillooets, the girl's mask was often made of goat-skin, covering her head, neck, shoulders and breast, and leaving only a narrow opening from the brow to the chin. During the nocturnal hours she performed many ceremonies. Thus she put two smooth stones in her bosom and ran, and as they fell down between her body and her clothes, she prayed, saying, " May I always have easy child-births ! " Now one of these stones represented her future child and the other represented the afterbirth. Also she dug trenches, praying that in the years to come she might be strong and tireless in digging roots ; she picked leaves and needles from the fir-trees, praying that her fingers might be nimble in picking berries ; and she tore sheets of birch-bark into

---

[1] James Teit, *The Thompson Indians of British Columbia*, pp. 311-317 (*The Jesup North Pacific Expedition, Memoir of the American Museum of Natural History*, New York, April, 1900). As to the customs observed among these Indians by the father of a girl at such times in order not to lose his luck in hunting, see *Spirits of the Corn and of the Wild*, ii. 268.

shreds, dropping the shreds as she walked and asking that her hands might never tire and that she might make neat and fine work of birch-bark.   Moreover, she ran and walked much that she might be light of foot.   And every evening, when the shadows were falling, and every morning, when the day was breaking, she prayed to the Dusk of the Evening or to the Dawn of Day, saying, "O Dawn of Day!" or "O Dusk," as it might be, "may I be able to dig roots fast and easily, and may I always find plenty!"   All her prayers were addressed to the Dusk of the Evening or the Dawn of Day.   She supplicated both, asking for long life, health, wealth, and happiness.[1]

Among the Shuswap Indians of British Columbia, who are neighbours of the Thompsons and Lillooets, "a girl on reaching maturity has to go through a great number of ceremonies.   She must leave the village and live alone in a small hut on the mountains.   She cooks her own food, and must not eat anything that bleeds.   She is forbidden to touch her head, for which purpose she uses a comb with three points.   Neither is she allowed to scratch her body, except with a painted deer-bone.   She wears the bone and the comb suspended from her belt.   She drinks out of a painted cup of birch-bark, and neither more nor less than the quantity it holds.   Every night she walks about her hut, and plants willow twigs, which she has painted, and to the ends of which she has attached pieces of cloth, into the ground.   It is believed that thus she will become rich in later life.   In order to become strong she should climb trees and try to break off their points.   She plays with *lehal* sticks that her future husbands might have good luck when gambling."[2]   During the day the girl stays in her hut and occupies herself in making miniature bags, mats, and baskets, in sewing and embroidery, in manufacturing thread, twine, and so forth ; in short she makes a beginning of all kinds of

---

[1] James Teit, *The Lillooet Indians* (Leyden and New York, 1906), pp. 263-265 (*The Jesup North Pacific Expedition, Memoir of the American Museum of Natural History*, New York).   Compare C. Hill Tout, " Report on the Ethnology of the Stlatlumh of British Columbia," *Journal of the Anthropological Institute*, xxxv. (1905) p. 136.

[2] Franz Boas, in *Sixth Report of the Committee on the North-Western Tribes of Canada*, pp. 89 *sq.* (separate reprint from the *Report of the British Association for the Advancement of Science*, Leeds meeting, 1890).

woman's work, in order that she may be a good housewife in after life. By night she roams the mountains and practises running, climbing, carrying burdens, and digging trenches, so that she may be expert at digging roots. If she has wandered far and daylight overtakes her, she hides herself behind a veil of fir branches; for no one, except her instructor or nearest relatives, should see her face during her period of seclusion. She wore a large robe painted red on the breast and sides, and her hair was done up in a knot at each ear.[1]

Seclusion of girls at puberty among the Delaware and Cheyenne Indians.

Ceremonies of the same general type were probably observed by girls at puberty among all the Indian tribes of North America. But the record of them is far less full for the Central and Eastern tribes, perhaps because the settlers who first came into contact with the Red Man in these regions were too busy fighting him to find leisure, even if they had the desire, to study his manners and customs. However, among the Delaware Indians, a tribe in the extreme east of the continent, we read that "when a Delaware girl has her first monthly period, she must withdraw into a hut at some distance from the village. Her head is wrapped up for twelve days, so that she can see nobody, and she must submit to frequent vomits and fasting, and abstain from all labor. After this she is washed and new clothed, but confined to a solitary life for two months, at the close of which she is declared marriageable." [2] Again, among the Cheyennes, an Indian tribe of the Missouri valley, a girl at her first menstruation is painted red all over her body and secluded in a special little lodge for four days. However, she may remain in her father's lodge provided that there are no charms ("medicine"), no sacred bundle, and no shield in it, or that these and all other objects invested with a sacred character have been removed. For four days she may not eat boiled meat; the flesh of which she partakes must be roasted over coals. Young men will not eat from the dish nor drink from the pot, which has been used by her; because

---

[1] James Teit, *The Shuswap* (Leyden and New York, 1909), pp. 587 *sq.* (*The Jesup North Pacific Expedition, Memoir of the American Museum of Natural History*, New York).

[2] G. H. Loskiel, *History of the Mission of the United Brethren among the Indians of North America* (London, 1794), Part i. pp. 56 *sq.*

they believe that were they to do so they would be wounded in the next fight. She may not handle nor even touch any weapon of war or any sacred object. If the camp moves, she may not ride a horse, but is mounted on a mare.[1]

Among the Esquimaux also, in the extreme north of the continent, who belong to an entirely different race from the Indians, the attainment of puberty in the female sex is, or used to be, the occasion of similar observances. Thus among the Koniags, an Esquimau people of Alaska, a girl at puberty was placed in a small hut in which she had to remain on her hands and knees for six months; then the hut was enlarged a little so as to allow her to straighten her back, but in this posture she had to remain for six months more. All this time she was regarded as an unclean being with whom no one might hold intercourse. At the end of the year she was received back by her parents and a great feast held.[2]   Again, among the Malemut, and southward from the lower Yukon and adjacent districts, when a girl reaches the age of puberty she is considered unclean for forty days and must therefore live by herself in a corner of the house with her face to the wall, always keeping her hood over her head and her hair hanging dishevelled over her eyes. But if it is summer, she commonly lives in a rough shelter outside the house. She may not go out by day, and only once at night, when every one else is asleep. At the end of the period she bathes and is clothed in new garments, whereupon she may be taken in marriage. During her seclusion she is supposed to be enveloped in a peculiar atmosphere of such a sort that were a young man to come near enough for it to touch him, it would render him visible to every animal he might hunt, so that his luck as a hunter would be gone.[3]

Seclusion of girls at puberty among the Esquimaux.

[1] G. B. Grinnell, "Cheyenne Woman Customs," *American Anthropologist*, New Series, iv. (New York, 1902) pp. 13 *sq.* The Cheyennes appear to have been at first settled on the Mississippi, from which they were driven westward to the Missouri. See *Handbook of American Indians north of Mexico*, edited by F. W. Hodge (Washington, 1907–1910), i. 250 *sqq.*

[2] H. J. Holmberg, "Ueber die Völker des Russischen Amerika," *Acta Societatis Scientiarum Fennicae*, iv. (Helsingfors, 1856) pp. 401 *sq.*; Ivan Petroff, *Report on the Population, Industries and Resources of Alaska*, p. 143.

[3] E. W. Nelson, "The Eskimo about Bering Strait," *Eighteenth Annual Report of the Bureau of American Ethnology*, Part i. (Washington, 1899) p. 291.

§ 5. *Seclusion of Girls at Puberty among the Indians of South America*

Seclusion of girls at puberty among the Guaranis, Chiriguanos, and Lengua Indians of South America.

When symptoms of puberty appeared on a girl for the first time, the Guaranis of Southern Brazil, on the borders of Paraguay, used to sew her up in her hammock, leaving only a small opening in it to allow her to breathe. In this condition, wrapt up and shrouded like a corpse, she was kept for two or three days or so long as the symptoms lasted, and during this time she had to observe a most rigorous fast. After that she was entrusted to a matron, who cut the girl's hair and enjoined her to abstain most strictly from eating flesh of any kind until her hair should be grown long enough to hide her ears. Meanwhile the diviners drew omens of her future character from the various birds or animals that flew past or crossed her path. If they saw a parrot, they would say she was a chatterbox ; if an owl, she was lazy and useless for domestic labours, and so on.[1] In similar circumstances the Chiriguanos of south-eastern Bolivia hoisted the girl in her hammock to the roof, where she stayed for a month : the second month the hammock was let half-way down from the roof ; and in the third month old women, armed with sticks, entered the hut and ran about striking everything they met, saying they were hunting the snake that had wounded the girl.[2] The Lengua Indians of the Paraguayan Chaco under similar circumstances hang the girl in her hammock from the roof of the house, but they leave her there only three days and nights, during which they give her nothing to eat but a little Paraguay tea or boiled maize. Only her mother or grandmother has access to her ; nobody else approaches or speaks to her. If she is obliged to leave the hammock for a little,

[1] Jose Guevara, "Historia del Paraguay, Rio de la Plata, y Tucuman," pp. 16 *sq.*, in Pedro de Angelis, *Coleccion de Obras y Documentos relativos a la Historia antigua y moderna de las Provincias del Rio de la Plata,* vol. ii. (Buenos-Ayres, 1836) ; J. F. Lafitau, *Mœurs des Sauvages Ameriquains* (Paris, 1724), i. 262 *sq.*

[2] Father Ignace Chomé, in *Lettres Édifiantes et Curieuses,* Nouvelle Édition (Paris, 1780–1783), viii. 333. As to the Chiriguanos, see C. F. Phil. von Martius, *Zur Ethnographie Amerika's, zumal Brasiliens* (Leipsic, 1867), pp. 212 *sqq.* ; Colonel G. E. Church, *Aborigines of South America* (London, 1912), pp. 207-227.

her friends take great care to prevent her from touching the *Boyrusu*, which is an imaginary serpent that would swallow her up. She must also be very careful not to set foot on the droppings of fowls or animals, else she would suffer from sores on the throat and breast. On the third day they let her down from the hammock, cut her hair, and make her sit in a corner of the room with her face turned to the wall. She may speak to nobody, and must abstain from flesh and fish. These rigorous observances she must practise for nearly a year. Many girls die or are injured for life in consequence of the hardships they endure at this time. Their only occupations during their seclusion are spinning and weaving.[1]

Among the Yuracares, an Indian tribe of Bolivia, at the eastern foot of the Andes, when a girl perceives the signs of puberty, she informs her parents. The mother weeps and the father constructs a little hut of palm leaves near the house. In this cabin he shuts up his daughter so that she cannot see the light, and there she remains fasting rigorously for four days. Meantime the mother, assisted by the women of the neighbourhood, has brewed a large quantity of the native intoxicant called *chicha*, and poured it into wooden troughs and palm leaves. On the morning of the fourth day, three hours before the dawn, the girl's father, having arrayed himself in his savage finery, summons all his neighbours with loud cries. The damsel is seated on a stone, and every guest in turn cuts off a lock of her hair, and running away hides it in the hollow trunk of a tree in the depths of the forest. When they have all done so and seated themselves again gravely in the circle, the girl offers

Seclusion of girls at puberty among the Yuracares of Bolivia.

---

[1] A. Thouar, *Explorations dans l'Amérique du Sud* (Paris, 1891), pp. 48 *sq.* ; G. Kurze, "Sitten und Gebräuche der Lengua-Indianer," *Mitteilungen der Geographischen Gesellschaft zu Jena*, xxiii. (1905) pp. 26 *sq.* The two accounts appear to be identical; but the former attributes the custom to the Chiriguanos, the latter to the Lenguas. As the latter account is based on the reports of the Rev. W. B. Grubb, a missionary who has been settled among the Indians of the Chaco for many years and is our principal authority on them, I assume that the ascription of the custom to the Lenguas is correct. However, in the volume on the Lengua Indians, which has been edited from Mr. Grubb's papers (*An Unknown People in an Unknown Land*, London, 1911), these details as to the seclusion of girls at puberty are not mentioned, though what seems to be the final ceremony is described (*op. cit.* pp. 177 *sq.*). From the description we learn that boys dressed in ostrich feathers and wearing masks circle round the girl with shrill cries, but are repelled by the women.

to each of them a calabash full of very strong *chicha*. Before the wassailing begins, the various fathers perform a curious operation on the arms of their sons, who are seated beside them. The operator takes a very sharp bone of an ape, rubs it with a pungent spice, and then pinching up the skin of his son's arm he pierces it with the bone through and through, as a surgeon might introduce a seton. This operation he repeats till the young man's arm is riddled with holes at regular intervals from the shoulder to the wrist. Almost all who take part in the festival are covered with these wounds, which the Indians call *culucute*. Having thus prepared themselves to spend a happy day, they drink, play on flutes, sing and dance till evening. Rain, thunder, and lightning, should they befall, have no effect in damping the general enjoyment or preventing its continuance till after the sun has set. The motive for perforating the arms of the young men is to make them skilful hunters ; at each perforation the sufferer is cheered by the promise of another sort of game or fish which the surgical operation will infallibly procure for him. The same operation is performed on the arms and legs of the girls, in order that they may be brave and strong ; even the dogs are operated on with the intention of making them run down the game better. For five or six months afterwards the damsel must cover her head with bark and refrain from speaking to men. The Yuracares think that if they did not submit a young girl to this severe ordeal, her children would afterwards perish by accidents of various kinds, such as the sting of a serpent, the bite of a jaguar, the fall of a tree, the wound of an arrow, or what not.[1]

Seclusion of girls at puberty among the Indians of the Gran Chaco.

Among the Matacos or Mataguayos, an Indian tribe of the Gran Chaco, a girl at puberty has to remain in seclusion for some time. She lies covered up with branches or other things in a corner of the hut, seeing no one and speaking to no one, and during this time she may eat neither flesh nor fish. Meantime a man beats a drum in front of the house.[2]

[1] Alcide d'Orbigny, *Voyage dans l'Amérique Méridionale*, vol. iii. 1re Partie (Paris and Strasburg, 1844), pp. 205 *sq*.

[2] A. Thouar, *Explorations dans*

l'Amérique du Sud (Paris, 1891) pp. 56 *sq*. ; Father Cardus, quoted in J. Pelleschi's *Los Indios Matacos* (Buenos Ayres, 1897), pp. 47 *sq*.

Similarly among the Tobas, another Indian tribe of the same region, when a chief's daughter has just attained to womanhood, she is shut up for two or three days in the house, all the men of the tribe scour the country to bring in game and fish for a feast, and a Mataco Indian is engaged to drum, sing, and dance in front of the house without cessation, day and night, till the festival is over. As the merry-making lasts for two or three weeks, the exhaustion of the musician at the end of it may be readily conceived. Meat and drink are supplied to him on the spot where he pays his laborious court to the Muses. The proceedings wind up with a saturnalia and a drunken debauch.[1] Among the Yaguas, an Indian tribe of the Upper Amazon, a girl at puberty is shut up for three months in a lonely hut in the forest, where her mother brings her food daily.[2] When a girl of the Peguenches tribe perceives in herself the first signs of womanhood, she is secluded by her mother in a corner of the hut screened off with blankets, and is warned not to lift up her eyes on any man. Next day, very early in the morning and again after sunset, she is taken out by two women and made to run till she is tired ; in the interval she is again secluded in her corner. On the following day she lays three packets of wool beside the path near the house to signify that she is now a woman.[3] Among the Passes, Mauhes, and other tribes of Brazil the young woman in similar circumstances is hung in her hammock from the roof and has to fast there for a month or as long as she can hold out.[4] One of the early settlers in Brazil, about the middle of the sixteenth century, has described the severe ordeal which damsels at puberty had to undergo among the Indians on the south-east coast of that country, near what is now Rio de Janeiro. When a girl had reached this critical period of life, her hair was burned or shaved off close to the head.

Seclusion of girls at puberty among the Indians of Brazil.

[1] A. Thouar, *op. cit.* p. 63.

[2] Francis de Castelnau, *Expédition dans les parties centrales de l'Amérique du Sud* (Paris, 1850–1851), v. 25.

[3] D. Luis de la Cruz, " Descripcion de la Naturaleza de los Terrenos que se comprenden en los Andes, poseidos por los Peguenches y los demas espacios hasta el rio de Chadileuba," p. 62, in Pedro de Angelis, *Coleccion de Obras y Documentos relativos a la Historia antigua y moderna de las Provincias del Rio de la Plata*, vol. i. (Buenos-Ayres, 1836). Apparently the Peguenches are an Indian tribe of Chili.

[4] J. B. von Spix und C. F. Ph. von Martius, *Reise in Brasilien* (Munich, 1823–1831), iii. 1186, 1187, 1318.

Then she was placed on a flat stone and cut with the tooth of an animal from the shoulders all down the back, till she ran with blood. Next the ashes of a wild gourd were rubbed into the wounds ; the girl was bound hand and foot, and hung in a hammock, being enveloped in it so closely that no one could see her. Here she had to stay for three days without eating or drinking. When the three days were over, she stepped out of the hammock upon the flat stone, for her feet might not touch the ground. If she had a call of nature, a female relation took the girl on her back and carried her out, taking with her a live coal to prevent evil influences from entering the girl's body. Being replaced in her hammock, she was now allowed to get some flour, boiled roots, and water, but might not taste salt or flesh. Thus she continued to the end of the first monthly period, at the expiry of which she was gashed on the breast and belly as well as all down the back. During the second month she still stayed in her hammock, but her rule of abstinence was less rigid, and she was allowed to spin. The third month she was blackened with a certain pigment and began to go about as usual.[1]

Seclusion of girls at puberty among the Indians of Guiana.

Amongst the Macusis of British Guiana, when a girl shews the first signs of puberty, she is hung in a hammock at the highest point of the hut. For the first few days she may not leave the hammock by day, but at night she must come down, light a fire, and spend the night beside it, else she would break out in sores on her neck, throat, and other parts of her body. So long as the symptoms are at their height, she must fast rigorously. When they have abated, she may come down and take up her abode in a little compartment that is made for her in the darkest corner of the hut. In the morning she may cook her food, but it must be at a separate fire and in a vessel of her own. After about ten days the magician comes and undoes the spell by muttering charms and breathing on her and on the more valuable of the things with which she has come in contact.

---

[1] André Thevet, *Cosmographie Universelle* (Paris, 1575), ii. 946 B [980] *sq.*; *id.*, *Les Singularitez de la France Antarctique, autrement nommée* *Amerique* (Antwerp, 1558), p. 76 ; J. F. Lafitau, *Mœurs des Sauvages Ameriquains* (Paris, 1724), i. 290 *sqq*,

The pots and drinking-vessels which she used are broken and the fragments buried. After her first bath, the girl must submit to be beaten by her mother with thin rods without uttering a cry. At the end of the second period she is again beaten, but not afterwards. She is now "clean," and can mix again with people.[1] Other Indians of Guiana, after keeping the girl in her hammock at the top of the hut for a month, expose her to certain large ants, whose bite is very painful.[2] Sometimes, in addition to being stung with ants, the sufferer has to fast day and night so long as she remains slung up on high in her hammock, so that when she comes down she is reduced to a skeleton. The intention of stinging her with ants is said to be to make her strong to bear the burden of maternity.[3] Amongst the Uaupes of Brazil a girl at puberty is secluded in the house for a month, and allowed only a small quantity of bread and water. Then she is taken out into the midst of her relations and friends, each of whom gives her four or five blows with pieces of *sipo* (an elastic climber), till she falls senseless or dead. If she recovers, the operation is repeated four times at intervals of six hours, and it is considered an offence to the parents not to strike hard. Meantime, pots of meats and fish have been made ready ; the *sipos* are dipped into them and then given to the girl to lick, who is now considered a marriageable woman.[4]

The custom of stinging the girl at such times with ants or beating her with rods is intended, we may be sure, not as a punishment or a test of endurance, but as a purification, the object being to drive away the malignant influences with which a girl in this condition is believed to be beset and enveloped. Examples of purification, by beating, by incisions in the flesh, and by

Marginal notes: Custom of beating the girls and of causing them to be stung by ants.

Custom in South America of causing young men to be stung with ants as an initiatory rite.

[1] R. Schomburgk, *Reisen in Britisch Guiana* (Leipsic, 1847–1848), ii. 315 *sq.* ; C. F. Ph. von Martius, *Zur Ethnographie Amerika's, zumal Brasiliens* (Leipsic, 1867), p. 644.

[2] Labat, *Voyage du Chevalier des Marchais en Guinée, Isles voisines, et à Cayenne,* iv. 365 *sq.* (Paris, 1730), pp. 17 *sq.* (Amsterdam, 1731).

[3] A. Caulin, *Historia Coro-graphica natural y evangelica dela Nueva Andalucia* (1779), p. 93. A similar custom, with the omission of the stinging, is reported of the Tamanaks in the region of the Orinoco. See F. S. Gilij, *Saggio di Storia Americana,* ii. (Rome, 1781), p. 133.

[4] A. R. Wallace, *Narrative of Travels on the Amazon and Rio Negro,* p. 496 (p. 345 of the Minerva Library edition, London, 1889).

stinging with ants, have already come before us.[1]   In some
Indian tribes of Brazil and Guiana young men do not rank
as warriors and may not marry till they have passed
through a terrible ordeal, which consists in being stung
by swarms of venomous ants whose bite is like fire.
Thus among the Mauhes on the Tapajos river, a southern
tributary of the Amazon, boys of eight to ten years are
obliged to thrust their arms into sleeves stuffed with great
ferocious ants, which the Indians call *tocandeira* (*Cryptocerus
atratus*, F.).   When the young victim shrieks with pain,
an excited mob of men dances round him, shouting and
encouraging him till he falls exhausted to the ground.
He is then committed to the care of old women, who treat
his fearfully swollen arms with fresh juice of the manioc ;
and on his recovery he has to shew his strength and skill
in bending a bow.   This cruel ordeal is commonly repeated
again and again, till the lad has reached his fourteenth year
and can bear the agony without betraying any sign of
emotion.   Then he is a man and can marry.   A lad's age
is reckoned by the number of times he has passed through
the ordeal.[2]   An eye-witness has described how a young
Mauhe hero bore the torture with an endurance more than
Spartan, dancing and singing, with his arms cased in the
terrible mittens, before every cabin of the great common
house, till pallid, staggering, and with chattering teeth he
triumphantly laid the gloves before the old chief and
received the congratulations of the men and the caresses
of the women ; then breaking away from his friends and
admirers he threw himself into the river and remained
in its cool soothing water till nightfall.[3]   Similarly among
the Ticunas of the Upper Amazon, on the border of Peru,
the young man who would take his place among the

[1] *Taboo and the Perils of the Soul*, pp.
105 *sqq.* ; *The Scapegoat*, pp. 259 *sqq.*

[2] J. B. von Spix and C. F. Ph. von
Martius, *Reise in Brasilien* (Munich,
1823–1831), iii. 1320.

[3] W. Lewis Herndon, *Exploration
of the Valley of the Amazon* (Washington, 1854), pp. 319 *sq.* The scene
was described to Mr. Herndon by a
French engineer and architect, M. de
Lincourt, who witnessed it at Mandu-

assu, a village on the Tapajos river.
Mr. Herndon adds : " The *Tocandeira*
ants not only bite, but are also armed
with a sting like the wasp ; but the
pain felt from it is more violent.   I
think it equal to that occasioned by
the sting of the black scorpion."   He
gives the name of the Indians as
Mahues, but I assume that they are
the same as the Mauhes described by
Spix and Martius.

warriors must plunge his arm into a sort of basket full of venomous ants and keep it there for several minutes without uttering a cry. He generally falls backwards and sometimes succumbs to the fever which ensues; hence as soon as the ordeal is over the women are prodigal of their attentions to him, and rub the swollen arm with a particular kind of herb.[1] Ordeals of this sort appear to be in vogue among the Indians of the Rio Negro as well as of the Amazon.[2] Among the Rucuyennes, a tribe of Indians in the north of Brazil, on the borders of Guiana, young men who are candidates for marriage must submit to be stung all over their persons not only with ants but with wasps, which are applied to their naked bodies in curious instruments of trellis-work shaped like fantastic quadrupeds or birds. The patient invariably falls down in a swoon and is carried like dead to his hammock, where he is tightly lashed with cords. As they come to themselves, they writhe in agony, so that their hammocks rock violently to and fro, causing the hut to shake as if it were about to collapse. This dreadful ordeal is called by the Indians a *maraké*.[3]

The same ordeal, under the same name, is also practised by the Wayanas, an Indian tribe of French Guiana, but with them, we are told, it is no longer deemed an indispensable preliminary to marriage ; "it is rather a sort of national medicine administered chiefly to the youth of both sexes." Applied to men, the *maraké*, as it is called, "sharpens them, prevents them from being heavy and lazy, makes them active, brisk, industrious, imparts strength, and helps them to shoot well with the bow ; without it the Indians would always be slack and rather sickly, would always have a little fever, and would lie perpetually in their hammocks. As for the women, the *maraké* keeps them from going to sleep, renders them active, alert, brisk,

Custom of causing men and women to be stung with ants to improve their character and health or to render them invulnerable.

---

[1] Francis de Castelnau, *Expédition dans les parties centrales de l'Amérique du Sud* (Paris, 1850–1851), v. 46.

[2] L'Abbé Durand, "Le Rio Negro du Nord et son bassin," *Bulletin de la Société de Géographie* (Paris), vi. Série, iii. (1872) pp. 21 *sq.* The writer says that the candidate has to keep his arms plunged up to the shoulders in vessels full of ants, "as in a bath of vitriol," for hours. He gives the native name of the ant as *issauba*.

[3] J. Crevaux, *Voyages dans l'Amérique du Sud* (Paris, 1883), pp. 245-250.

gives them strength and a liking for work, makes them good housekeepers, good workers at the stockade, good makers of *cachiri*. Every one undergoes the *maraké* at least twice in his life, sometimes thrice, and oftener if he likes. It may be had from the age of about eight years and upward, and no one thinks it odd that a man of forty should voluntarily submit to it."[1] Similarly the Indians of St. Juan Capistrano in California used to be branded on some part of their bodies, generally on the right arm, but sometimes on the leg also, not as a proof of manly fortitude, but because they believed that the custom " added greater strength to the nerves, and gave a better pulse for the management of the bow." Afterwards " they were whipped with nettles, and covered with ants, that they might become robust, and the infliction was always performed in summer, during the months of July and August, when the nettle was in its most fiery state. They gathered small bunches, which they fastened together, and the poor deluded Indian was chastised, by inflicting blows with them upon his naked limbs, until unable to walk ; and then he was carried to the nest of the nearest and most furious species of ants, and laid down among them, while some of his friends, with sticks, kept annoying the insects to make them still more violent. What torments did they not undergo ! What pain ! What hellish inflictions ! Yet their faith gave them power to endure all without a murmur, and they remained as if dead. Having undergone these dreadful ordeals, they were considered as invulnerable, and believed that the arrows of their enemies could no longer harm them."[2] Among the Alur, a tribe inhabiting the south-western region of the upper Nile, to bury a man in an ant-hill and leave him there for a while is the regular treatment for insanity.[3]

In like manner it is probable that beating or scourging as a religious or ceremonial rite was originally a

---

[1] H. Coudreau, *Chez nos Indiens : quatre années dans la Guyane Française* (Paris, 1895), p. 228. For details as to the different modes of administering the *maraké*, see *ibid.* pp. 228-235.

[2] Father Geronimo Boscana, "Chinigchinich," in *Life in California by an American* [A. Robinson] (New York, 1846), pp. 273 *sq.*

[3] F. Stuhlmann, *Mit Emin Pascha ins Herz von Afrika* (Berlin, 1894), p. 506.

mode of purification. It was meant to wipe off and drive away a dangerous contagion, whether personified as demoniacal or not, which was supposed to be adhering physically, though invisibly, to the body of the sufferer.[1] The pain inflicted on the person beaten was no more the object of the beating than it is of a surgical operation with us ; it was a necessary accident, that was all. In later times such customs were interpreted otherwise, and the pain, from being an accident, became the prime object of the ceremony, which was now regarded either as a test of endurance imposed upon persons at critical epochs of life, or as a mortification of the flesh well pleasing to the god. But asceticism, under any shape or form, is never primitive.

In such cases the beating or stinging was originally a purification ; at a later time it is interpreted as a test of courage and endurance.

[1] As a confirmation of this view it may be pointed out that beating or scourging is inflicted on inanimate objects expressly for the purpose indicated in the text. Thus the Indians of Costa Rica hold that there are two kinds of ceremonial uncleanness, *nya* and *bu-ku-rú*. Anything that has been connected with a death is *nya*. But *bu-ku-rú* is much more virulent. It can not only make one sick but kill. "*Bu-ku-rú* emanates in a variety of ways ; arms, utensils, even houses become affected by it after long disuse, and before they can be used again must be purified. In the case of portable objects left undisturbed for a long time, the custom is to beat them with a stick before touching them. I have seen a woman take a long walking-stick and beat a basket hanging from the roof of a house by a cord. On asking what that was for, I was told that the basket contained her treasures, that she would probably want to take something out the next day, and that she was driving off the *bu-ku-rú*. A house long unused must be swept, and then the person who is purifying it must take a stick and beat not only the movable objects, but the beds, posts, and in short every accessible part of the interior. The next day it is fit for occupation. A place not visited for a long time or reached for the first time is *bu-ku-rú*. On our return from the ascent of Pico Blanco, nearly all the party suffered from little calenturas, the result of extraordinary exposure to wet and cold and of want of food. The Indians said that the peak was especially *bu-ku-rú*, since nobody had ever been on it before." One day Mr. Gabb took down some dusty blow-guns amid cries of *bu-ku-rú* from the Indians. Some weeks afterwards a boy died, and the Indians firmly believed that the *bu-ku-rú* of the blow-guns had killed him. "From all the foregoing, it would seem that *bu-ku-rú* is a sort of evil spirit that takes possession of the object, and resents being disturbed ; but I have never been able to learn from the Indians that they consider it so. They seem to think of it as a property the object acquires. But the worst *bu-ku-rú* of all, is that of a young woman in her first pregnancy. She infects the whole neighbourhood. Persons going from the house where she lives, carry the infection with them to a distance, and all the deaths or other serious misfortunes in the vicinity are laid to her charge. In the old times, when the savage laws and customs were in full force, it was not an uncommon thing for the husband of such a woman to pay damages for casualties thus caused by his unfortunate wife." See Wm. M. Gabb, "On the Indian Tribes and Languages of Costa Rica," *Proceedings of the American Philosophical Society held at Philadelphia*, xiv. (Philadelphia, 1876) pp. 504 *sq.*

The savage, it is true, in certain circumstances will voluntarily subject himself to pains and privations which appear to us wholly needless ; but he never acts thus unless he believes that some solid temporal advantage is to be gained by so doing.   Pain for the sake of pain, whether as a moral discipline in this life or as a means of winning a glorious immortality hereafter, is not an object which he sets himself deliberately to pursue.

This explanation confirmed with reference to the beating of girls at puberty among the South American Indians.

If this view is correct, we can understand why so many Indian tribes of South America compel the youth of both sexes to submit to these painful and sometimes fatal ordeals. They imagine that in this way they rid the young folk of certain evils inherent in youth, especially at the critical age of puberty ; and when they picture to themselves the evils in a personal form as dangerous spirits or demons, the ceremony of their expulsion may in the strict sense be termed an exorcism.   This certainly appears to be the interpretation which the Banivas of the Orinoco put upon the cruel

Treatment of a girl at puberty among the Banivas of the Orinoco.

scourgings which they inflict on girls at puberty.   At her first menstruation a Baniva girl must pass several days and nights in her hammock, almost motionless and getting nothing to eat and drink but water and a little manioc. While she lies there, the suitors for her hand apply to her father, and he who can afford to give most for her or can prove himself the best man, is promised the damsel in marriage.   The fast over, some old men enter the hut, bandage the girl's eyes, cover her head with a bonnet of which the fringes fall on her shoulders, and then lead her forth and tie her to a post set up in an open place.   The head of the post is carved in the shape of a grotesque face. None but the old men may witness what follows.   Were a woman caught peeping and prying, it would go ill with her ; she would be marked out for the vengeance of the demon, who would make her expiate her crime at the very next moon by madness or death.   Every participant in the ceremony comes armed with a scourge of cords or of fish skins ; some of them reinforce the virtue of the instrument by tying little sharp stones to the end of the thongs.   Then, to the dismal and deafening notes of shell-trumpets blown by two or three supernumeraries, the men circle round and round the post, every one applying his scourge as he passes to the girl's back, till it streams with blood. At last the musicians, winding tremendous blasts on their trumpets against the demon, advance and touch the post in which he is supposed to be incorporate. Then the blows cease to descend ; the girl is untied, often in a fainting state, and carried away to have her wounds washed and simples applied to them. The youngest of the executioners, or rather of the exorcists, hastens to inform her betrothed husband of the happy issue of the exorcism. " The spirit," he says, " had cast thy beloved into a sleep as deep almost as that of death. But we have rescued her from his attacks, and laid her down in such and such a place. Go seek her." Then going from house to house through the village he cries to the inmates, " Come, let us burn the demon who would have taken possession of such and such a girl, our friend." The bridegroom at once carries his wounded and suffering bride to his own house ; and all the people gather round the post for the pleasure of burning it and the demon together. A great pile of firewood has meanwhile been heaped up about it, and the women run round the pyre cursing in shrill voices the wicked spirit who has wrought all this evil. The men join in with hoarser cries and animate themselves for the business in hand by deep draughts of an intoxicant which has been provided for the occasion by the parents-in-law. Soon the bridegroom, having committed the bride to the care of his mother, appears on the scene brandishing a lighted torch. He addresses the demon with bitter mockery and reproaches ; informs him that the fair creature on whom he, the demon, had nefarious designs, is now his, the bridegroom's, blooming spouse ; and shaking his torch at the grinning head on the post, he screams out, " This is how the victims of thy persecution take vengeance on thee !" With these words he puts a light to the pyre. At once the drums strike up, the trumpets blare, and men, women, and children begin to dance. In two long rows they dance, the men on one side, the women on the other, advancing till they almost touch and then retiring again. After that the two rows join hands, and forming a huge circle trip it round and round the blaze, till the post with its grotesque face is consumed in the flames and nothing of the pyre remains but a heap of red and glowing embers. "The evil spirit has been destroyed. Thus delivered from her persecutor, the young wife will be free from sickness, will not die in childbed, and will bear many children to her husband."[1] From this account it appears that the Banivas attribute the symptoms of puberty in girls to the wounds inflicted on them by an amorous devil, who, however, can be not only exorcised but burnt to ashes at the stake.

Symptoms of puberty in a girl regarded as wounds inflicted by a demon.

§ 6. *Seclusion of Girls at Puberty in India and Cambodia*

Seclusion of girls at puberty among the Hindoos.

When a Hindoo maiden reaches maturity she is kept in a dark room for four days, and is forbidden to see the sun. She is regarded as unclean ; no one may touch her. Her diet is restricted to boiled rice, milk, sugar, curd, and tamarind without salt. On the morning of the fifth day she goes to a neighbouring tank, accompanied by five women whose husbands are alive. Smeared with turmeric water, they all bathe and return home, throwing away the mat and other things that were in the room.[2] The Rarhi Brahmans of Bengal compel a girl at puberty to live alone, and do not allow her to see the face of any male. For three days she remains shut up in a dark room, and has to undergo certain penances. Fish, flesh, and sweetmeats are forbidden her ; she must live upon rice and ghee.[3] Among the Tiyans of Malabar a girl is thought to be polluted for four days from the beginning of her first menstruation. During this time she must keep to the north side of the house, where she sleeps on a grass mat of a particular kind, in a room festooned with garlands of young coco-nut leaves. Another girl keeps her company and sleeps with her, but she may

Seclusion of girls at puberty in Southern India.

---

[1] J. Chaffanjon, *L'Orénoque et le Caura* (Paris, 1889), pp. 213-215.

[2] Shib Chunder Bose, *The Hindoos as they are* (London and Calcutta, 1881), p. 86. Similarly, after a Brahman boy has been invested with the sacred thread, he is for three days strictly forbidden to see the sun. He may not eat salt, and he is enjoined to sleep either on a carpet or a deer's skin, without a mattress or mosquito curtain

(*ibid.* p. 186). In Bali, boys who have had their teeth filed, as a preliminary to marriage, are kept shut up in a dark room for three days (R. Van Eck, "Schetsen van het eiland Bali," *Tijdschrift voor Nederlandsch Indië*, N.S., ix. (1880) pp. 428 *sq.*).

[3] (Sir) H. H. Risley, *Tribes and Castes of Bengal, Ethnographic Glossary* (Calcutta, 1891–1892), i. 152.

not touch any other person, tree or plant.   Further, she may
not see the sky, and woe betide her if she catches sight of a
crow or a cat !   Her diet must be strictly vegetarian, without
salt, tamarinds, or chillies.   She is armed against evil spirits
by a knife, which is placed on the mat or carried on her
person.[1] Among the Kappiliyans of Madura and Tinnevelly
a girl at her first monthly period remains under pollution
for thirteen days, either in a corner of the house, which is
screened off for her use by her maternal uncle, or in a
temporary hut, which is erected by the same relative on the
common land of the village.   On the thirteenth day she
bathes in a tank, and, on entering the house, steps over a
pestle and a cake.   Near the entrance some food is placed
and a dog is allowed to partake of it ; but his enjoyment is
marred by suffering, for while he eats he receives a sound
thrashing, and the louder he howls the better, for the larger
will be the family to which the young woman will give birth ;
should there be no howls, there will be no children.   The
temporary hut in which the girl passed the days of her
seclusion is burnt down, and the pots which she used are
smashed to shivers.[2] Similarly among the Parivarams of
Madura, when a girl attains to puberty she is kept for sixteen
days in a hut, which is guarded at night by her relations ;
and when her sequestration is over the hut is burnt down
and the pots she used are broken into very small pieces,
because they think that if rain-water gathered in any of
them, the girl would be childless.[3] The Pulayars of Travancore build a special hut in the jungle for the use of a girl at
puberty ; there she remains for seven days.   No one else
may enter the hut, not even her mother.   Women stand a
little way off and lay down food for her.   At the end of the
time she is brought home, clad in a new or clean cloth, and
friends are treated to betel-nut, toddy, and arack.[4] Among
the Singhalese a girl at her first menstruation is confined to
a room, where she may neither see nor be seen by any male.
After being thus secluded for two weeks she is taken out,
with her face covered, and is bathed by women at the back

[1] Edgar Thurston, *Castes and Tribes
of Southern India* (Madras, 1909), vii.
63 *sq.*
    [2] Edgar Thurston, *op. cit.* iii. 218.

[3] Edgar Thurston, *op. cit.* vi. 157.

    [4] S. Mateer, *Native Life in Travan-
core* (London, 1883), p. 45.

of the house. Near the bathing-place are kept branches of any milk-bearing tree, usually of the *jak*-tree. In some cases, while the time of purification or uncleanness lasts, the maiden stays in a separate hut, which is afterwards burnt down.[1]

Seclusion of girls at puberty in Cambodia.

In Cambodia a girl at puberty is put to bed under a mosquito curtain, where she should stay a hundred days. Usually, however, four, five, ten, or twenty days are thought enough ; and even this, in a hot climate and under the close meshes of the curtain, is sufficiently trying.[2] According to another account, a Cambodian maiden at puberty is said to " enter into the shade." During her retirement, which, according to the rank and position of her family, may last any time from a few days to several years, she has to observe a number of rules, such as not to be seen by a strange man, not to eat flesh or fish, and so on. She goes nowhere, not even to the pagoda. But this state of seclusion is discontinued during eclipses ; at such times she goes forth and pays her devotions to the monster who is supposed to cause eclipses by catching the heavenly bodies between his teeth.[3] This permission to break her rule of retirement and appear abroad during an eclipse seems to shew how literally the injunction is interpreted which forbids maidens entering on womanhood to look upon the sun.

§ 7. *Seclusion of Girls at Puberty in Folk-tales*

Traces of the seclusion of girls at puberty in folk-tales. Danish story of the girl who might not see the sun.

A superstition so widely diffused as this might be expected to leave traces in legends and folk-tales. And it has done so. In a Danish story we read of a princess who was fated to be carried off by a warlock if ever the sun shone on her before she had passed her thirtieth year ; so the king her father kept her shut up in the palace, and had all the windows on the east, south, and west sides blocked up, lest a sunbeam should fall on his darling child, and he

---

[1] Arthur A. Perera, " Glimpses of Singhalese Social Life," *Indian Antiquary*, xxxi. (1902) p. 380.

[2] J. Moura, *Le Royaume du Cambodge* (Paris, 1883), i. 377.

[3] Étienne Aymonier, " Notes sur les coutumes et croyances superstitieuses des Cambodgiens," *Cochinchine Française: Excursions et Reconnaissances*, No. 16 (Saigon, 1883), pp. 193 *sq.* Compare *id.*, *Notice sur le Cambodge* (Paris, 1875), p. 50 ; *id.*, *Notes sur le Laos* (Saigon, 1885), p. 177.

should thus lose her for ever.   Only at evening, when the
sun was down, might she walk for a little in the beautiful
garden of the castle.   In time a prince came a-wooing,
followed by a train of gorgeous knights and squires on
horses all ablaze with gold and silver.   The king said the
prince might have his daughter to wife on condition that he
would not carry her away to his home till she was thirty
years old but would live with her in the castle, where the
windows looked out only to the north.   The prince agreed,
so married they were.   The bride was only fifteen, and
fifteen more long weary years must pass before she might
step out of the gloomy donjon, breathe the fresh air, and
see the sun.   But she and her gallant young bridegroom
loved each other and they were happy.   Often they sat
hand in hand at the window looking out to the north and
talked of what they would do when they were free.   Still it
was a little dull to look out always at the same window and
to see nothing but the castle woods, and the distant hills,
and the clouds drifting silently over them.   Well, one day
it happened that all the people in the castle had gone away
to a neighbouring castle to witness a tournament and other
gaieties, and the two young folks were left as usual all alone
at the window looking out to the north.   They sat silent
for a time gazing away to the hills.   It was a grey sad
day, the sky was overcast, and the weather seemed to
draw to rain.   At last the prince said, " There will be no
sunshine to-day.   What if we were to drive over and join
the rest at the tournament ? "   His young wife gladly con-
sented, for she longed to see more of the world than those
eternal green woods and those eternal blue hills, which were
all she ever saw from the window.   So the horses were put
into the coach, and it rattled up to the door, and in they
got and away they drove.   At first all went well.   The
clouds hung low over the woods, the wind sighed in the
trees, a drearier day you could hardly imagine.   So they
joined the rest at the other castle and took their seats to
watch the jousting in the lists.   So intent were they in
watching the gay spectacle of the prancing steeds, the
fluttering pennons, and the glittering armour of the knights,
that they failed to mark the change, the fatal change, in the

weather.   For the wind was rising and had begun to disperse
the clouds, and suddenly the sun broke through, and the
glory of it fell like an aureole on the young wife, and at
once she vanished away.   No sooner did her husband miss
her from his side than he, too, mysteriously disappeared.
The tournament broke up in confusion, the bereft father
hastened home, and shut himself up in the dark castle from
which the light of life had departed.   The green woods and
the blue hills could still be seen from the window that
looked to the north, but the young faces that had gazed out
of it so wistfully were gone, as it seemed, for ever.[1]

Tyrolese
story of the
girl who
might not
see the sun.   A Tyrolese story tells how it was the doom of a lovely
maiden with golden hair to be transported into the belly of a
whale if ever a sunbeam fell on her.   Hearing of the fame of
her beauty the king of the country sent for her to be his bride,
and her brother drove the fair damsel to the palace in a
carefully closed coach, himself sitting on the box and
handling the reins.   On the way they overtook two hideous
witches, who pretended they were weary and begged for a
lift in the coach.   At first the brother refused to take them
in, but his tender-hearted sister entreated him to have compassion on the two poor footsore women ; for you may easily
imagine that she was not acquainted with their true character.
So down he got rather surlily from the box, opened the
coach door, and in the two witches stepped, laughing in
their sleeves.   But no sooner had the brother mounted the
box and whipped up the horses, than one of the two wicked
witches bored a hole in the closed coach.   A sunbeam at
once shot through the hole and fell on the fair damsel.   So
she vanished from the coach and was spirited away into
the belly of a whale in the neighbouring sea.   You can
imagine the consternation of the king, when the coach door
opened and instead of his blooming bride out bounced two
hideous hags ! [2]

       In a modern Greek folk-tale the Fates predict that in her
fifteenth year a princess must be careful not to let the sun

[1] Svend Grundtvig, *Dänische Volks-
märchen*, übersetzt von A. Strodtmann,
Zweite Sammlung (Leipsic, 1879), pp.
199 *sqq.*

[2] Christian Schneller, *Märchen und
Sagen aus Wälschtirol* (Innsbruck.
1867), No. 22, pp. 51 *sqq.*

shine on her, for if this were to happen she would be turned
into a lizard.¹   In another modern Greek tale the Sun bestows
a daughter upon a childless woman on condition of taking
the child back to himself when she is twelve years old.   So,
when the child was twelve, the mother closed the doors and
windows, and stopped up all the chinks and crannies, to
prevent the Sun from coming to fetch away her daughter.
But she forgot to stop up the key-hole, and a sunbeam
streamed through it and carried off the girl.²   In a Sicilian
story a seer foretells that a king will have a daughter who,
in her fourteenth year, will conceive a child by the Sun.
So, when the child was born, the king shut her up in a
lonely tower which had no window, lest a sunbeam should
fall on her.   When she was nearly fourteen years old, it
happened that her parents sent her a piece of roasted kid,
in which she found a sharp bone.   With this bone she
scraped a hole in the wall, and a sunbeam shot through the
hole and got her with child.³

The old Greek story of Danae, who was confined by

¹ Bernhard Schmidt, *Griechische Märchen, Sagen und Volkslieder* (Leipsic, 1877), p. 98.

² J. G. von Hahn, *Griechische und albanesische Märchen* (Leipsic, 1864), No. 41, vol. i. pp. 245 *sqq.*

³ Laura Gonzenbach, *Sicilianische Märchen* (Leipsic, 1870), No. 28, vol. i. pp. 177 *sqq.*   The incident of the bone occurs in other folk-tales.   A prince or princess is shut up for safety in a tower and makes his or her escape by scraping a hole in the wall with a bone which has been accidentally conveyed into the tower; sometimes it is expressly said that care was taken to let the princess have no bones with her meat (J. G. von Hahn, *op. cit.* No. 15 ; L. Gonzenbach, *op. cit.* Nos. 26, 27 ; *Der Pentamerone, aus dem Neapolitanischen übertragen* von Felix Liebrecht (Breslau, 1846), No. 23, vol. i. pp. 294 *sqq.*).   From this we should infer that it is a rule with savages not to let women handle the bones of animals during their monthly seclusions.   We have already seen the great respect with which the savage treats the bones of game (*Spirits of the Corn and of the Wild*, ii. 238 *sqq.*, 256 *sqq.*) ; and women in their courses are specially forbidden to meddle with the hunter or fisher, as their contact or neighbourhood would spoil his sport (see below, pp. 77, 78 *sq.*, 87, 89 *sqq.*).   In folk-tales the hero who uses the bone is sometimes a boy ; but the incident might easily be transferred from a girl to a boy after its real meaning had been forgotten.   Amongst the Tinneh Indians a girl at puberty is forbidden to break the bones of hares (above, p. 48).   On the other hand, she drinks out of a tube made of a swan's bone (above, pp. 48, 49), and the same instrument is used for the same purpose by girls of the Carrier tribe of Indians (see below, p. 92).   We have seen that a Tlingit (Thlinkeet) girl in the same circumstances used to drink out of the wing-bone of a white-headed eagle (above, p. 45), and that among the Nootka and Shuswap tribes girls at puberty are provided with bones or combs with which to scratch themselves, because they may not use their fingers for this purpose (above, pp. 44, 53).

her father in a subterranean chamber or a brazen tower,
but impregnated by Zeus, who reached her in the shape
of a shower of gold,[1] perhaps belongs to the same class
of tales. It has its counterpart in the legend which the
Kirghiz of Siberia tell of their ancestry. A certain Khan had
a fair daughter, whom he kept in a dark iron house, that
no man might see her. An old woman tended her; and
when the girl was grown to maidenhood she asked the
old woman, "Where do you go so often?" "My child,"
said the old dame, "there is a bright world. In that bright
world your father and mother live, and all sorts of people
live there. That is where I go." The maiden said, "Good
mother, I will tell nobody, but shew me that bright world."
So the old woman took the girl out of the iron house. But
when she saw the bright world, the girl tottered and fainted;
and the eye of God fell upon her, and she conceived. Her
angry father put her in a golden chest and sent her floating
away (fairy gold can float in fairyland) over the wide sea.[2]
The shower of gold in the Greek story, and the eye of God in
the Kirghiz legend, probably stand for sunlight and the sun.

The idea that women may be impregnated by the sun
is not uncommon in legends. Thus, for example, among
the Indians of Guacheta in Colombia, it is said, a report
once ran that the sun would impregnate one of their maidens,
who should bear a child and yet remain a virgin. The
chief had two daughters, and was very desirous that one of
them should conceive in this miraculous manner. So every
day he made them climb a hill to the east of his house in
order to be touched by the first beams of the rising sun.
His wishes were fulfilled, for one of the damsels conceived
and after nine months gave birth to an emerald. So she
wrapped it in cotton and placed it in her bosom, and in a
few days it turned into a child, who received the name of
Garanchacha and was universally recognized as a son of the
sun.[3] Again, the Samoans tell of a woman named Manga-

[1] Sophocles, *Antigone*, 944 *sqq.*;
Apollodorus, *Bibliotheca*, ii. 4. 1;
Horace, *Odes*, iii. 16. 1 *sqq.*; Paus-
anias, ii. 23. 7.

[2] W. Radloff, *Proben der Volks-
litteratur der türkischen Stämme Süd-*

Sibiriens, iii. (St. Petersburg, 1870)
pp. 82 *sq.*

[3] H. Ternaux-Compans, *Essai sur
l'ancien Cundinamarca* (Paris, N.D.),
p. 18.

mangai, who became pregnant by looking at the rising sun. Her son grew up and was named "Child of the Sun." At his marriage he applied to his mother for a dowry, but she bade him apply to his father, the sun, and told him how to go to him. So one morning he took a long vine and made a noose in it ; then climbing up a tree he threw the noose over the sun and caught him fast. Thus arrested in his progress, the luminary asked him what he wanted, and being told by the young man that he wanted a present for his bride, the sun obligingly packed up a store of blessings in a basket, with which the youth descended to the earth.[1]

Even in the marriage customs of various races we may perhaps detect traces of this belief that women can be impregnated by the sun. Thus amongst the Chaco Indians of South America a newly married couple used to sleep the first night on a mare's or bullock's skin with their heads towards the west, " for the marriage is not considered ratified till the rising sun shines on their feet the succeeding morning." [2]   At old Hindoo marriages the first ceremony was the " Impregnation-rite " (*Garbhādhāna*) ; during the previous day the bride was made to look towards the sun or to be in some way exposed to its rays.[3]   Amongst the Turks of Siberia it was formerly the custom on the morning after the marriage to lead the young couple out of the hut to greet the rising sun. The same custom is said to be still practised in Iran and Central Asia under a belief that the beams of the rising sun are the surest means of impregnating the new bride.[4]   And as some people think that women may be gotten with child by the sun, so others imagine that they can conceive by the moon.   According to the Greenlanders

Traces in marriage customs of the belief that women can be impregnated by the sun.

Belief in the impregnation of women by the moon

[1] George Turner, LL.D., *Samoa, a Hundred Years ago and long before* (London, 1884), p. 200. For other examples of such tales, see Adolph Bastian, *Die Voelker des Oestlichen Asien*, i. 416, vi. 25 ; *Panjab Notes and Queries*, ii. p. 148, § 797 (June, 1885) ; A. Pfizmaier, "Nachrichten von den alten Bewohnern des heutigen Corea," *Sitzungsberichte der philosoph. histor. Classe der kaiser. Akademie der Wissenschaften* (Vienna), lvii. (1868) pp. 495 *sq.*

[2] Thomas J. Hutchinson, "On the Chaco and other Indians of South America," *Transactions of the Ethnological Society of London*, N.S. iii. (1865) p. 327. Amongst the Lengua Indians of the Paraguayan Chaco the marriage feast is now apparently extinct. See W. Barbrooke Grubb, *An Unknown People in an Unknown Land* (London, 1911), p. 179.

[3] Monier Williams, *Religious Thought and Life in India* (London, 1883), p. 354.

[4] H. Vambery, *Das Türkenvolk* (Leipsic, 1885), p. 112.

the moon is a young man, and he "now and then comes down to give their wives a visit and caress them ; for which reason no woman dare sleep lying upon her back, without she first spits upon her fingers and rubs her belly with it. For the same reason the young maids are afraid to stare long at the moon, imagining they may get a child by the bargain."[1] Similarly Breton peasants are reported to believe that women or girls who expose their persons to the moonlight may be impregnated by it and give birth to monsters.[2]

§ 8. *Reasons for the Seclusion of Girls at Puberty*

The reason for the seclusion of women at puberty is the dread of menstruous blood.

The motive for the restraints so commonly imposed on girls at puberty is the deeply engrained dread which primitive man universally entertains of menstruous blood. He fears it at all times but especially on its first appearance ; hence the restrictions under which women lie at their first menstruation are usually more stringent than those which they have to observe at any subsequent recurrence of the mysterious flow. Some evidence of the fear and of the customs based on it has been cited in an earlier part of this work ;[3] but as the terror, for it is nothing less, which the phenomenon periodically strikes into the mind of the savage has deeply influenced his life and institutions, it may be well to illustrate the subject with some further examples.

Dread and seclusion of menstruous women among the aborigines of Australia.

Thus in the Encounter Bay tribe of South Australia there is, or used to be, a " superstition which obliges a woman to separate herself from the camp at the time of her monthly illness, when, if a young man or boy should approach, she calls out, and he immediately makes a circuit to avoid her. If she is neglectful upon this point, she exposes herself to scolding, and sometimes to severe beating by her husband or nearest relation, because the boys are told from their infancy, that if they see the blood they will early become grey-headed, and their strength will fail prematurely."[4] And

---

[1] Hans Egede, *A Description of Greenland* (London, 1818), p. 209.

[2] *Revue des Traditions Populaires,* xv. (1900) p. 471.

[3] *Taboo and the Perils of the Soul,*

pp. 145 *sqq.*

[4] H. E. A. Meyer, " Manners and Customs of the Aborigines of the Encounter Bay Tribe, South Australia," *The Native Tribes of South Australia* (Adelaide, 1879), p. 186.

of the South Australian aborigines in general we read that there is a " custom requiring all boys and uninitiated young men to sleep at some distance from the huts of the adults, and to remove altogether away in the morning as soon as daylight dawns, and the natives begin to move about. This is to prevent their seeing the women, some of whom may be menstruating ; and if looked upon by the young males, it is supposed that dire results will follow." [1] And amongst these tribes women in their courses " are not allowed to eat fish of any kind, or to go near the water at all ; it being one of their superstitions, that if a female, in that state, goes near the water, no success can be expected by the men in fishing." [2] Similarly, among the natives of the Murray River, menstruous women " were not allowed to go near water for fear of frightening the fish. They were also not allowed to eat them, for the same reason. A woman during such periods would never cross the river in a canoe, or even fetch water for the camp. It was sufficient for her to say *Thama*, to ensure her husband getting the water himself." [3] The Dieri of Central Australia believe that if women at these times were to eat fish or bathe in a river, the fish would all die and the water would dry up. In this tribe a mark made with red ochre round a woman's mouth indicates that she has her courses ; no one would offer fish to such a woman. [4] The Arunta of Central Australia forbid menstruous women to gather the *irriakura* bulbs, which form a staple article of diet for both men and women. They believe that were a woman to break this rule, the supply of bulbs would fail. [5] Among the aborigines of Victoria the wife at her monthly periods had to sleep on the opposite side of the fire from her husband ; she might partake of nobody's food, and nobody would partake of hers, for people thought that if they ate or drank anything that had been touched by a woman in her courses, it would make them weak or ill. Unmarried girls

[1] E. J. Eyre, *Journals of Expeditions of Discovery into Central Australia* (London, 1845), ii. 304.

[2] E. J. Eyre, *op. cit.* ii. 295.

[3] R. Brough Smyth, *The Aborigines of Victoria* (Melbourne and London, 1878), i. 236.

[4] Samuel Gason, in *Journal of the* *Anthropological Institute*, xxiv. (1895) p. 171.

[5] Baldwin Spencer and F. J. Gillen, *Native Tribes of Central Australia* (London, 1899), p. 473 ; *iidem, Northern Tribes of Central Australia* (London, 1904), p. 615.

and widows at such times had to paint their heads and the upper parts of their bodies red,[1] no doubt as a danger signal.

Severe penalties inflicted for breaches of the custom of seclusion.

In some Australian tribes the seclusion of menstruous women was even more rigid, and was enforced by severer penalties than a scolding or a beating. Thus with regard to certain tribes of New South Wales and Southern Queensland we are told that " during the monthly illness, the woman is not allowed to touch anything that men use, or even to walk on a path that any man frequents, on pain of death." [2] Again, "there is a regulation relating to camps in the Wakelbura tribe which forbids the women coming into the encampment by the same path as the men. Any violation of this rule would in a large camp be punished with death. The reason for this is the dread with which they regard the menstrual period of women. During such a time, a woman is kept entirely away from the camp, half a mile at least. A woman in such a condition has boughs of some tree of her totem tied round her loins, and is constantly watched and guarded, for it is thought that should any male be so unfortunate as to see a woman in such a condition, he would die. If such a woman were to let herself be seen by a man, she would probably be put to death. When the woman has recovered, she is painted red and white, her head covered with feathers, and returns to the camp." [3]

Dread and seclusion of menstruous women in the Torres Straits Islands, New Guinea, Galela, and Sumatra.

In Muralug, one of the Torres Straits Islands, a menstruous woman may not eat anything that lives in the sea, else the natives believe that the fisheries would fail. Again, in Mabuiag, another of these islands, women who have their courses on them may not eat turtle flesh nor turtle eggs, probably for a similar reason. And during the season when the turtles are pairing the restrictions laid on

---

[1] James Dawson, *Australian Aborigines* (Melbourne, Sydney, and Adelaide, 1881), pp. ci. *sq.*

[2] Rev. William Ridley, " Report on Australian Languages and Traditions," *Journal of the Anthropological Institute*, ii. (1873) p. 268. Compare *id.*, *Kamilaroi and other Australian*

Languages (Sydney, 1875), p. 157.

[3] A. W. Howitt, *The Native Tribes of South-East Australia* (London, 1904), pp. 776 *sq.*, on the authority of Mr. J. C. Muirhead. The Wakelbura are in Central Queensland. Compare Captain W. E. Armit, quoted in *Journal of the Anthropological Institute*, ix. (1880) pp. 459 *sq.*

such a woman are much severer. She may not even enter a house in which there is turtle flesh, nor approach a fire on which the flesh is cooking ; she may not go near the sea and she should not walk on the beach below high-water mark. Nay, the infection extends to her husband, who may not himself harpoon or otherwise take an active part in catching turtle ; however, he is permitted to form one of the crew on a turtling expedition, provided he takes the precaution of rubbing his armpits with certain leaves, to which no doubt a disinfectant virtue is ascribed.[1] Among the Kai of German New Guinea women at their monthly sickness must live in little huts built for them in the forest ; they may not enter the cultivated fields, for if they did go to them, and the pigs were to taste of the blood, it would inspire the animals with an irresistible desire to go likewise into the fields, where they would commit great depredations on the growing crops. Hence the issue from women at these times is carefully buried to prevent the pigs from getting at it. And conversely, if the pigs often break into the fields, the blame is laid on the women who by the neglect of these elementary precautions have put temptation in the way of the swine.[2] In Galela, to the west of New Guinea, women at their monthly periods may not enter a tobacco-field, or the plants would be attacked by disease.[3] The Minangka-bauers of Sumatra are persuaded that if a woman in her unclean state were to go near a rice-field, the crop would be spoiled.[4]

The Bushmen of South Africa think that, by a glance of a girl's eye at the time when she ought to be kept in strict retirement, men become fixed in whatever position they happen to occupy, with whatever they were holding in their hands, and are changed into trees that talk.[5] Cattle-rearing

Dread and seclusion of menstruous women among the tribes of South Africa.

---

[1] *Reports of the Cambridge Anthropological Expedition to Torres Straits*, v. (Cambridge, 1904) pp. 196, 207.

[2] Ch. Keysser, "Aus dem Leben der Kaileute," in R. Neuhauss's *Deutsch Neu-Guinea* (Berlin, 1911), iii. 91.

[3] M. J. van Baarda, "Fabelen, Verhalen en Overleveringen der Galelareezen," *Bijdragen tot de Taal- Land-en Volkenkunde van Nederlandsch-*

Indië, xlv. (1895) p. 489.

[4] J. L. van der Toorn, "Het animisme bij den Minangkabauer der Padangsche Bovenlanden," *Bijdragen tot de Taal- Land- en Volkenkunde van Nederlandsch-Indië*, xxxix. (1890) p. 66.

[5] W. H. I. Bleek, *A Brief Account of Bushman Folk-lore* (London, 1875), p. 14 ; compare *ibid.*, p. 10.

tribes of South Africa hold that their cattle would die if the milk were drunk by a menstruous woman;[1] and they fear the same disaster if a drop of her blood were to fall on the ground and the oxen were to pass over it. To prevent such a calamity women in general, not menstruous women only, are forbidden to enter the cattle enclosure; and more than that, they may not use the ordinary paths in entering the village or in passing from one hut to another. They are obliged to make circuitous tracks at the back of the huts in order to avoid the ground in the middle of the village where the cattle stand or lie down. These women's tracks may be seen at every Caffre village.[2] Similarly among the Bahima, a cattle-breeding tribe of Ankole, in Central Africa, no menstruous woman may drink milk, lest by so doing she should injure the cows; and she may not lie on her husband's bed, no doubt lest she should injure him. Indeed she is forbidden to lie on a bed at all and must sleep on the ground. Her diet is restricted to vegetables and beer.[3] Among the Baganda, in like manner, no menstruous woman might drink milk or come into contact with any milk-vessel;[4] and she might not touch anything that belonged to her husband, nor sit on his mat, nor cook his food. If she touched anything of his at such a time it was deemed equivalent to wishing him dead or to actually working magic for his destruction.[5] Were she to handle any article of his, he would surely fall ill; were she to handle his weapons, he would certainly be killed in the next battle. Even a woman

Marginal note: Dread and seclusion of menstruous women among the tribes of Central and East Africa.

---

[1] Rev. James Macdonald, "Manners, Customs, Superstitions and Religions of South African Tribes," *Journal of the Anthropological Institute*, xx. (1891) p. 138; *id., Light in Africa*, Second Edition (London, 1890), p. 221.

[2] Dudley Kidd, *The Essential Kafir* (London, 1904), p. 238; Mr. Warren's Notes, in Col. Maclean's *Compendium of Kafir Laws and Customs* (Cape Town, 1866), p. 93; Rev. J. Macdonald, *Light in Africa*, p. 221; *id., Religion and Myth* (London, 1893), p. 198. Compare Henri A. Junod, "Les conceptions physiologiques des Bantou Sud-Africains et leurs tabous," *Revue d'Ethnographie et de Sociologie*, i. (1910) p. 139. The danger of death to the cattle from the blood of women is mentioned only by Mr. Kidd. The part of the village which is frequented by the cattle, and which accordingly must be shunned by women, has a special name, *inkundhla* (Mr. Warner's Notes, *l.c.*).

[3] Rev. J. Roscoe, "The Bahima, a Cow Tribe of Enkole," *Journal of the Royal Anthropological Institute*, xxxvii. (1907) p. 106.

[4] Rev. J. Roscoe, *The Baganda* (London, 1911), p. 419.

[5] Rev. J. Roscoe, *The Baganda*, p 96.

who did not menstruate was believed by the Baganda to be a source of danger to her husband, indeed capable of killing him. Hence, before he went to war, he used to wound her slightly with his spear so as to draw blood ; this was thought to ensure his safe return.[1] Apparently the notion was that if the wife did not lose blood in one way or another, her husband would be bled in war to make up for her deficiency ; so by way of guarding against this undesirable event, he took care to relieve her of a little superfluous blood before he repaired to the field of honour. Further, the Baganda would not suffer a menstruous woman to visit a well ; if she did so, they feared that the water would dry up, and that she herself would fall sick and die, unless she confessed her fault and the medicine-man made atonement for her.[2] Among the Akikuyu of British East Africa, if a new hut is built in a village and the wife chances to menstruate in it on the day she lights the first fire there, the hut must be broken down and demolished the very next day. The woman may on no account sleep a second night in it ; there is a curse (*thahu*) both on her and on it.[3] In the Suk tribe of British East Africa warriors may not eat anything that has been touched by menstruous women. If they did so, it is believed that they would lose their virility ; " in the rain they will shiver and in the heat they will faint." Suk men and women take their meals apart, because the men fear that one or more of the women may be menstruating.[4] The Anyanja of British Central Africa, at the southern end of Lake Nyassa, think that a man who should sleep with a woman in her courses would fall sick and die, unless some remedy were applied in time. And with them it is a rule that at such times a woman should not put any salt into the food she is cooking, otherwise the people who partook of the food salted by her would suffer from a certain disease called

[1] Rev. J. Roscoe, "Notes on the Manners and Customs of the Baganda," *Journal of the Anthropological Institute*, xxxi. (1901) p. 121 ; *id.*, "Further Notes on the Manners and Customs of the Baganda," *Journal of the Anthropological Institute*, xxxii. (1902) p. 39 ; *id.*, *The Baganda*, p. 352.

[2] Rev. J. Roscoe, *The Baganda*, p. 459.

[3] C. W. Hobley, "Further Researches into Kikuyu and Kamba Religious Beliefs and Customs," *Journal of the Royal Anthropological Institute*, xli. (1911) p. 409.

[4] Mervyn W. H. Beech, *The Suk, their Language and Folklore* (Oxford, 1911), p. 11.

tsempo ; hence to obviate the danger she calls a child to put the salt into the dish.[1]

Dread and seclusion of menstruous women among the tribes of West Africa.

Among the Hos, a tribe of Ewe negroes of Togo-land in West Africa, so long as a wife has her monthly sickness she may not cook for her husband, nor lie on his bed, nor sit on his stool ; an infraction of these rules would assuredly, it is believed, cause her husband to die. If her husband is a priest, or a magician, or a chief, she may not pass the days of her uncleanness in the house, but must go elsewhere till she is clean.[2] Among the Ewe negroes of this region each village has its huts where women who have their courses on them must spend their time secluded from intercourse with other people. Sometimes these huts stand by themselves in public places ; sometimes they are mere shelters built either at the back or front of the ordinary dwelling-houses. A woman is punishable if she does not pass the time of her monthly sickness in one of these huts or shelters provided for her use. Thus, if she shews herself in her own house or even in the yard of the house, she may be fined a sheep, which is killed, its flesh divided among the people, and its blood poured on the image of the chief god as a sin-offering to expiate her offence. She is also forbidden to go to the place where the villagers draw water, and if she breaks the rule, she must give a goat to be killed ; its flesh is distributed, and its blood, diluted with water and mixed with herbs, is sprinkled on the watering-place and on the paths leading to it. Were any woman to disregard these salutary precautions, the chief fetish-man in the village would fall sick and die, which would be an irreparable loss to society.[3]

Powerful influence ascribed to menstruous blood in Arab legend.

The miraculous virtue ascribed to menstruous blood is well illustrated in a story told by the Arab chronicler Tabari. He relates how Sapor, king of Persia, besieged the strong city of Atrae, in the desert of Mesopotamia, for several years without

[1] H. S. Stannus, "Notes on some Tribes of British Central Africa," *Journal of the Royal Anthropological Institute*, xl. (1910) p. 305 ; R. Sutherland Rattray, *Some Folk-lore Stories and Songs in Chinyanja* (London, 1907), p. 191. See above,

p. 27.

[2] Jakob Spieth, *Die Ewe-Stämme* (Berlin, 1906), p. 192.

[3] Anton Witte, "Menstruation und Pubertätsfeier der Mädchen in Kpan-dugebiet Togo," *Baessler-Archiv*, i. (1911) p. 279.

being able to take it. But the king of the city, whose name
was Daizan, had a daughter, and when it was with her after
the manner of women she went forth from the city and dwelt
for a time in the suburb, for such was the custom of the place.
Now it fell out that, while she tarried there, Sapor saw her
and loved her, and she loved him ; for he was a handsome
man and she a lovely maid. And she said to him, " What
will you give me if I shew you how you may destroy the
walls of this city and slay my father ? " And he said to her,
" I will give you what you will, and I will exalt you above
my other wives, and will set you nearer to me than them
all." Then she said to him, " Take a greenish dove with a
ring about its neck, and write something on its foot with the
menstruous blood of a blue-eyed maid ; then let the bird
loose, and it will perch on the walls of the city, and they
will fall down." For that, says the Arab historian, was the
talisman of the city, which could not be destroyed in any
other way. And Sapor did as she bade him, and the city
fell down in a heap, and he stormed it and slew Daizan on
the spot.[1]

According to the Talmud, if a woman at the beginning
of her period passes between two men, she thereby kills one
of them ; if she passes between them towards the end of her
period, she only causes them to quarrel violently.[2] Maimonides tells us that down to his time it was a common custom
in the East to keep women at their periods in a separate
house and to burn everything on which they had trodden ;
a man who spoke with such a woman or who was merely
exposed to the same wind that blew over her, became thereby
unclean.[3] Peasants of the Lebanon think that menstruous
women are the cause of many misfortunes ; their shadow

*Dread and
seclusion of
menstruous
women
among the
Jews and
in Syria.*

[1] Th. Nöldeke, *Geschichte der Perser
und Araber zur Zeit der Sassaniden,
aus der arabischen Chronik des Tabari
übersetzt* (Leyden, 1879), pp. 33-38.
I have to thank my friend Professor
A. A. Bevan for pointing out to me
this passage. Many ancient cities had
talismans on the preservation of which
their safety was believed to depend.
The Palladium of Troy is the most
familiar instance. See Chr. A. Lobeck,
Aglaophamus (Königsberg, 1829), pp.

278 *sqq.*, and my note on Pausanias,
viii. 47. 5 (vol. iv. pp. 433 *sq.*).

[2] J. Mergel, *Die Medezin der Tal-
mudisten* (Leipsic and Berlin, 1885),
pp. 15 *sq.*

[3] Maimonides, quoted by D. Chwol-
sohn, *Die Ssabier und der Ssabismus*
(St. Petersburg, 1856), ii. 483.
According to the editor (p. 735) by
the East Maimonides means India and
eastern countries generally.

causes flowers to wither and trees to perish, it even arrests
the movements of serpents ; if one of them mounts a horse,
the animal might die or at least be disabled for a long time.[1]
In Syria to this day a woman who has her courses on her
may neither salt nor pickle, for the people think that whatever she pickled or salted would not keep.[2]   The Toaripi of
New Guinea, doubtless for a similar reason, will not allow
women at such times to cook.[3]   The Bhuiyars, a Dravidian
tribe of South Mirzapur, are said to feel an intense dread of
menstrual pollution.   Every house has two doors, one of
which is used only by women in this condition.   During her
impurity the wife is fed by her husband apart from the rest
of the family, and whenever she has to quit the house she is
obliged to creep out on her hands and knees in order not to
defile the thatch by her touch.[4]   The Kharwars, another
aboriginal tribe of the same district, keep their women at
such seasons in the outer verandah of the house for eight
days, and will not let them enter the kitchen or the cow-
house ; during this time the unclean woman may not cook
nor even touch the cooking vessels.   When the eight days
are over, she bathes, washes her clothes, and returns to family
life.[5]   Hindoo women seclude themselves at their monthly
periods and observe a number of rules, such as not to drink
milk, not to milk cows, not to touch fire, not to lie on a high
bed, not to walk on common paths, not to cross the track
of animals, not to walk by the side of flowering plants, and
not to observe the heavenly bodies.[6]   The motive for these

Dread and
seclusion of
menstruous
women in
India.

[1] L'abbé Béchara Chémali, "Nais-
sance et premier âge au Liban," Anthropos, v. (1910) p. 735.

[2] Eijūb Abēla, " Beiträge zur Kennt-
niss abergläubischer Gebräuche in
Syrien," Zeitschrift des deutschen
Palaestina-Vereins, vii. (1884) p. 111.

[3] J. Chalmers, "Toaripi," Journal
of the Anthropological Institute, xxvii.
(1898) p. 328.

[4] W. Crooke, Tribes and Castes of
the North-Western Provinces and Oudh
(Calcutta, 1896), ii. 87.

[5] W. Crooke, in North Indian Notes
and Queries, i. p. 67, § 467 (July,
1891).

[6] L. K. Anantha Krishna Iyer,

The Cochin Tribes and Castes, i.
(Madras, 1909) pp. 201-203.   As to
the seclusion of menstruous women
among the Hindoos, see also Sonnerat,
Voyage aux Indes Orientales et à la
Chine (Paris, 1782), i. 31 ; J. A.
Dubois, Mœurs, Institutions et Céré-
monies des Peuples de l'Inde (Paris,
1825), i. 245 sq. Nair women in
Malabar seclude themselves for three
days at menstruation and prepare their
food in separate pots and pans.   See
Duarte Barbosa, Description of the
Coasts of East Africa and Malabar in
the beginning of the Sixteenth Century
(Hakluyt Society, London, 1866),
pp. 132 sq.

restrictions is not mentioned, but probably it is a dread of the baleful influence which is supposed to emanate from women at these times. The Parsees, who reverence fire, will not suffer menstruous women to see it or even to look on a lighted taper;[1] during their infirmity the women retire from their houses to little lodges in the country, whither victuals are brought to them daily; at the end of their seclusion they bathe and send a kid, a fowl, or a pigeon to the priest as an offering.[2] In Annam a woman at her monthly periods is deemed a centre of impurity, and contact with her is avoided. She is subject to all sorts of restrictions which she must observe herself and which others must observe towards her. She may not touch any food which is to be preserved by salting, whether it be fish, flesh, or vegetables; for were she to touch it the food would putrefy. She may not enter any sacred place, she may not be present at any religious ceremony. The linen which she wears at such times must be washed by herself at sunrise, never at night. On reaching puberty girls may not touch flowers or the fruits of certain trees, for touched by them the flowers would fade and the fruits fall to the ground. " It is on account of their reputation for impurity that the women generally live isolated. In every house they have an apartment reserved for them, and they never eat at the same table as the men. For the same reason they are excluded from all religious ceremonies. They may only be present at family ceremonies, but without ever officiating in them." [3]

Dread and seclusion of menstruous women in Annam.

The Guayquiries of the Orinoco think that when a woman has her courses, everything upon which she steps will die, and that if a man treads on the place where she has passed, his legs will immediately swell up.[4] Among the Guaraunos of the same great river, women at their periods are regarded as unclean and kept apart in special huts, where

Dread and seclusion of menstruous women among the Indians of South and Central America.

[1] G. Hoffman, *Auszüge aus Syrischen Akten persisischer Martyrer übersetzt* (Leipsic, 1880), p. 99. This passage was pointed out to me by my friend Professor A. A. Bevan.

[2] J. B. Tavernier, *Voyages en Turquie, en Perse, et aux Indes* (The Hague, 1718), i. 488.

[3] Paul Giran, *Magie et Religion Annamites* (Paris, 1912), pp. 107 *sq.*, 112.

[4] Joseph Gumilla, *Histoire Naturelle, Civile, et Géographique de l'Orenoque* (Avignon, 1758), i. 249.

all that they need is brought to them.[1]   In like manner among the Piapocos, an Indian tribe on the Guayabero, a tributary of the Orinoco, a menstruous woman is secluded from her family every month for four or five days.   She passes the time in a special hut, whither her husband brings her food ; and at the end of the time she takes a bath and resumes her usual occupations.[2]   So among the Indians of the Mosquito territory in Central America, when a woman is in her courses, she must quit the village for seven or eight days.   A small hut is built for her in the wood, and at night some of the village girls go and sleep with her to keep her company.   Or if the nights are dark and jaguars are known to be prowling in the neighbourhood, her husband will take his gun or bow and sleep in a hammock near her. She may neither handle nor cook food ; all is prepared and carried to her.   When the sickness is over, she bathes in the river, puts on clean clothes, and returns to her household duties.[3]   Among the Bri-bri Indians of Costa Rica a girl at her first menstruation retires to a hut built for the purpose in the forest, and there she must stay till she has been purified by a medicine-man, who breathes on her and places various objects, such as feathers, the beaks of birds, the teeth of beasts, and so forth, upon her body.   A married woman at her periods remains in the house with her husband, but she is reckoned unclean (*bukuru*) and must avoid all intimate relations with him.   She uses for plates only banana leaves, which, when she has done with them, she throws away in a sequestered spot ; for should a cow find and eat them, the animal would waste away and perish.   Also she drinks only out of a special vessel, because any person who should afterwards drink out of the same vessel would infallibly pine away and die.[4]

[1] Dr. Louis Plassard, " Les Guar-aunos et le delta de l'Orénoque," *Bulletin de la Société de Géographie* (Paris), v. Série, xv. (1868) p. 584.

[2] J. Crevaux, *Voyages dans l'Amérique du Sud* (Paris, 1883), p. 526. As to the customs observed at menstruation by Indian women in South America, see further A. d'Orbigny, *L'Homme Américain* (Paris, 1839), i. 237.

[3] Chas. N. Bell, " The Mosquito Territory," *Journal of the Royal Geographical Society*, xxxii. (1862) p. 254.

[4] H. Pittier de Fabrega, " Die Sprache der Bribri-Indianer in Costa Rica," *Sitzungsberichte der philosophischen-historischen Classe der Kaiserlichen Akademie der Wissenschaften* (Vienna), cxxxviii. (1898) pp. 19 *sq.*

Among most tribes of North American Indians the custom was that women in their courses retired from the camp or the village and lived during the time of their uncleanness in special huts or shelters which were appropriated to their use. There they dwelt apart, eating and sleeping by themselves, warming themselves at their own fires, and strictly abstaining from all communications with men, who shunned them just as if they were stricken with the plague. No article of furniture used in these menstrual huts might be used in any other, not even the flint and steel with which in the old days the fires were kindled. No one would borrow a light from a woman in her seclusion. If a white man in his ignorance asked to light his pipe at her fire, she would refuse to grant the request, telling him that it would make his nose bleed and his head ache, and that he would fall sick in consequence. If an Indian's wooden pipe cracked, his friends would think that he had either lit it at one of these polluted fires or had held some converse with a woman during her retirement, which was esteemed a most disgraceful and wicked thing to do. Decent men would not approach within a certain distance of a woman at such times, and if they had to convey anything to her they would stand some forty or fifty paces off and throw it to her. Everything which was touched by her hands during this period was deemed ceremonially unclean. Indeed her touch was thought to convey such pollution that if she chanced to lay a finger on a chief's lodge or his gun or anything else belonging to him, it would be instantly destroyed. If she crossed the path of a hunter or a warrior, his luck for that day at least would be gone. Were she not thus secluded, it was supposed that the men would be attacked by diseases of various kinds, which would prove mortal. In some tribes a woman who infringed the rules of separation might have to answer with her life for any misfortunes that might happen to individuals or to the tribe in consequence, as it was supposed, of her criminal negligence. When she quitted her tent or hut to go into retirement, the fire in it was extinguished and the ashes thrown away outside of the village, and a new fire was kindled, as if the old one had been defiled by her presence. At the end of their

Dread and seclusion of menstruous women among the Indians of North America.

seclusion the women bathed in running streams and returned to their usual occupations.[1]

Thus, to take examples, the Creek and kindred Indians of the United States compelled women at menstruation to live in separate huts at some distance from the village. There the women had to stay, at the risk of being surprised and cut off by enemies. It was thought "a most horrid and dangerous pollution" to go near the women at such times; and the danger extended to enemies who, if they slew the women, had to cleanse themselves from the pollution by means of certain sacred herbs and roots.[2] Similarly, the Choctaw women had to quit their huts during their monthly periods, and might not return till after they had been purified. While their uncleanness lasted they had to prepare their own food. The men believed that if they were to approach a menstruous woman, they would fall ill, and that some mishap would overtake them when they went to the wars.[3] When an Omaha woman has her courses on her, she retires from the family to a little shelter of bark or grass, supported by sticks, where she kindles a fire and cooks her victuals alone. Her seclusion lasts four days. During this time she may not approach or touch a horse, for the Indians believe that

[1] Gabriel Sagard, *Le Grand Voyage du Pays des Hurons*, Nouvelle Édition (Paris, 1865), p. 54 (original edition, Paris, 1632); J. F. Lafitau, *Mœurs des Sauvages Ameriquains* (Paris, 1724), i. 262; Charlevoix, *Histoire de la Nouvelle France* (Paris, 1744), v. 423 *sq.*; Captain Jonathan Carver, *Travels through the Interior Parts of North America*, Third Edition (London, 1781), pp. 236 *sq.*; Captains Lewis and Clark, *Expedition to the Sources of the Missouri*, etc. (London, 1905), iii. 90 (original edition, 1814); Rev. Jedidiah Morse, *Report to the Secretary of War of the United States on Indian Affairs* (New Haven, 1822), pp. 136 *sq.*; *Annales de l'Association de la Propagation de la Foi*, iv. (Paris and Lyons, 1830) pp. 483, 494 *sq.*; George Catlin, *Letters and Notes on the Manners, Customs, and Condition of the North American Indians*, Fourth Edition (London, 1844), ii. 233; H. R. Schoolcraft, *Indian Tribes of the United States* (Philadelphia, 1853–1856), v. 70; A. L. Kroeber, "The Religion of the Indians of California," *University of California Publications in American Archaeology and Ethnology*, vol. iv. No. 6 (Berkeley, September, 1907), pp. 323 *sq.*; Frank G. Speck, *Ethnology of the Yuchi Indians* (Philadelphia, 1909), p. 96. Among the Hurons of Canada women at their periods did not retire from the house or village, but they ate from small dishes apart from the rest of the family at these times (Gabriel Sagard, *l.c.*).

[2] James Adair, *History of the American Indians* (London, 1775), pp. 123 *sq.*

[3] Bossu, *Nouveaux Voyages aux Indes occidentales* (Paris, 1768), ii. 105.

such contamination would impoverish or weaken the animal.[1] Among the Potawatomis the women at their monthly periods "are not allowed to associate with the rest of the nation ; they are completely laid aside, and are not permitted to touch any article of furniture or food which the men have occasion to use. If the Indians be stationary at the time, the women are placed outside of the camp ; if on a march, they are not allowed to follow the trail, but must take a different path and keep at a distance from the main body." [2] Among the Cheyennes menstruous women slept in special lodges ; the men believed that if they slept with their wives at such times, they would probably be wounded in their next battle. A man who owned a shield had very particularly to be on his guard against women in their courses. He might not go into a lodge where one of them happened to be, nor even into a lodge where one of them had been, until a ceremony of purification had been performed. Sweet grass and juniper were burnt in the tent, and the pegs were pulled up and the covering thrown back, as if the tent were about to be struck. After this pretence of decamping from the polluted spot the owner of the shield might enter the tent.[3]

The Stseelis Indians of British Columbia imagined that if a menstruous woman were to step over a bundle of arrows, the arrows would thereby be rendered useless and might even cause the death of their owner ; and similarly that if she passed in front of a hunter who carried a gun, the weapon would never shoot straight again. Neither her husband nor her father would dream of going out to hunt while she was in this state ; and even if he had wished to do so, the other hunters would not go with him. Hence to keep them out of harm's way, the women, both married and unmarried, were secluded at these times for four days in shelters.[4] Among the Thompson

Dread and seclusion of menstruous women among the Indians of British Columbia.

[1] Edwin James, *Account of an Expedition from Pittsburgh to the Rocky Mountains* (London, 1823), i. 214.
[2] William H. Keating, *Narrative of an Expedition to the Source of St. Peter's River* (London, 1825), i. 132.
[3] G. B. Grinnell, "Cheyenne Woman Customs," *American Anthro-*

pologist, New Series, iv. (New York, 1902) p. 14.
[4] C. Hill Tout, "Ethnological Report on the Stseelis and Skaulits Tribes of the Halokmelem Division of the Salish of British Columbia," *Journal of the Anthropological Institute*, xxxiv. (1904) p. 320.

Indians of British Columbia every woman had to isolate herself from the rest of the people during every recurring period of menstruation, and had to live some little way off in a small brush or bark lodge made for the purpose. At these times she was considered unclean, must use cooking and eating utensils of her own, and was supplied with food by some other woman. If she smoked out of a pipe other than her own, that pipe would ever afterwards be hot to smoke. If she crossed in front of a gun, that gun would thenceforth be useless for the war or the chase, unless indeed the owner promptly washed the weapon in "medecine" or struck the woman with it once on each principal part of her body. If a man ate or had any intercourse with a menstruous woman, nay if he merely wore clothes or mocassins made or patched by her, he would have bad luck in hunting and the bears would attack him fiercely. Before being admitted again among the people, she had to change all her clothes and wash several times in clear water. The clothes worn during her isolation were hung on a tree, to be used next time, or to be washed. For one day after coming back among the people she did not cook food. Were a man to eat food cooked by a woman at such times, he would have incapacitated himself for hunting and exposed himself to sickness or death.[1]

Dread and seclusion of menstruous women among the Chippeway Indians.

Among the Chippeways and other Indians of the Hudson Bay Territory, menstruous women are excluded from the camp, and take up their abode in huts of branches. They wear long hoods, which effectually conceal the head and breast. They may not touch the household furniture nor any objects used by men ; for their touch "is supposed to defile them, so that their subsequent use would be followed by certain mischief or misfortune," such as disease or death. They must drink out of a swan's bone. They may not walk on the common paths nor cross the tracks of animals. They "are never permitted to walk on the ice of rivers or lakes, or near the part where the men are hunting beaver, or where a fishing-net is set, for fear of averting

[1] James Teit, *The Thompson Indians of British Columbia*, pp. 326 *sq.* (*The Jesup North Pacific Expedition, Memoir* of the American Museum of Natural History, New York, April, 1900).

their success.   They are also prohibited at those times from partaking of the head of any animal, and even from walking in or crossing the track where the head of a deer, moose, beaver, and many other animals have lately been carried, either on a sledge or on the back.   To be guilty of a violation of this custom is considered as of the greatest importance ; because they firmly believe that it would be a means of preventing the hunter from having an equal success in his future excursions." [1]   So the Lapps forbid women at menstruation to walk on that part of the shore where the fishers are in the habit of setting out their fish ; [2] and the Esquimaux of Bering Strait believe that if hunters were to come near women in their courses they would catch no game. [3]

But the beliefs and superstitions of this sort that prevail among the western tribes of the great Déné or Tinneh stock, to which the Chippeways belong, have been so well described by an experienced missionary, that I will give his description in his own words.   Prominent among the ceremonial rites of these Indians, he says, " are the observances peculiar to the fair sex, and many of them are remarkably analogous to those practised by the Hebrew women, so much so that, were it not savouring of profanity, the ordinances of the Déné ritual code might be termed a new edition ' revised and considerably augmented ' of the Mosaic ceremonial law.   Among the Carriers, [4] as soon as a girl has experienced the first flow of the menses which in the female constitution are a natural discharge, her father believed himself under the obligation of atoning for her supposedly sinful condition by a small impromptu distribution of clothes among the natives.   This periodical state of women was considered as one of legal impurity

Dread and seclusion of menstruous women among the Tinneh or Déné Indians.

Customs and beliefs of the Carrier Indians in regard to menstruous women.

---

[1] Samuel Hearne, *Journey from Prince of Wales's Fort in Hudson's Bay to the Northern Ocean* (London, 1795), pp. 314 *sq.* ; Alex. Mackenzie, *Voyages through the Continent of North America* (London, 1801), p. cxxiii. ; E. Petitot, *Monographie des Dènè-Dindjiè* (Paris, 1876), pp. 75 *sq.*

[2] C. Leemius, *De Lapponibus Finmarchiae eorumque lingua vita et religione pristina* (Copenhagen, 1767), p. 494.

[3] E. W. Nelson, "The Eskimo about Bering Strait," *Eighteenth Annual Report of the Bureau of American Ethnology*, Part i. (Washington, 1899) p. 440.

[4] The Carriers are a tribe of Déné or Tinneh Indians who get their name from a custom observed among them by widows, who carry, or rather used to carry, the charred bones of their dead husbands about with them in bundles.

fateful both to the man who happened to have any intercourse, however indirect, with her, and to the woman
herself who failed in scrupulously observing all the rites
prescribed by ancient usage for persons in her condition.

"Upon entering into that stage of her life, the maiden
was immediately sequestered from company, even that of
her parents, and compelled to dwell in a small branch hut
by herself away from beaten paths and the gaze of passers-
by. As she was supposed to exercise malefic influence on
any man who might inadvertently glance at her, she had to
wear a sort of head-dress combining in itself the purposes of
a veil, a bonnet, and a mantlet. It was made of tanned
skin, its forepart was shaped like a long fringe completely
hiding from view the face and breasts ; then it formed on
the head a close-fitting cap or bonnet, and finally fell in a
broad band almost to the heels. This head-dress was made
and publicly placed on her head by a paternal aunt, who
received at once some present from the girl's father. When,
three or four years later, the period of sequestration ceased,
only this same aunt had the right to take off her niece's
ceremonial head-dress. Furthermore, the girl's fingers,
wrists, and legs at the ankles and immediately below the
knees, were encircled with ornamental rings and bracelets of
sinew intended as a protection against the malign influences
she was supposed to be possessed with.[1] To a belt girding
her waist were suspended two bone implements called
respectively *Tsoenkuz* (bone tube) and *Tsiltsoet* (head
scratcher). The former was a hollowed swan bone to drink
with, any other mode of drinking being unlawful to her.
The latter was fork-like and was called into requisition
whenever she wanted to scratch her head—immediate contact of the fingers with the head being reputed injurious to
her health. While thus secluded, she was called *asta*, that

[1] Hence we may conjecture that the
similar ornaments worn by Mabuiag
girls in similar circumstances are also
amulets. See above, p. 36. Among
the aborigines of the Upper Yarra
river in Victoria, a girl at puberty
used to have cords tied very tightly
round several parts of her body. The
cords were worn for several days,
causing the whole body to swell very
much and inflicting great pain. The
girl might not remove them till she
was clean. See R. Brough Smyth,
Aborigines of Victoria (Melbourne and
London, 1878), i. 65. Perhaps the
cords were intended to arrest the flow
of blood.

is 'interred alive' in Carrier, and she had to submit to a rigorous fast and abstinence.   Her only allowed food consisted of dried fish boiled in a small bark vessel which nobody else must touch, and she had to abstain especially from meat of any kind, as well as fresh fish.   Nor was this all she had to endure ; even her contact, however remote, with these two articles of diet was so dreaded that she could not cross the public paths or trails, or the tracks of animals. Whenever absolute necessity constrained her to go beyond such spots, she had to be packed or carried over them lest she should contaminate the game or meat which had passed that way, or had been brought over these paths ; and also for the sake of self-preservation against tabooed, and consequently to her, deleterious food.   In the same way she was never allowed to wade in streams or lakes, for fear of causing death to the fish.

" It was also a prescription of the ancient ritual code for females during this primary condition to eat as little as possible, and to remain lying down, especially in course of each monthly flow, not only as a natural consequence of the prolonged fast and resulting weakness ; but chiefly as an exhibition of a becoming penitential spirit which was believed to be rewarded by long life and continual good health in after years.

" These mortifications or seclusion did not last less than three or four years.   Useless to say that during all that time marriage could not be thought of, since the girl could not so much as be seen by men.   When married, the same sequestration was practised relatively to husband and fellow-villagers—without the particular head-dress and rings spoken of—on the occasion of every recurring menstruation.   Sometimes it was protracted as long as ten days at a time, especially during the first years of cohabitation.   Even when she returned to her mate, she was not permitted to sleep with him on the first nor frequently on the second night, but would choose a distant corner of the lodge to spread her blanket, as if afraid to defile him with her dread uncleanness." [1]   Elsewhere the same writer tells us that most of

Seclusion of Carrier women at their monthly periods.

[1] Rev. Father A. G. Morice, " The Western Dénés, their Manners and   Customs," *Proceedings of the Canadian Institute, Toronto,* Third Series, vii.

Reasons
for the
seclusion of
menstruous
women
among the
Indians.

the devices to which these Indians used to resort for the
sake of ensuring success in the chase " were based on their
regard for continence and their excessive repugnance for,
and dread of, menstruating women."[1] But the strict observances imposed on Tinneh or Déné women at such times were
designed at the same time to protect the women themselves
from the evil consequences of their dangerous condition.
Thus it was thought that women in their courses could not
partake of the head, heart, or hind part of an animal that
had been caught in a snare without exposing themselves to
a premature death through a kind of rabies. They might
not cut or carve salmon, because to do so would seriously
endanger their health, and especially would enfeeble their
arms for life. And they had to abstain from cutting
up the grebes which are caught by the Carriers in great
numbers every spring, because otherwise the blood with
which these fowls abound would occasion hæmorrhage or an
unnaturally prolonged flux in the transgressor.[2] Similarly
Indian women of the Thompson tribe abstained from venison
and the flesh of other large game during menstruation,
lest the animals should be displeased and the menstrual
flow increased.[3] For a similar reason, probably, Shuswap
girls during their seclusion at puberty are forbidden to eat
anything that bleeds.[4] The same principle may perhaps
partly explain the rule, of which we have had some examples,
that women at such times should refrain from fish and flesh,
and restrict themselves to a vegetable diet.

The philosophic student of human nature will observe,
or learn, without surprise that ideas thus deeply ingrained

(1888–89) pp. 162-164. The writer
has repeated the substance of this
account in a later work, *Au pays de
l'Ours Noir : chez les sauvages de la
Colombie Britannique* (Paris and Lyons,
1897), pp. 72 *sq.*

[1] A. G. Morice, " Notes, Archaeological, Industrial, and Sociological, on
the Western Dénés," *Transactions of
the Canadian Institute*, iv. (1892–93)
pp. 106 *sq.* Compare Rev. Father
Julius Jetté, " On the Superstitions of
the Ten'a Indians," *Anthropos*, vi.
(1911) pp. 703 *sq.*, who tells us that

Tinneh women at these times may not
lift their own nets, may not step over
other people's nets, and may not pass
in a boat or canoe near a place where
nets are being set.

[2] A. G. Morice, in *Transactions of
the Canadian Institute*, iv. (1892–93)
pp. 107, 110.

[3] James Teit, *The Thompson Indians
of British Columbia*, p. 327 (*The Jesup
North Pacific Expedition, Memoir of
the American Museum of Natural
History*, New York, April 1900).

[4] See above, p. 53.

in the savage mind reappear at a more advanced stage of society in those elaborate codes which have been drawn up for the guidance of certain peoples by lawgivers who claim to have derived the rules they inculcate from the direct inspiration of the deity.   However we may explain it, the resemblance which exists between the earliest official utterances of the deity and the ideas of savages is unquestionably close and remarkable ; whether it be, as some suppose, that God communed face to face with man in those early days, or, as others maintain, that man mistook his wild and wandering thoughts for a revelation from heaven.   Be that as it may, certain it is that the natural uncleanness of woman at her monthly periods is a conception which has occurred, or been revealed, with singular unanimity to several ancient legislators.   The Hindoo lawgiver Manu, who professed to have received his institutes from the creator Brahman, informs us that the wisdom, the energy, the strength, the sight, and the vitality of a man who approaches a woman in her courses will utterly perish ; whereas, if he avoids her, his wisdom, energy, strength, sight, and vitality will all increase.[1] The Persian lawgiver Zoroaster, who, if we can take his word for it, derived his code from the mouth of the supreme being Ahura Mazda, devoted special attention to the subject. According to him, the menstrous flow, at least in its abnormal manifestations, is a work of Ahriman, or the devil.   Therefore, so long as it lasts, a woman " is unclean and possessed of the demon ; she must be kept confined, apart from the faithful whom her touch would defile, and from the fire which her very look would injure ; she is not allowed to eat as much as she wishes, as the strength she might acquire would accrue to the fiends.   Her food is not given her from hand to hand, but is passed to her from a distance, in a long leaden spoon." [2]   The Hebrew lawgiver Moses, whose divine legation is as little open to question as that of Manu and Zoroaster, treats the subject at still greater length ; but I must leave to the reader the task of comparing the inspired ordinances

Similar rules of seclusion enjoined on menstruous women in ancient Hindoo, Persian, and Hebrew codes.

---

[1] *Laws of Manu*, translated by G. Bühler (Oxford, 1886), ch. iv. 41 sq., p. 135 (*Sacred Books of the East*, vol. xxv.).

[2] *The Zend-Avesta*, translated by J. Darmesteter, i. (Oxford, 1880) p. xcii. (*Sacred Books of the East*, vol. iv.).   See *id.*, pp. 9, 181-185, *Fargard*, i. 18 and 19, xvi. 1-18.

on this head with the merely human regulations of the
Carrier Indians which they so closely resemble.

Supersti-
tions as to
menstruous
women in
ancient and
modern
Europe.

Amongst the civilized nations of Europe the superstitions which cluster round this mysterious aspect of
woman's nature are not less extravagant than those which
prevail among savages.   In the oldest existing cyclopaedia
—the *Natural History* of Pliny—the list of dangers apprehended from menstruation is longer than any furnished by
mere barbarians.   According to Pliny, the touch of a menstruous woman turned wine to vinegar, blighted crops, killed
seedlings, blasted gardens, brought down the fruit from trees,
dimmed mirrors, blunted razors, rusted iron and brass (especially at the waning of the moon), killed bees, or at least
drove them from their hives, caused mares to miscarry, and
so forth.[1]   Similarly, in various parts of Europe, it is still
believed that if a woman in her courses enters a brewery
the beer will turn sour ; if she touches beer, wine, vinegar,
or milk, it will go bad ; if she makes jam, it will not keep ;
if she mounts a mare, it will miscarry ; if she touches buds,
they will wither ; if she climbs a cherry tree, it will die.[2]
In Brunswick people think that if a menstruous woman
assists at the killing of a pig, the pork will putrefy.[3]   In the
Greek island of Calymnos a woman at such times may not

[1] Pliny, *Nat. Hist.* vii. 64 *sq.*, xxviii.
77 *sqq.*   Compare *Geoponica*, xii. 20. 5
and 25. 2 ; Columella, *De re rustica*,
xi. 357 *sqq.*

[2] August Schleicher, *Volkstümliches
aus Sonnenberg*(Weimar, 1858), p. 134;
B. Souché, *Croyances, Présages et
Traditions diverses* (Niort, 1880),
p. 11 ; A. Meyrac, *Traditions, Coutumes, Légendes et Contes des Ardennes*
(Charleville, 1890), p. 171 ; V. Fossel,
*Volksmedicin und medicinischer Aber-
glaube in Steiermark*[2] (Graz, 1886), p.
124.   A correspondent, who with-
holds her name, writes to me that in a
Suffolk village, where she used to live
some twenty or thirty years ago,
" every one pickled their own beef,
and it was held that if the pickling
were performed by a woman during
her menstrual period the meat would
not keep.   If the cook were incapaci-

tated at the time when the pickling
was due, another woman was sent for
out of the village rather than risk what
was considered a certainty."   Another
correspondent informs me that in some
of the dales in the north of Yorkshire
a similar belief prevailed down to
recent years with regard to the salting
of pork.   Another correspondent writes
to me : " The prohibition that a
menstruating woman must not touch
meat that is intended for keeping
appears to be common all over the
country ; at least I have met with it
as a confirmed and active custom in
widely separated parts of England. . . .
It is in regard to the salting of meat
for bacon that the prohibition is most
usual, because that is the commonest
process ; but it exists in regard to any
meat food that is required to be kept."

[3] R. Andree, *Braunschweiger Volkskunde* (Brunswick, 1896), p. 291.

go to the well to draw water, nor cross a running stream, nor enter the sea. Her presence in a boat is said to raise storms.[1]

Thus the object of secluding women at menstruation is to neutralize the dangerous influences which are supposed to emanate from them at such times. That the danger is believed to be especially great at the first menstruation appears from the unusual precautions taken to isolate girls at this crisis. Two of these precautions have been illustrated above, namely, the rules that the girl may not touch the ground nor see the sun. The general effect of these rules is to keep her suspended, so to say, between heaven and earth. Whether enveloped in her hammock and slung up to the roof, as in South America, or raised above the ground in a dark and narrow cage, as in New Ireland, she may be considered to be out of the way of doing mischief, since, being shut off both from the earth and from the sun, she can poison neither of these great sources of life by her deadly contagion. In short, she is rendered harmless by being, in electrical language, insulated. But the precautions thus taken to isolate or insulate the girl are dictated by a regard for her own safety as well as for the safety of others. For it is thought that she herself would suffer if she were to neglect the prescribed regimen. Thus Zulu girls, as we have seen, believe that they would shrivel to skeletons if the sun were to shine on them at puberty, and in some Brazilian tribes the young women think that a transgression of the rules would entail sores on the neck and throat. In short, the girl is viewed as charged with a powerful force which, if not kept within bounds, may prove destructive both to herself and to all with whom she comes in contact. To repress this force within the limits necessary for the safety of all concerned is the object of the taboos in question.

The same explanation applies to the observance of the same rules by divine kings and priests. The uncleanness, as it is called, of girls at puberty and the sanctity of holy men do not, to the primitive mind, differ materially from each other. They are only different manifestations of the same mysterious energy which, like energy in general, is in itself neither good

The intention of secluding menstruous women is to neutralize the dangerous influences which are thought to emanate from them in that condition.

Suspension between heaven and earth.

The same explanation applies to the similar rules of seclusion observed by divine

[1] W. R. Paton, in *Folk-lore*, i. (1890) p. 524.

nor bad, but becomes beneficent or maleficent according to its application.[1] Accordingly, if, like girls at puberty, divine personages may neither touch the ground nor see the sun, the reason is, on the one hand, a fear lest their divinity might, at contact with earth or heaven, discharge itself with fatal violence on either ; and, on the other hand, an apprehension that the divine being, thus drained of his ethereal virtue, might thereby be incapacitated for the future performance of those magical functions, upon the proper discharge of which the safety of the people and even of the

---

[1] The Greeks and Romans thought that a field was completely protected against insects if a menstruous woman walked round it with bare feet and streaming hair (Pliny, *Nat. Hist.* xvii. 266, xxviii. 78 ; Columella, *De re rustica*, x. 358 *sq.*, xi. 3. 64 ; Palladius, *De re rustica*, i. 35. 3 ; *Geoponica*, xii. 8. 5 *sq.* ; Aelian, *Nat. Anim.* vi. 36). A similar preventive is employed for the same purpose by North American Indians and European peasants. See H. R. Schoolcraft, *Indian Tribes of the United States* (Philadelphia, 1853–1856), v. 70 ; F. J. Wiedemann, *Aus dem inneren und äussern Leben der Ehsten* (St. Petersburg, 1876), p. 484. Compare J. Haltrich, *Zur Volkskunde der Siebenbürger Sachsen* (Vienna, 1885), p. 280 ; Adolph Heinrich, *Agrarische Sitten und Gebräuche unter den Sachsen Siebenbürgens* (Hermannstadt, 1880), p. 14 ; J. Grimm, *Deutsche Mythologie*,[4] iii. 468 ; G. Lammert, *Volksmedizin und medizinischer Aberglaube aus Bayern* (Würzburg, 1869), p. 147. Among the Western Dénés it is believed that one or two transverse lines tattooed on the arms or legs of a young man by a pubescent girl are a specific against premature weakness of these limbs. See A. G. Morice, " Notes, Archaeological, Industrial, and Sociological, on the Western Dénés," *Transactions of the Canadian Institute*, iv. (1892–93) p. 182. The Thompson Indians of British Columbia thought that the Dawn of Day could and would cure hernia if only an adolescent girl prayed to it to do so. Just before daybreak the girl would put some charcoal in her mouth, chew

it fine, and spit it out four times on the diseased place. Then she prayed : " O Day-dawn ! thy child relies on me to obtain healing from thee, who art mystery. Remove thou the swelling of thy child. Pity thou him, Day-Dawn ! " See James Teit, *The Thompson Indians of British Columbia*, pp. 345 *sq.* (*The Jesup North Pacific Expedition, Memoir of the American Museum of Natural History*, New York, April, 1900). To cure the painful and dangerous wound inflicted by a ray-fish, the Indians of the Gran Chaco smoke the wounded limb and then cause a woman in her courses to sit astride of it. See G. Pelleschi, *Eight Months on the Gran Chaco of the Argentine Republic* (London, 1886), p. 106. An ancient Hindoo method of securing prosperity was to swallow a portion of the menstruous fluid. See W. Caland, *Altindisches Zauberritual* (Amsterdam, 1900), pp. 57 *sq.* To preserve a new cow from the evil eye Scottish Highlanders used to sprinkle menstruous blood on the animal ; and at certain seasons of the year, especially at Beltane (the first of May) and Lammas (the first of August) it was their custom to sprinkle the same potent liquid on the doorposts and houses all round to guard them from harm. The fluid was applied by means of a wisp of straw, and the person who discharged this salutary office went round the house in the direction of the sun. See J. G. Campbell, *Superstitions of the Highlands and Islands of Scotland* (Glasgow, 1900), p. 248. These are examples of the beneficent application of the menstruous energy.

world is believed to hang. Thus the rules in question fall under the head of the taboos which we examined in the second part of this work ;[1] they are intended to preserve the life of the divine person and with it the life of his subjects and worshippers. Nowhere, it is thought, can his precious yet dangerous life be at once so safe and so harmless as when it is neither in heaven nor in earth, but, as far as possible, suspended between the two.[2]

Suspension between heaven and earth.

In legends and folk-tales, which reflect the ideas of earlier ages, we find this suspension between heaven and earth attributed to beings who have been endowed with the coveted yet burdensome gift of immortality. The wizened remains of the deathless Sibyl are said to have been preserved in a jar or urn which hung in a temple of Apollo at Cumae ; and when a group of merry children, tired, perhaps, of playing in the sunny streets, sought the shade of the temple and amused themselves by gathering underneath the familiar jar and calling out, " Sibyl, what do you wish ? " a hollow voice, like an echo, used to answer from the urn, " I wish to die." [3] A story, taken down from the lips of a German peasant at Thomsdorf, relates that once upon a time there was a girl in London who wished to live for ever, so they say :

Stories of immortality attained by suspension between heaven and earth.

> " *London, London is a fine town.*
> *A maiden prayed to live for ever.*"

And still she lives and hangs in a basket in a church, and every St. John's Day, about the hour of noon, she eats a roll of bread.[4] Another German story tells of a lady who

---

[1] *Taboo and the Perils of the Soul*, pp. 1 *sqq.*

[2] For a similar reason, perhaps, ancient Hindoo ritual prescribed that when the hair of a child's head was shorn in the third year, the clippings should be buried in a cow-stable, or near an *udumbara* tree, or in a clump of *darbha* grass, with the words, " Where Pushan, Brihaspati, Savitri, Soma, Agni dwell, they have in many ways searched where they should deposit it, between heaven and earth, the waters and heaven." See *The Grihya-Sûtras*, translated by H. Oldenberg,

Part ii. (Oxford, 1892) p. 218 (*Sacred Books of the East*, vol. xxx.).

[3] Petronius, *Sat.* 48 ; Pausanias, x. 12. 8 ; Justin Martyr, *Cohort ad Graecos*, 37, p. 34 C (ed. 1742). According to another account, the remains of the Sibyl were enclosed in an iron cage which hung from a pillar in an ancient temple of Hercules at Argyrus (Ampelius, *Liber Memorialis*, viii. 16).

[4] A. Kuhn und W. Schwartz, *Norddeutsche Sagen, Märchen und Gebräuche* (Leipsic, 1848), p. 70, No. 72. 1. This and the following German parallels

resided at Danzig and was so rich and so blest with all that life can give that she wished to live always. So when she came to her latter end, she did not really die but only looked like dead, and very soon they found her in a hollow of a pillar in the church, half standing and half sitting, motionless. She stirred never a limb, but they saw quite plainly that she was alive, and she sits there down to this blessed day. Every New Year's Day the sacristan comes and puts a morsel of the holy bread in her mouth, and that is all she has to live on. Long, long has she rued her fatal wish who set this transient life above the eternal joys of heaven.[1] A third German story tells of a noble damsel who cherished the same foolish wish for immortality. So they put her in a basket and hung her up in a church, and there she hangs and never dies, though many a year has come and gone since they put her there. But every year on a certain day they give her a roll, and she eats it and cries out, " For ever ! for ever ! for ever ! " And when she has so cried she falls silent again till the same time next year, and so it will go on for ever and for ever.[2] A fourth story, taken down near Oldenburg in Holstein, tells of a jolly dame that ate and drank and lived right merrily and had all that heart could desire, and she wished to live always. For the first hundred years all went well, but after that she began to shrink and shrivel up, till at last she could neither walk nor stand nor eat nor drink. But die she could not. At first they fed her as if she were a little child, but when she grew smaller and smaller they put her in a glass bottle and hung her up in the church. And there she still hangs, in the church of St. Mary, at Lübeck. She is as small as a mouse, but once a year she stirs.[3]

---

to the story of the Sibyl's wish were first indicated by Dr. M. R. James (*Classical Review*, vi. (1892) p. 74). I have already given the stories at length in a note on Pausanias, x. 12. 8 (vol. v. pp. 292 *sq.*).

[1] A. Kuhn und W. Schwartz, *op.*

cit. pp. 70 *sq.*, No. 72. 2.

[2] A. Kuhn und W. Schwartz, *op. cit.* p. 71, No. 72. 3.

[3] Karl Müllenhoff, *Sagen, Märchen und Lieder der Herzogthümer Holstein und Lauenburg* (Kiel, 1845), pp. 158 *sq.*, No. 217.

CHAPTER III

THE MYTH OF BALDER

A DEITY whose life might in a sense be said to be neither in heaven nor on earth but between the two, was the Norse Balder, the good and beautiful god, the son of the great god Odin, and himself the wisest, mildest, best beloved of all the immortals. The story of his death, as it is told in the younger or prose *Edda*, runs thus. Once on a time Balder dreamed heavy dreams which seemed to forebode his death. Thereupon the gods held a council and resolved to make him secure against every danger. So the goddess Frigg took an oath from fire and water, iron and all metals, stones and earth, from trees, sicknesses and poisons, and from all four-footed beasts, birds, and creeping things, that they would not hurt Balder. When this was done Balder was deemed invulnerable; so the gods amused themselves by setting him in their midst, while some shot at him, others hewed at him, and others threw stones at him. But whatever they did, nothing could hurt him; and at this they were all glad. Only Loki, the mischief-maker, was displeased, and he went in the guise of an old woman to Frigg, who told him that the weapons of the gods could not wound Balder, since she had made them all swear not to hurt him. Then Loki asked, " Have all things sworn to spare Balder? " She answered, " East of Walhalla grows a plant called mistletoe ; it seemed to me too young to swear." So Loki went and pulled the mistletoe and took it to the assembly of the gods. There he found the blind god Hother standing at the outside of the circle. Loki asked him, " Why do you not shoot at Balder? " Hother answered, " Because I do not see where he stands; besides I have no weapon." Then said Loki, " Do like the rest and shew Balder honour, as they all do. I will shew you where he stands, and do you shoot at him with this twig." Hother took the mistletoe and threw it at Balder, as Loki directed him. The mistletoe struck Balder and pierced him through and through, and he fell down dead. And that was the greatest misfortune that ever befell gods and men. For a while the gods stood speechless, then they lifted up their voices and wept bitterly. They took Balder's body and brought it to the sea-shore. There stood Balder's ship; it was called Ringhorn, and was the hugest of all ships. The gods wished to launch the ship and to burn Balder's body on it, but the ship would not stir. So they sent for a giantess called Hyrrockin. She came riding on a wolf and gave the ship such a push that fire flashed from the rollers and all the earth shook. Then Balder's body was taken and placed on the funeral pile upon his ship. When his wife Nanna saw that, her heart burst for sorrow and she died. So she was laid on the funeral pile with her husband, and fire was put to it. Balder's horse, too, with all its trappings, was burned on the pile.[1]

Tale of Balder in the older *Edda*.

In the older or poetic *Edda* the tragic tale of Balder is hinted at rather than told at length. Among the visions which the Norse Sibyl sees and describes in the weird prophecy known as the *Voluspa* is one of the fatal mistletoe. " I behold," says she, " Fate looming for Balder, Woden's son, the bloody victim. There stands the Mistletoe slender and delicate, blooming high above the ground. Out of this shoot, so slender to look on, there shall grow a harmful fateful shaft. Hod shall shoot it, but Frigga in Fen-hall shall weep over the woe of Wal-hall." [2] Yet looking far into

[1] *Die Edda*, übersetzt von K. Simrock [8] (Stuttgart, 1882), pp. 286-288. Compare pp. 8, 34, 264. Balder's story is told in a professedly historical form by the old Danish historian Saxo Grammaticus in his third book. See below, p. 103. In English the story is told at length by Professor (Sir) John Rhys, *Celtic Heathendom* (London and Edinburgh, 1888), pp. 529 *sqq.* It is elaborately discussed by Professor F. Kauffmann in a learned monograph,

Balder, Mythus und Sage (Strasburg, 1902).
[2] Gudbrand Vigfusson and F. York Powell, *Corpus Poeticum Boreale*, i. (Oxford, 1883) p. 197. Compare *Edda Rhythmica seu Antiquior, vulgo Saemundina dicta*, Pars iii. (Copenhagen, 1828) pp. 39 *sq.*; *Die Edda*, übersetzt von K. Simrock [8] (Stuttgart, 1882), p. 8; K. Müllenhoff, *Deutsche Altertumskunde*, v. Zweite Abteilung (Berlin, 1891), pp. 78 *sq.*; Fr. Kauffmann,

the future the Sibyl sees a brighter vision of a new heaven and a new earth, where the fields unsown shall yield their increase and all sorrows shall be healed ; then Balder will come back to dwell in Odin's mansions of bliss, in a hall brighter than the sun, shingled with gold, where the righteous shall live in joy for ever more.[1]

Writing about the end of the twelfth century, the old Danish historian Saxo Grammaticus tells the story of Balder in a form which professes to be historical. According to him, Balder and Hother were rival suitors for the hand of Nanna, daughter of Gewar, King of Norway. Now Balder was a demigod and common steel could not wound his sacred body. The two rivals encountered each other in a terrific battle, and though Odin and Thor and the rest of the gods fought for Balder, yet was he defeated and fled away, and Hother married the princess. Nevertheless Balder took heart of grace and again met Hother in a stricken field. But he fared even worse than before ; for Hother dealt him a deadly wound with a magic sword, which he had received from Miming, the Satyr of the woods ; and after lingering three days in pain Balder died of his hurt and was buried with royal honours in a barrow.[2]

The story of Balder as related by Saxo Grammaticus.

Balder, Mythus und Sage, pp. 20 *sq.* In this passage the words translated "bloody victim" (*blaupom tivor*) and "fate looming" (*ørløg fölgen*) are somewhat uncertain and have been variously interpreted. The word *tivor*, usually understood to mean "god," seems to be found nowhere else. Professor H. M. Chadwick has kindly furnished me with the following literal translation of the passage : "I saw (or ' have seen ') held in safe keeping the life of Balder, the bloody god, Othin's son. High above the fields (*i.e.* the surface of the earth) grew a mistletoe, slender and very beautiful. From a shaft (or ' stem ') which appeared slender, came a dangerous sorrow - bringing missile (*i.e.* the shaft became a . . . missile); Høðr proceeded to shoot. Soon was a brother of Balder born. He, Othin's son, proceeded to do battle when one day old. He did not wash his hands or comb his head before he brought Balder's antagonist on to the pyre.

But Frigg in Fen-salir (*i.e.* the Fen-abode) lamented the trouble of Valhǫll." In translating the words *ørlog fölgen* "held in safe keeping the life" Professor Chadwick follows Professor F. Kauffmann's rendering ("*das Leben verwahrt*"); but he writes to me that he is not quite confident about it, as the word *ørlǫg* usually means "fate" rather than "life." Several sentences translated by Professor Chadwick ("Soon was a brother of Balder born . . . he brought Balder's antagonist on the pyre") are omitted by some editors and translators of the *Edda*.
    [1] G. Vigfusson and F. York Powell, *Corpus Poeticum Boreale*, i. 200 *sq.* ; *Edda Rhythmica seu Antiquior, vulgo Saemundina dicta*, Pars iii. pp. 51-54 ; *Die Edda*, übersetzt von K. Simrock,[8] pp. 10 *sq.* ; K. Müllenhoff, *Deutsche Altertumskunde*, v. Zweite Abteilung, pp. 84 *sq.*
    [2] Saxo Grammaticus, *Historia Danica*, ed. P. E. Müller (Copen-

Whether he was a real or merely a mythical personage,
Balder was worshipped in Norway.   On one of the bays of
the beautiful Sogne Fiord, which penetrates far into the
depths of the solemn Norwegian mountains, with their
sombre pine-forests and their lofty cascades dissolving into
spray before they reach the dark water of the fiord far below,
Balder had a great sanctuary.   It was called Balder's Grove.
A palisade enclosed the hallowed ground, and within it stood
a spacious temple with the images of many gods, but none
of them was worshipped with such devotion as Balder.   So
great was the awe with which the heathen regarded the
place that no man might harm another there, nor steal his
cattle, nor defile himself with women.   But women cared for
the images of the gods in the temple ; they warmed them at
the fire, anointed them with oil, and dried them with cloths.[1]

It might be rash to affirm that the romantic figure of
Balder was nothing but a creation of the mythical fancy,
a radiant phantom conjured up as by a wizard's wand
to glitter for a time against the gloomy background of the
stern Norwegian landscape.   It may be so ; yet it is also
possible that the myth was founded on the tradition of a
hero, popular and beloved in his lifetime, who long survived
in the memory of the people, gathering more and more of
the marvellous about him as he passed from generation to
generation of story-tellers.   At all events it is worth while
to observe that a somewhat similar story is told of another
national hero, who may well have been a real man.   In
his great poem, *The Epic of Kings*, which is founded on
Persian traditions, the poet Firdusi tells us that in the combat
between Rustem and Isfendiyar the arrows of the former did
no harm to his adversary, " because Zerdusht had charmed
his body against all dangers, so that it was like unto brass."
But Simurgh, the bird of God, shewed Rustem the way he
should follow in order to vanquish his redoubtable foe.   He
rode after her, and they halted not till they came to the
sea-shore.   There she led him into a garden, where grew a

---

hagen, 1839–1858), *lib*. iii. vol. i.
pp. 110 *sqq.* ; *The First Nine Books
of the Danish History of Saxo Grammaticus*, translated by Oliver Elton
(London, 1894), pp. 83-93.

[1] *Fridthjofs Saga, aus dem Alt-
isländischen*, von J. C. Poestion
(Vienna, 1879), pp. 3 *sq.*, 14-17,
45-52.

tamarisk, tall and strong, and the roots thereof were in the ground, but the branches pierced even unto the sky.   Then the bird of God bade Rustem break from the tree a branch that was long and slender, and fashion it into an arrow, and she said, " Only through his eyes can Isfendiyar be wounded. If, therefore, thou wouldst slay him, direct this arrow unto his forehead, and verily it shall not miss its aim."   Rustem did as he was bid ; and when next he fought with Isfendiyar, he shot the arrow at him, and it pierced his eye, and he died.   Great was the mourning for Isfendiyar.   For the space of one year men ceased not to lament for him, and for many years they shed bitter tears for that arrow, and they said, " The glory of Iran hath been laid low." [1]

Whatever may be thought of an historical kernel under-lying a mythical husk in the legend of Balder, the details of the story suggest that it belongs to that class of myths which have been dramatized in ritual, or, to put it other-wise, which have been performed as magical ceremonies for the sake of producing those natural effects which they describe in figurative language.   A myth is never so graphic and precise in its details as when it is, so to speak, the book of the words which are spoken and acted by the performers of the sacred rite.   That the Norse story of Balder was a myth of this sort will become probable if we can prove that ceremonies resembling the incidents in the tale have been performed by Norsemen and other European peoples.   Now the main incidents in the tale are two—first, the pulling of the mistletoe, and second, the death and burning of the god ; and both of them may perhaps be found to have had their counterparts in yearly rites observed, whether separately or conjointly, by people in various parts of Europe.   These rites will be described and discussed in the following chapters.   We shall begin with the annual festivals of fire and shall reserve the pulling of the mistletoe for consideration later on.

The myth of Balder was perhaps acted as a magical ceremony. The two chief incidents of the myth, namely the pulling of the mistletoe and the death and burning of the god, have perhaps their counterparts in popular ritual.

[1] *The Epic of Kings, Stories retold from Firdusi,* by Helen Zimmern (London, 1883), pp. 325-331.   The parallel between Balder and Isfendiyar was pointed out in the " Lexicon Mythologicum " appended to the *Edda Rhythmica seu Antiquior, vulgo Sae-* *mundina dicta,* Pars iii. (Copenhagen, 1828) p. 513 note, with a reference to *Schah Nameh, verdeutscht von Görres,* ii. 324, 327 *sq.*   It is briefly mentioned by Dr. P. Wagler, *Die Eiche in alter und neuer Zeit,* ii. Teil (Berlin, 1891), p. 40.

CHAPTER IV

THE FIRE-FESTIVALS OF EUROPE

§ 1. *The Lenten Fires*

European custom of kindling bonfires on certain days of the year, dancing round them and leaping over them. Effigies are sometimes burnt in the fires. ALL over Europe the peasants have been accustomed from time immemorial to kindle bonfires on certain days of the year, and to dance round or leap over them. Customs of this kind can be traced back on historical evidence to the Middle Ages,[1] and their analogy to similar customs observed in antiquity goes with strong internal evidence to prove that their origin must be sought in a period long prior to the spread of Christianity. Indeed the earliest proof of their observance in Northern Europe is furnished by the attempts made by Christian synods in the eighth century to put them down as heathenish rites.[2] Not uncommonly effigies are burned in these fires, or a pretence is made of burning a living person in them ; and there are grounds for believing that anciently human beings were actually burned on these occasions. A general survey of the customs in question will bring out the traces of human sacrifice, and will serve at the same time to throw light on their meaning.[3]

Seasons of the year at which the bonfires are lit. The seasons of the year when these bonfires are most commonly lit are spring and midsummer ; but in some places they are kindled also at the end of autumn or during the

---

[1] See Jacob Grimm, *Deutsche Mythologie*[4] (Berlin, 1875–1878), i. 502, 510, 516.

[2] W. Mannhardt, *Der Baumkultus der Germanen und ihrer Nachbarstämme* (Berlin, 1875), pp. 518 *sq.*

[3] In the following survey of these fire-customs I follow chiefly W. Mannhardt, *Der Baumkultus*, kap. vi. pp.

497 *sqq.* Compare also J. Grimm, *Deutsche Mythologie*,[4] i. 500 *sqq.* ; Walter K. Kelly, *Curiosities of Indo-European Tradition and Folk-lore* (London, 1863), pp. 46 *sqq.* ; F. Vogt, " Scheibentreiben und Frühlingsfeuer," *Zeitschrift des Vereins für Volkskunde*, iii. (1893) pp. 349-369 ; *ibid.* iv. (1894) pp. 195-197.

course of the winter, particularly on Hallow E'en (the thirty-
first of October), Christmas Day, and the Eve of Twelfth
Day. We shall consider them in the order in which they
occur in the calendar year. The earliest of them is the
winter festival of the Eve of Twelfth Day (the fifth of
January); but as it has been already described in an earlier
part of this work[1] we shall pass it over here and begin
with the fire-festivals of spring, which usually fall on the
first Sunday of Lent (*Quadragesima* or *Invocavit*),[2] Easter
Eve, and May Day.

The custom of kindling bonfires on the first Sunday in
Lent has prevailed in Belgium, the north of France, and
many parts of Germany. Thus in the Belgian Ardennes
for a week or a fortnight before the " day of the great fire,"
as it is called, children go about from farm to farm collecting
fuel. At Grand Halleux any one who refuses their request
is pursued next day by the children, who try to blacken his
face with the ashes of the extinct fire. When the day has
come, they cut down bushes, especially juniper and broom,
and in the evening great bonfires blaze on all the heights.
It is a common saying that seven bonfires should be seen if
the village is to be safe from conflagrations. If the Meuse
happens to be frozen hard at the time, bonfires are lit also
on the ice. At Grand Halleux they set up a pole called
makral, or " the witch," in the midst of the pile, and the fire
is kindled by the man who was last married in the village.
In the neighbourhood of Morlanwelz a straw man is burnt
in the fire. Young people and children dance and sing
round the bonfires, and leap over the embers to secure good
crops or a happy marriage within the year, or as a means
of guarding themselves against colic. In Brabant on the
same Sunday, down to the beginning of the nineteenth
century, women and men disguised in female attire used to
go with burning torches to the fields, where they danced and
sang comic songs for the purpose, as they alleged, of driving
away " the wicked sower," who is mentioned in the Gospel
for the day. At Maeseyck and in many villages of Lim-

Custom of kindling bonfires on the first Sunday in Lent in the Belgian Ardennes.

----

[1] *The Scapegoat*, pp. 316 *sqq.*

[2] The first Sunday in Lent is known
as *Invocavit* from the first word of the

mass for the day (O. Frh. von Reinsberg-Düringsfeld, *Fest-Kalender aus
Böhmen*, p. 67).

burg, on the evening of the day children run through the streets carrying lighted torches ; then they kindle little fires of straw in the fields and dance round them.   At Ensival old folks tell young folks that they will have as many Easter eggs as they see bonfires on this day.[1]   At Pâturages, in the province of Hainaut, down to about 1840 the custom was observed under the name of *Escouvion* or *Scouvion.* Every year on the first Sunday of Lent, which was called the Day of the Little Scouvion, young folks and children used to run with lighted torches through the gardens and orchards.   As they ran they cried at the pitch of their voices,

> " *Bear apples, bear pears*
> *And cherries all black*
> *To Scouvion !* "

At these words the torch-bearer whirled his blazing brand and hurled it among the branches of the apple-trees, the pear-trees, and the cherry-trees.   The next Sunday was called the Day of the Great Scouvion, and the same race with lighted torches among the trees of the orchards was repeated in the afternoon till darkness fell.   The same custom was observed on the same two days at Wasmes.[2] In the neighbourhood of Liège, where the Lenten fires were put down by the police about the middle of the nineteenth century, girls thought that by leaping over the fires without being smirched they made sure of a happy marriage.   Elsewhere in order to get a good husband it was necessary to see seven of the bonfires from one spot.   In Famenne, a district of Namur, men and cattle who traversed the Lenten fires were thought to be safe from sickness and witchcraft. Anybody who saw seven such fires at once had nothing to fear from sorcerers.   An old saying ran, that if you do not light " the great fire," God will light it for you ; which seems to imply that the kindling of the bonfires was deemed a protection against conflagrations throughout the year.[3]

---

[1] Le Baron de Reinsberg-Düringsfeld, *Calendrier Belge* (Brussels, 1861–1862), i. 141-143 ; E. Monseur, *Le Folklore Wallon* (Brussels, N.D.), pp. 124 *sq.*

[2] Émile Hublard, *Fêtes du Temps Jadis, les Feux du Carême* (Mons, 1899), pp. 25.   For the loan of this work I am indebted to Mrs. Wherry of St. Peter's Terrace, Cambridge.

[3] É. Hublard, *op. cit.* pp. 27 *sq.*

In the French department of the Ardennes the whole village used to dance and sing round the bonfires which were lighted on the first Sunday in Lent.   Here, too, it was the person last married, sometimes a man and sometimes a woman, who put the match to the fire.   The custom is still kept up very commonly in the district.   Cats used to be burnt in the fire or roasted to death by being held over it ; and while they were burning the shepherds drove their flocks through the smoke and flames as a sure means of guarding them against sickness and witchcraft.   In some communes it was believed that the livelier the dance round the fire, the better would be the crops that year.[1]   In the Vosges Mountains it is still customary to light great fires on the heights and around the villages on the first Sunday in Lent ; and at Rupt and elsewhere the right of kindling them belongs to the person who was last married.   Round the fires the people dance and sing merrily till the flames have died out.   Then the master of the fire, as they call the man who kindled it, invites all who contributed to the erection of the pile to follow him to the nearest tavern, where they partake of good cheer.   At Dommartin they say that, if you would have the hemp tall, it is absolutely necessary that the women should be tipsy on the evening of this day.[2]   At Épinal in the Vosges, on the first Sunday in Lent, bonfires used to be kindled at various places both in the town and on the banks of the Moselle.   They consisted of pyramids of sticks and faggots, which had been collected some days earlier by young folks going from door to door.   When the flames blazed up, the names of various couples, whether young or old, handsome or ugly, rich or poor, were called out, and the persons thus linked in mock marriage were forced, whether they liked it or not, to march arm in arm round the fire amid the laughter and jests of the crowd.   The festivity lasted till the fire died out, and then the spectators dispersed through the streets, stopping under the windows of the houses and proclaiming the names of the

Bonfires on the first Sunday of Lent in the French department of the Ardennes.

---

[1] A. Meyrac, *Traditions, coutumes, légendes et contes des Ardennes* (Charleville, 1890), p. 68.

[2] L. F. Sauvé, *Le Folk-lore des Hautes-Vosges* (Paris, 1889), p. 56. The popular name for the bonfires in the Upper Vosges (*Hautes-Vosges*) is *chavandes*.

féchenots and *féchenottes* or Valentines whom the popular voice had assigned to each other. These couples had to exchange presents; the mock bridegroom gave his mock bride something for her toilet, while she in turn presented him with a cockade of coloured ribbon. Next Sunday, if the weather allowed it, all the couples, arrayed in their best attire and attended by their relations, repaired to the wood of Saint Antony, where they mounted a famous stone called the *danserosse* or *danseresse*. Here they found cakes and refreshments of all sorts, and danced to the music of a couple of fiddlers. The evening bell, ringing the Angelus, gave the signal to depart. As soon as its solemn chime was heard, every one quitted the forest and returned home. The exchange of presents between the Valentines went by the name of ransom or redemption (*rachat*), because it was supposed to redeem the couple from the flames of the bonfire. Any pair who failed thus to ransom themselves were not suffered to share the merrymaking at the great stone in the forest; and a pretence was made of burning them in small fires kindled before their own doors.[1]

In the French province of Franche-Comté, to the west of the Jura Mountains, the first Sunday of Lent is known as the Sunday of the Firebrands (*Brandons*), on account of the fires which it is customary to kindle on that day. On the Saturday or the Sunday the village lads harness themselves to a cart and drag it about the streets, stopping at the doors of the houses where there are girls and begging for a faggot. When they have got enough, they cart the fuel to a spot at some little distance from the village, pile it up, and set it on fire. All the people of the parish come out to see the bonfire. In some villages, when the bells have rung the Angelus, the signal for the observance is given by cries of, "To the fire! to the fire!" Lads, lasses, and children dance round the blaze, and when the flames have died down they vie with each other in leaping over the red embers. He or she who does so without singeing his or her garments will be married within the year. Young folk also carry lighted torches about the streets or the fields, and when they pass

---

[1] E. Cortet, *Essai sur les fêtes religieuses* (Paris, 1867), pp. 101 *sq.*   The local name for these bonfires is *bures*.

an orchard they cry out, "More fruit than leaves!" Down to recent years at Laviron, in the department of Doubs, it was the young married couples of the year who had charge of the bonfires. In the midst of the bonfire a pole was planted with a wooden figure of a cock fastened to the top. Then there were races, and the winner received the cock as a prize.[1]

In Auvergne fires are everywhere kindled on the evening of the first Sunday in Lent. Every village, every hamlet, even every ward, every isolated farm has its bonfire or *figo*, as it is called, which blazes up as the shades of night are falling. The fires may be seen flaring on the heights and in the plains; the people dance and sing round about them and leap through the flames. Then they proceed to the ceremony of the *Grannas-mias*. A *granno-mio*[2] is a torch of straw fastened to the top of a pole. When the pyre is half consumed, the bystanders kindle the torches at the expiring flames and carry them into the neighbouring orchards, fields, and gardens, wherever there are fruit-trees. As they march they sing at the top of their voices,

" Granno, mo mio,
Granno, mon pouère,
Granno, mo mouère!"

that is, "Grannus my friend, Grannus my father, Grannus my mother." Then they pass the burning torches under the branches of every tree, singing,

" Brando, brandounci
Tsaque brantso, in plan panei!"

Marginal note: Bonfires on the first Sunday of Lent in Auvergne.

---

[1] Charles Beauquier, *Les mois en Franche-Comté* (Paris, 1900), pp. 33 *sq*. In Bresse the custom was similar. See *La Bresse Louhannaise, Bulletin Mensuel, Organe de la Société d'Agriculture et d'Horticulture de l'Arrondissement de Louhans*, Mars, 1906, pp. 111 *sq.*; E. Cortet, *op. cit.* p. 100. The usual name for the bonfires is *chevannes* or *schvannes*; but in some places they are called *foulères*, *foualères*, *failles*, or *bourdifailles* (Ch. Beauquier, *op. cit.* p. 34). But the Sunday is called the Sunday of the *brandons*, *bures*, *bordes*, or *boidès*, according to the place. The *brandons* are the torches which are carried about the streets and the fields; the bonfires, as we have seen, bear another name. A curious custom, observed on the same Sunday in Franche-Comté, requires that couples married within the year should distribute boiled peas to all the young folks of both sexes who demand them at the door. The lads and lasses go about from house to house, making the customary request; in some places they wear masks or are otherwise disguised. See Ch. Beauquier, *op. cit.* pp. 31-33.

[2] Curiously enough, while the singular is *granno-mio*, the plural is *grannas-mias*.

that is, "Firebrand burn ; every branch a basketful ! " In some villages the people also run across the sown fields and shake the ashes of the torches on the ground ; also they put some of the ashes in the fowls' nests, in order that the hens may lay plenty of eggs throughout the year. When all these ceremonies have been performed, everybody goes home and feasts ; the special dishes of the evening are fritters and pancakes.[1] Here the application of the fire to the fruit-trees, to the sown fields, and to the nests of the poultry is clearly a charm intended to ensure fertility ; and the Granno to whom the invocations are addressed, and who gives his name to the torches, may possibly be, as Dr. Pommerol suggests,[2] no other than the ancient Celtic god Grannus, whom the Romans identified with Apollo, and whose worship is attested by inscriptions found not only in France but in Scotland and on the Danube.[3] If the name Grannus is derived, as the learned tell us, from a root meaning "to glow, burn, shine,"[4] the deity who bore the name and was identified with Apollo may well have been a sun-god ; and in that case the prayers addressed to him by the peasants of the Auvergne, while they wave the blazing, crackling torches about the fruit-trees, would be eminently appropriate. For who could ripen the fruit so well as the sun-god ? and what better process could be devised to draw the blossoms from the bare boughs than the application to them of that genial warmth which is ultimately derived from the solar beams ? Thus the fire-festival of the first Sunday in Lent, as it is observed in Auvergne, may be interpreted very naturally and simply as a religious or rather perhaps magical ceremony designed to procure a due supply of the sun's heat for plants and animals. At the same time we should remember that the employment of fire in this and kindred ceremonies may have been designed originally, not so much to stimulate growth and reproduction, as to burn and destroy all agencies.

The Granno invoked at these bonfires may be the old Celtic god Grannus, who was identified with Apollo.

---

[1] Dr. Pommerol, "La fête des Brandons et le dieu Gaulois Grannus," *Bulletins et Mémoires de la Société d'Anthropologie de Paris,* v. Série, ii. (1901) pp. 427-429.

[2] *Op. cit.* pp. 428 *sq.*

[3] H. Dessau, *Inscriptiones Latinae Selectae,* vol. ii. Pars i. (Berlin, 1902) pp. 216 *sq.,* Nos. 4646-4652.

[4] (Sir) John Rhys, *Celtic Heathendom* (London, 1888), pp. 22-25.

whether in the shape of vermin, witches, or what not, which threatened or were supposed to threaten the growth of the crops and the multiplication of animals. It is often difficult to decide between these two different interpretations of the use of fire in agricultural rites. In any case the fire-festival of Auvergne on the first Sunday in Lent may date from Druidical times.

The custom of carrying lighted torches of straw (*brandons*) about the orchards and fields to fertilize them on the first Sunday of Lent seems to have been common in France, whether it was accompanied with the practice of kindling bonfires or not. Thus in the province of Picardy " on the first Sunday of Lent people carried torches through the fields, exorcising the field-mice, the darnel, and the smut. They imagined that they did much good to the gardens and caused the onions to grow large. Children ran about the fields, torch in hand, to make the land more fertile. All that was done habitually in Picardy, and the ceremony of the torches is not entirely forgotten, especially in the villages on both sides the Somme as far as Saint-Valery." [1] " A very agreeable spectacle, said the curate of l'Étoile, is to survey from the portal of the church, situated almost on the top of the mountain, the vast plains of Vimeux all illuminated by these wandering fires. The same pastime is observed at Poix, at Conty, and in all the villages round about." [2] Again, in the district of Beauce a festival of torches (*brandons* or *brandelons*) used to be held both on the first and on the second Sunday in Lent; the first was called " the Great Torches " and the second " the Little Torches." The torches were, as usual, bundles of straw wrapt round poles. In the evening the village lads carried the burning brands through the country, running about in disorder and singing,

French custom of carrying lighted torches (brandons) about the orchards and fields to fertilize them on the first Sunday of Lent.

> " *Torches burn*
> *At these vines, at this wheat;*
> *Torches burn*
> *For the maidens that shall wed!*"

From time to time the bearers would stand still and smite

---

[1] Émile Hublard, *Fêtes du Temps Jadis, les Feux du Carême* (Mons, 1899), p. 38, quoting Dom Grenier, *Histoire de la Province de Picardie.*

[2] É. Hublard, *op. cit.* p. 39, quoting Dom Grenier.

the earth all together with the blazing straw of the torches, while they cried, "A sheaf of a peck and a half!" (*Gearbe à boissiaux*). If two torchbearers happened to meet each other on their rounds, they performed the same ceremony and uttered the same words. When the straw was burnt out, the poles were collected and a great bonfire made of them. Lads and lasses danced round the flames, and the lads leaped over them. Afterwards it was customary to eat a special sort of hasty - pudding made of wheaten flour. These usages were still in vogue at the beginning of the nineteenth century, but they have now almost disappeared. The peasants believed that by carrying lighted torches through the fields they protected the crops from field-mice, darnel, and smut.[1] "At Dijon, in Burgundy, it is the custom upon the first Sunday in Lent to make large fires in the streets, whence it is called Firebrand Sunday. This practice originated in the processions formerly made on that day by the peasants with lighted torches of straw, to drive away, as they called it, the bad air from the earth."[2] In some parts of France, while the people scoured the country with burning brands on the first Sunday in Lent, they warned the fruit-trees that if they did not take heed and bear fruit they would surely be cut down and cast into the fire.[3] On the same day peasants in the department of Loiret used to run about the sowed fields with burning torches in their hands, while they adjured the field-mice to quit the wheat on pain of having their whiskers burned.[4] In the department of Ain the great fires of straw and faggots which are kindled in the fields at this time are or were supposed to destroy the nests of the caterpillars.[5] At Verges, a lonely village surrounded by forests between the Jura and the Combe d'Ain, the torches used at this season were kindled in

[1] M. Desgranges, "Usages du Canton de Bonneval," *Mémoires de la Société Royale des Antiquaires de France*, i. (Paris, 1817) pp. 236-238; Felix Chapiseau, *Le folk - lore de la Beauce et du Perche* (Paris, 1902), i. 315 *sq.*

[2] John Brand, *Popular Antiquities of Great Britain* (London, 1882–1883), i. 100.

[3] E. Cortet, *Essai sur les fêtes re-* ligieuses (Paris, 1867), pp. 99 *sq.*; *La Bresse Louhannaise*, Mars, 1906, p. 111.

[4] A. de Nore, *Coutumes, mythes et traditions des provinces de France* (Paris and Lyons, 1846), pp. 283 *sq.* A similar, though not identical, custom prevailed at Valenciennes (*ibid.* p. 338).

[5] A. de Nore, *op. cit.* p. 302.

a peculiar manner.   The young people climbed to the top
of a mountain, where they placed three nests of straw in three
trees.   These nests being then set on fire, torches made of
dry lime-wood were lighted at them, and the merry troop
descended the mountain to their flickering light, and went
to every house in the village, demanding roasted peas and
obliging all couples who had been married within the year
to dance.[1]   In Berry, a district of central France, it appears
that bonfires are not lighted on this day, but when the sun
has set the whole population of the villages, armed with
blazing torches of straw, disperse over the country and scour
the fields, the vineyards, and the orchards.   Seen from afar,
the multitude of moving lights, twinkling in the darkness,
appear like will-o'-the-wisps chasing each other across the
plains, along the hillsides, and down the valleys.   While the
men wave their flambeaus about the branches of the fruit-
trees, the women and children tie bands of wheaten-straw
round the tree-trunks.   The effect of the ceremony is supposed to be to avert the various plagues from which the
fruits of the earth are apt to suffer ; and the bands of straw
fastened round the stems of the trees are believed to render
them fruitful.[2]   In the peninsula of La Manche the Norman
peasants used to spend almost the whole night of the first
Sunday in Lent rushing about the country with lighted
torches for the purpose, as they supposed, of driving away
the moles and field-mice ; fires were also kindled on some of
the dolmens.[3]

In Germany, Austria, and Switzerland at the same season
similar customs have prevailed.   Thus in the Eifel Mountains,
Rhenish Prussia, on the first Sunday in Lent young people
used to collect straw and brushwood from house to house.
These they carried to an eminence and piled up round a tall,
slim beech-tree, to which a piece of wood was fastened at

Bonfires on the first Sunday of Lent in Germany and Austria.

[1] Désiré Monnier, *Traditions populaires comparées* (Paris, 1854), pp.
191 *sq.*

[2] Laisnel de la Salle, *Croyances et
légendes du centre de la France* (Paris,
1875), i. 35 *sqq.*

[3] Jules Lecœur, *Esquisses du Bocage
Normand* (Condé-sur-Noireau, 1887),

ii. 131 *sq.*   For more evidence of
customs of this sort observed in various
parts of France on the first Sunday in
Lent, see Madame Clément, *Histoire
des Fêtes civiles et religieuses*, etc., *du
Département du Nord*[2] (Cambrai,
1836), pp. 351 *sqq.* ; Émile Hublard,
*Fêtes du Temps Jadis, les Feux du
Carême* (Mons, 1899), pp. 33 *sqq.*

right angles to form a cross. The structure was known as the " hut " or " castle." Fire was set to it and the young people marched round the blazing " castle " bareheaded, each carrying a lighted torch and praying aloud. Sometimes a straw-man was burned in the " hut." People observed the direction in which the smoke blew from the fire. If it blew towards the corn-fields, it was a sign that the harvest would be abundant. On the same day, in some parts of the Eifel, a great wheel was made of straw and dragged by three horses to the top of a hill. Thither the village boys marched at nightfall, set fire to the wheel, and sent it rolling down the slope. Two lads followed it with levers to set it in motion again, in case it should anywhere meet with a check. At Oberstattfeld the wheel had to be provided by the young man who was last married.[1] About Echternach in Luxemburg the same ceremony is called " burning the witch "; while it is going on, the older men ascend the heights and observe what wind is blowing, for that is the wind which will prevail the whole year.[2] At Voralberg in the Tyrol, on the first Sunday in Lent, a slender young fir-tree is surrounded with a pile of straw and firewood. To the top of the tree is fastened a human figure called the " witch," made of old clothes and stuffed with gunpowder. At night the whole is set on fire and boys and girls dance round it, swinging torches and singing rhymes in which the words " corn in the winnowing-basket, the plough in the earth " may be distinguished.[3] In Swabia on the first Sunday in Lent a figure called the " witch " or the " old wife " or " winter's grandmother " is made up of clothes and fastened to a pole. This is stuck in the middle of a pile of wood, to which fire is applied. While the " witch " is burning, the young people throw blazing discs into the air. The discs are thin round pieces of wood, a few inches in diameter, with notched edges to imitate the

Marginal notes: "Burning the witch." / Burning discs thrown into the air.

[1] J. H. Schmitz, *Sitten und Sagen, Lieder, Sprüchwörter und Räthsel des Eifler Volkes* (Trèves, 1856-1858), i. 21-25 ; N. Hocker, in *Zeitschrift für deutsche Mythologie und Sittenkunde*, i. (1853) p. 90; W. Mannhardt, *Der Baumkultus der Germanen*

und ihrer Nachbarstämme (Berlin, 1875), p. 501.
[2] N. Hocker, *op. cit.* pp. 89 *sq.* ; W. Mannhardt, *l.c.*
[3] F. J. Vonbun, *Beiträge zur deutschen Mythologie* (Chur, 1862), p. 20 ; W. Mannhardt, *l.c.*

rays of the sun or stars. They have a hole in the middle, by which they are attached to the end of a wand. Before the disc is thrown it is set on fire, the wand is swung to and fro, and the impetus thus communicated to the disc is augmented by dashing the rod sharply against a sloping board. The burning disc is thus thrown off, and mounting high into the air, describes a long fiery curve before it reaches the ground. A single lad may fling up forty or fifty of these discs, one ofter the other. The object is to throw them as high as possible. The wand by which they are hurled must, at least in some parts of Swabia, be of hazel. Sometimes the lads also leap over the fire brandishing lighted torches of pine-wood. The charred embers of the burned " witch " and discs are taken home and planted in the flax-fields the same night, in the belief that they will keep vermin from the fields.[1] At Wangen, near Molsheim in Baden, a like custom is observed on the first Sunday in Lent. The young people kindle a bonfire on the crest of the mountain above the village ; and the burning discs which they hurl into the air are said to present in the darkness the aspect of a continual shower of falling stars. When the supply of discs is exhausted and the bonfire begins to burn low, the boys light torches and run with them at full speed down one or other of the three steep and winding paths that descend the mountain-side to the village. Bumps, bruises, and scratches are often the result of their efforts to outstrip each other in the headlong race.[2] In the Rhön Mountains, situated on the borders of Hesse and Bavaria, the people used to march to the top of a hill or eminence on the first Sunday in Lent. Children and lads carried torches, brooms daubed with tar, and poles swathed in straw. A wheel, wrapt in combustibles, was kindled and rolled down

[1] Ernst Meier, *Deutsche Sagen, Sitten und Gebräuche aus Schwaben* (Stuttgart, 1852), pp. 380 *sqq.* ; Anton Birlinger, *Volksthümliches aus Schwaben* (Freiburg im Breisgau, 1861–1862), ii. 56 *sqq.*, 66 *sqq.* ; *Bavaria, Landes- und Volkskunde des Königreichs Bayern* (Munich, 1860–1867), ii. 2, pp. 838 *sq.* ; F. Panzer, *Beitrag zur deutschen Mythologie* (Munich, 1848–1855), i. 211, § 232 ; W. Mannhardt, *l.c.* One

of the popular German names for the first Sunday in Lent is White Sunday, which is not to be confused with the first Sunday after Easter, which also goes by the name of White Sunday (E. Meier, *op. cit.* p. 380 ; A. Birlinger, *op. cit.* ii. 56).

[2] H. Gaidoz, " Le dieu gaulois du soleil et le symbolisme de la roue," *Revue Archéologique*, iii. série, iv. (1884) pp. 139 *sq.*

Burning
wheels
rolled
down hill.
the hill ; and the young people rushed about the fields with
their burning torches and brooms, till at last they flung them
in a heap, and standing round them, struck up a hymn or a
popular song. The object of running about the fields with
the blazing torches was to " drive away the wicked sower."
Or it was done in honour of the Virgin, that she might
preserve the fruits of the earth throughout the year and
bless them.[1] In neighbouring villages of Hesse, between
the Rhön and the Vogel Mountains, it is thought that
wherever the burning wheels roll, the fields will be safe from
hail and storm.[2] At Konz on the Moselle, on the Thursday
before the first Sunday in Lent, the two guilds of the
butchers and the weavers used to repair to the Marxberg
and there set up an oak-tree with a wheel fastened to it.
On the following Sunday the people ascended the hill, cut
down the oak, set fire to the wheel, and sent both oak and
wheel rolling down the hillside, while a guard of butchers,
mounted on horses, fired at the flaming wheel in its descent.
If the wheel rolled down into the Moselle, the butchers were
rewarded with a waggon-load of wine by the archbishop of
Treves.[3]

Bonfires
on the first
Sunday in
Lent in
Switzer-
land.
In Switzerland, also, it is or used to be customary to
kindle bonfires on high places on the evening of the first
Sunday in Lent, and the day is therefore popularly known
as Spark Sunday. The custom prevailed, for example,
throughout the canton of Lucerne. Boys went about from
house to house begging for wood and straw, then piled the
fuel on a conspicuous mountain or hill round about a pole,
which bore a straw effigy called " the witch." At nightfall
the pile was set on fire, and the young folks danced wildly
round it, some of them cracking whips or ringing bells ; and
when the fire burned low enough, they leaped over it.   This

[1] August Witzschel, *Sagen, Sitten
und Gebräuche aus Thüringen* (Vienna,
1878), p. 189 ; F. Panzer, *Beitrag
zur deutschen Mythologie* (Munich,
1848–1855), ii. 207 ; W. Mannhardt,
Der Baumkultus, pp. 500 *sq.*

[2] W. Kolbe, *Hessiche Volks-Sitten
und Gebräuche* [2] (Marburg, 1888),
p. 36.

[3] Adalbert Kuhn, *Die Herabkunft des*

Feuers und des Göttertranks [2] (Gütersloh, 1886), p. 86, quoting Hocker,
*Des Mosellandes Geschichten, Sagen und
Legenden* (Trier, 1852), pp. 415 *sqq.*
Compare W. Mannhardt, *Der Baumkultus*, p. 501 ; and below, pp. 163 *sq.*
Thus it appears that the ceremony of
rolling the fiery wheel down hill was
observed twice a year at Konz, once
on the first Sunday in Lent, and once
at Midsummer.

was called "burning the witch." In some parts of the canton also they used to wrap old wheels in straw and thorns, put a light to them, and send them rolling and blazing down hill. The same custom of rolling lighted wheels down hill is attested by old authorities for the cantons of Aargau and Bâle. The more bonfires could be seen sparkling and flaring in the darkness, the more fruitful was the year expected to be ; and the higher the dancers leaped beside or over the fire, the higher, it was thought, would grow the flax. In the district of Freiburg and at Birseck in the district of Bâle it was the last married man or woman who must kindle the bonfire. While the bonfires blazed up, it was customary in some parts of Switzerland to propel burning discs of wood through the air by means of the same simple machinery which is used for the purpose in Swabia. Each lad tried to send his disc fizzing and flaring through the darkness as far as possible, and in discharging it he mentioned the name of the person to whose honour it was dedicated. But in Prättigau the words uttered in launching the fiery discs referred to the abundance which was apparently expected to follow the performance of the ceremony. Among them were, "Grease in the pan, corn in the fan, and the plough in the earth ! " [1] *Burning discs thrown into the air.*

It seems hardly possible to separate from these bonfires, kindled on the first Sunday in Lent, the fires in which, about the same season, the effigy called Death is burned as part of the ceremony of "carrying out Death." We have seen that at Spachendorf, in Austrian Silesia, on the morning of Rupert's Day (Shrove Tuesday ?), a straw-man, dressed in a fur coat and a fur cap, is laid in a hole outside the village and there burned, and that while it is blazing every one seeks to snatch a fragment of it, which he fastens to a branch of the highest tree in his garden or buries in his field, believing that this will make the crops to grow better. The ceremony is known as the "burying of Death." [2] Even *Connexion of these bonfires with the custom of "carrying out Death."*

---

[1] H. Herzog, *Schweizerische Volksfeste, Sitten und Gebräuche* (Aarau, 1884), pp. 214-216 ; E. Hoffmann-Krayer, "Fruchtbarkeitsriten im schweizerischen Volksbrauch," *Schweizerisches Archiv für Volkskunde*, xi. (1907) pp. 247-249; *id.*, *Feste und Bräuche des Schweizervolkes* (Zurich, 1913), pp. 135 *sq.*

[2] Theodor Vernaleken, *Mythen und Bräuche des Volkes in Oesterreich* (Vienna, 1859), pp. 293 *sq.* ; W. Mannhardt, *Der Baumkultus*, p. 498. See *The Dying God*, p. 250.

when the straw-man is not designated as Death, the meaning of the observance is probably the same; for the name Death, as I have tried to shew, does not express the original intention of the ceremony. At Cobern in the Eifel Mountains the lads make up a straw-man on Shrove Tuesday. The effigy is formally tried and accused of having perpetrated all the thefts that have been committed in the neighbourhood throughout the year. Being condemned to death, the straw-man is led through the village, shot, and burned upon a pyre. They dance round the blazing pile, and the last bride must leap over it.[1] In Oldenburg on the evening of Shrove Tuesday people used to make long bundles of straw, which they set on fire, and then ran about the fields waving them, shrieking, and singing wild songs. Finally they burned a straw-man on the field.[2] In the district of Düsseldorf the straw-man burned on Shrove Tuesday was made of an unthreshed sheaf of corn.[3] On the first Monday after the spring equinox the urchins of Zurich drag a straw-man on a little cart through the streets, while at the same time the girls carry about a May-tree. When vespers ring, the straw-man is burned.[4] In the district of Aachen on Ash Wednesday a man used to be encased in peas-straw and taken to an appointed place. Here he slipped quietly out of his straw casing, which was then burned, the children thinking that it was the man who was being burned.[5] In the Val di Ledro (Tyrol) on the last day of the Carnival a figure is made up of straw and brushwood and then burned. The figure is called the Old Woman, and the ceremony "burning the Old Woman."[6]

§ 2. The Easter Fires

Another occasion on which these fire-festivals are held is

---

[1] J. H. Schmitz, Sitten und Sagen, Lieder, Sprüchwörter und Räthsel des Eifler Volkes (Treves, 1856–1858), i. 20 ; W. Mannhardt, Der Baumkultus, p. 499.

[2] L. Strackerjan, Aberglaube und Sagen aus dem Herzogthum Oldenburg (Oldenburg, 1867), ii. 39, § 306 ; W. Mannhardt, Der Baumkultus, p.

498.

[3] W. Mannhardt, Der Baumkultus, p. 499.

[4] W. Mannhardt, op. cit. pp. 498 sq.

[5] W. Mannhardt, op. cit. p. 499.

[6] Christian Schneller, Märchen und Sagen aus Wälschtirol (Innsbruck, 1867), pp. 234 sq. ; W. Mannhardt, op. cit. pp. 499 sq.

Easter Eve, the Saturday before Easter Sunday. On that day it has been customary in Catholic countries to extinguish all the lights in the churches, and then to make a new fire, sometimes with flint and steel, sometimes with a burning-glass. At this fire is lit the great Paschal or Easter candle, which is then used to rekindle all the extinguished lights in the church. In many parts of Germany a bonfire is also kindled, by means of the new fire, on some open space near the church. It is consecrated, and the people bring sticks of oak, walnut, and beech, which they char in the fire, and then take home with them. Some of these charred sticks are thereupon burned at home in a newly-kindled fire, with a prayer that God will preserve the homestead from fire, lightning, and hail. Thus every house receives " new fire." Some of the sticks are kept throughout the year and laid on the hearth-fire during heavy thunder-storms to prevent the house from being struck by lightning, or they are inserted in the roof with the like intention. Others are placed in the fields, gardens, and meadows, with a prayer that God will keep them from blight and hail. Such fields and gardens are thought to thrive more than others; the corn and the plants that grow in them are not beaten down by hail, nor devoured by mice, vermin, and beetles; no witch harms them, and the ears of corn stand close and full. The charred sticks are also applied to the plough. The ashes of the Easter bonfire, together with the ashes of the consecrated palm-branches, are mixed with the seed at sowing. A wooden figure called Judas is sometimes burned in the consecrated bonfire, and even where this custom has been abolished the bonfire itself in some places goes by the name of " the burning of Judas." [1]

[1] John Brand, *Popular Antiquities of Great Britain* (London, 1882-1883), i. 157 *sq.* ; W. Mannhardt, *Der Baumkultus*, pp. 502-505 ; Karl Freiherr von Leoprechting, *Aus dem Lechrain* (Munich, 1855), pp. 172 *sq.* ; Anton Birlinger, *Volksthümliches aus Schwaben* (Freiburg im Breisgau, 1861-1862), i. 472 *sq.* ; Montanus, *Die deutschen Volksfeste, Volksbräuche und deutscher Volksglaube* (Iserlohn, N.D.), p. 26 ; F. Panzer, *Beitrag zur deut-schen Mythologie* (Munich, 1848-1855), ii. 241 *sq.* ; Ernst Meier, *Deutsche Sagen, Sitten und Gebräuche aus Schwaben* (Stuttgart, 1852), pp. 139 *sq.* ; *Bavaria, Landes- und Volkskunde des Königreichs Bayern* (Munich, 1860-1867), i. 371 ; A. Wuttke, *Der deutsche Volksaberglaube* [2] (Berlin, 1869), pp. 68 *sq.*, § 81 ; Ignaz V. Zingerle, *Sitten, Bräuche und Meinungen des Tiroler Volkes* [2] (Innsbruck, 1871), p. 149, §§ 1286-1289 ; W. Kolbe, *Hessische*

Easter fires
in Bavaria
and the
Abruzzi.

In the Hollertau, Bavaria, the young men used to light their lanterns at the newly - kindled Easter candle in the church and then race to the bonfire ; he who reached it first set fire to the pile, and next day, Easter Sunday, was rewarded at the church-door by the housewives, who presented him with red eggs. Great was the jubilation while the effigy of the traitor was being consumed in the flames. The ashes were carefully collected and thrown away at sunrise in running water.[1] In many parts of the Abruzzi, also, pious people kindle their fires on Easter Saturday with a brand brought from the sacred new fire in the church. When the brand has thus served to bless the fire on the domestic hearth, it is extinguished, and the re-mainder is preserved, partly in a cranny of the outer wall of the house, partly on a tree to which it is tied. This is done for the purpose of guarding the homestead against injury by storms. At Campo di Giove the people say that if you can get a piece of one of the three holy candles which the priest lights from the new fire, you should allow a few drops of the wax to fall into the crown of your hat ; for after that, if it should thunder and lighten, you have nothing to do but to clap the hat on your head, and no flash of lightning can possibly strike you.[2]

Water as well as fire conse-crated in the Abruzzi on Easter Saturday.

Further, it deserves to be noted that in the Abruzzi water as well as fire is, as it were, renewed and consecrated on Easter Saturday. Most people fetch holy water on

Volks-Sitten und Gebräuche[2] (Marburg, 1888), pp. 44 *sqq.* ; *County Folk-lore, Printed Extracts, Leicestershire and Rutland,* collected by C. J. Billson (London, 1895), pp. 75 *sq.* ; A. Tira-boschi, " Usi pasquali nel Berga-masco," *Archivio per lo Studio delle Tradizione Popolari,* i. (1892) pp. 442 *sq.* The ecclesiastical custom of light-ing the Paschal or Easter candle is very fully described by Mr. H. J. Feasey, *Ancient English Holy Week Ceremonial* (London, 1897), pp. 179 *sqq.* These candles were sometimes of prodigious size ; in the cathedrals of Norwich and Durham, for example, they reached almost to the roof, from which they had to be lighted. Often they went by the name of the Judas

Light or the Judas Candle ; and some-times small waxen figures of Judas were hung on them. See H. J. Feasey, *op. cit.* pp. 193, 213 *sqq.* As to the ritual of the new fire at St. Peter's in Rome, see R. Chambers, *The Book of Days* (London and Edin-burgh, 1886), i. 421 ; and as to the early history of the rite in the Catholic church, see Mgr. L. Duchesne, *Origines du Culte Chrétien*[3] (Paris, 1903), pp. 250-257.

[1] *Bavaria, Landes- und Volkskunde des Königreichs Bayern* (Munich, 1860–1867), i. 1002 *sq.*

[2] Gennaro Finamore, *Credenze, Usi e Costumi Abruzzesi* (Palermo, 1890), pp. 122 *sq.*

that day from the churches, and every member of the
family drinks a little of it, believing that it has power to
protect him or her against witchcraft, fever, and stomach-
aches of all sorts. And when the church bells ring again
after their enforced silence, the water is sprinkled about the
house, and especially under the beds, with the help of a palm-
branch. Some of this blessed water is also kept in the
house for use in great emergencies, when there is no time to
fetch a priest ; thus it may be employed to baptize a new-
born infant gasping for life or to sprinkle a sick man in the
last agony ; such a sprinkling is reckoned equal to priestly
absolution.[1] In Calabria the customs with regard to the *Water con-
new water, as it is called, on Easter Saturday are similar ; it *secrated in
*Calabria
is poured into a new vessel, adorned with ribbons and flowers, *on Easter
is blessed by the priest, and is tasted by every one of the *Saturday.*
household, beginning with the parents. And when the air
vibrates with the glad music of the church bells announcing
the resurrection, the people sprinkle the holy water about the
houses, bidding in a loud voice all evil things to go forth and
all good things to come in. At the same time, to emphasize
the exorcism, they knock on doors, window-shutters, chests,
and other domestic articles of furniture. At Cetraro people
who suffer from diseases of the skin bathe in the sea at this
propitious moment ; at Pietro in Guarano they plunge into
the river on the night of Easter Saturday before Easter
Sunday dawns, and while they bathe they utter never a word.
Moreover, the Calabrians keep the " new water " as a sacred
thing. They believe that it serves as a protection against
witchcraft if it is sprinkled on a fire or a lamp, when the
wood crackles or the wick sputters ; for they regard it as a
bad omen when the fire talks, as they say.[2] Among the *Water and
Germans of Western Bohemia, also, water as well as fire is *secrated
*fire con-
consecrated by the priest in front of the church on Easter *on Easter
Saturday. People bring jugs full of water to the church *Saturday
and set them beside the holy fire ; afterwards they use the *among the
*Germans of
water to sprinkle on the palm-branches which are stuck in *Bohemia.*
the fields. Charred sticks of the Judas fire, as it is popularly
called, are supposed to possess a magical and healing virtue ;

---

[1] G. Finamore, *op. cit.* pp. 123 *sq.*

[2] Vincenzo Dorsa, *La Tradizione*

*Greco-Latina negli Usi e nelle Credenze
Popolari della Calabria Citeriore*
(Cosenza, 1884), pp. 48 *sq.*

hence the people take them home with them, and even scuffle with each other for the still glowing embers in order to carry them, still glimmering, to their houses and so obtain "the light" or "the holy light."[1]   At Hildesheim, also, and the neighbouring villages of central Germany rites both of fire and water are or were till lately observed at Easter.   Thus on Easter night many people fetch water from the Innerste river and keep it carefully, believing it to be a remedy for many sorts of ailments both of man and beast.   In the villages on the Leine river servant men and maids used to go silently on Easter night between the hours of eleven and twelve and silently draw water in buckets from the river ; they mixed the water with the fodder and the drink of the cattle to make the animals thrive, and they imagined that to wash in it was good for human beings.   Many were also of opinion that at the same mystic hour the water turned to wine as far as the crowing of a cock could be heard, and in this belief they laid themselves flat on their stomachs and kept their tongues in the water till the miraculous change occurred, when they took a great gulp of the transformed water.   At Hildesheim, too, and the neighbouring villages fires used to blaze on all the heights on Easter Eve ; and embers taken from the bonfires were dipped in the cattle troughs to benefit the beasts and were kept in the houses to avert lightning.[2]

Easter rites of fire and water at Hildesheim.

In the Lesachthal, Carinthia, all the fires in the houses used to be extinguished on Easter Saturday, and rekindled with a fresh fire brought from the churchyard, where the priest had lit it by the friction of flint and steel and had bestowed his blessing on it.[3]   Such customs were probably widespread.   In a Latin poem of the sixteenth century, written by a certain Thomas Kirchmeyer and translated into English by Barnabe Googe, we read :—

New fire at Easter in Carinthia.

" *On Easter Eve the fire all is quencht in every place,*
  And fresh againe from out the flint is fetcht with solemne grace :

---

[1] Alois John, *Sitte, Brauch und Volksglaube im deutschen Westböhmen* (Prague, 1905), pp. 62 *sq.*

[2] K. Seifart, *Sagen, Märchen, Schwänke und Gebräuche aus Stadt und Stift Hildesheim* [2] (Hildesheim, 1889),

pp. 177 *sq.*, 179 *sq.*

[3] M. Lexer, " Volksüberlieferungen aus dem Lesachthal in Kärnten," *Zeitschrift für deutsche Mythologie und Sittenkunde,* iii. (1855) p. 31.

The priest doth halow this against great daungers many one,
A brande whereof doth every man with greedie mind take home,
That when the fearefull storme appeares, or tempest black arise,
By lighting this he safe may be from stroke of hurtful skies :
A taper great, the Paschall namde, with musicke then they blesse,
And franckensence herein they pricke, for greater holynesse :
This burneth night and day as signe of Christ that conquerde hell,
As if so be this foolish toye suffiseth this to tell.
Then doth the Bishop or the Priest, the water halow straight,
That for their baptisme is reservde : for now no more of waight
Is that they usde the yeare before, nor can they any more,
Yong children christen with the same, as they have done before.
With wondrous pompe and furniture, amid the Church they go,
With candles, crosses, banners, Chrisme, and oyle appoynted tho :
Nine times about the font they marche, and on the saintes doe call,
Then still at length they stande, and straight the Priest begins withall,
And thrise the water doth he touche, and crosses thereon make,
Here bigge and barbrous wordes he speakes, to make the devill quake :
And holsome waters conjureth, and foolishly doth dresse,
Supposing holyar that to make, which God before did blesse :
And after this his candle than, he thrusteth in the floode,
And thrise he breathes thereon with breath, that stinkes of former foode :
And making here an ende, his Chrisme he poureth thereupon,
The people staring hereat stande, amazed every one :
Beleeving that great powre is given to this water here,
By gaping of these learned men, and such like trifling gere.
Therefore in vessels brought they draw, and home they carie some,
Against the grieves that to themselves, or to their beastes may come.
Then Clappers ceasse, and belles are set againe at libertée,
And herewithall the hungrie times of fasting ended bée." [1]

It is said that formerly all the fires in Rome were lighted afresh from the holy fire kindled in St. Peter's on Easter Saturday.[2]

---

[1] *The Popish Kingdome or reigne of Antichrist, written in Latin verse by Thomas Naogeorgus and Englyshed by Barnabe Googe, 1570,* edited by R. C. Hope (London, 1880), p. 52, *recto.* The title of the original poem was *Regnum Papisticum.* The author, Thomas Kirchmeyer (Naogeorgus, as he called himself), died in 1577. The book is a satire on the abuses and superstitions of the Catholic Church. Only one perfect copy of Googe's translation is known to exist : it is in the University Library at Cambridge. See Mr. R. C. Hope's introduction to his reprint of this rare work, pp. xv. *sq.* The words, "Then Clappers ceasse, and belles are set againe at libertée," refer to the custom in Catholic countries of silencing the church bells for two days from noon on Maundy Thursday to noon on Easter Saturday and substituting for their music the harsh clatter of wooden rattles. See R. Chambers, *The Book of Days* (London and Edinburgh, 1886), i. 412 *sq.* According to another account the church bells are silent from midnight on the Wednesday preceding Maundy Thursday till matins on Easter Day. See W. Smith and S. Cheetham, *Dictionary of Christian Antiquities* (London, 1875–1880), ii. 1161, referring to *Ordo Roman. i. u.s.*

[2] R. Chambers, *The Book of Days* (London and Edinburgh, 1886), i. 421.

In Florence the ceremony of kindling the new fire on
Easter Eve is peculiar.   The holy flame is elicited from
certain flints which are said to have been brought by a
member of the Pazzi family from the Holy Land.   They are
kept in the church of the Holy Apostles on the Piazza del
Limbo, and on the morning of Easter Saturday the prior
strikes fire from them and lights a candle from the new
flame.   The burning candle is then carried in solemn
procession by the clergy and members of the municipality to
the high altar in the cathedral.   A vast crowd has meanwhile assembled in the cathedral and the neighbouring
square to witness the ceremony ; amongst the spectators are
many peasants drawn from the surrounding country, for it is
commonly believed that on the success or failure of the
ceremony depends the fate of the crops for the year.   Outside the door of the cathedral stands a festal car drawn by
two fine white oxen with gilded horns.   The body of the
car is loaded with a pyramid of squibs and crackers and is
connected by a wire with a pillar set up in front of the high
altar.   The wire extends down the middle of the nave at a
height of about six feet from the ground.   Beneath it a clear
passage is left, the spectators being ranged on either side and
crowding the vast interior from wall to wall.   When all is
ready, High Mass is celebrated, and precisely at noon, when
the first words of the *Gloria* are being chanted, the sacred
fire is applied to the pillar, which like the car is wreathed
with fireworks.   A moment more and a fiery dove comes
flying down the nave, with a hissing sound and a sputter of
sparks, between the two hedges of eager spectators.   If all
goes well, the bird pursues its course along the wire and out
at the door, and in another moment a prolonged series of
fizzes, pops and bangs announces to the excited crowd in
the cathedral that the fireworks on the car are going off.
Great is the joy accordingly, especially among the bumpkins,
who are now sure of an abundant harvest.   But if, as sometimes happens, the dove stops short in its career and fizzles
out, revealing itself as a stuffed bird with a packet of squibs
tied to its tail, great is the consternation, and deep the curses
that issue from between the set teeth of the clodhoppers, who
now give up the harvest for lost.   Formerly the unskilful

mechanician who was responsible for the failure would have
been clapped into gaol; but nowadays he is thought
sufficiently punished by the storm of public indignation and
the loss of his pay.   The disaster is announced by placards
posted about the streets in the evening ; and next morning
the newspapers are full of gloomy prognostications.[1]

Some of these customs have been transported by the
Catholic Church to the New World.   Thus in Mexico the
new fire is struck from a flint early in the morning of Easter
Saturday, and a candle which has been lighted at the sacred
flame is carried through the church by a deacon shouting
" *Lumen Christi.*"   Meantime the whole city, we are informed, has been converted into a vast place of execution.
Ropes stretch across the streets from house to house, and
from every house dangles an effigy of Judas, made of paper
pulp.   Scores or hundreds of them may adorn a single
street.   They are of all shapes and sizes, grotesque in form
and garbed in strange attire, stuffed with gunpowder, squibs
and crackers, sometimes, too, with meat, bread, soap, candy,
and clothing, for which the crowd will scramble and scuffle
while the effigies are burning.   There they hang grim, black,
and sullen in the strong sunshine, greeted with a roar of
execration by the pious mob.   A peal of bells from the
cathedral tower on the stroke of noon gives the signal for the
execution.   At the sound a frenzy seizes the crowd.   They
throw themselves furiously on the figures of the detested
traitor, cut them down, hurl them with curses into the fire,
and fight and struggle with each other in their efforts to tear
the effigies to tatters and appropriate their contents.   Smoke,
stink, sputter of crackers, oaths, curses, yells are now the
order of the day.   But the traitor does not perish unavenged.
For the anatomy of his frame has been cunningly contrived
so as in burning to discharge volleys of squibs into his
assailants ; and the wounds and burns with which their

The new fire and the burning of Judas on Easter Saturday in Mexico.

---

[1] Miss Jessie L. Weston, "The
Scoppio del Carro at Florence," *Folk-
lore*, xvi. (1905) pp. 182-184; "Lo
Scoppio del Carro," *Resurrezione,
Numero Unico del Sabato Santo*
(Florence, April, 1906), p. 1 (giving a
picture of the car with its pyramid of
fire-works).   The latter paper was
kindly sent to me from Florence by my
friend Professor W. J. Lewis.   I have
also received a letter on the subject
from Signor Carlo Placci, dated 4 (or
7) September, 1905, 1 Via Alfieri,
Firenze.

piety is rewarded form a feature of the morning's entertainment. The English Jockey Club in Mexico used to improve on this popular pastime by suspending huge figures of Judas, stuffed with copper coins, from ropes in front of their clubhouse. These were ignited at the proper moment and lowered within reach of the expectant rabble, and it was the privilege of members of the club, seated in the balcony, to watch the grimaces and to hear the shrieks of the victims, as they stamped and capered about with the hot coppers sticking to their hands, divided in their minds between an acute sense of pain and a thirst for filthy lucre.[1]

The burning of Judas at Easter in South America.

Scenes of the same sort, though on a less ambitious scale, are witnessed among the Catholics of South America on the same day. In Brazil the mourning for the death of Christ ceases at noon on Easter Saturday and gives place to an extravagant burst of joy at his resurrection. Shots are fired everywhere, and effigies of Judas are hung on trees or dragged about the streets, to be finally burned or otherwise destroyed.[2] In the Indian villages scattered among the wild valleys of the Peruvian Andes figures of the traitor, made of pasteboard and stuffed with squibs and crackers, are hanged on gibbets before the door of the church on Easter Saturday. Fire is set to them, and while they crackle and explode, the Indians dance and shout for joy at the destruction of their hated enemy.[3] Similarly at Rio Hacha, in Colombia, Judas is represented during Holy Week by life-sized effigies, and the people fire at them as if they were discharging a sacred duty.[4]

The new fire on Easter Saturday in the Church of

But usages of this sort are not confined to the Latin Church; they are common to the Greek Church also. Every year on the Saturday before Easter Sunday a new fire is miraculously kindled at the Holy Sepulchre in

[1] Frederick Starr, "Holy Week in Mexico," *The Journal of American Folk-lore,* xii. (1899) pp. 164 *sq.* ; C. Boyson Taylor, "Easter in Many Lands," *Everybody's Magazine,* New York, 1903, p. 293. I have to thank Mr. S. S. Cohen, of 1525 Walnut Street, Philadelphia, for sending me a cutting from the latter magazine.

[2] K. von den Steinen, *Unter aen*

Naturvölkern Zentral-Brasiliens (Berlin, 1894), pp. 458 *sq.* ; E. Montet, "Religion et Superstition dans l'Amérique du Sud," *Revue de l'Histoire des Religions,* xxxii. (1895) p. 145.

[3] J. J. von Tschudi, *Peru, Reiseskizzen aus den Jahren 1838–1842* (St. Gallen, 1846), ii. 189 *sq.*

[4] H. Candelier, *Rio-Hacha et les Indiens Goajires* (Paris, 1893), p. 85.

Jerusalem. It descends from heaven and ignites the
candles which the patriarch holds in his hands, while
with closed eyes he wrestles in prayer all alone in the
chapel of the Angel. The worshippers meanwhile wait
anxiously in the body of the church, and great are their
transports of joy when at one of the windows of the chapel,
which had been all dark a minute before, there suddenly
appears the hand of an angel, or of the partriarch, holding a
lighted taper. This is the sacred new fire ; it is passed out
to the expectant believers, and the desperate struggle which
ensues among them to get a share of its blessed influence is
only terminated by the intervention of the Turkish soldiery,
who restore peace and order by hustling the whole multitude
impartially out of the church. In days gone by many lives
were often lost in these holy scrimmages. For example, in
the year 1834, the famous Ibrahim Pasha witnessed the
frantic scene from one of the galleries, and, being moved
with compassion at the sight, descended with a few guards
into the arena in the chimerical hope of restoring peace and
order among the contending Christians. He contrived to
force his way into the midst of the dense crowd, but there
the heat and pressure were so great that he fainted away ;
a body of soldiers, seeing his danger, charged straight into
the throng and carried him out of it in their arms, trampling
under foot the dying and dead in their passage. Nearly two
hundred people were killed that day in the church. The
fortunate survivors on these occasions who succeeded in
obtaining a portion of the coveted fire applied it freely to
their faces, their beards, and their garments. The theory
was that the fire, being miraculous, could only bless and not
burn them ; but the practical results of the experiment were
often disappointing, for while the blessings were more or
less dubious, there could be no doubt whatever about the
burns.[1] The history of the miracle has been carefully

---

[1] Henry Maundrell, "A Journey
from Aleppo to Jerusalem at Easter,
A.D. 1697," in Bohn's *Early Travellers
in Palestine* (London, 1848), pp. 462-
465; Mgr. Auvergne, in *Annales de la
Propagation de la Foi*, x. (1837) pp.
23 *sq.* ; A. P. Stanley, *Sinai and
Palestine*, Second Edition (London,
1856), pp. 460-465 ; E. Cortet, *Essai
sur les Fêtes Religieuses* (Paris, 1867),
pp. 137-139; A. W. Kinglake, *Eothen*,
chapter xvi. pp. 158-163 (Temple
Classics edition) ; Father X. Abougit,
S.J., "Le feu du Saint-Sépulcre,"
Les Missions Catholiques, viii. (1876)
pp. 518 *sq.* ; Rev. C. T. Wilson,

investigated by a Jesuit father. The conclusions at which he arrives are that the miracle was a miracle indeed so long as the Catholics had the management of it ; but that since it fell into the hands of the heretics it has been nothing but a barefaced trick and imposture.[1] Many people will be disposed to agree with the latter conclusion who might hesitate to accept the former.

The new fire and the burning of Judas on Easter Saturday in Greece.

At Athens the new fire is kindled in the cathedral at midnight on Holy Saturday. A dense crowd with unlit candles in their hands fills the square in front of the cathedral ; the king, the archbishop, and the highest dignitaries of the church, arrayed in their gorgeous robes, occupy a platform ; and at the exact moment of the resurrection the bells ring out, and the whole square bursts as by magic into a blaze of light. Theoretically all the candles are lit from the sacred new fire in the cathedral, but practically it may be suspected that the matches which bear the name of Lucifer have some share in the sudden illumination.[2] Effigies of Judas used to be burned at Athens on Easter Saturday, but the custom has been forbidden by the Government. However, firing goes on more or less continuously all over the city both on Easter Saturday and Easter Sunday, and the cartridges used on this occasion are not always blank. The shots are aimed at Judas, but sometimes they miss him and hit other people. Outside of Athens the practice of burning Judas in effigy still survives in some places. For example, in Cos a straw image of the traitor is made on Easter Day, and after being hung up and shot at it is burned.[3] A similar custom

---

[1] *Peasant Life in the Holy Land* (London, 1906), pp. 45 *sq.* ; P. Saint-yves, "Le Renouvellement du Feu Sacré," *Revue des Traditions Populaires*, xxvii. (1912) pp. 449 *sqq.* The distribution of the new fire in the Church of the Holy Sepulchre is the subject of a picture by Holman Hunt. From some printed notes on the picture, with which Mrs. Holman Hunt was so kind as to furnish me, it appears that the new fire is carried by horsemen to Bethlehem and Jaffa, and that a Russian ship conveys it from Jaffa to Odessa, whence it is distributed all over the country.

[1] Father X. Abougit, S.J., "Le feu du Saint-Sépulcre," *Les Missions Catholiques*, viii. (1876) pp. 165-168.

[2] I have described the ceremony as I witnessed it at Athens, on April 13th, 1890. Compare *Folk-lore*, i. (1890) p. 275. Having been honoured, like other strangers, with a place on the platform, I did not myself detect Lucifer at work among the multitude below ; I merely suspected his insidious presence.

[3] W. H. D. Rouse, "Folk-lore from the Southern Sporades," *Folk-lore*, x. (1899) p. 178.

appears to prevail at Thebes ;[1] it used to be observed by the Macedonian peasantry, and it is still kept up at Therapia, a fashionable summer resort of Constantinople.[2]

In the Armenian Church the sacred new fire is kindled not at Easter but at Candlemas, that is, on the second of February, or on the eve of that festival. The materials of the bonfire are piled in an open space near a church, and they are generally ignited by young couples who have been married within the year. However, it is the bishop or his vicar who lights the candles with which fire is set to the pile. All young married pairs are expected to range themselves about the fire and to dance round it. Young men leap over the flames, but girls and women content themselves with going round them, while they pray to be preserved from the itch and other skin - diseases. When the ceremony is over, the people eagerly pick up charred sticks or ashes of the fire and preserve them or scatter them on the four corners of the roof, in the cattle-stall, in the garden, and on the pastures ; for these holy sticks and ashes protect men and cattle against disease, and fruit-trees against worms and caterpillars. Omens, too, are drawn from the direction in which the wind blows the flames and the smoke : if it carries them eastward, there is hope of a good harvest ; but if it inclines them westward, the people fear that the crops will fail.[3]

The new fire at Candlemas in Armenia.

In spite of the thin cloak of Christianity thrown over these customs by representing the new fire as an emblem of Christ and the figure burned in it as an effigy of Judas, we can hardly doubt that both practices are of pagan origin. Neither of them has the authority of Christ or of his disciples ; but both of them have abundant analogies in popular custom

The new fire and the burning of Judas at Easter are probably relics of paganism.

[1] Mrs. A. E. Gardner was so kind as to send me a photograph of a Theban Judas dangling from a gallows and partially enveloped in smoke. The photograph was taken at Thebes during the Easter celebration of 1891.

[2] G. F. Abbott, *Macedonian Folklore* (Cambridge, 1903) p. 37.

[3] Cirbied, " Mémoire sur le gouvernment et sur la religion des anciens Arméniens," *Mémoires publiées par la* *Société Royale des Antiquaires de France,* ii. (1820) pp. 285-287 ; Manuk Abeghian, *Der armenische Volksglaube* (Leipsic, 1899), pp. 72-74. The ceremony is said to be merely a continuation of an old heathen festival which was held at the beginning of spring in honour of the fire-god Mihr. A bonfire was made in a public place, and lamps kindled at it were kept burning throughout the year in each of the fire-god's temples.

and superstition. Some instances of the practice of annually extinguishing fires and relighting them from a new and sacred flame have already come before us ;[1] but a few examples may here be cited for the sake of illustrating the wide diffusion of a custom which has found its way into the ritual both of the Eastern and of the Western Church.

The new fire at the summer solstice among the Incas of Peru. The Incas of Peru celebrated a festival called Raymi, a word which their native historian Garcilasso de la Vega tells us was equivalent to our Easter. It was held in honour of the sun at the solstice in June. For three days before the festival the people fasted, men did not sleep with their wives, and no fires were lighted in Cuzco, the capital. The sacred new fire was obtained direct from the sun by concentrating his beams on a highly polished concave plate and reflecting them on a little cotton wool. With this holy fire the sheep and lambs offered to the sun were consumed, and the flesh of such as were to be eaten at the festival was roasted. Portions of the new fire were also conveyed to the temple of the sun and to the convent of the sacred virgins, where they were kept burning all the year, and it was an ill omen if the holy flame went out.[2] At a festival held in the last month of the old Mexican year all the fires both in the temples and in the houses were extinguished, and the priest kindled a new fire by rubbing two sticks against each other before the image of the fire-god.[3] The Zuñi Indians of New Mexico kindle a new fire by the friction of wood both at the winter and the summer solstice. At the winter solstice the chosen fire-maker collects a faggot of cedar-wood from every house in the village, and each person, as he hands the wood to the fire-maker, prays that the crops may be good in the coming year. For several days before the new fire is kindled, no

The new fire among the Indians of Mexico and New Mexico.

[1] *The Magic Art and the Evolution of Kings*, i. 32, ii. 243 ; *Spirits of the Corn and of the Wild*, ii. 65, 74, 75, 78, 136.

[2] Garcilasso de la Vega, *Royal Commentaries of the Yncas*, translated by (Sir) Clements R. Markham (Hakluyt Society, London, 1869–1871), vol. ii. pp. 155 - 163. Compare Juan de Velasco, " Histoire du Royaume de Quito," in H. Ternaux - Compans's *Voyages, Relations et Mémoires origi-*

naux pour servir à l'Histoire de la Découverte de l'Amérique, xviii. (Paris, 1840) p. 140.

[3] B. de Sahagun, *Histoire Générale des Choses de la Nouvelle Espagne*, traduite par D. Jourdanet et R. Simeon (Paris, 1880), bk. ii. chapters 18 and 37, pp. 76, 161; Brasseur de Bourbourg, *Histoire des Nations civilisées du Mexique et de l'Amérique-Centrale* (Paris, 1857–1859), iii. 136.

ashes or sweepings may be removed from the houses and no artificial light may appear outside of them, not even a burning cigarette or the flash of firearms. The Indians believe that no rain will fall on the fields of the man outside whose house a light has been seen at this season. The signal for kindling the new fire is given by the rising of the Morning Star. The flame is produced by twirling an upright stick between the hands on a horizontal stick laid on the floor of a sacred chamber, the sparks being caught by a tinder of cedar-dust. It is forbidden to blow up the smouldering tinder with the breath, for that would offend the gods. After the fire has thus been ceremonially kindled, the women and girls of all the families in the village clean out their houses. They carry the sweepings and ashes in baskets or bowls to the fields and leave them there. To the sweepings the woman says : " I now deposit you as sweepings, but in one year you will return to me as corn." And to the ashes she says : " I now deposit you as ashes, but in one year you will return to me as meal." At the summer solstice the sacred fire which has been procured by the friction of wood is used to kindle the grass and trees, that there may be a great cloud of smoke, while bull-roarers are swung and prayers offered that the Rain-makers up aloft will water the earth.[1] From this account we see how intimately the kindling of a new fire at the two turning-points of the sun's course is associated in the minds of these Indians with the fertility of the land, particularly with the growth of the corn. The rolling smoke is apparently an imitation of rain-clouds designed, on the principle of homoeopathic magic, to draw showers from the blue sky. Once a year the Iroquois priesthood supplied the people with a new fire. As a preparation for the annual rite

[1] Mrs. Matilda Coxe Stevenson, "The Zuñi Indians," *Twenty - third Annual Report of the Bureau of American Ethnology* (Washington, 1904), pp. 108-141, 148-162, especially pp. 108, 109, 114 *sq.*, 120 *sq.*, 130 *sq.*, 132, 148 *sq.*, 157 *sq.* I have already described these ceremonies in *Totemism and Exogamy*, iii. 237 *sq.* Among the Hopi (Moqui) Indians of Walpi, another pueblo village of this region, new fire is ceremonially kindled by friction in November. See Jesse Walter Fewkes, "The Tusayan New Fire Ceremony," *Proceedings of the Boston Society of Natural History*, xxvi. 422-458 ; *id.*, " The Group of Tusayan Ceremonials called *Katcinas*," *Fifteenth Annual Report of the Bureau of Ethnology* (Washington, 1897), p. 263 ; *id.*, " Hopi *Katcinas*," *Twenty - first Annual Report of the Bureau of American Ethnology* (Washington, 1903), p. 24.

the fires in all the huts were extinguished and the ashes scattered about.   Then the priest, wearing the insignia of his office, went from hut to hut relighting the fires by means of a flint.[1]   Among the Esquimaux with whom C. F. Hall resided, it was the custom that at a certain time, which answered to our New Year's Day, two men went about from house to house blowing out every light in the village.   One of the men was dressed to represent a woman.   Afterwards the lights were rekindled from a fresh fire.   An Esquimau woman being asked what all this meant, replied, " New sun—new light." [2] Among the Esquimaux of Iglulik, when the sun first rises above the horizon after the long night of the Arctic winter, the children who have watched for his reappearance run into the houses and blow out the lamps.   Then they receive from their mothers presents of pieces of wick.[3]

In the Sudanese kingdom of Wadai all the fires in the villages are put out and the ashes removed from the houses on the day which precedes the New Year festival.   At the beginning of the new year a new fire is lit by the friction of wood in the great straw hut where the village elders lounge away the sultry hours together ; and every man takes thence a burning brand with which he rekindles the fire on his domestic hearth.[4]   In the Bahr-el-Ghazal province of the Egyptian Sudan the people extinguish their old fires at the Arab New Year and bring in new fire.   On the same occasion they beat the walls of their huts, the grass thatches, and the walls of their enclosures in order to drive away the devil or evil spirits.   The beating of the walls and roofs is accompanied by the firing of guns, the shouting of men, and the shriller cries of the women.[5]   Thus these people combine

The new re among he Esqui- naux.

The new re in Vadai, among the Swahili, nd in other parts of Africa.

---

[1] Henry R. Schoolcraft, *Notes on the Iroquois* (Albany, 1847), p. 137. Schoolcraft did not know the date of the ceremony, but he conjectured that it fell at the end of the Iroquois year, which was a lunar year of twelve or thirteen months.   He says : " That the close of the lunar series should have been the period of putting out the fire, and the beginning of the next, the time of relumination, from new fire, is so consonant to analogy in the tropical tribes, as to be probable " (*op. cit.* p. 138).

[2] C. F. Hall, *Life with the Esquimaux* (London, 1864), ii. 323.

[3] Franz Boas, " The Eskimo of Baffin Land and Hudson Bay," *Bulletin of the American Museum of Natural History*, xv. Part i. (New York, 1901) p. 151.

[4] G. Nachtigal, *Sahárá und Súdân*, iii. (Leipsic, 1889) p. 251.

[5] Major C. Percival, " Tropical Africa, on the Border Line of Mohamedan Civilization," *The Geographical Journal*, xlii. (1913) pp. 253 *sq.*

an annual expulsion of demons with an annual lighting of a
new fire. Among the Swahili of East Africa the greatest
festival is that of the New Year, which falls in the second half
of August. At a given moment all the fires are extinguished
with water and afterwards relit by the friction of two dry
pieces of wood. The ashes of the old fires are carried out
and deposited at cross-roads. All the people get up very early
in the morning and bathe in the sea or some other water,
praying to be kept in good health and to live that they may
bathe again next year. Sham-fights form part of the amusements of the day ; sometimes they pass into grim reality.
Indeed the day was formerly one of general license ; every
man did that which was good in his own eyes. No awkward
questions were asked about any crimes committed on this
occasion, so some people improved the shining hour by
knocking a few poor devils on the head. Shooting still goes
on during the whole day, and at night the proceedings
generally wind up with a great dance.[1] The King of
Benametapa, as the early Portuguese traders called him, in
East Africa used to send commissioners annually to every
town in his dominions ; on the arrival of one of these officers
the inhabitants of each town had to put out all their fires and
to receive a new fire from him. Failure to comply with this
custom was treated as rebellion.[2] Some tribes of British
Central Africa carefully extinguish the fires on the hearths at

[1] Adrien Germain, " Note sur Zan-
zibar et la côte orientale de l'Afrique,"
Bulletin de la Société de Géographie
(Paris), v. Série xvi. (1868) p. 557 ;
Les Missions Catholiques, iii. (1870)
p. 270 ; Charles New, *Life, Wanderings,
and Labours in Eastern Africa* (London, 1873), p. 65 ; Jerome Becker,
La Vie en Afrique (Paris and Brussels,
1887), ii. 36 ; O. Baumann, *Usambara
und seine Nachbargebiete* (Berlin, 1891),
pp. 55 *sq.* ; C. Velten, *Sitten und
Gebräuche aer Suaheli* (Göttingen, 1903),
pp. 342-344.

[2] Duarte Barbosa, *Description of
the Coasts of East Africa and Malabar*
(Hakluyt Society, London, 1866), p.
8 ; *id.*, in *Records of South-Eastern
Africa*, collected by G. McCall Theal,

vol. i. (1898) p. 96 ; Damião de Goes,
"Chronicle of the Most Fortunate
King Dom Emanuel," in *Records of
South-Eastern Africa*, collected by G.
McCall Theal, vol. iii. (1899) pp. 130
sq. The name Benametapa (more
correctly *monomotapa*) appears to have
been the regular title of the paramount
chief, which the Portuguese took to be
the name of the country. The people
over whom he ruled seem to have been
the Bantu tribe of the Makalanga in
the neighbourhood of Sofala. See G.
McCall Theal, *Records of South-Eastern
Africa*, vii. (1901) pp. 481-484. It is
to their custom of annually extinguishing and relighting the fire that Mon-
taigne refers in his essay (i. 22, vol. i.
p. 140 of Charpentier's edition), though
he mentions no names.

the beginning of the hoeing season and at harvest ; the fires are afterwards rekindled by friction, and the people indulge in dances of various kinds.[1]

The Todas of the Neilgherry Hills, in Southern India, annually kindle a sacred new fire by the friction of wood in the month which begins with the October moon. The ceremony is performed by two holy dairymen at the foot of a high hill. When they have lighted the fire by rubbing two dry sticks together, and it begins to burn well, they stand a little way off and pray, saying, " May the young grass flower ! May honey flourish ! May fruit ripen ! " The purpose of the ceremony is to make the grass and honey plentiful. In ancient times the Todas lived largely on wild fruits, and then the rite of the new fire was very important. Now that they subsist chiefly on the milk of their buffaloes, the ceremony has lost much of its old significance.[2] When the Nagas of North-Eastern India have felled the timber and cut down the scrub in those patches of jungle which they propose to cultivate, they put out all the fires in the village and light a new fire by rubbing two dry pieces of wood together. Then having kindled torches at it they proceed with them to the jungle and ignite the felled timber and brushwood. The flesh of a cow or buffalo is also roasted on the new fire and furnishes a sacrificial meal.[3] Near the small town of Kahma in Burma, between Prome and Thayetmyo, certain gases escape from a hollow in the ground and burn with a steady flame during the dry season of the year. The people regard the flame as the forge of a spectral smith who here carried on his business after death had removed him from his old smithy in the village. Once a year all the household fires in Kahma are extinguished and then lighted afresh from the ghostly flame.[4]

In China every year, about the beginning of April, certain

[1] Sir H. H. Johnson, *British Central Africa* (London, 1897), pp. 426, 439.

[2] W. H. R. Rivers, *The Todas* (London, 1906), pp. 290-292.

[3] Lieut. R. Stewart, "Notes on Northern Cachar," *Journal of the Asiatic Society of Bengal*, xxiv. (1855) p. 612.

[4] A. Bastian, *Die Völker des östlichen Asien*, ii. (Leipsic, 1866) pp. 49 *sq.* ; Shway Yoe, *The Burman* (London, 1882), ii. 325 *sq.*

officials, called *Sz'hüen*, used of old to go about the country armed with wooden clappers.   Their business was to summon the people and command them to put out every fire.   This was the beginning of a season called *Han-shih-tsieh*, or " eating cold food."   For three days all household fires remained extinct as a preparation for the solemn renewal of the fire, which took place on the fifth or sixth day of April, being the hundred and fifth day after the winter solstice. The ceremony was performed with great pomp by the same officials, who procured the new fire from heaven by reflecting the sun's rays either from a metal mirror or from a crystal on dry moss.   Fire thus obtained is called by the Chinese heavenly fire, and its use is enjoined in sacrifices ; whereas fire elicited by the friction of wood is termed by them earthly fire, and its use is prescribed for cooking and other domestic purposes.   When once the new fire had thus been drawn from the sun, all the people were free to rekindle their domestic hearths ; and, as a Chinese distich has it—

"At the festival of the cold food there are a thousand white stalks among the flowers ;
On the day Tsing-ming, at sunrise, you may see the smoke of ten thousand houses."

According to a Chinese philosopher, the reason for thus renewing fire periodically is that the vital principle grows weaker and weaker in old fire, whereas in new fire it is young and vigorous.   This annual renewal of fire was a ceremony of very great antiquity in China, since it is known to have been observed in the time of the first dynasty, about two thousand years before Christ.   Under the Tcheou dynasty a change in the calendar led to shifting the fire-festival from spring to the summer solstice, but afterwards it was brought back to its original date.   Although the custom appears to have long fallen into disuse, the barbarous inhabitants of Hainan, an island to the south of China, still call a year " a fire," as if in memory of the time when the years were reckoned by the annually recurring ceremony of rekindling the sacred fire.[1]   " A Japanese book written two

[1] G. Schlegel, *Uranographie Chinoise* (The Hague and Leyden, 1875), pp. 139-143 ; C. Puini, " Il fuoco nella tradizione degli antichi Cinesi," *Giornale della Società Asiatica Italiana*, i. (1887) pp. 20-23 ; J. J. M. de Groot,

centuries ago informs us that sticks resembling the wands used for offerings at the purification ceremony were part shaven and set up in bundles at the four corners of the Gion shrine on the last day of the year. The priests, after prayers were recited, broke up the bundles and set fire to the sticks, which the people then carried home to light their household fires with for the New Year. The object of this ceremony was to avert pestilence." [1]

The new fire in ancient Greece and Rome.

In classical antiquity the Greek island of Lemnos was devoted to the worship of the smith-god Hephaestus, who was said to have fallen on it when Zeus hurled him from heaven.[2] Once a year every fire in the island was extinguished and remained extinct for nine days, during which sacrifices were offered to the dead and to the infernal powers. New fire was brought in a ship from the sacred isle of Delos, and with it the fires in the houses and the workshops were relit. The people said that with the new fire they made a new beginning of life. If the ship that bore the sacred flame arrived too soon, it might not put in to shore, but had to cruise in the offing till the nine days were expired.[3] At Rome the sacred fire in the temple of Vesta was kindled anew every year on the first of March, which used to be the beginning of the Roman year;[4] the task of lighting it was entrusted to the Vestal Virgins, and they performed it by drilling a hole in a board of lucky wood till the flame was elicited by friction. The new fire thus produced was carried into the temple of Vesta by one of the virgins in a bronze sieve.[5]

Les Fêtes annuellement célébrées à Émoui (*Amoy*) (Paris, 1886), i. 208 *sqq*. The notion that fire can be worn out with age meets us also in Brahman ritual. See the *Satapatha Brahmana*, translated by Julius Eggeling, Part i. (Oxford, 1882) p. 230 (*Sacred Books of the East*, vol. xii.).

[1] W. G. Aston, *Shinto, The Way of the Gods* (London, 1905), pp. 258 *sq*., compare p. 193. The wands in question are sticks whittled near the top into a mass of adherent shavings ; they go by the name of *kedzurikake* ("part-shaved"), and resemble the sacred *inao* of the Aino. See W. G. Aston,

op. cit. p. 191 ; and as to the *inao*, see *Spirits of the Corn and of the Wild*, ii. 185, with note [2].

[2] Ovid, *Fasti*, iii. 82 ; Homer, *Iliad*, i. 590, *sqq*.

[3] Philostratus, *Heroica*, xx. 24.

[4] Ovid, *Fasti*, iii. 143 *sq*. ; Macrobius, *Saturn.* i. 12. 6.

[5] Festus, ed. C. O. Müller (Leipsic, 1839), p. 106, *s.v.* "Ignis." Plutarch describes a method of rekindling the sacred fire by means of the sun's rays reflected from a hollow mirror (*Numa*, 9) ; but he seems to be referring to a Greek rather than to the Roman custom. The rule of celibacy imposed

Among the Celts of Ireland a new fire was annually The new fire at Hallow E'en among the old Celts of Ireland.
kindled on Hallowe'en or the Eve of Samhain, as they
called it, the last day of October, from which the Irish new
year began ; and all the hearths throughout the country
are said to have been relighted from the fresh fire. The place
where this holy flame was lit bore the name of Tlachtga
or Tlactga ; it has been identified with a rath or native
fort on the Hill of Ward near Athboy in the county of
Meath. "It was there," says the old Irish historian,
Geoffrey Keating, "that the Festival of the Fire of Tlactga
was ordered to be held, and it was thither that the Druids
of Ireland were wont to repair and to assemble, in solemn
meeting, on the eve of Samhain, for the purpose of making
a sacrifice to all the gods. It was in that fire at Tlactga,
that their sacrifice was burnt; and it was made obligatory,
under pain of punishment, to extinguish all the fires of
Ireland, on that eve ; and the men of Ireland were allowed
to kindle no other fire but that one ; and for each of the
other fires, which were all to be lighted from it, the king of
Munster was to receive a tax of a *sgreball*, that is, of three
pence, because the land, upon which Tlactga was built,
belongs to the portion of Meath which had been taken from
Munster."[1] In the villages near Moscow at the present The new fire on September 1st among the Russian peasants.
time the peasants put out all their fires on the eve of the
first of September, and next morning at sunrise a wise man
or a wise woman rekindles them with the help of muttered
incantations and spells.[2]

Instances of such practices might doubtless be multiplied, but the foregoing examples may suffice to render it

---

on the Vestals, whose duty it was to
relight the sacred fire as well as to
preserve it when it was once made, is
perhaps explained by a superstition
current among French peasants that
if a girl can blow up a smouldering
candle into a flame she is a virgin, but
that if she fails to do so, she is not.
See Jules Lecœur, *Esquisses du Bocage
Normand* (Condé-sur-Noireau, 1883–
1887), ii. 27 ; B. Souché, *Croyances,
Présages et Traditions diverses* (Niort,
1880), p. 12. At least it seems more
likely that the rule sprang from a
superstition of this sort than from a

simple calculation of expediency, as I
formerly suggested (*Journal of Philo-
logy*, xiv. (1885) p. 158). Compare
*The Magic Art and the Evolution of
Kings*, ii. 234 *sqq.*

[1] Geoffrey Keating, D.D., *The History
of Ireland, translated from the original
Gaelic, and copiously annotated*, by John
O'Mahony (New York, 1857), p. 300,
with the translator's note. Compare
(Sir) John Rhys, *Celtic Heathendom*
(London, 1888), pp. 514 *sq.*

[2] W. R. S. Ralston, *Songs of the
Russian People*, Second Edition (London, 1872), pp. 254 *sq.*

Thus the
ceremony
of the new
fire in the
Eastern
and
Western
Church is
probably a
relic of an
old heathen
rite.

probable that the ecclesiastical ceremony of lighting a sacred
new fire on Easter Saturday had originally nothing to do
with Christianity, but is merely one case of a world-wide
custom which the Church has seen fit to incorporate in its
ritual.   It might be supposed that in the Western Church
the custom was merely a survival of the old Roman usage of
renewing the fire on the first of March, were it not that the
observance by the Eastern Church of the custom on the
same day seems to point back to a still older period when
the ceremony of lighting a new fire in spring, perhaps at
the vernal equinox, was common to many peoples of the
Mediterranean area.   We may conjecture that wherever such
a ceremony has been observed, it originally marked the
beginning of a new year, as it did in ancient Rome and
Ireland, and as it still does in the Sudanese kingdom of
Wadai and among the Swahili of Eastern Africa.

The pagan
character
of the
Easter fire
appears
from the
super-
stitions
associated
with it,
such as the
belief that
the fire
fertilizes
the fields
and
protects
houses
from con-
flagration
and sick-
ness.

The essentially pagan character of the Easter fire festival
appears plainly both from the mode in which it is celebrated
by the peasants and from the superstitious beliefs which
they associate with it.   All over northern and central
Germany, from Altmark and Anhalt on the east, through
Brunswick, Hanover, Oldenburg, the Harz district, and Hesse
to Westphalia the Easter bonfires still blaze simultaneously
on the hill-tops.   As many as forty may sometimes be
counted within sight at once.   Long before Easter the
young people have been busy collecting firewood ; every
farmer contributes, and tar-barrels, petroleum cases, and so
forth go to swell the pile.   Neighbouring villages vie with
each other as to which shall send up the greatest blaze.   The
fires are always kindled, year after year, on the same hill,
which accordingly often takes the name of Easter Mountain.
It is a fine spectacle to watch from some eminence the bonfires flaring up one after another on the neighbouring heights.
As far as their light reaches, so far, in the belief of the
peasants, the fields will be fruitful, and the houses on which
they shine will be safe from conflagration or sickness.   At
Volkmarsen and other places in Hesse the people used to
observe which way the wind blew the flames, and then they
sowed flax seed in that direction, confident that it would grow
well.   Brands taken from the bonfires preserve houses from

being struck by lightning ; and the ashes increase the fertility of the fields, protect them from mice, and mixed with the drinking-water of cattle make the animals thrive and ensure them against plague. As the flames die down, young and old leap over them, and cattle are sometimes driven through the smouldering embers. In some places tar-barrels or wheels wrapt in straw used to be set on fire, and then sent rolling down the hillside. In others the boys light torches and wisps of straw at the bonfires and rush about brandishing them in their hands. Where the people are divided between Protestantism and Catholicism, as in Hildesheim, it has been observed that among Protestants the Easter bonfires are generally left to the boys, while in Catholic districts they are cared for by grown-up persons, and here the whole population will gather round the blazing pile and join in singing choral hymns, which echo far and wide in the stillness of night.[1]

In Münsterland these Easter fires are always kindled upon certain definite hills, which are hence known as Easter or Paschal Mountains. The whole community assembles about the fire. Fathers of families form an inner circle round it. An outer circle is composed of the young men and maidens, who, singing Easter hymns, march round and round the fire in the direction of the sun, till the blaze dies down. Then the girls jump over the fire in a line, one after the other, each supported by two young men who hold her hands and run beside her. When the fire has burned out, the whole assembly marches in solemn procession to the church, singing hymns. They go thrice round the church, and then break up. In the twilight boys with

The Easter fires in Münsterland, Oldenburg the Harz Mountains and the Altmark.

[1] A. Kuhn und W. Schwartz, *Norddeutsche Sagen, Märchen und Gebräuche* (Leipsic, 1848), p. 373 ; A. Kuhn, *Sagen, Gebräuche und Märchen aus Westfalen* (Leipsic, 1859), ii. 134 *sqq.* ; *id.*, *Märkische Sagen und Märchen* (Berlin, 1843), pp. 312 *sq.* ; J. D. H. Temme, *Die Volkssagen der Altmark* (Berlin, 1839), pp. 75 *sq.* ; K. Lynker, *Deutsche Sagen und Sitten in hessischen Gauen* [2] (Cassel and Göttingen, 1860), p. 240 ; H. Pröhle, *Harzbilder* (Leipsic, 1855), p. 63 ; R. Andree, *Braunschweiger Volkskunde* (Brunswick, 1896), pp. 240-242 ; W. Kolbe, *Hessische Volks-Sitten und Gebräuche* (Marburg, 1888), pp. 44-47; F. A. Reimann, *Deutsche Volksfeste* (Weimar, 1839), p. 37 ; " Sitten und Gebräuche in Duderstadt," *Zeitschrift für deutsche Mythologie und Sittenkunde*, ii. (1855) p. 107 ; K. Seifart, *Sagen, Märchen, Schwänke und Gebräuche aus Stadt und Stift Hildesheim* [2] (Hildesheim, 1889), pp. 177, 180 ; O. Hartung, "Zur Volkskunde aus Anhalt," *Zeitschrift des Vereins für Volkskunde*, vii. (1897) p. 76.

blazing bundles of straw run over the fields to make them fruitful.[1] At Delmenhorst, in Oldenburg, it used to be the custom to cut down two trees, plant them in the ground side by side, and pile twelve tar-barrels, one above the other, against each of the trees. Brushwood was then heaped about the trees, and on the evening of Easter Saturday the boys, after rushing about with blazing bean-poles in their hands, set fire to the whole. At the end of the ceremony the urchins tried to blacken each other and the clothes of grown-up people.[2] In Schaumburg the Easter bonfires may be seen blazing on all the mountains around for miles. They are made with a tar-barrel fastened to a pine-tree, which is wrapt in straw. The people dance singing round them.[3] In the Harz Mountains the fire is commonly made by piling brushwood about a tree and setting it on fire. At Osterode every one tries to snatch a brand from the bonfire and runs about with it ; the better it burns, the more lucky it is. In Grund there are torch-races.[4] In the Altmark the Easter bonfires are composed of tar-barrels, bee-hives, and so forth, piled round a pole. The young folk dance round the fire ; and when it has died out, the old folk come and collect the ashes, which they preserve as a remedy for the ailments of bees. It is also believed that as far as the blaze of the bonfire is visible, the corn will grow well throughout the year, and no conflagration will break out.[5] At Braunröde, in the Harz Mountains, it was the custom to burn squirrels in the Easter bonfire.[6] In the Altmark, bones were burned in it.[7]

[1] L. Strackerjan, *Aberglaube und Sagen aus dem Herzogthum Oldenburg* (Oldenburg, 1867), ii. pp. 43 *sq.*, § 313; W. Mannhardt, *Der Baumkultus der Germanen und ihrer Nachbarstämme* (Berlin, 1875), pp. 505 *sq.*

[2] L. Strackerjan, *op. cit.* ii. p. 43, § 313.

[3] J. Grimm, *Deutsche Mythologie,*[4] (Berlin, 1875–1878), i. 512; W. Mannhardt, *Der Baumkultus der Germanen und ihrer Nachbarstämme*, pp. 506 *sq.*

[4] H. Pröhle, *Harzbilder* (Leipsic, 1855), p. 63; *id.*, in *Zeitschrift für deutsche Mythologie und Sittenkunde*, i. (1853) p. 79; A. Kuhn und W.

Schwartz, *Norddeutsche Sagen, Märchen und Gebräuche* (Leipsic, 1848), p. 373; W. Mannhardt, *Der Baumkultus*, p. 507.

[5] A. Kuhn, *Märkische Sagen una Märchen* (Berlin, 1843), pp. 312 *sq.* ; W. Mannhardt, *l.c.*

[6] W. Mannhardt, *Der Baumkultus*, p. 508. Compare J. W. Wolf, *Beiträge zur deutschen Mythologie* (Göttingen, 1852–1857), i. 74; J. Grimm, *Deutsche Mythologie,*[4] i. 512. The two latter writers only state that before the fires were kindled it was customary to hunt squirrels in the woods.

[7] A. Kuhn, *l.c.* ; W. Mannhardt, *Der Baumkultus*, p. 508.

Further south the Easter fires are, or used to be, lit in many districts of Bavaria.   Thus on Easter Monday in some parts of Middle Franken the schoolboys collect all the old worn-out besoms they can lay hands on, and march with them in a long procession to a neighbouring height.   When the first chime of the evening bell comes up from the dale they set fire to the brooms, and run along the ridges waving them, so that seen from below the hills appear to be crested with a twinkling and moving chain of fire.[1]   In some parts of Upper Bavaria at Easter burning arrows or discs of wood were shot from hill-tops high into the air, as in the Swabian and Swiss customs already described.[2]   At Oberau, instead of the discs, an old cart-wheel was sometimes wrapt in straw, ignited, and sent rolling and blazing down the mountain.   The lads who hurled the discs received painted Easter eggs from the girls.[3]   Near Forchheim, in Upper Franken, a straw-man called the Judas used to be burned in the churchyards on Easter Saturday.   The whole village contributed wood to the pyre on which he perished, and the charred sticks were afterwards kept and planted in the fields on Walpurgis Day (the first of May) to preserve the wheat from blight and mildew.[4]   About a hundred years ago or more the custom at Althenneberg, in Upper Bavaria, used to be as follows.   On the afternoon of Easter Saturday the lads collected wood, which they piled in a cornfield, while in the middle of the pile they set up a tall wooden cross all swathed in straw. After the evening service they lighted their lanterns at the consecrated candle in the church, and ran with them at full speed to the pyre, each striving to get there first.   The first to arrive set fire to the heap.   No woman or girl might come near the bonfire, but they were allowed to watch it from a distance.   As the flames rose the men and lads rejoiced and made merry, shouting, " We are burning the Judas ! "   Two of them had to watch the glowing embers the whole night long, lest people should come and steal them.   Next morning at sunrise they carefully collected the

---

[1] *Bavaria, Landes- und Volkskunde des Königreichs Bayern* (Munich, 1860–1867), iii. 956.

[2] See above, pp. 116 *sq.*, 119.

[3] F. Panzer, *Beitrag zur deutschen Mythologie* (Munich, 1848–1855), i. pp. 211 *sq.*, § 233 ; W. Mannhardt, *Der Baumkultus*, pp. 507 *sq.*

[4] *Bavaria, Landes- und Volkskunde des Königreichs Bayern*, iii. 357.

ashes, and threw them into the running water of the Röten brook. The man who had been the first to reach the pyre and to kindle it was rewarded on Easter Sunday by the women, who gave him coloured eggs at the church door. Well-to-do women gave him two ; poorer women gave him only one. The object of the whole ceremony was to keep off the hail. About a century ago the Judas fire, as it was called, was put down by the police.[1] At Giggenhausen and Aufkirchen, two other villages of Upper Bavaria, a similar custom prevailed, yet with some interesting differences.

Here the ceremony, which took place between nine and ten at night on Easter Saturday, was called "burning the Easter Man." On a height about a mile from the village the young fellows set up a tall cross enveloped in straw, so that it looked like a man with his arms stretched out. This was the Easter Man. No lad under eighteen years of age might take part in the ceremony. One of the young men stationed himself beside the Easter Man, holding in his hand a consecrated taper which he had brought from the church and lighted. The rest stood at equal intervals in a great circle round the cross. At a given signal they raced thrice round the circle, and then at a second signal ran straight at the cross and at the lad with the lighted taper beside it ; the one who reached the goal first had the right of setting fire to the Easter Man. Great was the jubilation while he was burning. When he had been consumed in the flames, three lads were chosen from among the rest, and each of the three drew a circle on the ground with a stick thrice round the ashes. Then they all left the spot. On Easter Monday the villagers gathered the ashes and strewed them on their fields ; also they planted in the fields palm-branches which had been consecrated on Palm Sunday, and sticks which had been charred and hallowed on Good Friday, all for the purpose of protecting their fields against showers of hail. The custom of burning an Easter Man made of straw on Easter Saturday was observed also at Abensberg, in Lower Bavaria.[2] In some parts of Swabia the Easter fires might

[1] F. Panzer, *Beitrag zur deutschen Mythologie* (Munich, 1848–1855), i. pp. 212 *sq.*, § 236.

[2] F. Panzer, *op. cit.* ii. pp. 78 *sq.*,

§§ 114, 115. The customs observed at these places and at Althenneberg are described together by W. Mannhardt, *Der Baumkultus*, p. 505.

not be kindled with iron or steel or flint, but only by the friction of wood.[1]

The Easter fires in Baden.

In Baden bonfires are still kindled in the churchyards on Easter Saturday, and ecclesiastical refuse of various sorts, such as candle-ends, old surplices, and the wool used by the priest in the application of extreme unction, is consumed in the flames. At Zoznegg down to about 1850 the fire was lighted by the priest by means of a flint which had never been used before. People bring sticks, especially oaken sticks, char them in the fire, and then carry them home and keep them in the house as a preservative against lightning. At Zoznegg these oaken sticks were sword-shaped, each about an ell and a half long, and they went by the name of " weather or thunder poles " (*Wetterpfähle*). When a thunder-storm threatened to break out, one of the sticks was put into a small fire, in order that the hallowed smoke, ascending to the clouds, might ward off the lightning from the house and the hail from the fields and gardens. At Schöllbronn the oaken sticks, which are thus charred in the Easter bonfire and kept in the house as a protective against thunder and lightning, are three in number, perhaps with an allusion to the Trinity ; they are brought every Easter to be consecrated afresh in the bonfire, till they are quite burnt away. In the lake district of Baden it is also customary to burn one of these holy sticks in the fire when a heavy thunderstorm is raging.[2] Hence it seems that the ancient association of the oak with the thunder[3] persists in the minds of German peasants to the present day.

" Thunder poles."

Easter fires in Holland and Sweden.

Thus the custom of the Easter fires appears to have prevailed all over central and western Germany from north to south. We find it also in Holland, where the fires were kindled on the highest eminences, and the people danced round them and leaped through the flames or over the glowing embers. Here too, as so often in Germany, the materials for the bonfire were collected by the young folk

[1] A. Birlinger, *Volksthümliches aus Schwaben* (Freiburg im Breisgau, 1861-1862), ii. p. 82, § 106 ; W. Mann-hardt, *Der Baumkultus*, p. 508.

[2] Elard Hugo Meyer, *Badisches*

Volksleben (Strasburg, 1900), pp. 97 sq.

[3] *The Magic Art and the Evolution of Kings*, ii. 349 *sqq.* See further below, vol. ii. pp. 298 *sqq.*

from door to door.[1] In many parts of Sweden firearms are, as at Athens, discharged in all directions on Easter eve, and huge bonfires are lighted on hills and eminences. Some people think that the intention is to keep off the Troll and other evil spirits who are especially active at this season.[2]

The burn-
ing of
Judas in
Bohemia. When the afternoon service on Good Friday is over, German children in Bohemia drive Judas out of the church by running about the sacred edifice and even the streets shaking rattles and clappers. Next day, on Easter Saturday, the remains of the holy oil are burnt before the church door in a fire which must be kindled with flint and steel. This fire is called "the burning of Judas," but in spite of its evil name a beneficent virtue is ascribed to it, for the people scuffle for the cinders, which they put in the roofs of their houses as a safeguard against fire and lightning.[3]

§ 3. *The Beltane Fires*

The
Beltane
fires on the
first of May
in the
Highlands
of Scot-
land. In the central Highlands of Scotland bonfires, known as the Beltane fires, were formerly kindled with great ceremony on the first of May, and the traces of human sacrifices at them were particularly clear and unequivocal. The custom of lighting the bonfires lasted in various places far into the eighteenth century, and the descriptions of the ceremony by writers of that period present such a curious and interesting picture of ancient heathendom surviving in our own country that I will reproduce them in the words of their authors.

Descrip-
tion of the
Beltane
fires by The fullest of the descriptions, so far as I know, is the one bequeathed to us by John Ramsay, laird of Ochtertyre, near Crieff, the patron of Burns and the friend of Sir

---

[1] J. W. Wolf, *Beiträge zur deutschen Mythologie*, i. 75 *sq.* ; W. Mannhardt, *Der Baumkultus*, p. 506.

[2] L. Lloyd, *Peasant Life in Sweden* (London, 1870), p. 228.

[3] W. Müller, *Beiträge zur Volks-kunde der Deutschen in Mähren* (Vienna and Olmütz, 1893), pp. 321, 397 *sq.* In Wagstadt, a town of Austrian Silesia, a boy in a red waistcoat used to play the part of Judas on the Wednesday before Good Friday. He was

chased from before the church door by the other school children, who pursued him through the streets with shouts and the noise of rattles and clappers till they reached a certain suburb, where they always caught and beat him because he had betrayed the Redeemer. See Anton Peter, *Volks-thümliches aus österreichisch-Schlesien* (Troppau, 1865–1867), ii. 282 *sq.* ; Paul Drechsler, *Sitte, Brauch und Volksglaube in Schlesien* (Leipsic, 1903–1906), i. 77 *sq.*

Walter Scott. From his voluminous manuscripts, written in John Ramsay of Ochtertyre in the eighteenth century. the last quarter of the eighteenth century, a selection was published in the latter part of the nineteenth century. The following account of Beltane is extracted from a chapter dealing with Highland superstitions. Ramsay says : " But the most considerable of the Druidical festivals is that of Beltane, or May-day, which was lately observed in some parts of the Highlands with extraordinary ceremonies. Of later years it is chiefly attended to by young people, persons advanced in years considering it as inconsistent with their gravity to give it any countenance. Yet a number of circumstances relative to it may be collected from tradition, or the conversation of very old people, who witnessed this feast in their youth, when the ancient rites were better observed.

" This festival is called in Gaelic *Beal-tene—i.e.*, the fire of Bel. . . . Like the other public worship of the Druids, the Beltane feast seems to have been performed on hills or eminences. They thought it degrading to him whose temple is the universe, to suppose that he would dwell in any house made with hands. Their sacrifices were therefore offered in the open air, frequently upon the tops of hills, where they were presented with the grandest views of nature, and were nearest the seat of warmth and order. And, according to tradition, such was the manner of celebrating this festival in the Highlands within the last hundred years. But since the decline of superstition, it has been celebrated by the people of each hamlet on some hill or rising ground around which their cattle were pasturing. Thither the young folks repaired in the morning, and cut a trench, on the summit of which a seat of turf was formed for the company. And in the middle a pile of wood or other fuel was placed, which of old they kindled with *tein-eigin — i.e.*, forced-fire or *need-fire*. Need fire Although, for many years past, they have been contented with common fire, yet we shall now describe the process, because it will hereafter appear that recourse is still had to the *tein-eigin* upon extraordinary emergencies.

" The night before, all the fires in the country were Need-fire kindled by the friction of oak wood. carefully extinguished, and next morning the materials for exciting this sacred fire were prepared. The most primitive method seems to be that which was used in the islands of

Skye, Mull, and Tiree. A well-seasoned plank of oak was procured, in the midst of which a hole was bored. A wimble of the same timber was then applied, the end of which they fitted to the hole. But in some parts of the mainland the machinery was different. They used a frame of green wood, of a square form, in the centre of which was an axle-tree. In some places three times three persons, in others three times nine, were required for turning round by turns the axle-tree or wimble. If any of them had been guilty of murder, adultery, theft, or other atrocious crime, it was imagined either that the fire would not kindle, or that it would be devoid of its usual virtue. So soon as any sparks were emitted by means of the violent friction, they applied a species of agaric which grows on old birch-trees, and is very combustible. This fire had the appearance of being immediately derived from heaven, and manifold were the virtues ascribed to it. They esteemed it a preservative against witchcraft, and a sovereign remedy against malignant diseases, both in the human species and in cattle ; and by it the strongest poisons were supposed to have their nature changed.

The Beltane cake and the Beltane carline (*cailleach*).

" After kindling the bonfire with the *tein-eigin* the company prepared their victuals. And as soon as they had finished their meal, they amused themselves a while in singing and dancing round the fire. Towards the close of the entertainment, the person who officiated as master of the feast produced a large cake baked with eggs and scalloped round the edge, called *am bonnach beal-tine—i.e.*, the Beltane cake. It was divided into a number of pieces, and distributed in great form to the company. There was one particular piece which whoever got was called *cailleach beal-tine—i.e.*, the Beltane *carline*, a term of great reproach. Upon his being known, part of the company laid hold of him and made a show of putting him into the fire ; but the majority interposing, he was rescued. And in some places they laid him flat on the ground, making as if they would quarter him. Afterwards, he was pelted with egg-shells, and retained the odious appellation during the whole year. And while the feast was fresh in people's memory, they affected to speak of the *cailleach beal-tine* as dead.

"This festival was longest observed in the interior Local differences in the Beltane cakes. Highlands, for towards the west coast the traces of it are faintest. In Glenorchy and Lorne, a large cake is made on that day, which they consume in the house ; and in Mull it has a large hole in the middle, through which each of the cows in the fold is milked. In Tiree it is of a triangular form. The more elderly people remember when this festival was celebrated without-doors with some solemnity in both these islands. There are at present no vestiges of it in Skye or the Long Island, the inhabitants of which have substituted the *connach Micheil* or St. Michael's cake. It is made at Michaelmas with milk and oatmeal, and some eggs are sprinkled on its surface. Part of it is sent to the neighbours.

"It is probable that at the original Beltane festival there Evidence of two fires at Beltane. were two fires kindled near one another. When any person is in a critical dilemma, pressed on each side by unsurmountable difficulties, the Highlanders have a proverb, *The e' eada anda theine bealtuin*—*i.e.*, he is between the two Beltane fires. There are in several parts small round hills, which, it is like, owe their present names to such solemn uses. One of the highest and most central in Icolmkil is called *Cnoch-nan-ainneal*—*i.e.*, the hill of the fires. There is another of the same name near the kirk of Balquhidder ; and at Killin there is a round green eminence which seems to have been raised by art. It is called *Tom - nan - ainneal*—*i.e.*, the eminence of the fires. Around it there are the remains of a circular wall about two feet high. On the top a stone stands upon end. According to the tradition of the inhabitants, it was a place of Druidical worship ; and it was afterwards pitched on as the most venerable spot for holding courts of justice for the country of Breadalbane. The earth of this eminence is still thought to be possessed of some healing virtue, for when cattle are observed to be diseased some of it is sent for, which is rubbed on the part affected." [1]

[1] *Scotland and Scotsmen in the Eighteenth Century*, from the MSS. of John Ramsay, Esq., of Ochtertyre, edited by Alexander Allardyce (Edinburgh and London, 1888), ii. 439-445. As to the *tein-eigin* or need- fire, see below, pp. 269 *sqq*. The etymology of the word Beltane is uncertain ; the popular derivation of the first part from the Phoenician Baal is absurd. See, for example, John Graham Dalyell, *The Darker Super-*

In the parish of Callander, a beautiful district of western Perthshire, the Beltane custom was still in vogue towards the end of the eighteenth century. It has been described as follows by the parish minister of the time: "Upon the first day of May, which is called *Beltan*, or *Bal-tein* day, all the boys in a township or hamlet, meet in the moors. They cut a table in the green sod, of a round figure, by casting a trench in the ground, of such circumference as to hold the whole company. They kindle a fire, and dress a repast of eggs and milk in the consistence of a custard. They knead a cake of oatmeal, which is toasted at the embers against a stone. After the custard is eaten up, they divide the cake into so many portions, as similar as possible to one another in size and shape, as there are persons in the company. They daub one of these portions all over with charcoal, until it be perfectly black. They put all the bits of the cake into a bonnet. Every one, blindfold, draws out a portion. He who holds the bonnet, is entitled to the last bit. Whoever draws the black bit, is the *devoted* person who is to be sacrificed to *Baal*,[1] whose favour they mean to implore, in

---

stitions of Scotland (Edinburgh, 1834), pp. 176 *sq.* : " The recognition of the pagan divinity Baal, or Bel, the Sun, is discovered through innumerable etymological sources. In the records of Scottish history, down to the sixteenth or seventeenth centuries, multiplied prohibitions were issued from the fountains of ecclesiastical ordinances, against kindling *Bailfires*, of which the origin cannot be mistaken. The festival of this divinity was commemorated in Scotland until the latest date." Modern scholars are not agreed as to the derivation of the name Beltane. See Rev. John Gregorson Campbell, *Witchcraft and Second Sight in the Highlands and Islands of Scotland* (Glasgow, 1902), pp. 268 *sq.* ; J. A. MacCulloch, *The Religion of the Ancient Celts* (Edinburgh, 1911), p. 264.

[1] "*Bal-tein* signifies the *fire of Baal. Baal* or *Ball* is the only word in Gaelic for *a globe*. This festival was probably in honour of the sun, whose return, in his apparent annual course, they cele-

brated, on account of his having such a visible influence, by his genial warmth, on the productions of the earth. That the Caledonians paid a superstitious respect to the sun, as was the practice among many other nations, is evident, not only by the sacrifice at Baltein, but upon many other occasions. When a Highlander goes to bathe, or to drink waters out of a consecrated fountain, he must always approach by going round the place, *from east to west on the south side*, in imitation of the apparent diurnal motion of the sun. When the dead are laid in the earth, the grave is approached by going round in the same manner. The bride is conducted to her future spouse, in the presence of the minister, and the glass goes round a company, in the course of the sun. This is called, in Gaelic, going round the right, or the *lucky way*. The opposite course is the wrong, or the *unlucky* way. And if a person's meat or drink were to affect the wind-pipe, or come against his breath, they instantly cry out *deisheal !*

rendering the year productive of the sustenance of man and

which is an ejaculation praying that it may go by the right way" (Rev. J. Robertson, in Sir John Sinclair's *Statistical Account of Scotland*, xi. 621 note). Compare J. G. Campbell, *Superstitions of the Highlands and Islands of Scotland* (Glasgow, 1900), pp. 229 *sq.* : "*The Right-hand Turn (Deiseal)*.—This was the most important of all the observances. The rule is ' *Deiseal (i.e.* the right-hand turn) for everything,' and consists in doing all things with a motion corresponding to the course of the sun, or from left to right. This is the manner in which screw-nails are driven, and is common with many for no reason but its convenience. Old men in the Highlands were very particular about it. The coffin was taken *deiseal* about the grave, when about to be lowered ; boats were turned to sea according to it, and drams are given to the present day to a company. When putting a straw rope on a house or corn-stack, if the assistant went *tuaitheal* (*i.e.* against the course of the sun), the old man was ready to come down and thrash him. On coming to a house the visitor should go round it *deiseal* to secure luck in the object of his visit. After milking a cow the dairy-maid should strike it *deiseal* with the shackle, saying ' out and home' (*mach 'us dachaigh*). This secures its safe return. The word is from *deas*, right-hand, and *iul*, direction, and of itself contains no allusion to the sun." Compare M. Martin, "Description of the Western Islands of Scotland," in J. Pinkerton's *Voyages and Travels*, iii. 612 *sq.*: "There was an ancient custom in the island of Lewis, to make a fiery circle about the houses, corn, cattle, etc., belonging to each particular family : a man carried fire in his right hand, and went round, and it was called *dessil*, from the right hand, which in the ancient language is called *dess.* . . . There is another way of the *dessil*, or carrying fire round about women before they are churched, after child-bearing ; and it is used likewise about children until they are christened; both which are performed in the morn-

ing and at night. This is only practised now by some of the ancient midwives : I enquired their reason for this custom, which I told them was altogether unlawful ; this disobliged them mightily, insomuch that they would give me no satisfaction. But others, that were of a more agreeable temper, told me that fire-round was an effectual means to preserve both the mother and the infant from the power of evil spirits, who are ready at such times to do mischief, and sometimes carry away the infant ; and when they get them once in their possession, return them poor meagre skeletons ; and these infants are said to have voracious appetites, constantly craving for meat. In this case it was usual with those who believed that their children were thus taken away, to dig a grave in the fields upon quarter-day, and there to lay the fairy skeleton till next morning ; at which time the parents went to the place, where they doubted not to find their own child instead of this skeleton. Some of the poorer sort of people in these islands retain the custom of performing these rounds sunways about the persons of their benefactors three times, when they bless them, and wish good success to all their enterprizes. Some are very careful when they set out to sea that the boat be first rowed about sun-ways ; and if this be neglected, they are afraid their voyage may prove unfortunate." Probably the superstition was based entirely on the supposed luckiness of the right hand, which accordingly, in making a circuit round an object, is kept towards the centre. As to a supposed worship of the sun among the Scottish Highlanders, compare J. G. Campbell, *Witchcraft and Second Sight in the Highlands and Islands of Scotland*, p. 304 : " Both the sun (*a Ghrian*) and moon (*a Ghealach*) are feminine in Gaelic, and the names are simply descriptive of their appearance. There is no trace of a Sun-God or Moon-Goddess." As to the etymology of Beltane, see above, p. 149 note.

beast.   There is little doubt of these inhuman sacrifices having been once offered in this country, as well as in the east, although they now pass from the act of sacrificing, and only compel the *devoted* person to leap three times through the flames ; with which the ceremonies of this festival are closed."[1]

Pennant's
description
of the
Beltane
fires and
cakes in
Perthshire.

Thomas Pennant, who travelled in Perthshire in the year 1769, tells us that " on the first of May, the herdsmen of every village hold their Bel-tien, a rural sacrifice. They cut a square trench on the ground, leaving the turf in the middle ; on that they make a fire of wood, on which they dress a large caudle of eggs, butter, oatmeal and milk ; and bring besides the ingredients of the caudle, plenty of beer and whisky ; for each of the company must contribute something.   The rites begin with spilling some of the caudle on the ground, by way of libation : on that every one takes a cake of oatmeal, upon which are raised nine square knobs, each dedicated to some particular being, the supposed pre-server of their flocks and herds, or to some particular animal, the real destroyer of them : each person then turns his face to the fire, breaks off a knob, and flinging it over his shoulders, says, ' This I give to thee, preserve thou my horses ; this to thee, preserve thou my sheep ; and so on.'   After that, they use the same ceremony to the noxious animals : ' This I give to thee, O fox ! spare thou my lambs ; this to thee, O hooded crow ! this to thee, O eagle !'   When the ceremony is over, they dine on the caudle ; and after the feast is finished, what is left is hid by two persons deputed for that purpose ; but on the next Sunday they re-assemble, and finish the reliques of the first entertainment."[2]

Beltane
cakes and
fires in the
parishes of
Logierait
and Kirk-
michael.

Another writer of the eighteenth century has described the Beltane festival as it was held in the parish of Logierait in Perthshire.   He says : " On the first of May, O.S., a festival called *Beltan* is annually held here.   It is chiefly celebrated by the cow-herds, who assemble by scores in the fields, to dress a dinner for themselves, of boiled milk

[1] Rev. James Robertson (Parish Minister of Callander), in Sir John Sinclair's *Statistical Account of Scotland* (Edinburgh, 1791–1799), xi. 620 *sq.*

[2] Pennant's "Tour in Scotland," in John Pinkerton's *Voyages and Travels* (London, 1808–1814), iii. 49.

and eggs. These dishes they eat with a sort of cakes baked for the occasion, and having small lumps in the form of *nipples*, raised all over the surface." [1]   In this last account no mention is made of bonfires, but they were probably lighted, for a contemporary writer informs us that in the parish of Kirkmichael, which adjoins the parish of Logierait on the east, the custom of lighting a fire in the fields and baking a consecrated cake on the first of May was not quite obsolete in his time. [2]   We may conjecture that the cake with knobs was formerly used for the purpose of determining who should be the " Beltane carline " or victim doomed to the flames.   A trace of this custom survived, perhaps, in the custom of baking oatmeal cakes of a special kind and rolling them down hill about noon on the first of May ; for it was thought that the person whose cake broke as it rolled would die or be unfortunate within the year.   These cakes, or bannocks as we call them in Scotland, were baked in the usual way, but they were washed over with a thin batter composed of whipped egg, milk or cream, and a little oatmeal.   This custom appears to have prevailed at or near Kingussie in Inverness-shire.   At Achterneed, near Strathpeffer in Ross-shire, the Beltane bannocks were called *tcharnican* or hand-cakes, because they were kneaded entirely in the hand, and not on a board or table like common cakes ; and after being baked they might not be placed anywhere but in the hands of the children who were to eat them. [3]

Omens drawn from the cakes.

In the north-east of Scotland the Beltane fires were still kindled in the latter half of the eighteenth century ; the herdsmen of several farms used to gather dry wood, kindle it, and dance three times "southways" about the burning

Beltane fires in the north-east of Scotland to burn the witches.

[1] Rev. Dr. Thomas Bisset, in Sir John Sinclair's *Statistical Account of Scotland*, v. 84.

[2] Rev. Allan Stewart, in Sir John Sinclair's *Statistical Account of Scotland*, xv. 517 note.

[3] Rev. Walter Gregor, "Notes on Beltane Cakes," *Folk-lore*, vi. (1895) pp. 2 *sq.* The Beltane cakes with the nine knobs on them remind us of the cakes with twelve knobs which the Athenians offered to Cronus and other deities (see *The Scapegoat*, p. 351). The King of the Bean on Twelfth Night was chosen by means of a cake, which was broken in as many pieces as there were persons present, and the person who received the piece containing a bean or a coin became king. See J. Boemus, *Mores, leges et ritus omnium gentium* (Lyons, 1541), p. 222 ; John Brand, *Popular Antiquities of Great Britain* (London, 1882–1883), i. 22 *sq.* ; *The Scapegoat*, pp. 313 *sqq.*

pile.[1]   But in this region, according to a later authority, the Beltane fires were lit not on the first but on the second of May, Old Style.   They were called bone-fires.   The people believed that on that evening and night the witches were abroad and busy casting spells on cattle and stealing cows' milk.   To counteract their machinations, pieces of rowan-tree and woodbine, but especially of rowan-tree, were placed over the doors of the cow-houses, and fires were kindled by every farmer and cottar.   Old thatch, straw, furze, or broom was piled in a heap and set on fire a little after sunset. While some of the bystanders kept tossing the blazing mass, others hoisted portions of it on pitchforks or poles and ran hither and thither, holding them as high as they could. Meantime the young people danced round the fire or ran through the smoke shouting, " Fire ! blaze and burn the witches ; fire ! fire ! burn the witches."   In some districts a large round cake of oat or barley meal was rolled through the ashes.   When all the fuel was consumed, the people scattered the ashes far and wide, and till the night grew quite dark they continued to run through them, crying, " Fire ! burn the witches." [2]

In the Hebrides " the Beltane bannock is smaller than that made at St. Michael's, but is made in the same way ; it is no longer made in Uist, but Father Allan remembers seeing his grandmother make one about twenty-five years ago.   There was also a cheese made, generally on the first of May, which was kept to the next Beltane as a sort of charm against the bewitching of milk-produce.   The Beltane customs seem to have been the same as elsewhere. Every fire was put out and a large one lit on the top of the hill, and the cattle driven round it sunwards (*dessil*), to keep off murrain all the year.   Each man would take home fire wherewith to kindle his own." [3]

Burning the witches.

The Beltane cake.

Beltane cakes and fires in the Hebrides.

[1] Shaw, in Pennant's " Tour in Scotland," printed in J. Pinkerton's *Voyages and Travels*, iii. 136.   The part of Scotland to which Shaw's description applies is what he calls the province or country of Murray, extending from the river Spey on the east to the river Beauly on the west, and south-west to Loch Lochy.

[2] Rev. Walter Gregor, *Notes on the Folk-lore of the North-East of Scotland* (London, 1881), p. 167.
[3] A. Goodrich-Freer, " More Folk-lore from the Hebrides," *Folk-lore*, xiii. (1902) p. 41.   The St. Michael's cake (*Strùthan na h'eill Micheil*), referred to in the text, is described as " the size of a quern " in circumference.

In Wales also the custom of lighting Beltane fires at
the beginning of May used to be observed, but the day on
which they were kindled varied from the Eve of May Day
to the third of May.   The flame was sometimes elicited by
the friction of two pieces of oak, as appears from the following description.   "The fire was done in this way.   Nine
men would turn their pockets inside out, and see that every
piece of money and all metals were off their persons.
Then the men went into the nearest woods, and collected
sticks of nine different kinds of trees.   These were carried
to the spot where the fire had to be built.   There a circle
was cut in the sod, and the sticks were set crosswise.   All
around the circle the people stood and watched the proceedings.   One of the men would then take two bits of oak,
and rub them together until a flame was kindled.   This
was applied to the sticks, and soon a large fire was made.
Sometimes two fires were set up side by side.   These fires,
whether one or two, were called *coelcerth* or bonfire.   Round
cakes of oatmeal and brown meal were split in four, and
placed in a small flour-bag, and everybody present had to
pick out a portion.   The last bit in the bag fell to the lot
of the bag-holder.   Each person who chanced to pick up a
piece of brown-meal cake was compelled to leap three times
over the flames, or to run thrice between the two fires, by
which means the people thought they were sure of a
plentiful harvest.   Shouts and screams of those who had
to face the ordeal could be heard ever so far, and those who
chanced to pick the oatmeal portions sang and danced and
clapped their hands in approval, as the holders of the
brown bits leaped three times over the flames, or ran three
times between the two fires.   As a rule, no danger attended

" It is kneaded simply with water, and
marked across like a scone, dividing
it into four equal parts, and then placed
in front of the fire resting on a quern.
It is not polished with dry meal as is
usual in making a cake, but when it is
cooked a thin coating of eggs (four in
number), mixed with buttermilk, is
spread first on one side, then on the
other, and it is put before the fire
again.   An earlier shape, still in use,
which tradition associates with the
female sex, is that of a triangle with
the corners cut off.   A *strùthan* or
strùdhan (the word seems to be used
for no other kind of cake) is made for
each member of the household, including servants and herds.   When harvest
is late, an early patch of corn is mown
on purpose for the *strùthan*" (A.
Goodrich-Freer, *op. cit.* pp. 44 *sq.*).

these curious celebrations, but occasionally somebody's clothes caught fire, which was quickly put out. The greatest fire of the year was the eve of May, or May first, second, or third. The Midsummer Eve fire was more for the harvest. Very often a fire was built on the eve of November. The high ground near the Castle Ditches at Llantwit Major, in the Vale of Glamorgan, was a familiar spot for the Beltane on May third and on Midsummer Eve. . . . Sometimes the Beltane fire was lighted by the flames produced by stone instead of wood friction. Charred logs and faggots used in the May Beltane were carefully preserved, and from them the next fire was lighted. May fires were always started with old faggots of the previous year, and midsummer from those of the last summer. It was unlucky to build a midsummer fire from May faggots. People carried the ashes left after these fires to their homes, and a charred brand was not only effectual against pestilence, but magical in its use. A few of the ashes placed in a person's shoes protected the wearer from any great sorrow or woe."[1]

Welsh belief that passage over or between the fires ensured good crops. From the foregoing account we learn that bonfires were kindled in Wales on Midsummer Eve and Hallowe'en (the thirty-first of October), as well as at the beginning of May, but that the Beltane fires in May were deemed the most important. To the Midsummer Eve and Hallowe'en fires we shall return presently. The belief of the people that by leaping thrice over the bonfires or running thrice between them they ensured a plentiful harvest is worthy of note. The mode in which this result was supposed to be brought about is indicated by another writer on Welsh folk-lore, according to whom it used to be held that "the bonfires lighted in May or Midsummer protected the lands from sorcery, so that good crops would follow. The ashes were also considered valuable as charms."[2] Hence it appears that the heat of the fires was thought to fertilize the fields, not directly by quickening the seeds in the ground, but indirectly by counteracting the baleful influence

---

[1] Marie Trevelyan, *Folk-lore and Folk-stories of Wales* (London, 1909), pp. 22-24.

[2] Jonathan Ceredig Davies, *Folk-lore of West and Mid-Wales* (Aberystwyth, 1911), p. 76.

of witchcraft or perhaps by burning up the persons of the witches.

"The Druidical anniversary of Beil or Baal is still celebrated in the Isle of Man. On the first of May, 1837, the Baal fires were, as usual on that day, so numerous as to give the island the appearance of a general conflagration."[1] By May Day in Manx folk-lore is meant May Day Old Style, or *Shenn Laa Boaldyn*, as it is called in Manx. The day was one on which the power of elves and witches was particularly dreaded, and the people resorted to many precautions in order to protect themselves against these mischievous beings. Hence at daybreak they set fire to the ling or gorse, for the purpose of burning out the witches, who are wont to lurk in the form of hares.[2] On the Hemlock Stone, a natural pillar of sandstone standing on Stapleford Hill in Nottinghamshire, a fire used to be solemnly kindled every year on Beltane Eve. The custom seems to have survived down to the beginning of the nineteenth century; old people could remember and describe the ceremony long after it had fallen into desuetude.[3]

The Beltane fires appear to have been kindled also in Ireland, for Cormac, "or somebody in his name, says that *belltaine*, May-day, was so called from the 'lucky fire,' or the 'two fires,' which the druids of Erin used to make on that day with great incantations; and cattle, he adds, used to be brought to those fires, or to be driven between them, as a safeguard against the diseases of the year."[4] Again, a very ancient Irish poem, enumerating the May Day celebrations, mentions among them a bonfire on a hill (*tendal ar cnuc*); and another old authority says that these fires were kindled in the name of the idol-god Bel.[5] From an old life of St. Patrick we learn that on a day

Marginal notes:
Beltane fires in the Isle of Man to burn the witches.

Beltane fires in Nottinghamshire

Beltane fires in Ireland.

[1] Joseph Train, *An Historical and Statistical Account of the Isle of Man* (Douglas, Isle of Man, 1845), i. 314 *sq.*

[2] (Sir) John Rhys, *Celtic Folk-lore, Welsh and Manx* (Oxford, 1901), i. 309; *id.*, "The Coligny Calendar," *Proceedings of the British Academy, 1909-1910*, pp. 261 *sq.* See further *The Magic Art and the Evolution of Kings*, ii. 53 *sq.*

[3] Professor Frank Granger, "Early Man," in *The Victoria History of the County of Nottingham*, edited by William Page, i. (London, 1906) pp. 186 *sq.*

[4] (Sir) John Rhys, *Celtic Folk-lore, Welsh and Manx* (Oxford, 1901), i. 310; *id.*, "Manx Folk-lore and Superstitions," *Folk-lore*, ii. (1891) pp. 303 *sq.*

[5] P. W. Joyce, *A Social History of Ancient Ireland* (London, 1903), i. 290 *sq.*, referring to Kuno Meyer, *Hibernia Minora*, p. 49 and *Glossary*, 23.

in spring the heathen of Ireland were wont to extinguish
all their fires until a new fire was kindled with solemn
ceremony in the king's house at Tara. In the year in
which St. Patrick landed in Ireland it chanced that the
night of the extinguished fires coincided with the Eve of
Easter ; and the saint, ignorant of this pagan superstition,
resolved to celebrate his first Easter in Ireland after the
true Christian fashion by lighting the holy Paschal fire on
the hill of Slane, which rises high above the left bank of the
Boyne, about twelve miles from the mouth of the river.
So that night, looking from his palace at Tara across the
darkened landscape, the king of Tara saw the solitary fire
flaring on the top of the hill of Slane, and in consternation he asked his wise men what that light meant. They
warned him of the danger that it betokened for the ancient
faith of Erin.[1] In spite of the difference of date between
Easter and Beltane, we may suspect that the new fire
annually kindled with solemn ceremony about Easter in the
king of Ireland's palace at Tara was no other than the Beltane
fire. We have seen that in the Highlands of Scotland down
to modern times it was customary to extinguish all fires
in the neighbourhood before proceeding to kindle the sacred
flame.[2] The Irish historian Geoffrey Keating, who wrote in
the first part of the seventeenth century, tells us that the men
of Ireland held a great fair every year in the month of May
at Uisnech (*Ushnagh*) in the county of Meath, "and at it
they were wont to exchange their goods and their wares and
their jewels. At it, they were, also, wont to make a sacrifice
to the Arch-God that they adored, whose name was Bèl
(*bayl*). It was, likewise, their usage to light two fires to Bèl,
in every district of Ireland, at this season, and to drive a pair
of each kind of cattle that the district contained, between
those two fires, as a preservative to guard them against all
the diseases of that year. It is from that fire, thus made in
honour of Bèl, that the day [the first of May] on which the
noble feast of the apostles, Philip and James, is held, has
been called Bèltaini, or Bèaltaine (*Bayltinnie*) ; for Beltaini
is the same as Bèil-teinè, *i.e.* Teiné Bhèil (*Tinnie Vayl*) or

[1] J. B. Bury, *The Life of St. Patrick* (London, 1905), pp. 104 *sqq.*
[2] Above, p. 147.

Bèl's Fire." [1]   The custom of driving cattle through or
between fires on May Day or the eve of May Day persisted
in Ireland down to a time within living memory.   Thus Sir
John Rhys was informed by a Manxman that an Irish cattle-
dealer of his acquaintance used to drive his cattle through
fire on May Day so as to singe them a little, since he believed
that it would preserve them from harm.   When the Manxman was asked where the dealer came from, he answered,
" From the mountains over there," pointing to the Mourne
Mountains then looming faintly in the mists on the western
horizon.[2]

The first of May is a great popular festival in the more
midland and southern parts of Sweden.   On the eve of the
festival, huge bonfires, which should be lighted by striking
two flints together, blaze on all the hills and knolls.   Every
large hamlet has its own fire, round which the young people
dance in a ring.   The old folk notice whether the flames
incline to the north or to the south.   In the former case, the
spring will be cold and backward ; in the latter, it will be
mild and genial.[3]   Similarly, in Bohemia, on the eve of
May Day, young people kindle fires on hills and eminences,
at crossways, and in pastures, and dance round them.   They
leap over the glowing embers or even through the flames.
The ceremony is called " burning the witches."   In some
places an effigy representing a witch used to be burnt in
the bonfire.[4]   We have to remember that the eve of May
Day is the notorious Walpurgis Night, when the witches are
everywhere speeding unseen· through the air on their hellish

*Fires on
the Eve of
May Day
in Sweden*

*Fires on
the Eve
of May
Day in
Austria
and Saxony
for the
purpose of
burning
the witches*

---

[1] Geoffrey Keating, D.D., *The
History of Ireland*, translated by John
O'Mahony (New York, 1857), pp.
300 *sq.*

[2] (Sir) John Rhys, " Manx Folk-lore
and Superstition," *Folk-lore*, ii. (1891)
p. 303 ; *id.*, *Celtic Folk-lore, Welsh
and Manx* (Oxford, 1901), i. 309.
Compare P. W. Joyce, *A Social History
of Ancient Ireland* (London, 1903), i.
291 : " The custom of driving cattle
through fires against disease on the eve
of the 1st of May, and on the eve of
the 24th June (St. John's Day), continued in Ireland, as well as in the
Scottish Highlands, to a period within

living memory." In a footnote Mr.
Joyce refers to Carmichael, *Carmina
Gadelica*, ii. 340, for Scotland, and
adds, " I saw it done in Ireland."

[3] L. Lloyd, *Peasant Life in Sweden*
(London, 1870), pp. 233 *sq.*

[4] Reinsberg - Düringsfeld, *Fest-Kalender aus Böhmen* (Prague, N.D.), pp.
211 *sq.* ; Br. Jelínek, " Materialien
zur Vorgeschichte und Volkskunde
Böhmens," *Mittheilungen der anthropologischen Gesellschaft in Wien*, xxi.
(1891) p. 13 ; Alois John, *Sitte,
Brauch, und Volksglaube im deutschen
Westböhmen* (Prague, 1905), p. 71.

errands. On this witching night children in Voigtland also light bonfires on the heights and leap over them. Moreover, they wave burning brooms or toss them into the air. So far as the light of the bonfire reaches, so far will a blessing rest on the fields. The kindling of the fires on Walpurgis Night is called "driving away the witches."[1] The custom of kindling fires on the eve of May Day (Walpurgis Night) for the purpose of burning the witches is, or used to be, widespread in the Tyrol, Moravia, Saxony and Silesia.[2]

§ 4. *The Midsummer Fires*

The great season for fire-festivals in Europe is the summer solstice, Midsummer Eve or Midsummer Day, which the church has dedicated to St. John the Baptist.

But the season at which these fire-festivals have been mostly generally held all over Europe is the summer solstice, that is Midsummer Eve (the twenty-third of June) or Midsummer Day (the twenty-fourth of June). A faint tinge of Christianity has been given to them by naming Midsummer Day after St. John the Baptist, but we cannot doubt that the celebration dates from a time long before the beginning of our era. The summer solstice, or Midsummer Day, is the great turning-point in the sun's career, when, after climbing higher and higher day by day in the sky, the luminary stops and thenceforth retraces his steps down the heavenly road. Such a moment could not but be regarded with anxiety by primitive man so soon as he began to observe and ponder the courses of the great lights across the celestial vault ; and having still to learn his own powerlessness in face of the vast cyclic changes of nature, he may have fancied that he could help the sun in his seeming decline—could prop his failing

[1] J. A. E. Köhler, *Volksbrauch, Aberglauben, Sagen und andre alte Ueberlieferungen im Voigtlande* (Leipsic, 1867), p. 373. The superstitions relating to witches at this season are legion. For instance, in Saxony and Thuringia any one who labours under a physical blemish can easily rid himself of it by transferring it to the witches on Walpurgis Night. He has only to go out to a cross-road, make three crosses on the blemish, and say, " In the name of God the Father, the Son, and the Holy Ghost." Thus the blemish, whatever it may be, is left behind him at the cross-road, and when the witches sweep by on their way to the Brocken, they must take it with them, and it sticks to them henceforth. Moreover, three crosses chalked up on the doors of houses and cattle-stalls on Walpurgis Night will effectually prevent any of the infernal crew from entering and doing harm to man or beast. See E. Sommer, *Sagen, Märchen und Gebräuche aus Sachsen und Thüringen* (Halle, 1846), pp. 148 *sq.* ; *Die gestriegelte Rockenphilosophie* (Chemnitz, 1759), p. 116.

[2] See *The Scapegoat*, pp. 158 *sqq.*

steps and rekindle the sinking flame of the red lamp in his feeble hand.   In some such thoughts as these the midsummer festivals of our European peasantry may perhaps have taken their rise.   Whatever their origin, they have prevailed all over this quarter of the globe, from Ireland on the west to Russia on the east, and from Norway and Sweden on the north to Spain and Greece on the south.[1]   According to a mediæval writer, the three great features of the midsummer celebration were the bonfires, the procession with torches round the fields, and the custom of rolling a wheel.   He tells us that boys burned bones and filth of various kinds to make a foul smoke, and that the smoke drove away certain noxious dragons which at this time, excited by the summer heat, copulated in the air and poisoned the wells and rivers by dropping their seed into them ; and he explains the custom of trundling a wheel to mean that the sun, having now reached the highest point in the ecliptic, begins thenceforward to descend.[2]

The bonfires, the torches, and the burning wheels of the festival.

[1] As to the Midsummer Festival of Europe in general see the evidence collected in the " Specimen Calendarii Gentilis," appended to the *Edda Rhythmica seu Antiquior, vulgo Saemundina dicta*, Pars iii. (Copenhagen, 1828) pp. 1086-1097.

[2] John Mitchell Kemble, *The Saxons in England*, New Edition (London, 1876), i. 361 *sq.*, quoting " an ancient MS. written in England, and now in the Harleian Collection, No. 2345, fol. 50." The passage is quoted in part by J. Brand, *Popular Antiquities of Great Britain* (London, 1882-1883), i. 298 *sq.*, by R. T. Hampson, *Medii Aevi Kalendarium* (London, 1841), i. 300, and by W. Mannhardt, *Der Baumkultus*, p. 509. The same explanations of the Midsummer fires and of the custom of trundling a burning wheel on Midsummer Eve are given also by John Beleth, a writer of the twelfth century.   See his *Rationale Divinorum Officiorum* (appended to the *Rationale Divinorum Officiorum* of G. [W.] Durandus, Lyons, 1584), p. 556 *recto* : " *Solent porro hoc tempore* [the Eve of St. John the Baptist] *ex veteri consuetudine mortuorum animalium ossa comburi, quod hujusmodi*

habet originem.   Sunt enim animalia, quae dracones appellamus. . . . Haec inquam animalia in aere volant, in aquis natant, in terra ambulant.   Sed quando in aere ad libidinem concitantur (quod fere fit) saepe ipsum sperma vel in puteos, vel in aquas fluviales ejiciunt ex quo lethalis sequitur annus.   Adversus haec ergo hujusmodi inventum est remedium, ut videlicet rogus ex ossibus construeretur, et ita fumus hujusmodi animalia fugaret.   Et quia istud maxime hoc tempore fiebat, idem etiam modo ab omnibus observatur. . . . Consuetum item est hac vigilia ardentes deferri faculas quod Johannes fuerit ardens lucerna, et qui vias Domini praeparaverit.   Sed quod etiam rota vertatur hinc esse putant quia in eum circulum tunc Sol descenderit ultra quem progredi nequit, a quo cogitur paulatim descendere."   The substance of the passage is repeated in other words by G. Durandus (Wilh. Durantis), a writer of the thirteenth century, in his *Rationale Divinorum Officiorum*, lib. vii. cap. 14 (p. 442 *verso*, ed. Lyons, 1584). Compare J. Grimm, *Deutsche Mythologie*,[4] i. 516.

With the notion that the air is poisoned at midsummer we may

Th. Kirch-
meyer's
description
of the Mid-
summer
festival.

A good general account of the midsummer customs, together with some of the reasons popularly alleged for observing them, is given by Thomas Kirchmeyer, a writer of the sixteenth century, in his poem *The Popish King-dome* :—

" *Then doth the joyfull feast of John the Baptist take his turne,*
When bonfiers great with loftie flame, in every towne doe burne;
And yong men round about with maides, doe daunce in every streete,
With garlands wrought of Motherwort, or else with Vervain sweete,
And many other flowres faire, with Violets in their handes,
Whereas they all do fondly thinke, that whosoever standes,
And thorow the flowres beholds the flame, his eyes shall feele no paine.
When thus till night they daunced have, they through the fire amaine
With striving mindes doe runne, and all their hearbes they cast therin,
And then with wordes devout and prayers, they solemnely begin,
Desiring God that all their illes may there consumed bee,
Whereby they thinke through all that yeare from Agues to be free.
Some others get a rotten wheele, all worne and cast aside,
Which covered round about with strawe, and tow, they closely hide :
And caryed to some mountaines top, being all with fire light,
They hurle it downe with violence, when darke appeares the night :

---

compare the popular belief that it is similarly infected at an eclipse. Thus among the Esquimaux on the Lower Yukon river in Alaska "it is believed that a subtle essence or unclean influence descends to the earth during an eclipse, and if any of it is caught in utensils of any kind it will produce sickness. As a result, immediately on the commencement of an eclipse, every woman turns bottom side up all her pots, wooden buckets, and dishes" (E. W. Nelson, "The Eskimo about Bering Strait," *Eighteenth Annual Report of the Bureau of American Ethnology,* Part i. (Washington, 1899) p. 431). Similar notions and practices prevail among the peasantry of southern Germany. Thus the Swabian peasants think that during an eclipse of the sun poison falls on the earth ; hence at such a time they will not sow, mow, gather fruit or eat it, they bring the cattle into the stalls, and refrain from business of every kind. If the eclipse lasts long, the people get very anxious, set a burning candle on the mantel-shelf of the stove, and pray to be delivered from

the danger. See Anton Birlinger, *Volks-thümliches aus Schwaben* (Freiburg im Breisgau, 1861–1862), i. 189. Similarly Bavarian peasants imagine that water is poisoned during a solar eclipse (F. Panzer, *Beitrag zur deutschen Mythologie,* ii. 297) ; and Thuringian bumpkins cover up the wells and bring the cattle home from pasture during an eclipse either of the sun or of the moon ; an eclipse is particularly poisonous when it happens to fall on a Wednesday. See August Witzschel, *Sagen, Sitten und Gebräuche aus Thüringen* (Vienna, 1878), p. 287. As eclipses are commonly supposed by the ignorant to be caused by a monster attacking the sun or moon (E. B. Tylor, *Primitive Culture,*[2] London, 1873, i. 328 *sqq.*), we may surmise, on the analogy of the explanation given of the Midsummer fires, that the unclean influence which is thought to descend on the earth at such times is popularly attributed to seed discharged by the monster or possibly by the sun or moon then in conjunction with each other.

Resembling much the Sunne, that from the heavens downe should fal,
A straunge and monstrous sight it seemes, and fearfull to them all :
But they suppose their mischiefes all are likewise throwne to hell,
And that from harmes and daungers now, in safetie here they dwell." [1]

From these general descriptions, which to some extent still hold good, or did so till lately, we see that the main features of the midsummer fire-festival resemble those which we have found to characterize the vernal festivals of fire. The similarity of the two sets of ceremonies will plainly appear from the following examples.

A writer of the first half of the sixteenth century informs us that in almost every village and town of Germany public bonfires were kindled on the Eve of St. John, and young and old, of both sexes, gathered about them and passed the time in dancing and singing. People on this occasion wore chaplets of mugwort and vervain, and they looked at the fire through bunches of larkspur which they held in their hands, believing that this would preserve their eyes in a healthy state throughout the year. As each departed, he threw the mugwort and vervain into the fire, saying, " May all my ill-luck depart and be burnt up with these." [2] At Lower Konz, a village prettily situated on a hillside overlooking the Moselle, in the midst of a wood of walnut-trees and fruit-trees, the midsummer festival used to be celebrated as follows. A quantity of straw was collected on the top of the steep Stromberg Hill. Every inhabitant, or at least every householder, had to contribute his share of straw to the pile ; a recusant was looked at askance, and if in the course of the year he happened to break a leg or lose a child, there was not a gossip in the village but knew the reason why. At nightfall the whole male population, men and boys, mustered on the top of the hill ; the women and girls were not allowed to join them, but had to take up their position at a certain spring half-way down the slope. On the summit stood a huge wheel completely encased in some of the straw which had been jointly contributed by the villagers ; the rest of the

The Midsummer fires in Germany.

The celebration at Konz on the Moselle : the rolling of a burning wheel down hill.

---

[1] *The Popish Kingdome or reigne of Antichrist, written in Latin verse by Thomas Naogeorgus and Englyshed by Barnabe Googe, 1570,* edited by R. C. Hope (London, 1880), p. 54 *verso.*

As to this work see above, p. 125 note [1].

[2] J. Boemus, *Mores, leges et ritus omnium gentium* (Lyons, 1541), pp. 225 *sq.*

straw was made into torches.   From each side of the wheel
the axle-tree projected about three feet, thus furnishing
handles to the lads who were to guide it in its descent.   The
mayor of the neighbouring town of Sierck, who always
received a basket of cherries for his services, gave the signal;
a lighted torch was applied to the wheel, and as it burst into
flame, two young fellows, strong-limbed and swift of foot,
seized the handles and began running with it down the
slope.   A great shout went up.   Every man and boy waved
a blazing torch in the air, and took care to keep it alight so
long as the wheel was trundling down the hill.   Some of
them followed the fiery wheel, and watched with amusement
the shifts to which its guides were put in steering it round
the hollows and over the broken ground on the mountain-
side.   The great object of the young men who guided the
wheel was to plunge it blazing into the water of the Moselle ;
but they rarely succeeded in their efforts, for the vineyards
which cover the greater part of the declivity impeded their
progress, and the wheel was often burned out before it
reached the river.   As it rolled past the women and girls at
the spring, they raised cries of joy which were answered by
the men on the top of the mountain ; and the shouts were
echoed by the inhabitants of neighbouring villages who
watched the spectacle from their hills on the opposite bank
of the Moselle.   If the fiery wheel was successfully conveyed
to the bank of the river and extinguished in the water, the
people looked for an abundant vintage that year, and the
inhabitants of Konz had the right to exact a waggon-load of
white wine from the surrounding vineyards.   On the other
hand, they believed that, if they neglected to perform the
ceremony, the cattle would be attacked by giddiness and
convulsions and would dance in their stalls.[1]

The Mid-
summer
fires in
Bavaria.

Down at least to the middle of the nineteenth century
the midsummer fires used to blaze all over Upper Bavaria.

[1] Tessier, " Sur la fête annuelle de
la roue flamboyante de la Saint-Jean, à
Basse-Kontz, arrondissement de Thion-
ville," *Mémoires et dissertations publiés
par la Société Royale des Antiquaires de
France*, v. (1823) pp. 379-393.   Tessier
witnessed the ceremony, 23rd June 1822
(not 1823, as is sometimes stated).   His

account has been reproduced more or
less fully by J. Grimm (*Deutsche Mythologie*,[4] i.   515 *sq.*), W.   Mannhardt
(*Der Baumkultus*, pp. 510 *sq.*), and
H. Gaidoz (" Le dieu gaulois du Soleil
et le symbolisme de la Roue," *Revue
Archéologique*, iii. Série, iv. (1884) pp.
24 *sq.*).

They were kindled especially on the mountains, but also far
and wide in the lowlands, and we are told that in the darkness and stillness of night the moving groups, lit up by
the flickering glow of the flames, presented an impressive
spectacle.   In some places the people shewed their sense of
the sanctity of the fires by using for fuel the trees past which
the gay procession had defiled, with fluttering banners, on
Corpus Christi Day.   In others the children collected the
firewood from door to door on the eve of the festival, singing
their request for fuel at every house in doggerel verse.   Cattle *Cattle driven through the fire.*
were driven through the fire to cure the sick animals and to
guard such as were sound against plague and harm of every
kind throughout the year.   Many a householder on that *The new fire.*
day put out the fire on the domestic hearth and rekindled
it by means of a brand taken from the midsummer bonfire.
The people judged of the height to which the flax would *Omens of the harvest drawn from the fires.*
grow in the year by the height to which the flames of the
bonfire rose ; and whoever leaped over the burning pile was
sure not to suffer from backache in reaping the corn at
harvest.   But it was especially the practice for lovers to
spring over the fire hand in hand, and the way in which
each couple made the leap was the subject of many a jest
and many a superstition.   In one district the custom of
kindling the bonfires was combined with that of lighting
wooden discs and hurling them in the air after the manner
which prevails at some of the spring festivals.[1]   In many
parts of Bavaria it was believed that the flax would grow as
high as the young people leaped over the fire.[2]   In others
the old folk used to plant three charred sticks from the
bonfire in the fields, believing that this would make the flax
grow tall.[3]   Elsewhere an extinguished brand was put in
the roof of the house to protect it against fire.   In the towns
about Würzburg the bonfires used to be kindled in the
market-places, and the young people who jumped over them
wore garlands of flowers, especially of mugwort and vervain,
and carried sprigs of larkspur in their hands.   They thought

[1] *Bavaria, Landes- und Volkskunde des Königreichs Bayern* (Munich, 1860-1867), i. 373 *sq.* ; compare *id.*, iii. 327 *sq.*   As to the burning discs at the spring festivals, see above, pp. 116 *sq.*, 119, 143.

[2] *Op. cit.* ii. 260 *sq.*, iii. 936, 956, iv. 2. p. 360.

[3] *Op. cit.* ii. 260.

that such as looked at the fire holding a bit of larkspur before their face would be troubled by no malady of the eyes throughout the year.[1]   Further, it was customary at Würzburg, in the sixteenth century, for the bishop's followers to throw burning discs of wood into the air from a mountain which overhangs the town.   The discs were discharged by means of flexible rods, and in their flight through the darkness presented the appearance of fiery dragons.[2]

In the valley of the Lech, which divides Upper Bavaria from Swabia, the midsummer customs and beliefs are, or used to be, very similar.   Bonfires are kindled on the mountains on Midsummer Day ; and besides the bonfire a tall beam, thickly wrapt in straw and surmounted by a cross-piece, is burned in many places.   Round this cross as it burns the lads dance with loud shouts ; and when the flames have subsided, the young people leap over the fire in pairs, a young man and a young woman together.   If they escape unsmirched, the man will not suffer from fever, and the girl will not become a mother within the year.   Further, it is believed that the flax will grow that year as high as they leap over the fire ; and that if a charred billet be taken from the fire and stuck in a flax-field it will promote the growth of the flax.[3]   Similarly in Swabia, lads and lasses, hand in hand, leap over the midsummer bonfire, praying that the hemp may grow three ells high, and they set fire to wheels of straw and send them rolling down the hill. Among the places where burning wheels were thus bowled down hill at Midsummer were the Hohenstaufen mountains in Wurtemberg and the Frauenberg near Gerhausen.[4] At Deffingen, in Swabia, as the people sprang over the mid-

Burning discs thrown into the air.

The Midsummer fires in Swabia.

Omens drawn from the leaps over the fires.

Burning wheels rolled down hill.

---

[1] *Op. cit.* iv. 1. p. 242.   We have seen (p. 163) that in the sixteenth century these customs and beliefs were common in Germany.   It is also a German superstition that a house which contains a brand from the midsummer bonfire will not be struck by lightning (J. W. Wolf, *Beiträge zur deutschen Mythologie,* i. p. 217, § 185).

[2] J. Boemus, *Mores, leges et ritus omnium gentium* (Lyons, 1541), p. 226.

[3] Karl Freiherr von Leoprechting,

Aus dem Lechrain (Munich, 1855), pp. 181 *sqq.* ; W. Mannhardt, *Der Baumkultus,* p. 510.

[4] A. Birlinger, *Volksthümliches aus Schwaben* (Freiburg im Breisgau, 1861–1862), ii. pp. 96 *sqq.,* § 128, pp. 103 *sq.,* § 129; *id., Aus Schwaben* (Wiesbaden, 1874), ii. 116-120; E. Meier, *Deutsche Sagen, Sitten und Gebräuche aus Schwaben* (Stuttgart, 1852), pp. 423 *·qq.* ; W. Mannhardt, *Der Baumkultus,* p. 510.

summer bonfire they cried out, "Flax, flax! may the flax
this year grow seven ells high!"[1] At Rottenburg in Burning
Swabia, down to the year 1807 or 1808, the festival was the Angel-
Man at
marked by some special features. About mid-day troops Rotten-
of boys went about the town begging for firewood at the burg.
houses. In each troop there were three leaders, one of
whom carried a dagger, a second a paper banner, and a
third a white plate covered with a white cloth. These three
entered each house and recited verses, in which they expressed an intention of roasting Martin Luther and sending him to the devil ; and for this meritorious service they
expected to be paid, the contributions being received in
the cloth-covered plate. In the evening they counted up
their money and proceeded to "behead the Angel-man."
For this ceremony an open space was chosen, sometimes in
the middle of the town. Here a stake was thrust into the
ground and straw wrapt about it, so as to make a rude
effigy of human form with arms, head, and face. Every
boy brought a handful of nosegays and fastened them to
the straw-man, who was thus enveloped in flowers. Fuel
was heaped about the stake and set on fire. When the
Angel-man, as the straw-effigy was called, blazed up, all the
boys of the neighbourhood, who had gathered expectantly
around, fell upon him with their wooden swords and hewed
him to pieces. As soon as he had vanished in smoke and
flame, the lads leaped backward and forward over the glowing embers, and later in the evening they feasted on the
proceeds of their collection.[2] Here the Angel-man burnt
in the fire appears to be identified with Martin Luther, to
whom, as we have seen, allusion was made during the
house-to-house visitation. The identification was probably
modern, for we may assume that the custom of burning
an effigy in the Midsummer bonfire is far older than the
time of Luther.

In Baden the children used to collect fuel from house The Mid-
to house for the Midsummer bonfire on St. John's Day ; summer
fires in
and lads and lasses leaped over the fire in couples. Here, Baden.

[1] F. Panzer, *Beitrag zur deutschen
Mythologie* (Munich, 1848–1855), i.
pp. 215 *sq.*, § 242 ; *id.*, ii. 549.

[2] A. Birlinger, *Volksthümliches aus
Schwaben* (Freiburg im Breisgau, 1861–
1862), ii. 99-101.

Omens
drawn from
leaps over
the fires. as elsewhere, a close connexion was traced between these bonfires and the harvest. In some places it was thought that those who leaped over the fires would not suffer from backache at reaping. Sometimes, as the young folk sprang over the flames, they cried, "Grow, that the hemp may be three ells high!" This notion that the hemp or the corn would grow as high as the flames blazed or as the people jumped over them, seems to have been widespread in Baden. It was held that the parents of the young people who bounded highest over the fire would have the most abundant harvest; and on the other hand, if a man contributed nothing to the bonfire, it was imagined that there would be no blessing on his crops, and that his hemp in particular would never grow.[1] In the neighbourhood of Bühl and Achern the St. John's fires were kindled on the tops of hills; only the unmarried lads of the village brought the fuel, and only the unmarried young men and women sprang through the flames. But most of the villagers, old and young, gathered round the bonfires, leaving a clear space for the leapers to take their run. One of the bystanders would call out the names of a pair of sweethearts; on which the two would step out from the throng, take each other by the hand, and leap high and lightly through the swirling smoke and flames, while the spectators watched them critically and drew omens of their married life from the height to which each of them bounded. Such an invitation to jump together over the bonfire was regarded as tantamount to a public betrothal.[2] Near Offenburg, in the Black Forest, on Midsummer Day the village boys used to collect faggots and straw on some steep and conspicuous height, and they spent some time in making circular wooden discs by slicing the trunk of a pine-tree across. When darkness had fallen, they kindled the

Burning
discs
thrown into
the air. bonfire, and then, as it blazed up, they lighted the discs at it, and, after swinging them to and fro at the end of a stout and supple hazel-wand, they hurled them one after the other, whizzing and flaming, into the air, where they described

---

[1] Elard Hugo Mayer, *Badisches Volksleben* (Strasburg, 1900), pp. 103 *sq.*, 225 *sq.*

[2] W. von Schulenberg, in *Verhand-* *lungen der Berliner Gesellschaft für Anthropologie, Ethnologie und Urgeschichte, Jahrgang 1897*, pp. 494 *sq.* (bound up with *Zeitschrift für Ethnologie*, xxix. 1897).

great arcs of fire, to fall at length, like shooting-stars, at the foot of the mountain.[1] In many parts of Alsace and Lorraine the midsummer fires still blaze annually or did so not very many years ago.[2] At Speicher in the Eifel, a district which lies on the middle Rhine, to the west of Coblentz, a bonfire used to be kindled in front of the village on St. John's Day, and all the young people had to jump over it. Those who failed to do so were not allowed to join the rest in begging for eggs from house to house. Where no eggs were given, they drove a wedge into the keyhole of the door. On this day children in the Eifel used also to gather flowers in the fields, weave them into garlands, and throw the garlands on the roofs or hang them on the doors of the houses. So long as the flowers remained there, they were supposed to guard the house from fire and lightning.[3] In the southern Harz district and in Thuringia the Midsummer or St. John's fires used to be commonly lighted down to about the middle of the nineteenth century, and the custom has probably not died out. At Edersleben, near Sangerhausen, a high pole was planted in the ground and a tar-barrel was hung from it by a chain which reached to the ground. The barrel was then set on fire and swung round the pole amid shouts of joy.[4]

Midsummer fires in Alsace, Lorraine, the Eifel, the Harz districts and Thuringia.

Burning barrel swung round a pole.

According to one account, German tradition required that the midsummer fire should be lighted, not from a common hearth, but by the friction of two sorts of wood, namely oak and fir.[5] In some old farm-houses of the Surenthal and Winenthal, in Switzerland, a couple of holes or a whole row of them may be seen facing each other in the door-posts of the barn or stable. Sometimes the holes are smooth and

Midsummer fires kindled by the friction of wood in Germany and Switzerland.

[1] H. Gaidoz, "Le dieu Gaulois du Soleil et le symbolisme de la Roue," *Revue Archéologique*, iii. Série, iv. (1884) pp. 29 *sq.*

[2] Bruno Stehle, "Volksglauben, Sitten und Gebräuche in Lothringen," *Globus*, lix. (1891) pp. 378 *sq.*; "Die Sommerwendfeier im St. Amarinthale," *Der Urquell*, N.F., i. (1897) pp. 181 *sqq.*

[3] J. H. Schmitz, *Sitten und Sagen, Lieder, Sprüchwörter und Räthsel des Eifler Volkes* (Treves, 1856–1858), i. 40 *sq.* According to one writer, the garlands are composed of St. John's wort (Montanus, *Die deutschen Volksfeste, Volksbräuche und deutscher Volksglaube*, Iserlohn, N.D., p. 33). As to the use of St. John's wort at Midsummer, see below, vol. ii. pp. 54 *sqq.*

[4] A. Kuhn und W. Schwartz, *Norddeutsche Sagen, Märchen und Gebräuche* (Leipsic, 1848), p. 390.

[5] Montanus, *Die deutschen Volksfeste, Volksbräuche und deutscher Volksglaube* (Iserlohn, N.D.), pp. 33 *sq.*

round ; sometimes they are deeply burnt and blackened.
The explanation of them is this.   About midsummer, but
especially on Midsummer Day, two such holes are bored
opposite each other, into which the extremities of a strong
pole are fixed.   The holes are then stuffed with tow steeped
in resin and oil ; a rope is looped round the pole, and two
young men, who must be brothers or must have the same
baptismal name, and must be of the same age, pull the ends
of the rope backwards and forwards so as to make the pole
revolve rapidly, till smoke and sparks issue from the two
holes in the door-posts.   The sparks are caught and blown
up with tinder, and this is the new and pure fire, the
appearance of which is greeted with cries of joy.   Heaps of
combustible materials are now ignited with the new fire, and
blazing bundles are placed on boards and sent floating down
the brook.   The boys light torches at the new fire and run
to fumigate the pastures.   This is believed to drive away all
the demons and witches that molest the cattle.   Finally the
torches are thrown in a heap on the meadow and allowed to
burn out.   On their way back the boys strew the ashes over
the fields, which is supposed to make them fertile.   If a
farmer has taken possession of a new house, or if servants
have changed masters, the boys fumigate the new abode and
are rewarded by the farmer with a supper.[1]

In Silesia, from the south-eastern part of the Sudeten
range and north-westward as far as Lausitz, the mountains
are ablaze with bonfires on Midsummer Eve ; and from the
valleys and the plains round about Leobschütz, Neustadt,
Zülz, Oels, and other places answering fires twinkle through
the deepening gloom.   While they are smouldering and
sending forth volumes of smoke across the fields, young men
kindle broom-stumps, soaked in pitch, at the bonfires and
then, brandishing the stumps, which emit showers of sparks,
they chase one another or dance with the girls round the
burning pile.   Shots, too, are fired, and shouts raised.   The
fire, the smoke, the shots, and the shouts are all intended to
scare away the witches, who are let loose on this witching
day, and who would certainly work harm to the crops and the
cattle, if they were not deterred by these salutary measures.

*Driving
away
demons
and
witches.*

*Mid-
summer
fires in
Silesia.*

*Scaring
away the
witches.*

---

[1] C. L. Rochholz, *Deutscher Glaube und Brauch* (Berlin, 1867), ii. 144 *sqq.*

Mere contact with the fire brings all sorts of blessings. Hence when the bonfire is burning low, the lads leap over it, and the higher they bound, the better is the luck in store for them.   He who surpasses his fellows is the hero of the day and is much admired by the village girls.   It is also thought to be very good for the eyes to stare steadily at the bonfire without blinking ; moreover he who does so will not drowse and fall asleep betimes in the long winter evenings.   On Midsummer Eve the windows and doors of houses in Silesia are crowned with flowers, especially with the blue corn-flowers and the bright corn-cockles ; in some villages long strings of garlands and nosegays are stretched across the streets.   The people believe that on that night St. John comes down from heaven to bless the flowers and to keep all evil things from house and home.[1]

In Denmark and Norway also Midsummer fires were kindled on St. John's Eve on roads, open spaces, and hills. People in Norway thought that the fires banished sickness from among the cattle.[2]   Even yet the fires are said to be lighted all over Norway on the night of June the twenty-third, Midsummer Eve, Old Style.   As many as fifty or sixty bonfires may often be counted burning on the hills round Bergen.   Sometimes fuel is piled on rafts, ignited, and allowed to drift blazing across the fiords in the darkness of night.   The fires are thought to be kindled in order to keep off the witches, who are said to be flying from all parts that night to the Blocksberg, where the big witch lives.[3]

The Midsummer fires in Denmark and Norway.

Keeping off the witches.

[1] Philo vom Walde, *Schlesien in Sage und Brauch* (Berlin, N.D.), p. 124 ; Paul Drechsler, *Sitte, Brauch, und Volksglaube in Schlesien* (Leipsic, 1903–1906), i. 136 *sq.*

[2] J. Grimm, *Deutsche Mythologie*,[4] i. 517 *sq.*

[3] From information supplied by Mr. Sigurd K. Heiberg, engineer, of Bergen, Norway, who in his boyhood regularly collected fuel for the fires.   I have to thank Miss Anderson, of Bar-skimming, Mauchline, Ayrshire, for kindly procuring the information for me from Mr. Heiberg.

The Blocksberg, where German as well as Norwegian witches gather for

their great Sabbaths on the Eve of May Day (Walpurgis Night) and Mid-summer Eve, is commonly identified with the Brocken, the highest peak of the Harz mountains. But in Mecklen-burg, Pomerania, and probably else-where, villages have their own local Blocksberg, which is generally a hill or open place in the neighbourhood ; a number of places in Pomerania go by the name of the Blocksberg.   See J. Grimm, *Deutsche Mythologie*,[4] ii. 878 *sq.* ; Ulrich Jahn, *Hexenwesen und Zauberei in Pommern* (Breslau, 1886), pp. 4 *sq.* ; *id.*, *Volkssagen aus Pommern und Rügen* (Stettin, 1886), p. 329.

The Mid-
summer
fires in
Sweden.
In Sweden the Eve of St. John (St. Hans) is the most joyous night of the whole year. Throughout some parts of the country, especially in the provinces of Bohus and Scania and in districts bordering on Norway, it is celebrated by the frequent discharge of firearms and by huge bonfires, formerly called Balder's Balefires (*Balder's Bålar*), which are kindled at dusk on hills and eminences and throw a glare of light over the surrounding landscape. The people dance round the fires and leap over or through them. In parts of Norrland on St. John's Eve the bonfires are lit at the cross-roads. The fuel consists of nine different sorts of wood, and the spectators cast into the flames a kind of toad-stool (*Bäran*) in order to counteract the power of the Trolls and other evil spirits, who are believed to be abroad that night ; for at that mystic season the mountains open and from their cavernous depths the uncanny crew pours forth to dance and disport themselves for a time. The peasants believe that should any of the Trolls be in the vicinity they will shew themselves ; and if an animal, for example a he or she goat, happens to be seen near the blazing, crackling pile, the peasants are firmly persuaded that it is no other than the Evil One in person.[1] Further, it deserves to be remarked that in Sweden St. John's Eve is a festival of water as well as of fire ; for certain holy springs are then supposed to be endowed with wonderful medicinal virtues, and many sick people resort to them for the healing of their infirmities.[2]

The Mid-
summer
fires in
Switzer-
land and
Austria.
In Switzerland on Midsummer Eve fires are, or used to be, kindled on high places in the cantons of Bern, Neuchatel, Valais, and Geneva.[3] In Austria the midsummer customs and superstitions resemble those of Germany. Thus in some parts of the Tyrol bonfires are kindled and burning discs hurled into the air.[4] In the lower valley of the Inn a tatterdemalion effigy is carted about the village on Midsummer

---

[1] L. Lloyd, *Peasant Life in Sweden* (London, 1870), pp. 259, 265.

[2] L. Lloyd, *op. cit.* pp. 261 *sq.* These springs are called "sacrificial fonts" (*Offer källor*) and are "so named because in heathen times the limbs of the slaughtered victim, whether man or beast, were here washed prior to

immolation" (L. Lloyd, *op. cit.* p. 261).

[3] E. Hoffmann-Krayer, *Feste und Bräuche des Schweizervolkes* (Zurich, 1913), p. 164.

[4] Ignaz V. Zingerle, *Sitten, Bräuche und Meinungen des Tiroler Volkes*[2] (Innsbruck, 1871), ii. p. 159, § 1354.

Day and then burned.   He is called the *Lotter*, which has   Effigies
been corrupted into Luther.   At Ambras, one of the villages   burnt in
                                                                the fires
where Martin Luther is thus burned in effigy, they say that
if you go through the village between eleven and twelve on
St. John's Night and wash yourself in three wells, you will
see all who are to die in the following year.[1]   At Gratz on
St. John's Eve (the twenty-third of June) the common people
used to make a puppet called the *Tatermann*, which they
dragged to the bleaching ground, and pelted with burning
besoms till it took fire.[2]   At Reutte, in the Tyrol, people
believed that the flax would grow as high as they leaped
over the midsummer bonfire, and they took pieces of charred
wood from the fire and stuck them in their flax-fields the
same night, leaving them there till the flax harvest had
been got in.[3]   In Lower Austria fires are lit in the fields,
commonly in front of a cross, and the people dance and
sing round them and throw flowers into the flames.   Before
each handful of flowers is tossed into the fire, a set speech
is made ;   then the dance is resumed and the dancers sing
in chorus the last words of the speech.   At evening bonfires
are kindled on the heights, and the boys caper round
them, brandishing lighted torches drenched in pitch.   Whoever jumps thrice across the fire will not suffer from fever
within the year.   Cart-wheels are often smeared with pitch,   Burning
ignited, and sent rolling and blazing down the hillsides.[4]   wheels
                                                                rolled
    All over Bohemia bonfires still burn on Midsummer   down hill
Eve.   In the afternoon boys go about with handcarts   Mid-
from house to house collecting fuel, such as sticks, brush-   summer
                                                                fires in
wood, old besoms, and so forth.   They make their request   Bohemia.
at each house in rhyming verses, threatening with evil
consequences the curmudgeons who refuse them a dole.
Sometimes the young men fell a tall straight fir in the
woods and set it up on a height, where the girls deck it
with nosegays, wreaths of leaves, and red ribbons.   Then
brushwood is piled about it, and at nightfall the whole is set
on fire.   While the flames break out, the young men climb

---

[1] I. V. Zingerle, *op. cit.* p. 159,
§§ 1353, 1355, 1356 ; W. Mannhardt,
Der Baumkultus, p. 513.

[2] W. Mannhardt, *l.c.*

[3] F. Panzer, *Beitrag zur deutschen*

Mythologie (Munich, 1848–1855), i. p.
210, § 231.

[4] Theodor Vernaleken, *Mythen und
Bräuche des Volkes in Oesterreich*
(Vienna, 1859), pp. 307 *sq.*

the tree and fetch down the wreaths which the girls had
placed on it.   After that, lads and lasses stand on opposite
sides of the fire and look at one another through the wreaths
to see whether they will be true to each other and marry
within the year.   Also the girls throw the wreaths across
the flames to the men, and woe to the awkward swain who
fails to catch the wreath thrown him by his sweetheart.
When the blaze has died down, each couple takes hands,
and leaps thrice across the fire.   He or she who does so
will be free from ague throughout the year, and the flax
will grow as high as the young folks leap.   A girl who sees
nine bonfires on Midsummer Eve will marry before the year
is out.   The singed wreaths are carried home and carefully
preserved throughout the year.   During thunderstorms a
bit of the wreath is burned on the hearth with a prayer;
some of it is given to kine that are sick or calving, and some
of it serves to fumigate house and cattle-stall, that man and
beast may keep hale and well.   Sometimes an old cart-
wheel is smeared with resin, ignited, and sent rolling down
the hill.   Often the boys collect all the worn-out besoms
they can get hold of, dip them in pitch, and having set them
on fire wave them about or throw them high into the air.
Or they rush down the hillside in troops, brandishing the
flaming brooms and shouting, only however to return to the
bonfire on the summit when the brooms have burnt out.
Embers of
the fire
stuck in
fields,
gardens,
and houses
as a
talisman
against
lightning
and con-
flagration.

Use of
mugwort.
The stumps of the brooms and embers from the fire are
preserved and stuck in cabbage gardens to protect the
cabbages from caterpillars and gnats.   Some people insert
charred sticks and ashes from the bonfire in their sown
fields and meadows, in their gardens and the roofs of their
houses, as a talisman against lightning and foul weather;
or they fancy that the ashes placed in the roof will prevent
any fire from breaking out in the house.   In some districts
they crown or gird themselves with mugwort while the
midsummer fire is burning, for this is supposed to be a protection against ghosts, witches, and sickness; in particular,
a wreath of mugwort is a sure preventive of sore eyes.
Sometimes the girls look at the bonfires through garlands
of wild flowers, praying the fire to strengthen their eyes and
eyelids.   She who does this thrice will have no sore eyes

all that year. In some parts of Bohemia they used to drive Cattle protected against witchcraft. the cows through the midsummer fire to guard them against witchcraft.[1]

The Germans of Moravia in like manner still light The Midsummer fires in Moravia, Austrian Silesia, and the district of Cracow. bonfires on open grounds and high places on Midsummer Eve ; and they kindle besoms in the flames and then stick the charred stumps in the cabbage - fields as a powerful protection against caterpillars. On the same mystic evening Moravian girls gather flowers of nine sorts and lay them under their pillow when they go to sleep ; then they dream every one of him who is to be her partner for life. For in Moravia maidens in their beds as well as poets by haunted streams have their Midsummer Night's dreams.[2] In Austrian Silesia the custom also prevails of lighting great bonfires on hilltops on Midsummer Eve, and here too the boys swing blazing besoms or hurl them high in the air, while they shout and leap and dance wildly. Next morning every door is decked with flowers and birchen saplings.[3] In the district of Cracow, especially towards the Carpathian Mountains, great fires are kindled by the peasants in the fields or on the heights at nightfall on Midsummer Eve, which among them goes by the name of Kupalo's Night. The fire must be kindled by the friction Fire kindled by the friction of wood. of two sticks. The young people dance round or leap over it ; and a band of sturdy fellows run a race with lighted torches, the winner being rewarded with a peacock's feather, which he keeps throughout the year as a distinction. Cattle also are driven round the fire in the belief that this is a charm against pestilence and disease of every sort.[4]

---

[1] J. Grimm, *Deutsche Mythologie*,[4] i. 519 ; Theodor Vernaleken, *Mythen und Bräuche des Volkes in Oesterreich* (Vienna, 1859), p. 308 ; Joseph Virgil Grohmann, *Aberglauben und Gebräuche aus Böhmen und Mähren* (Prague and Leipsic, 1864), p. 80, § 636 ; Reinsberg-Düringsfeld, *Fest-Kalender aus Bohmen* (Prague, N.D.), pp. 306-311 ; Br. Jelínek, "Materialien zur Vorgeschichte und Volkskunde Böhmens," *Mittheilungen der anthropologischen Gesellschaft in Wien*, xxi. (1891) p. 13 ; Alois John, *Sitte, Brauch und Volksglaube im deutschen Westböhmen* (Prague, 1905), pp. 84-86.

[2] Willibald Müller, *Beiträge zur Volkskunde der Deutschen in Mähren* (Vienna and Olmutz, 1893), pp. 263-265.

[3] Anton Peter, *Volksthümliches aus Österreichisch - Schlesien* (Troppau, 1865-1867), ii. 287.

[4] Th. Vernaleken, *Mythen und Bräuche des Volkes in Oesterreich* (Vienna, 1859), pp. 308 *sq.*

The Midsummer fires among the Slavs of Russia.

The name of Kupalo's Night, applied in this part of Galicia to Midsummer Eve, reminds us that we have now passed from German to Slavonic ground ; even in Bohemia the midsummer celebration is common to Slavs and Germans. We have already seen that in Russia the summer solstice or Eve of St. John is celebrated by young men and maidens, who jump over a bonfire in couples carrying a straw effigy of Kupalo in their arms.[1] In some parts of Russia an image of Kupalo is burnt or thrown into a stream on St. John's Night.[2] Again, in some districts of Russia the young folk wear garlands of flowers and girdles of holy herbs when they spring through the smoke

Cattle protected against witchcraft.

or flames ; and sometimes they drive the cattle also through the fire in order to protect the animals against wizards and witches, who are then ravenous after milk.[3] In Little Russia a stake is driven into the ground on St. John's Night, wrapt in straw, and set on fire. As the flames rise the peasant women throw birchen boughs into them,

The fires lighted by the friction of wood.

saying, " May my flax be as tall as this bough ! "[4] In Ruthenia the bonfires are lighted by a flame procured by the friction of wood. While the elders of the party are engaged in thus " churning " the fire, the rest maintain a respectful silence ; but when the flame bursts from the wood, they break forth into joyous songs. As soon as the bonfires are kindled, the young people take hands and leap in pairs through the smoke, if not through the flames ; and after that the cattle in their turn are driven through the fire.[5]

The Midsummer fires in Prussia and Lithuania thought to protect against witchcraft, thunder, hail, and cattle disease.

In many parts of Prussia and Lithuania great fires are kindled on Midsummer Eve. All the heights are ablaze with them, as far as the eye can see. The fires are supposed to be a protection against witchcraft, thunder, hail, and cattle disease, especially if next morning the cattle are driven over the places where the fires burned. Above all, the bonfires ensure the farmer against the arts of witches, who try to steal the milk from his cows by charms and

[1] *The Dying God*, p. 262. Compare M. Kowalewsky, in *Folk-lore*, i. (1890) p. 467.

[2] W. R. S. Ralston, *Songs of the Russian People*, Second Edition (London, 1872), p. 240.

[3] J. Grimm, *Deutsche Mythologie*,[4] i. 519 ; W. R. S. Ralston, *Songs of the Russian People* (London, 1872), pp. 240, 391.

[4] W. R. S. Ralston, *op. cit.* p. 240.

[5] W. R. S. Ralston, *l.c.*

spells.   That is why next morning you may see the young
fellows who lit the bonfire going from house to house and
receiving jugfuls of milk.   And for the same reason they
stick burs and mugwort on the gate or the hedge through
which the cows go to pasture, because that is supposed to
be a preservative against witchcraft.[1]   In Masuren, a district   The fire
of Eastern Prussia inhabited by a branch of the Polish   kindled by
                                                           the friction
family, it is the custom on the evening of Midsummer Day   of wood.
to put out all the fires in the village.   Then an oaken stake
is driven into the ground and a wheel is fixed on it as on
an axle.   This wheel the villagers, working by relays, cause
to revolve with great rapidity till fire is produced by friction.
Every one takes home a lighted brand from the new fire
and with it rekindles the fire on the domestic hearth.[2]
In the sixteenth century Martin of Urzedow, a Polish priest,
denounced the heathen practices of the women who on St.
John's Eve (Midsummer Eve) kindled fires by the friction
of wood, danced, and sang songs in honour of the devil.[3]

Among the Letts who inhabit the Baltic provinces of   The Mid-
Russia the most joyful festival of the year is held on Mid-   summer
                                                              fires among
summer Day.   The people drink and dance and sing and   the Letts of
adorn themselves and their houses with flowers and branches.   Russia.
Chopped boughs of fir are strewn about the rooms, and
leaves are stuck in the roofs.   In every farm-yard a birch
tree is set up, and every person of the name of John who
enters the farm that day must break off a twig from the tree
and hang up on its branches in return a small present for
the family.   When the serene twilight of the summer night
has veiled the landscape, bonfires gleam on all the hills, and
wild shouts of " Ligho ! Ligho !" echo from the woods and
fields.   In Riga the day is a festival of flowers.   From all
the neighbourhood the peasants stream into the city laden
with flowers and garlands.   A market of flowers is held in
an open square and on the chief bridge over the river ; here
wreaths of immortelles, which grow wild in the meadows
and woods, are sold in great profusion and deck the houses

[1] W. J. A. von Tettau und J. D. H.
Temme, *Die Volkssagen Ostpreussens,
Litthauens und Westpreussens* (Berlin,
1837), p. 277.
[2] M. Töppen, *Aberglauben aus*
Masuren[2] (Danzig, 1867), p. 71.

[3] F.   S.   Krauss,   " Altslavische
Feuergewinnung," *Globus*, lix. (1891)
p. 318.

of Riga for long afterwards.   Roses, too, are now at the
prime of their beauty, and masses of them adorn the flower-
stalls.   Till far into the night gay crowds parade the streets
to music or float on the river in gondolas decked with

flowers.[1]   So long ago in ancient Rome barges crowned
with flowers and crowded with revellers used to float down
the Tiber on Midsummer Day, the twenty-fourth of June,[2] and
no doubt the strains of music were wafted as sweetly across
the water to listeners on the banks as they still are to the
throngs of merrymakers at Riga.

Bonfires are commonly kindled by the South Slavonian
peasantry on Midsummer Eve, and lads and lasses dance
and shout round them in the usual way.   The very names
of St. John's Day (*Ivanje*) and the St. John's fires (*kries*)
are said to act like electric sparks on the hearts and minds
of these swains, kindling a thousand wild, merry, and happy
fancies and ideas in their rustic breasts.   At Kamenagora
in Croatia the herdsmen throw nine three-year old vines into
the bonfire, and when these burst into flames the young men
who are candidates for matrimony jump through the blaze.
He who succeeds in leaping over the fire without singeing
himself will be married within the year.   At Vidovec in
Croatia parties of two girls and one lad unite to kindle a
Midsummer bonfire and to leap through the flames ; he or
she who leaps furthest will soonest wed.   Afterwards lads
and lasses dance in separate rings, but the ring of lads
bumps up against the ring of girls and breaks it, and the
girl who has to let go her neighbour's hand will forsake her
true love hereafter.[3]   In Servia on Midsummer Eve herdsmen light torches of birch bark and march round the
sheepfolds and cattle-stalls ; then they climb the hills and
there allow the torches to burn out.[4]

Among the Magyars in Hungary the midsummer fire-
festival is marked by the same features that meet us in so
many parts of Europe.   On Midsummer Eve in many

---

[1] J. G. Kohl, *Die deutsch-russischen Ostseeprovinzen* (Dresden and Leipsic, 1841), i. 178-180, ii. 24 *sq.*   Ligho was an old heathen deity, whose joyous festival used to fall in spring.

[2] Ovid, *Fasti*, vi. 775 *sqq.*

[3] Friederich S. Krauss, *Sitte und Brauch der Südslaven* (Vienna, 1885), pp. 176 *sq.*

[4] J. Grimm, *Deutsche Mythologie*,[4] i. 519.

places it is customary to kindle bonfires on heights and to leap over them, and from the manner in which the young people leap the bystanders predict whether they will marry soon. At Nograd-Ludany the young men and women, each carrying a truss of straw, repair to a meadow, where they pile the straw in seven or twelve heaps and set it on fire. Then they go round the fire singing, and hold a bunch of iron-wort in the smoke, while they say, " No boil on my body, no sprain in my foot ! " This holding of the flowers over the flames is regarded, we are told, as equally important with the practice of walking through the fire barefoot and stamping it out. On this day also many Hungarian swineherds make fire by rotating a wheel round a wooden axle wrapt in hemp, and through the fire thus made they drive their pigs to preserve them from sickness.[1] In villages on the Danube, where the population is a cross between Magyar and German, the young men and maidens go to the high banks of the river on Midsummer Eve ; and while the girls post themselves low down the slope, the lads on the height above set fire to little wooden wheels and, after swinging them to and fro at the end of a wand, send them whirling through the air to fall into the Danube. As he does so, each lad sings out the name of his sweetheart, and she listens well pleased down below.[2]

The Esthonians of Russia, who, like the Magyars, belong to the great Turanian family of mankind, also celebrate the summer solstice in the usual way. On the Eve of St. John all the people of a farm, a village, or an estate, walk solemnly in procession, the girls decked with flowers, the men with leaves and carrying bundles of straw under their arms. The lads carry lighted torches or flaming hoops steeped in tar at the top of long poles. Thus they go singing to the cattle-sheds, the granaries, and so forth, and afterwards march thrice round the dwelling-house. Finally, preceded by the shrill music of the bagpipes and shawms, they repair to a neighbouring hill, where the materials of a bonfire have

The Midsummer fires among the Esthonians.

---

[1] H. von Wlislocki, *Volksglaube und religiöser Brauch der Magyar* (Münster i. W., 1893), pp. 40-44.

[2] A. von Ipolyi, " Beiträge zur deutschen Mythologie aus Ungarn," *Zeitschrift für deutsche Mythologie und Sittenkunde,* i. (1853) pp. 270 *sq.*

been collected. Tar-barrels filled with combustibles are hung on poles, or the trunk of a felled tree has been set up with a great mass of juniper piled about it in the form of a pyramid. When a light has been set to the pile, old and young gather about it and pass the time merrily with song and music till break of day. Every one who comes brings fresh fuel for the fire, and they say, " Now we all gather together, where St. John's fire burns. He who comes not to St. John's fire will have his barley full of thistles, and his oats full of weeds." Three logs are thrown into the fire with special ceremony ; in throwing the first they say, " Gold of pleasure (a plant with yellow flowers) into the fire ! " in throwing the second they say, " Weeds to the unploughed land ! " but in throwing the third they cry, " Flax on my field ! " The fire is said to keep the witches from the cattle.[1] According to others, it ensures that for the whole year the milk shall be " as pure as silver and as the stars in the sky, and the butter as yellow as the sun and the fire and the gold." [2] In the Esthonian island of Oesel, while they throw fuel into the midsummer fire, they call out, " Weeds to the fire, flax to the field," or they fling three billets into the flames, saying, " Flax grow long ! " And they take charred sticks from the bonfire home with them and keep them to make the cattle thrive. In some parts of the island the bonfire is formed by piling brushwood and other combustibles round a tree, at the top of which a flag flies. Whoever succeeds in knocking down the flag with a pole before it begins to burn will have good luck. Formerly the festivities lasted till daybreak, and ended in scenes of debauchery which looked doubly hideous by the growing light of a summer morning.[3]

Still farther north, among a people of the same Turanian

The Midsummer fires in Oesel.

[1] J. G. Kohl, *Die deutsch-russischen Ostseeprovinzen*, ii. 268 *sq.* ; F. J Wiedemann, *Aus dem inneren und äusseren Leben der Ehsten* (St. Petersburg, 1876), p. 362. The word which I have translated " weeds " is in Esthonian *kaste-heinad*, in German *Thaugras*. Apparently it is the name of a special kind of weed.

[2] Fr. Kreutzwald und H. Neus,

Mythische und Magische Lieder der Ehsten (St. Petersburg, 1854), p. 62.

[3] J. B. Holzmayer, " Osiliana," *Verhandlungen der gelehrten Estnischen Gesellschaft zu Dorpat*, vii. (1872) pp. 62 *sq.* Wiedemann also observes that the sports in which young couples engage in the woods on this evening are not always decorous (*Aus dem inneren und äusseren Leben der Ehsten*, p. 362).

stock, we learn from an eye-witness that Midsummer Night
used to witness a sort of witches' sabbath on the top of every
hill in Finland. The bonfire was made by setting up four tall
birches in a square and piling the intermediate space with fuel.
Round the roaring flames the people sang and drank and
gambolled in the usual way.[1] Farther east, in the valley of the
Volga, the Cheremiss celebrate about midsummer a festival
which Haxthausen regarded as identical with the midsummer
ceremonies of the rest of Europe. A sacred tree in the
forest, generally a tall and solitary oak, marks the scene of
the solemnity. All the males assemble there, but no woman
may be present. A heathen priest lights seven fires in a
row from north-west to south-east ; cattle are sacrificed and
their blood poured in the fires, each of which is dedicated to
a separate deity. Afterwards the holy tree is illumined by
lighted candles placed on its branches ; the people fall on
their knees and with faces bowed to the earth pray that
God would be pleased to bless them, their children, their
cattle, and their bees, grant them success in trade, in travel,
and in the chase, enable them to pay the Czar's taxes, and
so forth.[2]

When we pass from the east to the west of Europe we
still find the summer solstice celebrated with rites of the
same general character. Down to about the middle of the
nineteenth century the custom of lighting bonfires at midsummer prevailed so commonly in France that there was
hardly a town or a village, we are told, where they were not
kindled.[3] Though the pagan origin of the custom may be
regarded as certain, the Catholic Church threw a Christian
cloak over it by boldly declaring that the bonfires were lit
in token of the general rejoicing at the birth of the Baptist,
who opportunely came into the world at the solstice of
summer, just as his greater successor did at the solstice of
winter ; so that the whole year might be said to revolve on

---

[1] J. G. Kohl, *Die deutsch-russischen Ostseeprovinzen*, ii. 447 *sq.*

[2] J. G. Georgi, *Beschreibung aller Nationen des russischen Reichs* (St. Petersburg, 1776), p. 36 ; August Freiherr von Haxthausen, *Studien über die innere Zustände das Volksleben und*

insbesondere die ländlichen Einricht-ungen Russlands (Hanover, 1847), i. 446 *sqq.*

[3] Alfred de Nore, *Coutumes, Mythes et Traditions des Provinces de France* (Paris and Lyons, 1846), p. 19.

the golden hinges of these two great birthdays.[1] Writing
in the seventeenth century Bishop Bossuet expressly affirms
this edifying theory of the Midsummer bonfires, and he
tells his catechumens that the Church herself participated
in the illumination, since in several dioceses, including
his own diocese of Meaux, a number of parishes kindled
what were called ecclesiastical fires for the purpose of
banishing the superstitions practised at the purely mundane
bonfires.   These superstitions, he goes on to say, consisted in dancing round the fire, playing, feasting, singing
ribald songs, throwing herbs across the fire, gathering herbs
at noon or while fasting, carrying them on the person,
preserving them throughout the year, keeping brands or
cinders of the fire, and other similar practices.[2]   However
excellent the intentions of the ecclesiastical authorities may
have been, they failed of effecting their purpose ; for the
superstitions as well as the bonfires survived in France far
into the nineteenth century, if indeed they are extinct even
now at the beginning of the twentieth.   Writing in the
latter part of the nineteenth century Mr. Ch. Cuissard tells
us that he himself witnessed in Touraine and Poitou the
superstitious practices which he describes as follows : " The
most credulous examine the ways in which the flame burns
and draw good or bad omens accordingly.   Others, after
leaping through the flames crosswise, pass their little children
through them thrice, fully persuaded that the little ones will
then be able to walk at once.   In some places the shepherds
make their sheep tread the embers of the extinct fire in order
to preserve them from the foot-rot.   Here you may see
about midnight an old woman grubbing among the cinders
of the pyre to find the hair of the Holy Virgin or Saint

[1] It is notable that St. John is the
only saint whose birthday the Church
celebrates with honours like those which
she accords to the nativity of Christ.
Compare Edmond Doutté, *Magie et
Religion dans l'Afrique du Nord*
(Algiers, 1908), p. 571 note 1.

[2] Bossuet, *Œuvres* (Versailles, 1815-
1819), vi. 276 (" Catéchisme du
diocèse de Meaux "). His description
of the superstitions is, in his own words,

as follows : " *Danser à l'entour du feu,
jouer, faire des festins, chanter des
chansons deshonnètes, jeter des herbes
par-dessus le feu, en cueillir avant midi
ou à jeun, en porter sur soi, les conserver
le long de l'année, garder des tisons ou
des charbons du feu, et autres sembla-
bles.*"   This and other evidence of the
custom of kindling Midsummer bonfires
in France is cited by Ch. Cuissard in
his tract *Les Feux de la Saint-Jean*
(Orleans, 1884).

John, which she deems an infallible specific against fever. There, another woman is busy plucking the roots of the herbs which have been burned on the surface of the ground ; she intends to eat them, imagining that they are an infallible preservative against cancer. Elsewhere a girl wears on her neck a flower which the touch of St. John's fire has turned for her into a talisman, and she is sure to marry within the year. Shots are fired at the tree planted in the midst of the fire to drive away the demons who might purpose to send sicknesses about the country. Seats are set round about the bonfire, in order that the souls of dead relations may come and enjoy themselves for a little with the living." [1]

In Brittany, apparently, the custom of the Midsummer bonfires is kept up to this day. Thus in Lower Brittany every town and every village still lights its *tantad* or bonfire on St. John's Night. When the flames have died down, the whole assembly kneels round about the bonfire and an old man prays aloud. Then they all rise and march thrice round the fire ; at the third turn they stop and every one picks up a pebble and throws it on the burning pile. After that they disperse.[2] In Finistère the bonfires of St. John's Day are kindled by preference in an open space near a chapel of St. John ; but if there is no such chapel, they are lighted in the square facing the parish church and in some districts at cross-roads. Everybody brings fuel for the fire, it may be a faggot, a log, a branch, or an armful of gorse. When the vespers are over, the parish priest sets a light to the pile. All heads are bared, prayers recited, and hymns sung. Then the dancing begins. The young folk skip round the blazing pile and leap over it, when the flames have died down. If anybody makes a false step and falls or rolls in the hot embers, he or she is greeted with hoots and retires abashed from the circle of dancers. Brands are carried home from the bonfire to protect the houses against lightning, conflagrations, and certain maladies and spells. The precious talisman is carefully kept in a cupboard till

The Mid summer fires in Brittany.

---

[1] Ch. Cuissard, *Les Feux de la Saint-Jean* (Orleans, 1884), pp. 40 *sq.*

[2] A. Le Braz, *La Légende de la Mort en Basse-Bretagne* (Paris, 1893), p. 279. For an explanation of the custom of throwing a pebble into the fire, see below, p. 240.

St. John's Day of the following year.[1]   At Quimper, and in
the district of Léon, chairs used to be placed round the midsummer bonfire, that the souls of the dead might sit on them
and warm themselves at the blaze.[2]   At Brest on this day
thousands of people used to assemble on the ramparts towards evening and brandish lighted torches, which they swung
in circles or flung by hundreds into the air.   The closing of
the town gates put an end to the spectacle, and the lights
might be seen dispersing in all directions like wandering will-
o'-the-wisps.[3]   In Upper Brittany the materials for the midsummer bonfires, which generally consist of bundles of furze and
heath, are furnished by voluntary contributions, and piled on
the tops of hills round poles, each of which is surmounted by
a nosegay or a crown.   This nosegay or crown is generally
provided by a man named John or a woman named Jean,
and it is always a John or a Jean who puts a light to the
bonfire.   While the fire is blazing the people dance and sing
round it, and when the flames have subsided they leap over
the glowing embers.   Charred sticks from the bonfire are
thrown into wells to improve the water, and they are also
taken home as a protection against thunder.[4]   To make
them thoroughly effective, however, against thunder and
lightning you should keep them near your bed, between a
bit of a Twelfth Night cake and a sprig of boxwood which
has been blessed on Palm Sunday.[5]   Flowers from the nosegay or crown which overhung the fire are accounted charms
against disease and pain, both bodily and spiritual ; hence
girls hang them at their breast by a thread of scarlet wool.
In many parishes of Brittany the priest used to go in procession
with the crucifix and kindle the bonfire with his own hands ;

Uses
made of
the charred
sticks and
flowers.

[1] M. Quellien, quoted by Alexandre
Bertrand, *La Religion des Gaulois*
(Paris, 1897), pp. 116 *sq.*

[2] Collin de Plancy, *Dictionnaire
Infernal* (Paris, 1825–1826), iii. 40 ;
J. W. Wolf, *Beiträge zur deutschen
Mythologie* (Göttingen, 1852–1857), i.
p. 217, § 185 ; A. Breuil, "Du Culte
de St. Jean Baptiste," *Mémoires de la
Société des Antiquaires de Picardie*,
viii. (Amiens, 1845) pp. 189 *sq.*

[3] Eugène Cortet, *Essai sur les Fêtes
Religieuses* (Paris, 1867), p. 216 ; Ch.

Cuissard, *Les Feux de la Saint-Jean*
(Orleans, 1884), p. 24.

[4] Paul Sébillot, *Coutumes populaires
de la Haute-Bretagne* (Paris, 1886),
pp. 192-195.   In Upper Brittany
these bonfires are called *rieux* or
raviers.

[5] A. de Nore, *Coutumes, Mythes et
Traditions des Provinces de France*
(Paris and Lyons, 1846), p. 219 ; E.
Cortet, *Essai sur les Fêtes Religieuses*,
p. 216.

and farmers were wont to drive their flocks and herds through
the fire in order to preserve them from sickness till midsummer
of the following year.   Also it was believed that every girl
who danced round nine of the bonfires would marry within
the year.[1]

In Normandy the midsummer fires have now almost
disappeared, at least in the district known as the Bocage,
but they used to shine on every hill.   They were commonly
made by piling brushwood, broom, and ferns about a tall
tree, which was decorated with a crown of moss and sometimes with flowers.   While they burned, people danced
and sang round them, and young folk leaped over the
flames or the glowing ashes.   In the valley of the Orne
the custom was to kindle the bonfire just at the moment
when the sun was about to dip below the horizon ; and the
peasants drove their cattle through the fires to protect them
against witchcraft, especially against the spells of witches
and wizards who attempted to steal the milk and butter.[2]
At Jumièges in Normandy, down to the first half of the
nineteenth century, the midsummer festival was marked by
certain singular features which bore the stamp of a very high
antiquity.   Every year, on the twenty-third of June, the Eve
of St. John, the Brotherhood of the Green Wolf chose a new
chief or master, who had always to be taken from the hamlet
of Conihout.   On being elected, the new head of the brotherhood assumed the title of the Green Wolf, and donned a
peculiar costume consisting of a long green mantle and a
very tall green hat of a conical shape and without a brim.
Thus arrayed he stalked solemnly at the head of the brothers,
chanting the hymn of St. John, the crucifix and holy banner
leading the way, to a place called Chouquet.   Here the
procession was met by the priest, precentors, and choir, who
conducted the brotherhood to the parish church.   After
hearing mass the company adjourned to the house of the
Green Wolf, where a simple repast, such as is required by
the church on fast-days, was served up to them.   Then they

The Mid-
summer
fires in
Normandy,

The fires
as a pro-
tection
against
witchcraft

The
Brother-
hood of
the Green
Wolf at
Jumièges.

---

[1] A. de Nore, *Coutumes, Mythes et
Traditions des Provinces de France*, pp.
219, 228, 231 ; E. Cortet, *op. cit.* pp.
215 *sq.*

[2] J. Lecœur, *Esquisses du Bocage
Normand* (Condé-sur-Noireau, 1883–
1887), ii. 219-224.

danced before the door till it was time to light the bonfire. Night being come, the fire was kindled to the sound of hand-bells by a young man and a young woman, both decked with flowers. As the flames rose, the *Te Deum* was sung, and a villager thundered out a parody in the Norman dialect of the hymn *ut queant laxis*. Meantime the Green Wolf and his brothers, with their hoods down on their shoulders and holding each other by the hand, ran round the fire after the man who had been chosen to be the Green

Pretence of throwing the Green Wolf into the fire.

Wolf of the following year. Though only the first and the last man of the chain had a hand free, their business was to surround and seize thrice the future Green Wolf, who in his efforts to escape belaboured the brothers with a long wand which he carried. When at last they succeeded in catching him they carried him to the burning pile and made as if they would throw him on it. This ceremony over, they returned to the house of the Green Wolf, where a supper, still of the most meagre fare, was set before them. Up till midnight a sort of religious solemnity prevailed. No unbecoming word might fall from the lips of any of the company, and a censor, armed with a hand-bell, was appointed to mark and punish instantly any infraction of the rule. But at the stroke of twelve all this was changed. Constraint gave way to license ; pious hymns were replaced by Bacchanalian ditties, and the shrill quavering notes of the village fiddle hardly rose above the roar of voices that went up from the merry brotherhood of the Green Wolf. Next day, the twenty-fourth of June or Midsummer Day, was celebrated by the same personages with the same noisy gaiety. One of the ceremonies consisted in parading, to the sound of musketry, an enormous loaf of consecrated bread, which, rising in tiers, was surmounted by a pyramid of verdure adorned with ribbons. After that the holy hand-bells, deposited on the step of the altar, were entrusted as insignia of office to the man who was to be the Green Wolf next year.[1]

---

[1] This description is quoted by Madame Clément (*Histoire des fêtes civiles et religieuses*, etc., *de la Belgique Méridionale*, Avesnes, 1846, pp. 394-396) ; F. Liebrecht (*Des Gervasius von Tilbury Otia Imperialia*, Hanover, 1856, pp. 209 *sq.*) ; and W. Mannhardt (*Antike Wald und Feldkulte*, Berlin, 1877, pp. 323 *sqq.*) from the *Magazin pittoresque*, Paris, viii. (1840)

In the canton of Breteuil in Picardy (department of Oise) the priest used to kindle the midsummer bonfire, and the people marched thrice round it in procession. Some of them took ashes of the fire home with them to protect the houses against lightning.[1] The custom is, or was down to recent years, similar at Vorges, near Laon. An enormous pyre, some fifty or sixty feet high, supported in the middle by a tall pole, is constructed every year on the twenty-third of June, the Eve of St. John. It stands at one end of the village, and all the inhabitants contribute fuel to it : a cart goes round the village in the morning, by order of the mayor, collecting combustibles from house to house : no one would dream of refusing to comply with the customary obligation. In the evening, after a service in honour of St. John has been performed in the church, the clergy, the mayor, the municipal authorities, the rural police, and the fire-brigade march in procession to the bonfire, accompanied by the inhabitants and a crowd of idlers drawn by curiosity from the neighbouring villages. After addressing the throng in a sermon, to which they pay little heed, the parish priest sprinkles the pyre with holy water, and taking a lighted torch from the hand of an assistant sets fire to the pile. The enormous blaze, flaring up against the dark sky of the summer night, is seen for many miles around, particularly from the hill of Laon. When it has died down into a huge heap of glowing embers and grey ashes, every one carries home a charred stick or some cinders ; and the fire-brigade, playing their hose on what remains, extinguishes the smouldering fire. The people preserve the charred sticks and cinders throughout the year, believing that these relics of St. John's bonfire have power to guard them from light- ning and from contagious diseases.[2] At Château-Thierry, a town of the department of Aisne, between Paris and Reims, the custom of lighting bonfires and dancing round them at the midsummer festival of St. John lasted down to about 1850 ; the fires were kindled especially when June had

---

pp. 287 *sqq.* A slightly condensed account is given, from the same source, by E. Cortet (*Essai sur les Fêtes Reli- gieuses,* pp. 221 *sq.*).

[1] Bazin, quoted by Breuil, in

Mémoires de la Société d'Antiquaires de Picardie, viii. (1845) p. 191 note.

[2] Correspondents quoted by A. Ber- trand, *La Religion des Gaulois* (Paris, 1897), pp. 118, 406.

been rainy, and the people thought that the lighting of the bonfires would cause the rain to cease.[1]

In Beauce and Perche, two neighbouring districts of France to the south-west of Paris, the midsummer bonfires have nearly or wholly disappeared, but formerly they were commonly kindled and went by the name of the "fires of St. John." The site of the bonfire was either the village square or beside the cross in the cemetery. Here a great pile of faggots, brushwood, and grass was accumulated about a huge branch, which bore at the top a crown of fresh flowers. The priest blessed the bonfire and the people danced round it. When it blazed and crackled, the bystanders thrust their heads into the puffs of smoke, in the belief that it would preserve them from a multitude of ills ; and when the fire was burnt out, they rushed upon the charred embers and ashes and carried them home, imagining that they had a secret virtue to guard their houses from
being struck by lightning or consumed by fire. Some of the Perche farmers in the old days, not content with the public bonfire, used to light little private bonfires in their farmyards and make all their cattle pass through the smoke and flames for the purpose of protecting them against witchcraft or disease.[2]

In the department of the Ardennes every one was wont to contribute his faggot to the midsummer bonfire, and the clergy marched at the head of the procession to kindle it. Failure to light the fires would, in the popular belief, have exposed the fields to the greatest danger. At Revin the young folk, besides dancing round the fire to the strains of the village fiddler, threw garlands of flowers across the flames to each other.[3] In the Vosges it is still customary to kindle bonfires upon the hill-tops on Midsummer Eve ; the people believe that the fires help to preserve the fruits of the earth and ensure good crops.[4] In the Jura Mountains the mid-

[1] Correspondent quoted by A. Bertrand, *op. cit.* p. 407.

[2] Felix Chapiseau, *Le Folk-lore de la Beauce et du Perche* (Paris, 1902), i. 318-320. In Perche the midsummer bonfires were called *marolles*. As to the custom formerly observed at Bullou, near Chateaudun, see a correspondent

quoted by A. Bertrand, *La Religion des Gaulois* (Paris, 1897), p. 117.

[3] Albert Meyrac, *Traditions, Coutumes, Légendes, et Contes des Ardennes* (Charleville, 1890), pp. 88 *sq.*

[4] L. F. Sauvé, *Le Folk-lore des Hautes-Vosges* (Paris, 1889), p. 186.

summer bonfires went by the name of *bâ* or *beau*. They
were lit on the most conspicuous points of the landscape.[1]
Near St. Jean, in the Jura, it appears that at this season
young people still repair to the cross-roads and heights, and
there wave burning torches so as to present the appearance
of fiery wheels in the darkness.[2]   In Franche-Comté, the
province of France which lies immediately to the west of
the Jura mountains, the fires of St. John still shone on the
saint's day in several villages down to recent years.   They
were generally lit on high ground and the young folks of
both sexes sang and danced round them, and sprang over
the dying flames.[3]   In Bresse bonfires used to be kindled
on Midsummer Eve (the twenty-third of June) and the
people danced about them in a circle.   Devout persons,
particularly old women, circumambulated the fires fourteen
times, telling their beads and mumbling seven *Paters* and
seven *Aves* in the hope that thereby they would feel no
pains in their backs when they stooped over the sickle in
the harvest field.[4]   In Berry, a district of Central France,
the midsummer fire was lit on the Eve of St. John and
went by the name of the *jônée, joannée,* or *jouannée*.   Every
family according to its means contributed faggots, which
were piled round a pole on the highest ground in the neighbourhood.   In the hamlets the office of kindling the fire
devolved on the oldest man, but in the towns it was the
priest or the mayor who discharged the duty.   Here, as in
Brittany, people supposed that a girl who had danced round
nine of the midsummer bonfires would marry within the
year.   To leap several times over the fire was regarded as a
sort of purification which kept off sickness and brought good
luck to the leaper.   Hence the nimble youth bounded through
the smoke and flames, and when the fire had somewhat abated
parents jumped across it with their children in their arms
in order that the little ones might also partake of its bene-

*The Mid-
summer
fires in
Franche-
Comté,*

*The Mid-
summer
fires in
Berry and
other parts
of Central
France.*

1 Désiré Monnier, *Traditions populaires comparées* (Paris, 1854), pp. 207
sqq. ; E. Cortet, *Essai sur les Fêtes
Religieuses*, pp. 217 *sq.*

2 Bérenger - Féraud, *Réminiscences
populaires de la Provence* (Paris, 1885),
p. 142.

3 Charles Beauquier, *Les Mois en*

Franche-Comté (Paris, 1900), p. 89.
The names of the bonfires vary with
the place ; among them are *failles,
bourdifailles, bâs* or *baux, feulères* or
folières, and *chavannes*.

4 *La Bresse Louhannaise*, Juin,
1906, p. 207.

ficent influence.   Embers from the extinct bonfire were taken home, and after being dipped in holy water were kept as a talisman against all kinds of misfortune, but especially against lightning.[1]   The same virtue was ascribed to the ashes and charred sticks of the midsummer bonfire in Périgord, where everybody contributed his share of fuel to the pile and the whole was crowned with flowers, especially with roses and lilies.[2]   On the borders of the departments of Creuse and Corrèze, in Central France, the fires of St. John used to be lit on the Eve of the saint's day (the twenty-third of June) ; the custom seems to have survived till towards the end of the nineteenth century.   Men, women, and children assembled round the fires, and the young people jumped over them.   Children were brought by their parents or elder brothers into contact with the flames in the belief that this would save them from fever.   Older people girded themselves with stalks of rye taken from a neighbouring field, because they fancied that by so doing they would not grow weary in reaping the corn at harvest.[3]

The Mid-summer fires in Poitou.

Bonfires were lit in almost all the hamlets of Poitou on the Eve of St. John.   People marched round them thrice, carrying a branch of walnut in their hand.   Shepherdesses and children passed sprigs of mullein (*verbascum*) and nuts across the flames; the nuts were supposed to cure toothache, and the mullein to protect the cattle from sickness and sorcery.   When the fire died down people took some of the ashes home with them, either to keep them in the house as a preservative against thunder or to scatter them on the fields for the purpose of destroying corn-cockles and darnel.   Stones were also placed round the fire, and it was believed that the first to lift one of these stones next morning would find under it the hair of St. John.[4]   In Poitou also it used to be

[1] Laisnel de la Salle, *Croyances et Légendes du Centre de la France* (Paris, 1875), i. 78 *sqq.*   The writer adopts the absurd derivation of *jônée* from Janus.   Needless to say that our old friend Baal, Bel, or Belus figures prominently in this and many other accounts of the European fire-festivals.

[2] A. de Nore, *Coutumes, Mythes et Traditions des Provinces de France*

(Paris and Lyons, 1846), p. 150.

[3] Correspondent, quoted by A. Bertrand, *La Religion des Gaulois* (Paris, 1897), p. 408.

[4] Guerry, "Sur les usages et traditions du Poitou," *Mémoires et dissertations publiés par la Société Royale des Antiquaires de France*, viii. (1829) pp. 451 *sq.*

customary on the Eve of St. John to trundle a blazing wheel wrapt in straw over the fields to fertilize them.[1] This last custom is said to be now extinct,[2] but it is still usual, or was so down to recent years, in Poitou to kindle fires on this day at cross-roads or on the heights. The oldest or youngest person present sets a light to the pile, which consists of broom, gorse, and heath. A bright and crackling blaze shoots up, but soon dies down, and over it the young folk leap. They also throw stones into it, picking the stone according to the size of the turnips that they wish to have that year. It is said that "the good Virgin" comes and sits on the prettiest of the stones, and next morning they see there her beautiful golden tresses. At Lussac, in Poitou, the lighting of the midsummer bonfire is still an affair of some ceremony. A pyramid of faggots is piled round a tree or tall pole on the ground where the fair is held ; the priest goes in procession to the spot and kindles the pile. When prayers have been said and the clergy have withdrawn, the people continue to march round the fire, telling their beads, but it is not till the flames have begun to die down that the youth jump over them. A brand from the midsummer bonfire is supposed to be a preservative against thunder.[3]

In the department of Vienne the bonfire was kindled by the oldest man, and before the dance round the flames began it was the custom to pass across them a great bunch of mullein (*bouillon blanc*) and a branch of walnut, which next morning before sunrise were fastened over the door of the chief cattle-shed.[4] A similar custom prevailed in the neighbouring department of Deux-Sèvres ; but here it was the priest who kindled the bonfire, and old men used to put embers of the fire in their wooden shoes as a preservative

The Midsummer fires in the departments of Vienne and Deux-Sèvres and in the provinces of Saintonge and Aunis.

---

[1] Breuil, in *Mémoires de la Société des Antiquaires de Picardie*, viii. (1845) p. 206 ; E. Cortet, *Essai sur les Fêtes Religieuses*, p. 216 ; Laisnel de la Salle, *Croyances et Légendes du Centre de la France*, i. 83 ; J. Lecœur, *Esquisses du Bocage Normand*, ii. 225.

[2] H. Gaidoz, " Le dieu gaulois du soleil et le symbolisme de la roue," *Revue Archéologique*, iii. Série, iv. (1884) p. 26, note 3.

[3] L. Pineau, *Le Folk-lore du Poitou* (Paris, 1892), pp. 499 *sq.* In Périgord the ashes of the midsummer bonfire are searched for the hair of the Virgin (E. Cortet, *Essai sur les Fêtes Religieuses*, p. 219).

[4] A. de Nore, *Coutumes Mythes et Traditions des Provinces de France*, pp. 149 *sq.* ; E. Cortet, *op. cit.* pp. 218 *sq.*

against many evils.[1]　In some towns and villages of Saintonge and Aunis, provinces of Western France now mostly
comprised in the department of Charente Inférieure, the fires
of St. John are still kindled on Midsummer Eve, but the
custom is neither so common nor carried out with so much
pomp and ceremony as formerly.　Great quantities of wood
used to be piled on an open space round about a huge post
or a tree stripped of its leaves and branches.　Every one
took care to contribute a faggot to the pile, and the whole
population marched to the spot in procession with the
crucifix at their head and the priest bringing up the rear.
The squire, or other person of high degree, put the torch to
the pyre, and the priest blessed it.　In the southern and
eastern parts of Saintonge children and cattle were passed
through the smoke of the bonfires to preserve them from
contagious diseases, and when the fire had gone out the
people scuffled for the charred fragments of the great post,
which they regarded as talismans against thunder.　Next
morning, on Midsummer Day, every shepherdess in the
neighbourhood was up very early, for the first to drive her
sheep over the blackened cinders and ashes of the great
bonfire was sure to have the best flock all that year.　Where
the shepherds shrunk from driving their flocks through the
smoke and flames of the bonfire they contented themselves
with marking the hinder-quarters of the animals with a broom
which had been blackened in the ashes.[2]

The Mid-
summer
fires in
Southern
France.

　　In the mountainous part of Comminges, a province of
Southern France, now comprised in the department of Haute
Garonne, the midsummer fire is made by splitting open the
trunk of a tall tree, stuffing the crevice with shavings, and
igniting the whole.　A garland of flowers is fastened to
the top of the tree, and at the moment when the fire is
lighted the man who was last married has to climb up a
ladder and bring the flowers down.　In the flat parts of
the same district the materials of the midsummer bonfires
consist of fuel piled in the usual way; but they must be

[1] Dupin, "Notice sur quelques fêtes
et divertissemens populaires du département des Deux-Sèvres," *Mémoires et
Dissertations publiés par la Société
Royale des Antiquaires de France*, iv.

(1823) p. 110.

[2] J. L. M. Noguès, *Les mœurs
d'autrefois en Saintonge et en Aunis*
(Saintes, 1891), pp. 72, 178 *sq.*

put together by men who have been married since the last
midsummer festival, and each of these benedicts is obliged
to lay a wreath of flowers on the top of the pile.[1]   At the
entrance of the valley of Aran young people set up on the
banks of the Garonne a tree covered with ribbons and
garlands ; at the end of a year the withered tree and faded
flowers furnish excellent fuel.   So on the Eve of St. John
the villagers assemble, and an old man or a child kindles
the fire which is to consume tree and garlands together.
While the blaze lasts the people sing and dance ; and the
burnt tree is then replaced by another which will suffer the
same fate after the lapse of a year.[2]   In some districts of
the French Pyrenees it is deemed necessary to leap nine
times over the midsummer fire if you would be assured
of prosperity.[3]   A traveller in Southern France at the
beginning of the nineteenth century tells us that "the Eve
of St. John is also a day of joy for the Provençals.   They
light great fires and the young folk leap over them.   At
Aix they shower squibs and crackers on the passers-by,
which has often had disagreeable consequences.   At Marseilles they drench each other with scented water, which is
poured from the windows or squirted from little syringes ;
the roughest jest is to souse passers-by with clean water,
which gives rise to loud bursts of laughter."[4]   At Draguig-
nan, in the department of Var, fires used to be lit in every
street on the Eve of St. John, and the people roasted pods
of garlic at them ; the pods were afterwards distributed to
every family.   Another diversion of the evening was to pour
cans of water from the houses on the heads of people in
the streets.[5]   In Provence the midsummer fires are still
popular.   Children go from door to door begging for fuel,
and they are seldom sent empty away.   Formerly the priest,
the mayor, and the aldermen used to walk in procession to
the bonfire, and even deigned to light it ; after which the
assembly marched thrice round the burning pile, while the

*Mid-
summer
festival of
fire and
water in
Provence*

---

[1] H. Gaidoz, "Le dieu soleil et le
symbolisme de la roue," *Revue Archéologique*, iii. Série, iv. (1884) p. 30.

[2] Ch. Cuissard, *Les Feux de la
Saint-Jean* (Orleans, 1884), pp. 22 *sq.*

[3] A. de Nore, *Coutumes, Mythes et*

Traditions des Provinces de France, p.
127.

[4] Aubin-Louis Millin, *Voyage dans
les Départemens du Midi de la France*
(Paris, 1807–1811), iii. 341 *sq.*

[5] Aubin-Louis Millin, *op. cit.* iii. 28.

church bells pealed and rockets fizzed and sputtered in the
air.   Dancing began later, and the bystanders threw water

Bathing in the sea at Mid-summer.

on each other.   At Ciotat, while the fire was blazing, the
young people plunged into the sea and splashed each other
vigorously.   At Vitrolles they bathed in a pond in order
that they might not suffer from fever during the year, and
at Saintes-Maries they watered the horses to protect them

Temporary Mid-summer kings at Aix and Marseilles.

from the itch.[1]   At Aix a nominal king, chosen from among
the youth for his skill in shooting at a popinjay, presided
over the festival.   He selected his own officers, and escorted
by a brilliant train marched to the bonfire, kindled it, and
was the first to dance round it.   Next day he distributed
largesse to his followers.   His reign lasted a year, during
which he enjoyed certain privileges.   He was allowed to
attend the mass celebrated by the commander of the Knights
of St. John on St. John's Day : the right of hunting was
accorded to him ; and soldiers might not be quartered in his
house.   At Marseilles also on this day one of the guilds chose
a king of the *badache* or double axe ; but it does not appear
that he kindled the bonfire, which is said to have been lighted
with great ceremony by the préfet and other authorities.[2]

The Mid-summer fires in Belgium.

In Belgium the custom of kindling the midsummer
bonfires has long disappeared from the great cities, but it
is still kept up in rural districts and small towns of Brabant,
Flanders, and Limburg.   People leap across the fires to
protect themselves against fever, and in eastern Flanders
women perform similar leaps for the purpose of ensuring
an easy delivery.   At Termonde young people go from
door to door collecting fuel for the fires and reciting
verses, in which they beg the inmates to give them " wood
of St. John " and to keep some wood for St. Peter's Day
(the twenty-ninth of June) ; for in Belgium the Eve of St.
Peter's Day is celebrated by bonfires and dances exactly like
those which commemorate St. John's Eve.   The ashes of

[1] A. de Nore, *op. cit.* pp. 19 *sq.* ;
Bérenger-Féraud, *Reminiscences populaires de la Provence* (Paris, 1885), pp.
135-141. As to the custom at Toulon,
see Poncy, quoted by Breuil, *Mémoires
de la Société des Antiquaires de Picardie,*
viii. (1845) p. 190 note. The custom of
drenching people on this occasion with

water used to prevail in Toulon, as well
as in Marseilles and other towns in
the south of France. The water was
squirted from syringes, poured on the
heads of passers-by from windows, and
so on. See Breuil, *op. cit.* pp. 237 *sq.*

[2] A. de Nore, *op. cit.* pp. 20 *sq.* ;
E. Cortet, *op. cit.* pp. 218, 219 *sq.*

the St. John's fires are deemed by Belgian peasants an excellent remedy for consumption, if you take a spoonful or two of them, moistened with water, day by day.   People also burn vervain in the fires, and they say that in the ashes of the plant you may find, if you look for it, the " Fool's Stone." [1]   In many parts of Brabant St. Peter's bonfire used to be much larger than that of his rival St. John.   When it had burned out, both sexes engaged in a game of ball, and the winner became the King of Summer or of the Ball and had the right to choose his Queen.   Sometimes the winner was a woman, and it was then her privilege to select her royal mate.   This pastime was well known at Louvain and it continued to be practised at Grammont and Mespelaer down to the second half of the nineteenth century.   At Mespelaer, which is a village near Termonde, a huge pile of eglantine, reeds, and straw was collected in a marshy meadow for the bonfire ; and next evening after vespers the young folk who had lit it assembled at the " Good Life " tavern to play the game.   The winner was crowned with a wreath of roses, and the rest danced and sang in a ring about him.   At Grammont, while the bonfire was lit and the dances round it took place on St. Peter's Eve, the festival of the " Crown of Roses " was deferred till the following Sunday.   The young folk arranged among themselves beforehand who should be King and Queen of the Roses : the rosy wreaths were hung on cords across the street : the dancers danced below them, and at a given moment the wreaths fell on the heads of the chosen King and Queen, who had to entertain their fellows at a feast. According to some people the fires of St. Peter, like those of St. John, were lighted in order to drive away dragons.[2] In French Flanders down to 1789 a straw figure representing a man was always burned in the midsummer bonfire, and the figure of a woman was burned on St. Peter's Day.[3] In Belgium people jump over the midsummer bonfires as a

Bonfires on St. Peter's Day in Brabant.

The King and Queen of the Roses.

Effigies burnt in the Midsummer fires.

---

[1] Le Baron de Reinsberg-Düringsfeld, *Calendrier Belge* (Brussels, 1861–1862), i. 416 *sq.*, 439.

[2] Le Baron de Reinsberg-Düringsfeld, *op. cit.* i. 439-442.

[3] Madame Clément, *Histoire des*

fêtes civiles et religieuses, etc., *du Département du Nord* (Cambrai, 1836), p. 364; J. W. Wolf, *Beiträge zur deutschen Mythologie* (Göttingen, 1852–1857), ii. 392 ; W. Mannhardt, *Der Baumkultus*, p. 513.

preventive of colic, and they keep the ashes at home to hinder fire from breaking out.[1]

The Midsummer fires in England.

The custom of lighting bonfires at midsummer has been observed in many parts of our own country. " On the Vigil of Saint John the Baptist, commonly called Midsummer Eve, it was usual in most country places, and also in towns and cities, for the inhabitants, both old and young, and of both sexes, to meet together, and make merry by the side of a large fire made in the middle of the street, or in some open and convenient place, over which the young men frequently leaped by way of frolic, and also exercised themselves with various sports and pastimes, more especially with running, wrestling, and dancing. These diversions they continued till midnight, and sometimes till cock-crowing." [2] In the streets of London the midsummer fires were lighted in the time of Queen Elizabeth down to the end of the sixteenth century,

Stow's description of the Midsummer fires in London.

as we learn from Stow's description, which runs thus : " In the months of June and July, on the vigils of festival days, and on the same festival days in the evenings after the sun setting, there were usually made bonfires in the streets, every man bestowing wood or labour towards them ; the wealthier sort also, before their doors near to the said bonfires, would set out tables on the vigils furnished with sweet bread and good drink, and on the festival days with meats and drinks plentifully, whereunto they would invite their neighbours and passengers also to sit and be merry with them in great familiarity, praising God for His benefits bestowed on them. These were called bonfires as well of good amity amongst neighbours that being before at controversy, were there, by the labour of others, reconciled, and made of bitter enemies loving friends ; and also for the virtue that a great fire hath to purge the infection of the air. On the vigil of St. John the Baptist, and on St. Peter and Paul the Apostles, every man's door being shadowed with green birch, long fennel, St. John's wort, orpin, white lilies, and such like, garnished upon with garlands of beautiful flowers, had also lamps of glass, with oil burning in them all the night ; some hung

[1] E. Monseur, Folklore Wallon (Brussels, N.D.), p. 130, §§ 1783, 1786, 1787.

[2] Joseph Strutt, The Sports and Pastimes of the People of England, New Edition, by W. Hone (London, 1834), p. 359.

out branches of iron curiously wrought, containing hundreds
of lamps alight at once, which made a goodly show, namely,
in New Fish Street, Thames Street, etc."[1]   In the sixteenth century the Eton boys used to kindle a bonfire on
the east side of the church both on St. John's Day and on
St. Peter's Day.[2]   Writing in the second half of the
seventeenth century, the antiquary John Aubrey tells us
that bonfires were still kindled in many places on St.
John's Night, but that the civil wars had thrown many of
these old customs out of fashion.   Wars, he adds, extinguish superstition as well as religion and laws, and there is
nothing like gunpowder for putting phantoms to flight.[3]

The Mid-
summer
fires at
Eton.

In the north of England these fires used to be lit
in the open streets.   Young and old gathered round them,
and while the young leaped over the fires and engaged
in games, their elders looked on and probably remembered
with regret the days when they used to foot it as nimbly.
Sometimes the fires were kindled on the tops of high hills.
The people also carried firebrands about the fields.[4]   The
custom of kindling bonfires on Midsummer Eve prevailed
all over Cumberland down to the second half of the
eighteenth century.[5]   In Northumberland the custom seems
to have lasted into the first quarter of the nineteenth century ;
the fires were lit in the villages and on the tops of high hills,
and the people sported and danced round them.[6]   Moreover,
the villagers used to run with burning brands round their

The Mid-
summer
fires in the
north of
England.

The Mid-
summer
fires in
Northum-
berland.

---

[1] John Stow, *A Survey of London*,
edited by Henry Morley (London, N.D.),
pp. 126 *sq.* Stow's *Survay* was written
in 1598.

[2] John Brand, *Popular Antiquities
of Great Britain* (London, 1882–1883),
i. 338 ; T. F. Thiselton Dyer, *British
Popular Customs* (London, 1876), p.
331.   Both writers refer to *Status
Scholae Etonensis* (A.D. 1560).

[3] John Aubrey, *Remaines of Gentilisme and Judaisme* (London, 1881), p.
26.

[4] J. Brand, *Popular Antiquities of
Great Britain* (London, 1882–1883),
i. 300 *sq.*, 318, compare pp. 305, 306,
308 *sq.* ; W. Mannhardt, *Der Baumkultus*, p. 512.   Compare W. Hutchinson, *View of Northumberland*, vol.

ii. (Newcastle, 1778), Appendix, p.
(15), under the head "Midsummer ":—
" It is usual to raise fires on the tops
of high hills and in the villages, and
sport and danse around them ; this is
of very remote antiquity, and the first
cause lost in the distance of time."

[5] Dr. Lyttelton, Bishop of Carlisle,
quoted by William Borlase, *Antiquities,
Historical and Monumental, of the
County of Cornwall* (London, 1769),
p. 135 note.

[6] *County Folk-lore*, vol. iv. *Northumberland*, collected by M. C. Balfour
(London, 1904), p. 76, quoting E.
Mackenzie, *An Historical, Topographical, and Descriptive View of the County
of Northumberland*, Second Edition
(Newcastle, 1825), i. 217.

fields and to snatch ashes from a neighbour's fire, saying as they did so, "We have the flower (or flour) of the wake." [1]   At Sandhill bonfires were kindled on the Eve of St. Peter as well as on Midsummer Eve ; the custom is attested for the year 1575, when it was described as ancient. [2]   We are told that "on Midsummer's eve, reckoned according to the old style, it was formerly the custom of the inhabitants, young and old, not only of Whalton, but of most of the adjacent villages, to collect a large cartload of whins and other combustible materials, which was dragged by them with great rejoicing (a fiddler being seated on the top of the cart) into the village and erected into a pile.   The people from the surrounding country assembled towards evening, when it was set on fire ; and whilst the young danced around it, the elders looked on smoking their pipes and drinking their beer, until it was consumed.   There can be little doubt that this curious old custom dates from a very remote antiquity."   In a law-suit, which was tried in 1878, the rector of Whalton gave evidence of the constant use of the village green for the ceremony since 1843.   " The bonfire," he said, "was lighted a little to the north-east of the well at Whalton, and partly on the footpath, and people danced round it and jumped through it.   That was never interrupted."   The Rev. G. R. Hall, writing in 1879, says that " the fire festivals or bonfires of the summer solstice at the Old Midsummer until recently were commemorated on Christenburg Crags and elsewhere by leaping through and dancing round the fires, as those who have been present have told me." [3]   Down to the early part of the nineteenth century bonfires called Beal-fires used to be lit on Midsummer Eve all over the wolds in the East Riding of Yorkshire. [4]

The Midsummer fires at Whalton in Northumberland.

[1] *County Folk-lore*, vol. iv. *Northumberland*, collected by M. C. Balfour, p. 75.

[2] *County Folk-lore*, vol. iv. *Northumberland*, collected by M. C. Balfour, p. 75.

[3] *The Denham Tracts*, edited by J. Hardy (London, 1892–1895), ii. 342 *sq.*, quoting *Archæologia Aeliana*, N.S., viii. 73, and the *Proceedings* of the

Berwickshire Naturalists' Club, vi. 242 *sq.* ; *County Folk-lore*, vol. iv. *Northumberland*, collected by M. C. Balfour (London, 1904), pp. 75 *sq.* Whalton is a village of Northumberland, not far from Morpeth.

[4] *County Folk-lore*, vol. vi. *East Riding of Yorkshire*, collected and edited by Mrs. Gutch (London, 1912), p. 102.

In Herefordshire and Somersetshire the peasants used to make fires in the fields on Midsummer Eve "to bless the apples."[1]   In Devonshire the custom of leaping over the midsummer fires was also observed.[2]   "In Cornwall, the festival fires, called bonfires, are kindled on the Eves of St. John Baptist and St. Peter's day ; and Midsummer is thence, in the Cornish tongue, called *Goluan,* which signifies both light and rejoicing.   At these fires the Cornish attend with lighted torches, tarred and pitched at the end, and make their perambulations round their fires, going from village to village and carrying their torches before them ; this is certainly the remains of Druid superstition ; for, *Faces praeferre,* to carry lighted torches was reckoned a kind of gentilism, and as such particularly prohibited by the Gallick Councils."[3]   At Penzance and elsewhere in the county the people danced and sang about the bonfires on Midsummer Eve.   On Whiteborough, a large tumulus near Launceston, a huge bonfire used to be kindled on Midsummer Eve ; a tall summer pole with a large bush at the top was fixed in the centre of the bonfire.[4]   The Cornish fires at this season appear to have been commonly lit on high and conspicuous hills, such as Tregonan, Godolphin, Carnwarth, and Carn Brea.   When it grew dusk on Midsummer Eve, old men would hobble away to some height whence they counted the fires and drew a presage from their number.[5]   "It is the immemorial usage in Penzance, and the neighbouring towns and villages, to kindle bonfires and torches on Midsummer-eve ; and on Midsummer-day to hold a fair on Penzance quay, where the country folks assemble from the adjoining parishes in great numbers to make excursions on the water.   St. Peter's Eve

[1] John Aubrey, *Remaines of Gentilisme and Judaisme* (London, 1881), p. 96, compare *id.*, p. 26.

[2] J. Brand, *Popular Antiquities of Great Britain* (London, 1882–1883), i. 311.

[3] William Borlase, LL.D., *Antiquities, Historical and Monumental, of the County of Cornwall* (London, 1769), pp. 135 *sq.* The Eve of St. Peter is June 28th.   Bonfires have been lit elsewhere on the Eve or the day of St. Peter.   See above, pp. 194 *sq.*, 196 *sq.*, and below, pp. 199 *sq.*, 202, 207.

[4] J. Brand, *op. cit.* i. 318, 319 ; T. F. Thiselton Dyer, *British Popular Customs* (London, 1876), p. 315.

[5] William Bottrell, *Traditions and Hearthside Stories of West Cornwall* (Penzance, 1870), pp. 8 *sq.*, 55 *sq.* ; James Napier, *Folk-lore, or Superstitious Beliefs in the West of Scotland* (Paisley, 1879), p. 173.

The
Cornish
fires on
Mid-
summer
Eve and
St. Peter's
Eve.
[the twenty-eighth of June] is distinguished by a similar display of bonfires and torches, although the ' quay-fair ' on St. Peter's-day [the twenty-ninth of June], has been discontinued upwards of forty years.   On these eves a line of tar-barrels, relieved occasionally by large bonfires, is seen in the centre of each of the principal streets in Penzance.   On either side of this line young men and women pass up and down, swinging round their heads heavy torches made of large pieces of folded canvas steeped in tar, and nailed to the ends of sticks between three and four feet long ; the flames of some of these almost equal those of the tar-barrels. Rows of lighted candles, also, when the air is calm, are fixed outside the windows or along the sides of the streets.   In St. Just, and other mining parishes, the young miners, mimicking their fathers' employments, bore rows of holes in the rocks, load them with gunpowder, and explode them in rapid succession by trains of the same substance.   As the holes are not deep enough to split the rocks, the same little batteries serve for many years.   On these nights, Mount's Bay has a most animating appearance, although not equal to what was annually witnessed at the beginning of the present century, when the whole coast, from the Land's End to the Lizard, wherever a town or a village existed, was lighted up with these stationary or moving fires.   In the early part of the evening, children may be seen wearing wreaths of flowers—a custom in all probability originating from the ancient use of these ornaments when they danced around the fires.   At the close of the fireworks in Penzance, a great number of persons of both sexes, chiefly from the neighbourhood of the quay, used always, until within the last few years, to join hand in hand, forming a long string, and run through the streets, playing ' thread the needle,' heedless of the fireworks showered upon them, and oftentimes leaping over the yet glowing embers.   I have on these occasions seen boys following one another, jumping through flames higher than themselves." [1]

In Wales the midsummer fires were kindled on St. John's

[1] Richard   Edmonds,   *The Land's End District* (London, 1862), pp. 66 *sq.* ;   Robert Hunt, *Popular Romances* of the West of England, Third Edition (London, 1881), pp. 207 *sq.*

Eve and on St. John's Day.   Three or nine different kinds of The Mid-
summer
fires in
Wales and
the Isle of
Man.
wood and charred faggots carefully preserved from the last
midsummer were deemed necessary to build the bonfire, which
was generally done on rising ground.   Various herbs were
thrown into the blaze ; and girls with bunches of three or
nine different kinds of flowers would take the hands of boys,
who wore flowers in their buttonholes and hats, and together
the young couples would leap over the fires.   On the same
two midsummer days roses and wreaths of flowers were
hung over the doors and windows.   " Describing a midsummer fire, an old inhabitant, born in 1809, remembered
being taken to different hills in the Vale of Glamorgan to
see festivities in which people from all parts of the district
participated.   She was at that time about fourteen, and old
enough to retain a vivid recollection of the circumstances.
People conveyed trusses of straw to the top of the hill, where
men and youths waited for the contributions.   Women and
girls were stationed at the bottom of the hill.   Then a large Burning
wheel
rolled
down hill
cart-wheel was thickly swathed with straw, and not an inch
of wood was left in sight.   A pole was inserted through the
centre of the wheel, so that long ends extended about a yard
on each side.   If any straw remained, it was made up into
torches at the top of tall sticks.   At a given signal the
wheel was lighted, and sent rolling downhill.   If this fire-
wheel went out before it reached the bottom of the hill, a
very poor harvest was promised.   If it kept lighted all the
way down, and continued blazing for a long time, the harvest
would be exceptionally abundant.   Loud cheers and shouts
accompanied the progress of the wheel." [1]   At Darowen in
Wales small bonfires were kindled on Midsummer Eve. [2]   On
the same day people in the Isle of Man were wont to light
fires to the windward of every field, so that the smoke might
pass over the corn ; and they folded their cattle and carried
blazing furze or gorse round them several times. [3]

A writer of the last quarter of the seventeenth century

[1] Marie Trevelyan, *Folk-lore and
Folk-stories of Wales* (London, 1909),
pp. 27 *sq.*   Compare Jonathan Ceredig
Davies, *Folk-lore of West and Mid-
Wales* (Aberystwyth, 1911), p. 76.

[2] J. Brand, *Popular Antiquities of*
Great Britain (London, 1882–1883),
i. 318.

[3] Joseph Train, *Account of the Isle
of Man* (Douglas, Isle of Man, 1845),
ii. 120.

The Midsummer fires in Ireland.

tells us that in Ireland, "on the Eves of St. John Baptist and St. Peter, they always have in every town a bonfire, late in the evenings, and carry about bundles of reeds fast tied and fired ; these being dry, will last long, and flame better than a torch, and be a pleasing divertive prospect to the distant beholder ; a stranger would go near to imagine the whole country was on fire." [1] Another writer says of the South of Ireland : " On Midsummer's Eve, every eminence, near which is a habitation, blazes with bonfires ; and round these they carry numerous torches, shouting and dancing, which affords a beautiful sight." [2] An author who described Ireland in the first quarter of the eighteenth century says : " On the vigil of St. John the Baptist's Nativity, they make bonfires, and run along the streets and fields with wisps of straw blazing on long poles to purify the air, which they think infectious, by believing all the devils, spirits, ghosts, and hobgoblins fly abroad this night to hurt mankind." [3] Another writer states that he witnessed the festival in Ireland in 1782 : " At the house where I was entertained, it was told me, that we should see, at midnight, the most singular sight in Ireland, which was the lighting of fires in honour of the sun. Accordingly, exactly at midnight, the fires began to appear; and taking the advantage of going up to the leads of the house, which had a widely extended view, I saw on a radius of thirty miles, all around, the fires burning on every eminence which the country afforded. I had a farther satisfaction in learning, from undoubted authority, that the people danced round the fires, and at the close went through these fires, and made their sons and daughters, together with their cattle, pass through the fire ; and the whole was conducted with religious solemnity." [4] That the custom prevailed in full force as late as 1867 appears from a notice in a newspaper of that date, which runs thus : " The old pagan fire-worship still survives in Ireland, though nomi-

Passage of people and cattle through the fires.

---

[1] Sir Henry Piers, *Description of the County of Westmeath*, written in 1682, published by (General) Charles Vallancey, *Collectanea de Rebus Hibernicis*, i. (Dublin, 1786) pp. 123 *sq.*

[2] J. Brand, *Popular Antiquities of Great Britain* (London, 1882-1883), i. 303, quoting the author of the *Survey of the South of Ireland*, p. 232.

[3] J. Brand, *op. cit.* i. 305, quoting the author of the *Comical Pilgrim's Pilgrimage into Ireland* (1723), p. 92.

[4] *The Gentleman's Magazine*, vol. lxv. (London, 1795) pp. 124 *sq.* The writer dates the festival on June 21st, which is probably a mistake.

nally in honour of St. John.   On Sunday night bonfires were observed throughout nearly every county in the province of Leinster.   In Kilkenny, fires blazed on every hillside at intervals of about a mile.   There were very many in the Queen's County, also in Kildare and Wexford.   The effect in the rich sunset appeared to travellers very grand.   The people assemble, and dance round the fires, the children jump through the flames, and in former times live coals were carried into the corn-fields to prevent blight."[1]   In County Leitrim on St. John's Eve, which is called Bonfire Day, fires are still lighted after dusk on the hills and along the sides of the roads.[2]   All over Kerry the same thing continues to be done, though not so commonly as of old.   Small fires were made across the road, and to drive through them brought luck for the year.   Cattle were also driven through the fires.   On Lettermore Island, in South Connemara, some of the ashes from the midsummer bonfire are thrown on the fields to fertilize them.[3]   One writer informs us that in Munster and Connaught a bone must always be burned in the fire ; for otherwise the people believe that the fire will bring no luck.   He adds that in many places sterile beasts and human beings are passed through the fire, and that as a boy he himself jumped through the fire "for luck."[4]   An eye-witness has described as follows a remarkable ceremony observed in Ireland on Midsummer Eve : "When the fire burned for some hours, and got low, an indispensable part of the ceremony commenced.   Every one present of the peasantry passed through it, and several children were thrown across the sparkling embers ; while a wooden frame, of some eight feet long, with a horse's head fixed to one end, and a large white sheet thrown over it concealing the wood and the man on whose head it was carried, made its appearance.   This was greeted with loud shouts of 'The white horse!' and having been safely carried by the skill of its

Marginal notes: Cattle driven through the fire ; ashes used to fertilize the fields. The White Horse at the Midsummer fire.

[1] T. F. Thiselton Dyer, *British Popular Customs* (London, 1876), pp. 321 *sq.*, quoting the *Liverpool Mercury* of June 29th, 1867.

[2] L. L. Duncan, "Further Notes from County Leitrim," *Folk-lore*, **v.** (1894) p. 193.

[3] A. C. Haddon, "A Batch of Irish Folk-lore," *Folk-lore*, iv. (1893) pp. 351, 359.

[4] G. H. Kinahan, "Notes on Irish Folk-lore," *Folk-lore Record*, iv. (1881) p. 97.

bearer several times through the fire with a bold leap, it pursued the people, who ran screaming and laughing in every direction. I asked what the horse was meant for, and was told that it represented ' all cattle.' "[1]

Lady Wilde's account of the midsummer festival in Ireland is picturesque and probably correct in substance, although she does not cite her authorities. As it contains some interesting features which are not noticed by the other writers on Ireland whom I have consulted, I will quote the greater part of it in full. " In ancient times," she says, " the sacred fire was lighted with great ceremony on Midsummer Eve ; and on that night all the people of the adjacent country kept fixed watch on the western promontory of Howth, and the moment the first flash was seen from that spot the fact of ignition was announced with wild cries and cheers repeated from village to village, when all the local fires began to blaze, and Ireland was circled by a cordon of flame rising up from every hill. Then the dance and song began round every fire, and the wild hurrahs filled the air with the most frantic revelry. Many of these ancient customs are still continued, and the fires are still lighted on St. John's Eve on every hill in Ireland. When the fire has burned down to a red glow the young men strip to the waist and leap over or through the flames ; this is done backwards and forwards several times, and he who braves the greatest blaze is considered the victor over the powers of evil, and is greeted with tremendous applause. When the fire burns still lower, the young girls leap the flame, and those who leap clean over three times back and forward will be certain of a speedy marriage and good luck in after-life, with many children. The married women then walk through the lines of the burning embers ; and when the fire is nearly burnt and trampled down, the yearling cattle are driven through the hot ashes, and their back is singed with a lighted hazel twig. These rods are kept safely afterwards, being considered of immense power to drive the cattle to and from the watering places. As the fire diminishes the shouting grows fainter, and the song and the dance commence ; while pro-

---

[1] Charlotte Elizabeth, *Personal Recollections*, quoted by Rev. Alexander   Hislop, *The Two Babylons* (Edinburgh, 1853), p. 53.

fessional story-tellers narrate tales of fairy-land, or of the good old times long ago, when the kings and princes of Ireland dwelt amongst their own people, and there was food to eat and wine to drink for all comers to the feast at the king's house. When the crowd at length separate, every one carries home a brand from the fire, and great virtue is attached to the lighted *brone* which is safely carried to the house without breaking or falling to the ground. Many contests also arise amongst the young men ; for whoever enters his house first with the sacred fire brings the good luck of the year with him." [1]

In Ireland, as elsewhere, water was also apparently thought to acquire a certain mystical virtue at midsummer. "At Stoole, near Downpatrick, there is a ceremony commencing at twelve o'clock at night on Midsummer Eve. Its sacred mount is consecrated to St. Patrick ; the plain contains three wells, to which the most extraordinary virtues are attributed. Here and there are heaps of stones, around some of which appear great numbers of people, running with as much speed as possible ; around others crowds of worshippers kneel with bare legs and feet as an indispensable part of the penance. The men, without coats, with handkerchiefs on their heads instead of hats, having gone seven times round each heap, kiss the ground, cross themselves, and proceed to the hill ; here they ascend, on their bare knees, by a path so steep and rugged that it would be difficult to walk up. Many hold their hands clasped at the back of their necks, and several carry large stones on their heads. Having repeated this ceremony seven times, they go to what is called St. Patrick's Chair, which are two great flat stones fixed upright in the hill ; here they cross and bless themselves as they step in between these stones, and, while repeating prayers, an old man, seated for the purpose, turns them round on their feet three times, for which he is paid ; the devotee then goes to conclude his penance at a pile of stones, named the Altar. While this busy scene is continued by the multitude, the wells and streams issuing from them are thronged by crowds of halt, maimed, and blind, pressing

Holy wells resorted to on Midsummer Eve in Ireland.

to wash away their infirmities with water consecrated by their patron saint, and so powerful is the impression of its efficacy on their minds, that many of those who go to be healed, and who are not totally blind, or altogether crippled, really believe for a time that they are by means of its miraculous virtues perfectly restored." [1]

The Midsummer fires in Scotland.

In Scotland the traces of midsummer fires are few. We are told by a writer of the eighteenth century that "the midsummer-even fire, a relict of Druidism," was kindled in some parts of the county of Perth.[2] Another writer of the same period, describing what he calls the Druidical festivals of the Highlanders, says that "the least considerable of them is that of midsummer. In the Highlands of Perthshire there are some vestiges of it. The cowherd goes three times round the fold, according to the course of the sun, with a burning torch in his hand. They imagined this rite had a tendency to purify their herds and flocks, and to prevent diseases. At their return the landlady makes an entertainment for the cowherd and his associates." [3] In the north-east of Scotland, down to the latter half of the eighteenth century, farmers used to go round their lands with burning torches about the middle of June.[4] On the hill of Cairnshee, in the parish of Durris, Kincardineshire, the herdsmen of the country round about annually kindle a bonfire at sunset on Midsummer Day (the twenty-fourth of June); the men or lads collect the fuel and push each other through the smoke and flames. The custom is kept up through the benefaction of a certain Alexander Hogg, a native of the parish, who died about 1790 and left a small sum for the maintenance of a midsummer bonfire on the spot, because as

---

[1] T. F. Thiselton Dyer, *British Popular Customs* (London, 1876), pp. 322 *sq.*, quoting the *Hibernian Magazine*, July 1817. As to the worship of wells in ancient Ireland, see P. W. Joyce, *A Social History of Ancient Ireland* (London, 1903), i. 288 *sq.*, 366 *sqq.*

[2] Rev. A. Johnstone, describing the parish of Monquhitter in Perthshire, in Sir John Sinclair's *Statistical Account of Scotland* (Edinburgh, 1791–1799), xxi. 145. Mr. W. Warde Fowler writes that in Scotland "before the bonfires were kindled on mid-

summer eve, the houses were decorated with foliage brought from the woods" (*Roman Festivals of the Period of the Republic*, London, 1899, pp. 80 *sq.*). For his authority he refers to *Chambers' Journal*, July, 1842.

[3] John Ramsay, of Ochtertyre, *Scotland and Scotsmen in the Eighteenth Century*, edited by A. Allardyce (Edinburgh, 1888), ii. 436.

[4] Rev. Mr. Shaw, Minister of Elgin, in Pennant's "Tour in Scotland," printed in John Pinkerton's *Voyages and Travels* (London, 1808–1814), iii. 136.

a boy he had herded cattle on the hill.   We may conjecture
that in doing so he merely provided for the continuance
of an old custom which he himself had observed in the
same place in his youth.[1]   At the village of Tarbolton in
Ayrshire a bonfire has been annually kindled from time
immemorial on the evening of the first Monday after the
eleventh of June.   A noted cattle-market was formerly
held at the fair on the following day.   The bonfire is still
lit at the gloaming by the lads and lasses of the village on
a high mound or hillock just outside of the village.   Fuel
for it is collected by the lads from door to door.   The
youth dance round the fire and leap over the fringes of it.
The many cattle-drovers who used to assemble for the fair
were wont to gather round the blazing pile, smoke their
pipes, and listen to the young folk singing in chorus on the
hillock.   Afterwards they wrapped themselves in their
plaids and slept round the bonfire, which was intended to
last all night.[2]   Thomas Moresin of Aberdeen, a writer of
the sixteenth century, says that on St. Peter's Day, which is
the twenty-ninth of June, the Scotch ran about at night with
lighted torches on mountains and high grounds, "as Ceres
did when she roamed the whole earth in search of Proserpine" ;[3] and towards the end of the eighteenth century the
parish minister of Loudoun, a district of Ayrshire whose
"bonny woods and braes" have been sung by Burns, wrote
that "the custom still remains amongst the herds and young
people to kindle fires in the high grounds in honour of
Beltan.   *Beltan,* which in Gaelic signifies *Baal,* or *Bel's-fire,*
was antiently the time of this solemnity.   It is now kept on
St. Peter's day."[4]

Fires on St. Peter's Day (the twenty-ninth of June).

---

[1] A. Macdonald, "Midsummer Bonfires," *Folk-lore,* xv. (1904) pp. 105 *sq.*

[2] From notes kindly furnished to me
by the Rev. J. C. Higgins, parish
minister of Tarbolton. Mr. Higgins
adds that he knows of no superstition
connected with the fire, and no tradition of its origin. I visited the scene
of the bonfire in 1898, but, as Pausanias says (viii. 41. 6) in similar circumstances, "I did not happen to
arrive at the season of the festival."
Indeed the snow was falling thick as

I trudged to the village through the
beautiful woods of "the Castle o'
Montgomery" immortalized by Burns.
From a notice in *The Scotsman* of 26th
June, 1906 (p. 8) it appears that the
old custom was observed as usual that
year.

[3] Thomas Moresinus, *Papatus seu
Depravatae Religionis Origo et Incre-
mentum* (Edinburgh, 1594), p. 56.

[4] Rev. Dr. George Lawrie, in Sir
John Sinclair's *Statistical Account of
Scotland,* iii. (Edinburgh, 1792) p. 105.

All over Spain great bonfires called *lumes* are still lit on Midsummer Eve. They are kept up all night, and the children leap over them in a certain rhythmical way which is said to resemble the ancient dances. On the coast, people at this season plunge into the sea; in the inland districts the villagers go and roll naked in the dew of the meadows, which is supposed to be a sovereign preservative against diseases of the skin. On this evening, too, girls who would pry into the future put a vessel of water on the sill outside their window; and when the clocks strike twelve, they break an egg in the water and see, or fancy they see, in the shapes assumed by the pulp, as it blends with the liquid, the likeness of future bridegrooms, castles, coffins, and so forth. But generally, as might perhaps have been anticipated, the obliging egg exhibits the features of a bridegroom.[1] In the Azores, also, bonfires are lit on Midsummer Eve (St. John's Eve), and boys jump over them for luck. On that night St. John himself is supposed to appear in person and bless all the seas and waters, driving out the devils and demons who had been disporting themselves in them ever since the second day of November; that is why in the interval between the second of November and the twenty-third of June nobody will bathe in the sea or in a hot spring. On Midsummer Eve, too, you can always see the devil, if you will go into a garden at midnight. He is invariably found standing near a mustard-plant. His reason for adopting this posture has not been ascertained; perhaps in the chilly air of the upper world he is attracted by the genial warmth of the mustard. Various forms of divination are practised by people in the Azores on Midsummer Eve. Thus a new-laid egg is broken

[1] Letter from Dr. Otero Acevado of Madrid, published in *Le Temps*, September 1898. An extract from the newspaper was sent me, but without mention of the day of the month when it appeared. The fires on St. John's Eve in Spain are mentioned also by J. Brand, *Popular Antiquities of Great Britain*, i. 317. Jacob Grimm inferred the custom from a passage in a romance (*Deutsche Mythologie*,[4] i. 518). The custom of washing or bathing on the morning of St. John's Day is mentioned by the Spanish historian Diego Duran, *Historia de las Indias de Nueva España*, edited by J. F. Ramirez (Mexico, 1867–1880), vol. ii. p. 293. To roll in the dew on the morning of St. John's Day is a cure for diseases of the skin in Normandy, Périgord, and the Abruzzi, as well as in Spain. See J. Lecœur, *Esquisses du Bocage Normand*, ii. 8; A. de Nore, *Coutumes, Mythes et Traditions des Provinces de France*, p. 150; Gennaro Finamore, *Credenze, Usi e Costumi Abruzzesi* (Palermo, 1890), p. 157.

into a glass of water, and the shapes which it assumes fore-
shadow the fate of the person concerned.   Again, seven
saucers are placed in a row, filled respectively with water,
earth, ashes, keys, a thimble, money, and grass, which things
signify travel, death, widowhood, housekeeping, spinsterhood,
riches, and farming.   A blindfolded person touches one or
other of the saucers with a wand and so discovers his or her
fate.   Again, three broad beans are taken ; one is left in its
skin, one is half peeled, and the third is peeled outright.
The three denote respectively riches, competence, and
poverty.   They are hidden and searched for ; and he who
finds one of them knows accordingly whether he will be rich,
moderately well-off, or poor.   Again, girls take slips of
paper and write the names of young men twice over on them.
These they fold up and crumple and place one set under their
pillows and the other set in a saucer full of water.   In the
morning they draw one slip of paper from under their pillow,
and see whether one in the water has opened out.   If the
names on the two slips are the same, it is the name of her
future husband.   Young men do the same with girls' names.
Once more, if a girl rises at sunrise, goes out into the street,
and asks the first passer-by his Christian name, that will be
her husband's name.[1]   Some of these modes of divination
resemble those which are or used to be practised in Scotland
at Hallowe'en.[2]   In Corsica on the Eve of St. John the
people set fire to the trunk of a tree or to a whole tree, and
the young men and maidens dance round the blaze, which is
called *fucaraia*.[3]   We have seen that at Ozieri, in Sardinia,
a great bonfire is kindled on St. John's Eve, and that the
young people dance round it.[4]

Passing to Italy, we find that the midsummer fires are
still lighted on St. John's Eve in many parts of the Abruzzi.
They are commonest in the territory which was inhabited in
antiquity by the Vestini ; they are rarer in the land of the
ancient Marsi, and they disappear entirely in the lower valley

---

[1] M. Longworth Dames and Mrs. E.
Seemann, " Folklore of the Azores,"
Folk-lore, xiv. (1903) pp. 142 *sq.* ;
Theophilo Braga, *O Povo Portuguez
nos seus Costumes, Crenças e Tradiçoes*
(Lisbon, 1885), ii. 304 *sq.*, 307 *sq.*

[2] See below, pp. 234 *sqq.*

[3] Angelo de Gubernatis, *Mythologie
des Plantes* (Paris, 1878–1882), i. 185
note [1].

[4] *Adonis, Attis, Osiris,* Second
Edition, pp. 202 *sq.*

of the Sangro.   For the most part, the fires are fed with straw and dry grass, and are kindled in the fields near the villages or on high ground.   As they blaze up, the people dance round or over them.   In leaping across the flames the boys cry out, " St. John, preserve my thighs and legs ! " Formerly it used to be common to light the bonfires also in the towns in front of churches of St. John, and the remains of the sacred fire were carried home by the people ; but this custom has mostly fallen into disuse.   However, at Celano the practice is still kept up of taking brands and ashes from the bonfires to the houses, although the fires are no longer kindled in front of the churches, but merely in the streets.[1]

Bathing on Midsummer Eve in the Abruzzi. In the Abruzzi water also is supposed to acquire certain marvellous and beneficent properties on St. John's Night. Hence many people bathe or at least wash their faces and hands in the sea or a river at that season, especially at the moment of sunrise.   Such a bath is said to be an excellent cure for diseases of the skin.   At Castiglione a Casauria the people, after washing in the river or in springs, gird their waists and wreath their brows with sprigs of briony in order to keep them from aches and pains.[2]   In various parts of Sicily, also, fires are kindled on Midsummer Eve (St. John's Eve), the twenty-third of June.   On the Madonie mountains, in the north of the island, the herdsmen kindle them at intervals, so that the crests of the mountains are seen ablaze in the darkness for many miles.   About Acireale, on the east coast of the island, the bonfires are lit by boys, who jump over them.   At Chiaromonte the witches that night acquire extraordinary powers ; hence everybody then puts a broom outside of his house, because a broom is an excellent protective against witchcraft.[3]   At Orvieto the midsummer fires were specially excepted from the prohibition directed against bonfires in general.[4]

The Midsummer fires in Sicily.

The witches at Midsummer.

In Malta also the people celebrate Midsummer Eve

[1] G. Finamore, *Credenze, Usi e Costumi Abruzzesi* (Palermo, 1890), pp. 154 *sq.*

[2] G. Finamore, *Credenze, Usi e Costumi Abruzzesi*, pp. 158-160. We may compare the Provençal and Spanish customs of bathing and splashing water at midsummer.   See above, pp. 193

sq., 208.

[3] Giuseppe Pitrè, *Spettacoli e Feste Popolari Siciliane* (Palermo, 1881), pp. 246, 308 *sq.* ; *id.*, *Usi e Costumi, Credenze e Pregiudizi del Popolo Siciliano* (Palermo, 1889), pp. 146 *sq.*

[4] J. Grimm, *Deutsche Mythologie,*[4] i. 518.

(St. John's Eve) " by kindling great fires in the public
streets, and giving their children dolls to carry in their arms
on this day, in order to make good the prophecy respecting
the Baptist, *Multi in nativitate ejus gaudebunt.* Days and
even weeks before this festival, groups of children are seen
going out into the country fields to gather straw, twigs, and
all sorts of other combustibles, which they store up for
St. John's Eve. On the night of the twenty-third of June,
the day before the festival of the Saint, great fires are kindled
in the streets, squares, and market places of the towns and
villages of the Island, and as fire after fire blazes out of the
darkness of that summer night, the effect is singularly
striking. These fires are sometimes kept up for hours, being
continually fed by the scores of bystanders, who take great
delight in throwing amidst the flames some old rickety piece
of furniture which they consider as lumber in their houses.
Lots of happy and reckless children, and very often men, are
seen merrily leaping in succession over and through the
crackling flames. At the time of the Order of St. John of
Jerusalem, the Grand Master himself, soon after the *Angelus*,
used to leave his palace, accompanied by the Grand Prior,
the Bishop, and two bailiffs, to set fire to some pitch barrels
which were placed for the occasion in the square facing the
sacred Hospital. Great crowds used to assemble here in
order to assist at this ceremony. The setting ablaze of the
five casks, and later on of the eight casks, by the Grand
Master, was a signal for the others to kindle their fires in the
different parts of the town." [1]

In Greece, the custom of kindling fires on St. John's Eve
and jumping over them is said to be still universal. One
reason assigned for it is a wish to escape from the fleas.[2]
According to another account, the women cry out, as they
leap over the fire, " I leave my sins behind me." [3] In Lesbos
the fires on St. John's Eve are usually lighted by threes, and

[1] V. Busuttil, *Holiday Customs in Malta, and Sports, Usages, Ceremonies, Omens, and Superstitions of the Maltese People* (Malta, 1894), pp. 56 *sqq.* The extract was kindly sent to me by Mr. H. W. Underwood (letter dated 14th November, 1902, Birbeck Bank Chambers, Southampton Buildings, Chancery Lane, W.C.). See *Folk-lore*, xiv. (1903) pp. 77 *sq.*

[2] W. R. Paton, in *Folk-lore*, ii. (1891) p. 128. The custom was reported to me when I was in Greece in 1890 (*Folk-lore*, i. (1890) p. 520).

[3] J. Grimm, *Deutsche Mythologie*,[4] i. 519.

the people spring thrice over them, each with a stone on his head, saying, " I jump the hare's fire, my head a stone ! " On the morning of St. John's Day those who dwell near the coast go to bathe in the sea. As they go they gird themselves with osiers, and when they are in the water they let the osiers float away, saying, " Let my maladies go away ! " Then they look for what is called " the hairy stone," which possesses the remarkable property not only of keeping moths from clothes but even of multiplying the clothes in the chest where it is laid up, and the more hairs on the stone the more will the clothes multiply in the chest.[1] In Calymnos the midsummer fire is supposed to ensure abundance in the coming year as well as deliverance from fleas. The people dance round the fires singing, with stones on their heads, and then jump over the blaze or the glowing embers. When the fire is burning low, they throw the stones into it ; and when it is nearly out, they make crosses on their legs and then go straightway and bathe in the sea.[2] In Cos the lads and lasses dance round the bonfires on St. John's Eve. Each of the lads binds a black stone on his head, signifying that he wishes to become as strong as the stone. Also they make the sign of the cross on their feet and legs and jump over the fire.[3] On Midsummer Eve the Greeks of Macedonia light fires after supper in front of their gates. The garlands, now faded, which were hung over the doors on May Day, are taken down and cast into the flames, after which the young folk leap over the blaze, fully persuaded that St. John's fire will not burn them.[4] In Albania fires of dry herbage are, or used to be, lit everywhere on St. John's Eve ; young and old leap over them, for such a leap is thought to be good for the health.[5]

From the Old World the midsummer fires have been

The Midsummer fires in Macedonia and Albania.

---

[1] G. Georgeakis et L. Pineau, *Le Folk-lore de Lesbos* (Paris, 1894), pp. 308 *sq.*

[2] W. R. Paton, in *Folk-lore*, vi. (1895) p. 94. From the stones cast into the fire omens may perhaps be drawn, as in Scotland, Wales, and probably Brittany. See above, p. 183, and below, pp. 230 *sq.*, 239, 240.

[3] W. H. D. Rouse, "Folklore from the Southern Sporades," *Folk-lore*, x. (1899) p. 179.

[4] Lucy M. J. Garnett, *The Women of Turkey and their Folk-lore, the Christian Women* (London, 1890), p. 122 ; G. F. Abbott, *Macedonian Folk-lore* (Cambridge, 1903), p. 57.

[5] J. G. von Hahn, *Albanesische Studien* (Jena, 1854), i. 156.

carried across the Atlantic to America. In Brazil people jump over the fires of St. John, and at this season they can take hot coals in their mouths without burning themselves.[1] In Bolivia on the Eve of St. John it is usual to see bonfires lighted on the hills and even in the streets of the capital La Paz. As the city stands at the bottom of an immense ravine, and the Indians of the neighbourhood take a pride in kindling bonfires on heights which might seem inaccessible, the scene is very striking when the darkness of night is suddenly and simultaneously lit up by hundreds of fires, which cast a glare on surrounding objects, producing an effect at once weird and picturesque.[2]

The custom of kindling bonfires on Midsummer Day or on Midsummer Eve is widely spread among the Mohammedan peoples of North Africa, particularly in Morocco and Algeria; it is common both to the Berbers and to many of the Arabs or Arabic-speaking tribes. In these countries Midsummer Day (the twenty-fourth of June, Old Style) is called *l 'ánṣăra*. The fires are lit in the court-yards, at cross-roads, in the fields, and sometimes on the threshing-floors. Plants which in burning give out a thick smoke and an aromatic smell are much sought after for fuel on these occasions; among the plants used for the purpose are giant-fennel, thyme, rue, chervil-seed, camomile, geranium, and penny-royal. People expose themselves, and especially their children, to the smoke, and drive it towards the orchards and the crops. Also they leap across the fires; in some places everybody ought to repeat the leap seven times. Moreover they take burning brands from the fires and carry them through the houses in order to fumigate them. They pass things through the fire, and bring the sick into contact with it, while they utter prayers for their recovery. The ashes of the bonfires are also reputed to possess beneficial properties; hence in some places people rub their hair or their bodies with them.[3] For example, the Andjra

[1] K. von den Steinen, *Unter den Natur - Völkern Zentral - Brasiliens* (Berlin, 1894), p. 561.

[2] Alcide d'Orbigny, *Voyage dans l'Amérique Méridionale*, ii. (Paris and Strasbourg, 1839–1843), p. 420; D.

Forbes, "On the Aymara Indians of Bolivia and Peru," *Journal of the Ethnological Society of London*, ii. (1870) p. 235.

[3] Edmond Doutté, *Magie et Religion dans l'Afrique du Nord* (Algiers, 1908),

mountaineers of Morocco kindle large fires in open places of their villages on Midsummer Day. Men, women, and children jump over the flames or the glowing embers, believing that by so doing they rid themselves of all misfortune which may be clinging to them; they imagine, also, that such leaps cure the sick and procure offspring for childless couples. Moreover, they burn straw, together with some marjoram and alum, in the fold where the cattle, sheep, and goats are penned for the night; the smoke, in their opinion, will make the animals thrive. On Midsummer Day the Arabs of the Mnasara tribe make fires outside their tents, near their animals, on their fields, and in their gardens. Large quantities of penny-royal are burned in these fires, and over some of them the people leap thrice to and fro. Sometimes small fires are also kindled inside the tents. They say that the smoke confers blessings on everything with which it comes into contact. At Salee, on the Atlantic coast of Morocco, persons who suffer from diseased eyes rub them with the ashes of the midsummer fire; and in Casablanca and Azemmur the people hold their faces over the fire, because the smoke is thought to be good for the eyes. The Arab tribe Ulad Bu Aziz, in the Dukkala province of Morocco, kindle midsummer bonfires, not for themselves and their cattle, but only for crops and fruit; nobody likes to reap his crops before Midsummer Day, because if he did they would lose the benefit of the blessed influence which flows from the smoke of the bonfires.

---

pp. 566 *sq.* For an older but briefer notice of the Midsummer fires in North Africa, see Giuseppe Ferraro, *Superstizioni, Usi e Proverbi Monferrini* (Palermo, 1886), pp. 34 *sq.* : "Also in Algeria, among the Mussalmans, and in Morocco, as Alvise da Cadamosto reports in his *Relazione dei viaggi d'Africa,* which may be read in Ramusio, people used to hold great festivities on St. John's Night; they kindled everywhere huge fires of straw (the *Palilia* of the Romans), in which they threw incense and perfumes the whole night long in order to invoke the divine blessing on the fruit-trees." See also Budgett Meakin, *The Moors* (London, 1902), p. 394 : "The Berber festivals are mainly those of Islam, though a few traces of their predecessors are observable. Of these the most noteworthy is Midsummer or St. John's Day, still celebrated in a special manner, and styled *El 'Ansarah.* In the Rif it is celebrated by the lighting of bonfires only, but in other parts there is a special dish prepared of wheat, raisins, etc., resembling the frumenty consumed at the New Year. It is worthy of remark that the Old Style Gregorian calendar is maintained among them, with corruptions of Latin names."

Again, the Beni Mgild, a Berber tribe of Morocco, light fires
of straw on Midsummer Eve and leap thrice over them to
and fro.   They let some of the smoke pass underneath their
clothes, and married women hold their breasts over the fire,
in order that their children may be strong.   Moreover, they
paint their eyes and lips with some black powder, in which
ashes of the bonfire are mixed.   And in order that their
horses may also benefit by the fires, they dip the right fore-
legs of the animals in the smoke and flames or in the hot
embers, and they rub ashes on the foreheads and between
the nostrils of the horses.   Berbers of the Rif province, in
northern Morocco, similarly make great use of fires at
midsummer for the good of themselves, their cattle, and
their fruit-trees.   They jump over the bonfires in the belief
that this will preserve them in good health, and they light
fires under fruit-trees to keep the fruit from falling untimely.
And they imagine that by rubbing a paste of the ashes on
their hair they prevent the hair from falling off their heads.[1]

In all these Moroccan customs, we are told, the beneficial Beneficial
effect is attributed wholly to the smoke, which is supposed effect
to be endued with a magical quality that removes misfortune to the
from men, animals, fruit-trees, and crops.   But in some parts the fires.
of Morocco people at midsummer kindle fires of a different Ill luck
sort, not for the sake of fumigation, but in order to burn up supposed
misfortune in the flames.   Thus on Midsummer Eve the in the Mid-
Berber tribe of the Beni Mgild burn three sheaves of fires.
unthreshed wheat or barley, "one for the children, one for
the crops, and one for the animals."   On the same occasion
they burn the tent of a widow who has never given birth to
a child ; by so doing they think to rid the village of ill luck.
It is said that at midsummer the Zemmur burn a tent, which
belongs to somebody who was killed in war during a feast ;
or if there is no such person in the village, the schoolmaster's
tent is burned instead.   Among the Arabic-speaking Beni
Ahsen it is customary for those who live near the river Sbu
to make a little hut of straw at midsummer, set it on fire,

[1] Edward   Westermarck,   "Mid-   *culture, Certain Dates of the Solar*
summer Customs in Morocco," *Folk-*   *Year, and the Weather* (Helsingfors,
lore, xvi. (1905) pp. 28-30 ; *id., Cere-*   1913), pp. 79-83.
monies and Beliefs connected with Agri-

and let it float down the river.   Similarly the inhabitants of
Salee burn a straw hut on the river which flows past their
town.[1]

The Mid-
summer
festival in
North
Africa
comprises
rites con-
cerned with
water as
well as with
fire.
Further it deserves to be noticed that in Northern
Africa, as in Southern Europe, the midsummer festival
comprises rites concerned with water as well as with fire.
For example, among the Beni-Snous the women light a fire in
an oven, throw perfumes into it, and circumambulate a tank,
which they also incense after a fashion.   In many places on
the coast, as in the province of Oran and particularly in the
north of Morocco, everybody goes and bathes in the sea at
midsummer ; and in many towns of the interior, such as
Fez, Mequinez, and especially Merrakech, people throw water
over each other on this day ; and where water is scarce, earth
is used instead, according to the Mohammedan principle
which permits ablutions to be performed with earth or sand
when water cannot be spared for the purpose.[2]   People of
the Andjra district in Morocco not only bathe themselves in
the sea or in rivers at midsummer, they also bathe their
animals, their horses, mules, donkeys, cattle, sheep, and
goats ; for they think that on that day water possesses a
blessed virtue (*baraka*), which removes sickness and misfortune.   In Aglu, again, men, women, and children bathe in
the sea or springs or rivers at midsummer, alleging that by
so doing they protect themselves against disease for the
whole year.   Among the Berbers of the Rif district the
custom of bathing on this day is commonly observed, and
animals share the ablutions.[3]

The Mid-
summer
festival in
North
Africa is
probably
older than
Moham-
medanism.
The celebration of a midsummer festival by Mohammedan peoples is particularly remarkable, because the
Mohammedan calendar, being purely lunar and uncorrected
by intercalation, necessarily takes no note of festivals
which occupy fixed points in the solar year ; all strictly
Mohammedan feasts, being pinned to the moon, slide

---

[1] E. Westermarck, " Midsummer
Customs in Morocco," *Folk-lore*, xvi.
(1905) pp. 30 *sq.* ; *id.*, *Ceremonies and
Beliefs connected with Agriculture*, etc.,
pp. 83 *sq.*

[2] Edmond Doutté, *Magie et Religion*

dans l'Afrique du Nord (Algiers, 1908),
pp. 567 *sq.*

[3] E. Westermarck, " Midsummer
Customs in Morocco," *Folk-lore*, xvi.
(1905) pp. 31 *sq.* ; *id.*, *Ceremonies and
Beliefs connected with Agriculture*, etc.,
pp. 84-86.

gradually with that luminary through the whole period of the earth's revolution about the sun.   This fact of itself seems to prove that among the Mohammedan peoples of Northern Africa, as among the Christian peoples of Europe, the midsummer festival is quite independent of the religion which the people publicly profess, and is a relic of a far older paganism.   There are, indeed, independent grounds for thinking that the Arabs enjoyed the advantage of a comparatively well-regulated solar year before the prophet of God saddled them with the absurdity and inconvenience of a purely lunar calendar.[1]   Be that as it may, it is notable that some Mohammedan people of North Africa kindle fires and bathe in water at the movable New Year of their lunar calendar instead of at the fixed Midsummer of the solar year ; while others again practise these observances at both seasons.   New Year's Day, on which the rites are celebrated, is called *Ashur* ; it is the tenth day of Moharram, the first month of the Mohammedan calendar.   On that day bonfires are kindled in Tunis and also at Merrakech and among some tribes of the neighbourhood.[2]   At Demnat, in the Great Atlas mountains, people kindle a large bonfire on New Year's Eve and leap to and fro over the flames, uttering words which imply that by these leaps they think to purify themselves from all kinds of evil.   At Aglu, in the province of Sus, the fire is lighted at three different points by an unmarried girl, and when it has died down the young men leap over the glowing embers, saying, " We shook on you, O Lady Ashur, fleas, and lice, and the illnesses of the heart, as also those of the bones ; we shall pass through you again next year and the following years with safety and health."   Both at Aglu and Glawi, in the Great Atlas, smaller fires are also kindled, over which the animals

Some Moham-
medans
of North
Africa
kindle fires
and observe
water cere-
monies at
their mov-
able New
Year.

---

[1] See K. Vollers, in Dr. James Hastings's *Encyclopaedia of Religion and Ethics*, iii. (Edinburgh, 1910) *s.v.* " Calendar (Muslim)," pp. 126 *sq.* However, L. Ideler held that even before the time of Mohammed the Arab year was lunar and vague, and that intercalation was only employed in order to fix the pilgrimage month in autumn, which, on account of the milder weather and the abundance of food, is the best time for pilgrims to go to Mecca.   See L. Ideler, *Handbuch der mathematischen und techischen Chronologie* (Berlin, 1825–1826), ii. 495 *sqq.*

[2] E. Doutté, *Magie et Religion dans l'Afrique du Nord*, pp. 496, 509, 532, 543, 569.   It is somewhat remarkable that the tenth, not the first, day of the first month should be reckoned New Year's Day.

are driven. At Demnat girls who wish to marry wash themselves in water which has been boiled over the New Year fire ; and in Dukkala people use the ashes of that fire to rub sore eyes with. New Year fires appear to be commonly kindled among the Berbers who inhabit the western portion of the Great Atlas, and also among the Arabic-speaking tribes of the plains ; but Dr. Westermarck found no traces of such fires among the Arabic-speaking mountaineers of Northern Morocco and the Berbers of the Rif province.

Water ceremonies at New Year in Morocco.

Further, it should be observed that water ceremonies like those which are practised at Midsummer are very commonly observed in Morocco at the New Year, that is, on the tenth day of the first month. On the morning of that day (*Ashur*) all water or, according to some people, only spring water is endowed with a magical virtue (*baraka*), especially before sunrise. Hence at that time the people bathe and pour water over each other ; in some places they also sprinkle their animals, tents, or rooms. In Dukkala some of the New Year water is preserved at home till New Year's Day (*Ashur*) of next year ; some of it is kept to be used as medicine, some of it is poured on the place where the corn is threshed, and some is used to water the money which is to be buried in the ground ; for the people think that the earth-spirits will not be able to steal the buried treasures which have thus been sanctified with the holy water.[1]

The rites of fire and water at Midsummer and New Year in Morocco seem to be identical in character ; the duplication of the festival is probably due to a conflict between

Thus the rites of fire and water which are observed in Morocco at Midsummer and New Year appear to be identical in character and intention, and it seems certain that the duplication of the rites is due to a conflict between two calendars, namely the old Julian calendar of the Romans, which was based on the sun, and the newer Mohammedan calendar of the Arabs, which is based on the moon. For not only was the Julian calendar in use throughout the whole of Northern Africa under the Roman Empire ; to this day it is everywhere employed among Mohammedans for the regulation of agriculture and all the affairs of daily life ; its practical convenience has made it indispensable,

[1] E. Westermarck, "Midsummer Customs in Morocco," *Folk-lore*, xvi. (1905) pp. 40-42.

and the lunar calendar of orthodox Mohammedanism is
scarcely used except for purposes of chronology.   Even the
old Latin names of the months are known and employed,
in slightly disguised forms, throughout the whole Moslem
world ; and little calendars of the Julian year circulate in
manuscript among Mohammedans, permitting them to combine the practical advantages of pagan science with a
nominal adherence to orthodox absurdity.[1]   Thus the
heathen origin of the midsummer festival is too palpable to
escape the attention of good Mohammedans, who accordingly frown upon the midsummer bonfires as pagan superstitions, precisely as similar observances in Europe have often
been denounced by orthodox Christianity.   Indeed, many
religious people in Morocco entirely disapprove of the
whole of the midsummer ceremonies, maintaining that they
are all bad ; and a conscientious schoolmaster will even
refuse his pupils a holiday at midsummer, though the
boys sometimes offer him a bribe if he will sacrifice
his scruples to his avarice.[2]   As the midsummer customs
appear to flourish among all the Berbers of Morocco
but to be unknown among the pure Arabs who have not
been affected by Berber influence, it seems reasonable to
infer with Dr. Westermarck that the midsummer festival has
belonged from time immemorial to the Berber race, and that
so far as it is now observed by the Arabs of Morocco, it has
been learned by them from the Berbers, the old indigenous
inhabitants of the country.   Dr. Westermarck may also be
right in holding that, in spite of the close similarity which
obtains between the midsummer festival of Europe and the
midsummer festival of North Africa, the latter is not a copy
of the former, but that both have been handed down independently from a time beyond the purview of history,
when such ceremonies were common to the Mediterranean
race.[3]

the solar calendar of the Romans and the lunar calendar of the Arabs.

The Mid-summer festival in Morocco seems to be of Berber origin.

[1] E. Doutté, *Magie et Religion dans l'Afrique du Nord* (Algiers, 1908), pp. 541 *sq.*

[2] E. Westermarck, "Midsummer Customs in Morocco," *Folk-lore*, xvi. (1905) p. 42 ; *id.*, *Ceremonies and Beliefs connected with Agriculture, Certain Dates of the Solar Year, and*

the Weather in Morocco (Helsingfors, 1913), p. 101.

[3] E. Westermarck, "Midsummer Customs in Morocco," *Folk-lore*, xvi. (1905), pp. 42 *sq.*, 46 *sq.* ; *id.*, *Ceremonies and Beliefs connected with Agriculture*, etc., *in Morocco*, pp. 99 *sqq.*

§ 5. The Autumn Fires

Festivals of fire in August.

In the months which elapse between midsummer and the setting in of winter the European festivals of fire appear to be few and unimportant. On the evening of the first day of August, which is the Festival of the Cross, bonfires are commonly lit in Macedonia and boys jump over them, shouting, " Dig up! bury!" but whom or what they wish to dig up or bury they do not know.[1] The Russians hold the feast of two martyrs, Florus and Laurus, on the eighteenth day of August, Old Style. "On this day the Russians lead their horses round the church of their village, beside which on the foregoing evening they dig a hole with two mouths. Each horse has a bridle made of the bark of the linden-tree. The horses go through this hole one after the other, opposite to one of the mouths of which the priest stands with a sprinkler in his hand, with which he sprinkles them. As soon as the horses have passed by their bridles are taken off, and they are made to go between two fires that they kindle, called by the Russians *Givoy Agon*, that is to say, living fires, of which I shall give an account. I shall before remark, that the Russian peasantry throw the bridles of their horses into one of these fires to be consumed. This is the manner of their lighting these *givoy agon*, or living fires. Some men hold the ends of a stick made of the plane-tree, very dry, and about a fathom long. This stick they hold firmly over one of birch, perfectly dry, and rub with violence and quickly against the former; the birch, which is somewhat softer than the plane, in a short time inflames, and serves them to light both the fires I have described."[2]

Russian feast of Florus and Laurus on August 18th.

" Living fire " made by the friction of wood.

Feast of the Nativity of the Virgin on

The Feast of the Nativity of the Virgin on the eighth day of September is celebrated at Naples and Capri with fireworks, bonfires, and assassinations. On this subject my

---

[1] G. F. Abbott, *Macedonian Folk-lore* (Cambridge, 1903), pp. 60 *sq.*

[2] " Narrative of the Adventures of four Russian Sailors, who were cast in a storm upon the uncultivated island of East Spitzbergen," translated from the German of P. L. Le Roy, in John Pinkerton's *Voyages and Travels* (London, 1808–1814), i. 603. This passage is quoted from the original by (Sir) Edward B. Tylor, *Researches into the Early History of Mankind*, Third Edition (London, 1878), pp. 259 *sq.*

friend Professor A. E. Housman, who witnessed the celebration in different years at both places, has kindly furnished
me with the following particulars : " In 1906 I was in the
island of Capri on September the eighth, the feast of the
Nativity of the Virgin.   The anniversary was duly solemn-
ised by fire-works at nine or ten in the evening, which I suppose were municipal ; but just after sundown the boys outside
the villages were making small fires of brushwood on waste
bits of ground by the wayside.   Very pretty it looked, with
the flames blowing about in the twilight ; but what took
my attention was the listlessness of the boys and their lack
of interest in the proceeding.   A single lad, the youngest,
would be raking the fire together and keeping it alight, but
the rest stood lounging about and looking in every other
direction, with the air of discharging mechanically a traditional
office from which all zest had evaporated."   " The pious orgy
at Naples on September the eighth went through the following phases when I witnessed it in 1897.   It began at eight
in the evening with an illumination of the façade of Santa
Maria Piedigrotta and with the whole population walking
about blowing penny trumpets.   After four hours of this I
went to bed at midnight, and was lulled to sleep by barrel-
organs, which supersede the trumpets about that hour.   At
four in the morning I was waked by detonations as if the
British fleet were bombarding the city, caused, I was afterwards told, by dynamite rockets.   The only step possible
beyond this is assassination, which accordingly takes place
about peep of day : I forget now the number of the slain,
but I think the average is eight or ten, and I know that
in honour of my presence they murdered a few more than
usual."

It is no doubt possible that these illuminations and fireworks, like the assassinations, are merely the natural and
spontaneous expressions of that overflowing joy with which
the thought of the birth of the Virgin must fill every
pious heart ; but when we remember how often the Church
has skilfully decanted the new wine of Christianity into the
old bottles of heathendom, we may be allowed to conjecture
that the ecclesiastical authorities adroitly timed the Nativity
of the Virgin so as to coincide with an old pagan festival

of that day, in which fire, noise, and uproar, if not broken heads and bloodshed, were conspicuous features. The penny trumpets blown on this occasion recall the like melodious instruments which figure so largely in the celebration of Befana (the Eve of Epiphany) at Rome.[1]

§ 6. *The Hallowe'en Fires*

The coincidence of the Midsummer festival with the summer solstice implies that the founders of the festival regulated their calendar by observation of the sun.

From the foregoing survey we may infer that among the heathen forefathers of the European peoples the most popular and widespread fire-festival of the year was the great celebration of Midsummer Eve or Midsummer Day. The coincidence of the festival with the summer solstice can hardly be accidental. Rather we must suppose that our pagan ancestors purposely timed the ceremony of fire on earth to coincide with the arrival of the sun at the highest point of his course in the sky. If that was so, it follows that the old founders of the midsummer rites had observed the solstices or turning-points of the sun's apparent path in the sky, and that they accordingly regulated their festal calendar to some extent by astronomical considerations.

On the other hand the Celts divided their year, not by the solstices, but by the beginning of summer (the first of May) and the beginning of winter (the first of November).

But while this may be regarded as fairly certain for what we may call the aborigines throughout a large part of the continent, it appears not to have been true of the Celtic peoples who inhabited the Land's End of Europe, the islands and promontories that stretch out into the Atlantic ocean on the North-West. The principal fire-festivals of the Celts, which have survived, though in a restricted area and with diminished pomp, to modern times and even to our own day, were seemingly timed without any reference to the position of the sun in the heaven. They were two in number, and fell at an interval of six months, one being celebrated on the eve of May Day and the other on Allhallow Even or Hallowe'en, as it is now commonly called, that is, on the thirty-first of October, the day preceding All Saints' or Allhallows' Day. These dates coincide with none of the four great hinges on which the solar year revolves, to wit, the solstices and the equinoxes. Nor do they agree with the principal seasons of the agri-

[1] See *The Scapegoat*, pp. 166 *sq.*

cultural year, the sowing in spring and the reaping in autumn.   For when May Day comes, the seed has long been committed to the earth ; and when November opens, the harvest has long been reaped and garnered, the fields lie bare, the fruit-trees are stripped, and even the yellow leaves are fast fluttering to the ground.   Yet the first of May and the first of November mark turning-points of the year in Europe ; the one ushers in the genial heat and the rich vegetation of summer, the other heralds, if it does not share, the cold and barrenness of winter.   Now these par-ticular points of the year, as has been well pointed out by a learned and ingenious writer,[1] while they are of com-paratively little moment to the European husbandman, do deeply concern the European herdsman ; for it is on the approach of summer that he drives his cattle out into the open to crop the fresh grass, and it is on the approach of winter that he leads them back to the safety and shelter of the stall.   Accordingly it seems not improbable that the Celtic bisection of the year into two halves at the beginning of May and the beginning of November dates from a time when the Celts were mainly a pastoral people, dependent for their subsistence on their herds, and when accordingly the great epochs of the year for them were the days on which the cattle went forth from the homestead in early summer and returned to it again in early winter.[2] Even in Central Europe, remote from the region now occupied by the Celts, a similar bisection of the year may be clearly traced in the great popularity, on the one hand, of May Day and its Eve (Walpurgis Night), and, on the other hand, of the Feast of All Souls at the beginning of November,

The divi-sion seems to have been neither astronomi-cal nor agri-cultural but pastoral, being de-termined by the times when cattle are driven to and from their summer pasture.

---

[1] E. K. Chambers, *The Mediaeval Stage* (Oxford, 1903), i. 110 *sqq.*

[2] In Eastern Europe to this day the great season for driving out the cattle to pasture for the first time in spring is St. George's Day, the twenty-third of April, which is not far removed from May Day.   See *The Magic Art and the Evolution of Kings*, ii. 324 *sqq.* As to the bisection of the Celtic year, see the old authority quoted by P. W. Joyce, *The Social History of Ancient*

Ireland (London, 1903), ii. 390 : "The whole year was [originally] divided into two parts—Summer from 1st May to 1st November, and Winter from 1st November to 1st May."   On this subject compare (Sir) John Rhys, *Celtic Heathendom* (London and Edin-burgh, 1888), pp. 460, 514 *sqq.* ; *id.*, *Celtic Folk-lore, Welsh and Manx* (Ox-ford, 1901), i. 315 *sqq.* ; J. A. Mac-Culloch, in Dr. James Hastings's *Encyclopaedia of Religion and Ethics*, iii. (Edinburgh, 1910) p. 80.

which under a thin Christian cloak conceals an ancient pagan festival of the dead.[1]   Hence we may conjecture that everywhere throughout Europe the celestial division of the year according to the solstices was preceded by what we may call a terrestrial division of the year according to the beginning of summer and the beginning of winter.

The two great Celtic festivals, Beltane and Hallowe'en.

Be that as it may, the two great Celtic festivals of May Day and the first of November or, to be more accurate, the Eves of these two days, closely resemble each other in the manner of their celebration and in the superstitions associated with them, and alike, by the antique character impressed upon both, betray a remote and purely pagan origin.   The festival of May Day or Beltane, as the Celts called it, which ushered in summer, has already been described ;[2] it remains to give some account of the corresponding festival of Hallowe'en, which announced the arrival of winter.

Hallowe'en (the evening of October 31st) seems to have marked the beginning of the Celtic year.

Of the two feasts Hallowe'en was perhaps of old the more important, since the Celts would seem to have dated the beginning of the year from it rather than from Beltane. In the Isle of Man, one of the fortresses in which the Celtic language and lore longest held out against the siege of the Saxon invaders, the first of November, Old Style, has been regarded as New Year's day down to recent times.   Thus Manx mummers used to go round on Hallowe'en (Old Style), singing, in the Manx language, a sort of Hogmanay song which began "To-night is New Year's Night, *Hogunnaa*!"[3]   One of Sir John Rhys's Manx informants, an old man of sixty-seven, "had been a farm servant from the age of sixteen till he was twenty-six to the same man, near Regaby, in the parish of Andreas, and he remembers his master and a near neighbour of his discussing the term New Year's Day as applied to the first of November, and explaining to the younger men that it had always been so in old

[1] See below, p. 225.

[2] Above, pp. 146 *sqq.* ; *The Magic Art and the Evolution of Kings*, ii. 59 *sqq.*

[3] (Sir) John Rhys, *Celtic Folk-lore, Manx and Welsh* (Oxford, 1901), i. 316, 317 *sq.* ; J. A. MacCulloch, in Dr. James Hastings's *Encyclopaedia of Religion and Ethics*, iii. (Edinburgh, 1910) *s.v.* "Calendar," p. 80, referring to Kelly, *English and Manx Dictionary* (Douglas, 1866), *s.v.* "Blein." Hogmanay is the popular Scotch name for the last day of the year. See Dr. J. Jamieson, *Etymological Dictionary of the Scottish Language*, New Edition (Paisley, 1879-1882), ii. 602 *sq.*

times. In fact, it seemed to him natural enough, as all
tenure of land ends at that time, and as all servant men
begin their service then." [1]   In ancient Ireland, as we saw,
a new fire used to be kindled every year on Hallowe'en or
the Eve of Samhain, and from this sacred flame all the fires
in Ireland were rekindled.[2]   Such a custom points strongly
to Samhain or All Saints' Day (the first of November)
as New Year's Day ; since the annual kindling of a new
fire takes place most naturally at the beginning of the year,
in order that the blessed influence of the fresh fire may last
throughout the whole period of twelve months.   Another
confirmation of the view that the Celts dated their year from
the first of November is furnished by the manifold modes of
divination which, as we shall see presently, were commonly
resorted to by Celtic peoples on Hallowe'en for the purpose
of ascertaining their destiny, especially their fortune in the
coming year ; for when could these devices for prying into
the future be more reasonably put in practice than at the
beginning of the year ?   As a season of omens and auguries
Hallowe'en seems to have far surpassed Beltane in the
imagination of the Celts ; from which we may with some
probability infer that they reckoned their year from
Hallowe'en rather than Beltane.   Another circumstance of
great moment which points to the same conclusion is the
association of the dead with Hallowe'en.   Not only among
the Celts but throughout Europe, Hallowe'en, the night
which marks the transition from autumn to winter, seems to
have been of old the time of year when the souls of the
departed were supposed to revisit their old homes in order
to warm themselves by the fire and to comfort themselves
with the good cheer provided for them in the kitchen or the
parlour by their affectionate kinsfolk.[3]   It was, perhaps, a

The many forms of divination resorted to at Hallowe'en are appropriate to the beginning of a New Year.

Hallowe'en also a festival of the dead.

[1] (Sir) John Rhys, *Celtic Folk-lore,
Welsh and Manx*, i. 316 *sq.*

[2] Above, p. 139.

[3] See *Adonis, Attis, Osiris*, Second
Edition, pp. 309-318.   As I have
there pointed out, the Catholic Church
succeeded in altering the date of the
festival by one day, but not in changing
the character of the festival.   All
Souls' Day is now the second instead
of the first of November.   But we can

hardly doubt that the Saints, who
have taken possession of the first of
November, wrested it from the Souls
of the Dead, the original proprietors.
After all, the Saints are only one particular class of the Souls of the Dead ;
so that the change which the Church
effected, no doubt for the purpose of
disguising the heathen character of the
festival, is less great than appears at
first sight.

natural thought that the approach of winter should drive the poor shivering hungry ghosts from the bare fields and the leafless woodlands to the shelter of the cottage with its familiar fireside.[1] Did not the lowing kine then troop back from the summer pastures in the forests and on the hills to be fed and cared for in the stalls, while the bleak winds whistled among the swaying boughs and the snow drifts deepened in the hollows? and could the good-man and the good-wife deny to the spirits of their dead the welcome which they gave to the cows?

Fairies and hobgoblins let loose at Hallowe'en. But it is not only the souls of the departed who are supposed to be hovering unseen on the day "when autumn to winter resigns the pale year." Witches then speed on their errands of mischief, some sweeping through the air on besoms, others galloping along the roads on tabby-cats, which for that evening are turned into coal-black steeds.[2] The fairies, too, are all let loose, and hobgoblins of every sort roam freely about. In South Uist and Eriskay there is a saying :—

> *" Hallowe'en will come, will come,*
> *Witchcraft [or divination] will be set agoing,*
> *Fairies will be at full speed,*
> *Running in every pass.*
> *Avoid the road, children, children."* [3]

In Cardiganshire on November Eve a bogie sits on every stile.[4] On that night in Ireland all the fairy hills are thrown wide open and the fairies swarm forth; any man who is bold enough may then peep into the open green hills and see the treasures hidden in them. Worse than that, the cave of Cruachan in Connaught, known as "the Hell-gate of Ireland," is unbarred on Samhain Eve or Hallowe'en, and a host of horrible fiends and goblins used to rush forth, particularly a flock of copper-red birds, which

---

[1] In Wales "it was firmly believed in former times that on All Hallows' Eve the spirit of a departed person was to be seen at midnight on every cross-road and on every stile" (Marie Trevelyan, *Folk-lore and Folk-stories of Wales*, London, 1909, p. 254).

[2] E. J. Guthrie, *Old Scottish Cus-*

toms (London and Glasgow, 1885), p. 68.

[3] A. Goodrich-Freer, "More Folk-lore from the Hebrides," *Folk-lore*, xiii. (1902) p. 53.

[4] (Sir) John Rhys, *Celtic Heathendom* (London and Edinburgh, 1888), p. 516.

blighted crops and killed animals by their poisonous breath.[1]
The Scotch Highlanders have a special name *Samhanach*
(derived from *Samhain*, "All-hallows") for the dreadful
bogies that go about that night stealing babies and com-
mitting other atrocities.[2] And though the fairies are a
kindlier folk, it is dangerous to see even them at their revels
on Hallowe'en. A melancholy case of this sort is reported Dancing
with the
fairies
at Hal-
lowe'en.
from the Ferintosh district of the Highlands, though others
say that it happened at the Slope of Big Stones in Harris.
Two young men were coming home after nightfall on
Hallowe'en, each with a jar of whisky on his back, when
they saw, as they thought, a house all lit up by the roadside,
from which proceeded the sounds of music and dancing. In
reality it was not a house at all but a fairy knoll, and it was
the fairies who were jigging it about there so merrily. But
one of the young men was deceived and stepping into the
house joined in the dance, without even stopping to put
down the jar of whisky. His companion was wiser ; he had
a shrewd suspicion that the place was not what it seemed,
and on entering he took the precaution of sticking a needle
in the door. That disarmed the power of the fairies, and
he got away safely. Well, that day twelve months he came
back to the spot and what should he see but his poor friend
still dancing away with the jar of whisky on his back ? A
weary man was he, as you may well believe, but he begged
to be allowed to finish the reel which he was in the act of
executing, and when they took him out into the open air,
there was nothing of him left but skin and bones.[3] Again,
the wicked fairies are apt to carry off men's wives with them
to fairyland ; but the lost spouses can be recovered within a
year and a day when the procession of the fairies is defiling
past on Hallowe'en, always provided that the mortals did not
partake of elfin food while they were in elfinland.[4]

Sometimes valuable information may be obtained from
the fairies on Hallowe'en. There was a young man named

[1] P. W. Joyce, *A Social History of Ancient Ireland* (London, 1903), i. 264 *sq.*, ii. 556.

[2] (Sir) John Rhys, *Celtic Heathendom*, p. 516.

[3] Rev. John Gregorson Campbell, *Superstitions of the Highlands and Islands of Scotland* (Glasgow, 1900), pp. 61 *sq.*

[4] Ch. Rogers, *Social Life in Scotland* (Edinburgh, 1884–1886), iii. 258-260.

Guleesh
and the
revels of
the fairies
at Hal-
lowe'en.
Guleesh in the County of Mayo.   Near his house was a *rath*
or old fort with a fine grass bank running round it.   One
Hallowe'en, when the darkness was falling, Guleesh went to
the rath and stood on a gray old flag.   The night was calm
and still ; there was not a breath of wind stirring, nor a
sound to be heard except the hum of the insects flitting past,
or the whistle of the plovers, or the hoarse scream of the
wild geese as they winged their way far overhead.   Above
the white fog the moon rose like a knob of fire in the east,
and a thousand thousand stars were twinkling in the sky.
There was a little frost in the air, the grass was white and
crisp and crackled under foot.   Guleesh expected to see the
fairies, but they did not come.   Hour after hour wore away,
and he was just bethinking him of going home to bed, when
his ear caught a sound far off coming towards him, and he
knew what it was in a moment.   The sound grew louder
and louder ; at first it was like the beating of waves on a
stony shore, then it was like the roar of a waterfall, at last
it was like a mighty rushing wind in the tops of the trees,
then the storm burst upon the rath, and sure enough the
fairies were in it.   The rout went by so suddenly that
Guleesh lost his breath ; but he came to himself and
listened.   The fairies were now gathered within the grassy
bank of the rath, and a fine uproar they made.   But Guleesh
listened with all his ears, and he heard one fairy saying to
another that a magic herb grew by Guleesh's own door, and
that Guleesh had nothing to do but pluck it and boil it
and give it to his sweetheart, the daughter of the King of
France, and she would be well, for just then she was lying
very ill.   Guleesh took the hint, and everything went as the
fairy had said.   And he married the daughter of the King
of France ; and they had never a cark nor a care, a sickness
nor a sorrow, a mishap nor a misfortune to the day of their
death.[1]

Divination
resorted to
in Celtic
countries
at Hal-
lowe'en.
In all Celtic countries Hallowe'en seems to have been
the great season of the year for prying into the future ; all
kinds of divination were put in practice that night.   We
read that Dathi, a king of Ireland in the fifth century,

[1] Douglas Hyde, *Beside the Fire, a*   (London, 1890), pp. 104, 105, 121-
Collection of Irish Gaelic Folk Stories   128.

happening to be at the Druids' Hill (*Cnoc-nan-druad*) in the county of Sligo one Hallowe'en, ordered his druid to forecast for him the future from that day till the next Hallowe'en should come round. The druid passed the night on the top of the hill, and next morning made a prediction to the king which came true.[1] In Wales Hallowe'en was the weirdest of all the *Teir Nos Ysbrydion*, or Three Spirit Nights, when the wind, "blowing over the feet of the corpses," bore sighs to the houses of those who were to die within the year. People thought that if on that night they went out to a cross-road and listened to the wind, they would learn all the most important things that would befall them during the next twelve months.[2] In Wales, too, not so long ago women used to congregate in the parish churches on the night of Hallowe'en and read their fate from the flame of the candle which each of them held in her hand ; also they heard the names or saw the coffins of the parishioners who would die within the year, and many were the sad scenes to which these gloomy visions gave rise.[3] And in the Highlands of Scotland anybody who pleased could hear proclaimed aloud the names of parishioners doomed to perish within the next twelve months, if he would only take a three-legged stool and go and sit on it at three cross-roads, while the church clock was striking twelve at midnight on Hallowe'en. It was even in his power to save the destined victims from their doom by taking with him articles of wearing apparel and throwing them away, one by one, as each name was called out by the mysterious voice.[4]

But while a glamour of mystery and awe has always clung to Hallowe'en in the minds of the Celtic peasantry, the popular celebration of the festival has been, at least in modern times, by no means of a prevailingly gloomy cast ; on the contrary it has been attended by picturesque features and

Hallowe'en bonfires in the Highlands of Scotland.

---

[1] P. W. Joyce, *Social History of Ancient Ireland,* i. 229.

[2] Marie Trevelyan, *Folk-lore and Folk-stories of Wales* (London, 1909), p. 254.

[3] (Sir) John Rhys, *Celtic Heathen-dom*, pp. 514 *sq.* In order to see the apparitions all you had to do was to run thrice round the parish church

and then peep through the key-hole of the door. See Marie Trevelyan, *op. cit.* p. 254 ; J. C. Davies, *Folk-lore of West and Mid-Wales* (Aberystwyth, 1911), p. 77.

[4] Miss E. J. Guthrie, *Old Scottish Customs* (London and Glasgow, 1885), p. 75.

merry pastimes, which rendered it the gayest night of all the year.   Amongst the things which in the Highlands of Scotland contributed to invest the festival with a romantic beauty were the bonfires which used to blaze at frequent intervals on the heights.   " On the last day of autumn children gathered ferns, tar-barrels, the long thin stalks called *gàinisg*, and everything suitable for a bonfire.   These were placed in a heap on some eminence near the house, and in the evening set fire to.   The fires were called *Samhnagan*.   There was one for each house, and it was an object of ambition who should have the biggest.   Whole districts were brilliant with bonfires, and their glare across a Highland loch, and from many eminences, formed an exceedingly picturesque scene." [1]   Like the Beltane fires on the first of May, the Hallowe'en bonfires seem to have been kindled most commonly in the Perthshire Highlands.   Travelling in the parish of Moulin, near Pitlochrie, in the year 1772, the Englishman Thomas Pennant writes that " Hallow Eve is also kept sacred : as soon as it is dark, a person sets fire to a bush of broom fastened round a pole, and, attended with a crowd, runs about the village.   He then flings it down, heaps great quantity of combustible matters on it, and makes a great bonfire.   A whole tract is thus illuminated at the same time, and makes a fine appearance." [2]   The custom has been described more fully by a Scotchman of the eighteenth century, John Ramsay of Ochtertyre.   On the evening of Hallowe'en " the young people of every hamlet assembled upon some eminence near the houses.   There they made a bonfire of ferns or other fuel, cut the same day, which from the feast was called *Samh-nag* or *Savnag*, a fire of rest and pleasure.   Around it was placed a circle of stones, one for each person of the families to whom they belonged.   And when it grew dark the bonfire was kindled, at which a loud shout was set up.   Then each person taking a torch of ferns or sticks in his hand, ran round the fire exulting ; and some-

John Ramsay's account of the Hallowe'en bonfires.

---

[1] Rev. John Gregorson Campbell, *Witchcraft and Second Sight in the Highlands and Islands of Scotland* (Glasgow, 1902), p. 282.

[2] Thomas Pennant, " Tour in Scot-

land, and Voyage to the Hebrides in 1772," in John Pinkerton's *Voyages and Travels*, iii. (London, 1809) pp. 383 *sq.*   In quoting the passage I have corrected what seem to be two misprints.

times they went into the adjacent fields, where, if there was
another company, they visited the bonfire, taunting the
others if inferior in any respect to themselves.   After the
fire was burned out they returned home, where a feast was
prepared, and the remainder of the evening was spent in
mirth and diversions of various kinds.   Next morning they
repaired betimes to the bonfire, where the situation of the
stones was examined with much attention.   If any of them
were misplaced, or if the print of a foot could be discerned
near any particular stone, it was imagined that the person
for whom it was set would not live out the year.   Of late
years this is less attended to, but about the beginning of the
present century it was regarded as a sure prediction.   The
Hallowe'en fire is still kept up in some parts of the Low
country ; but on the western coast and in the Isles it is
never kindled, though the night is spent in merriment and
entertainments." [1]   In the Perthshire parish of Callander,
which includes the now famous pass of the Trossachs opening out on the winding and wooded shores of the lovely
Loch Katrine, the Hallowe'en bonfires were still kindled
down to near the end of the eighteenth century.   When the
fire had died down, the ashes were carefully collected in the
form of a circle, and a stone was put in, near the circumference, for every person of the several families interested
in the bonfire.   Next morning, if any of these stones was
found to be displaced or injured, the people made sure that
the person represented by it was *fey* or devoted, and that
he could not live twelve months from that day. [2]   In the
parish of Logierait, which covers the beautiful valley of the
Tummel, one of the fairest regions of all Scotland, the
Hallowe'en fire was somewhat different.   Faggots of heath,
broom, and the dressings of flax were kindled and carried on
poles by men, who ran with them round the villages, attended
by a crowd.   As soon as one faggot was burnt out, a fresh
one was lighted and fastened to the pole.   Numbers of these
blazing faggots were often carried about together, and when

Marginal notes:
Divination from stones at the fire.

Hallowe'en fires in the parishes of Callander and Logierait.

Divination from stones.

[1] John Ramsay, of Ochtertyre, *Scotland and Scotsmen in the Eighteenth
Century*, edited by Alexander Allardyce (Edinburgh and London, 1888),
ii. 437 *sq.*   This account was written
in the eighteenth century.

[2] Rev. James Robertson, Parish
minister of Callander, in Sir John Sinclair's *Statistical Account of Scotland*,
xi. (Edinburgh, 1794), pp. 621 *sq.*

the night happened to be dark, they formed a splendid illumination.[1]

Nor did the Hallowe'en fires die out in Perthshire with the end of the eighteenth century. Journeying from Dunkeld to Aberfeldy on Hallowe'en in the first half of the nineteenth century, Sheriff Barclay counted thirty fires blazing on the hill tops, and saw the figures of the people dancing like phantoms round the flames.[2] Again, " in 1860, I was residing near the head of Loch Tay during the season of the Hallowe'en feast. For several days before Hallowe'en, boys and youths collected wood and conveyed it to the most prominent places on the hill sides in their neighbourhood. Some of the heaps were as large as a corn-stack or hay-rick. After dark on Hallowe'en, these heaps were kindled, and for several hours both sides of Loch Tay were illuminated as far as the eye could see. I was told by old men that at the beginning of this century men as well as boys took part in getting up the bonfires, and that, when the fire was ablaze, all joined hands and danced round the fire, and made a great noise ; but that, as these gatherings generally ended in drunkenness and rough and dangerous fun, the ministers set their faces against the observance, and were seconded in their efforts by the more intelligent and well-behaved in the community ; and so the practice was discontinued by adults

and relegated to school boys." [3] At Balquhidder down to the latter part of the nineteenth century each household kindled its bonfire at Hallowe'en, but the custom was chiefly observed by children. The fires were lighted on any high knoll near the house ; there was no dancing round them.[4]

Hallowe'en fires were also lighted in some districts of the north-east of Scotland, such as Buchan. Villagers and farmers alike must have their fire. In the villages the boys went from house to house and begged a peat from each householder, usually with the words, " Ge's a peat t' burn

---

[1] Rev. Dr. Thomas Bisset, in Sir John Sinclair's *Statistical Account of Scotland*, v. (Edinburgh, 1793) pp. 84 *sq.*

[2] Miss E. J. Guthrie, *Old Scottish Customs* (London and Glasgow, 1885), p. 67.

[3] James Napier, *Folk Lore, or Superstitious Beliefs in the West of Scotland within this Century* (Paisley, 1879), p. 179.

[4] J. G. Frazer, " Folk-lore at Balquhidder," *The Folk-lore Journal*, vi. (1888) p. 270.

the witches." In some villages the lads collected the peats
in a cart, some of them drawing it along and the others
receiving the peats and loading them on the cart.   Along
with the peats they accumulated straw, furze, potato haulm,
everything that would burn quickly, and when they had got
enough they piled it all in a heap and set it on fire.   Then
each of the youths, one after another, laid himself down on
the ground as near to the fire as he could without being
scorched, and thus lying allowed the smoke to roll over him.
The others ran through the smoke and jumped over their
prostrate comrade.   When the heap was burned down, they
scattered the ashes.   Each one took a share in this part of
the ceremony, giving a kick first with the right foot and
then with the left ; and each vied with the other who should
scatter the most.   After that some of them still continued
to run through the scattered ashes and to pelt each other
with the half-burned peats.   At each farm a spot as high as
possible, not too near the steading, was chosen for the fire,
and the proceedings were much the same as at the village
bonfire.   The lads of one farm, when their own fire was
burned down and the ashes scattered, sometimes went to a
neighbouring fire and helped to kick the ashes about.[1]   Referring to this part of Scotland, a writer at the end of the
eighteenth century observes that "the Hallow-even fire,
another relict of druidism, was kindled in Buchan.   Various
magic ceremonies were then celebrated to counteract the
influence of witches and demons, and to prognosticate to
the young their success or disappointment in the matrimonial
lottery.   These being devoutly finished, the hallow fire was
kindled, and guarded by the male part of the family.
Societies were formed, either by pique or humour, to scatter
certain fires, and the attack and defence were often
conducted with art and with fury."[2]   Down to about the
middle of the nineteenth century "the Braemar Highlanders
made the circuit of their fields with lighted torches at
Hallowe'en to ensure their fertility in the coming year.

Proces-
sions with
torches at
Hallowe'en
in the
Braemar
Highlands.

[1] Rev. Walter Gregor, *Notes on the
Folk-lore of the North-East of Scotland*
(London, 1881), pp. 167 *sq.*
[2] Rev. A. Johnstone, as to the

parish of Monquhitter, in Sir John
Sinclair's *Statistical Account of Scotland*, xxi. (Edinburgh, 1799) pp. 145
sq.

At that date the custom was as follows : Every member of the family (in those days households were larger than they are now) was provided with a bundle of fir 'can'les' with which to go the round. The father and mother stood at the hearth and lit the splints in the peat fire, which they passed to the children and servants, who trooped out one after the other, and proceeded to tread the bounds of their little property, going slowly round at equal distances apart, and invariably with the sun. To go 'withershins' seems to have been reserved for cursing and excommunication. When the fields had thus been circumambulated the remaining spills were thrown together in a heap and allowed to burn out."[1]

Divination at Hallowe'en in the Highlands and Lowlands of Scotland. In the Highlands of Scotland, as the evening of Hallowe'en wore on, young people gathered in one of the houses and resorted to an almost endless variety of games, or rather forms of divination, for the purpose of ascertaining the future fate of each member of the company. Were they to marry or remain single, was the marriage to take place that year or never, who was to be married first, what sort of husband or wife she or he was to get, the name, the trade, the colour of the hair, the amount of property of the future spouse—these were questions that were eagerly canvassed and the answers to them furnished never-failing entertainment.[2] Nor were these modes of divination at Hallowe'en confined to the Highlands, where the bonfires were kindled ; they were practised with equal faith and in practically the same forms in the Lowlands, as we learn, for example, from Burns's poem *Hallowe'en*, which describes the auguries drawn from a variety of omens by the Ayrshire peasantry. These Lowlanders of Saxon descent may well have inherited the rites from the Celts who preceded them
The stolen kail. in the possession of the south country. A common practice at Hallowe'en was to go out stealthily to a neighbour's kailyard and there, with shut eyes, to pull up the first kail

---

[1] A. Macdonald, "Some former Customs of the Royal Parish of Crathie, Scotland," *Folk-lore*, xviii. (1907) p. 85. The writer adds : "In this way the 'faulds' were purged of evil spirits." But it does not appear whether this expresses the belief of the people or only the interpretation of the writer.

[2] Rev. John Gregorson Campbell, *Witchcraft and Second Sight in the Highlands and Islands of Scotland* (Glasgow, 1902), pp. 282 *sq.*

stock that came to hand. It was necessary that the plants
should be stolen without the knowledge or consent of their
owner ; otherwise they were quite useless for the purpose
of divination. Strictly speaking, too, the neighbour upon
whose garden the raid was made should be unmarried,
whether a bachelor or a spinster. The stolen kail was
taken home and examined, and according to its height,
shape, and features would be the height, shape, and features
of the future husband or wife. The taste of the *custock*,
that is, the heart of the stem, was an infallible indication
of his or her temper ; and a clod of earth adhering to the
root signified, in proportion to its size, the amount of property which he or she would bring to the common stock.
Then the kail-stock or *runt*, as it was called in Ayrshire,
was placed over the lintel of the door ; and the baptismal
name of the young man or woman who first entered the
door after the kail was in position would be the baptismal
name of the husband or wife.[1] Again, young women sowed Sowing
hemp seed over nine ridges of ploughed land, saying, " I hemp seed.
sow hemp seed, and he who is to be my husband, let him
come and harrow it." On looking back over her left shoulder
the girl would see the figure of her future mate behind her
in the darkness. In the north-east of Scotland lint seed was
used instead of hemp seed and answered the purpose quite
as well.[2] Again, a mode of ascertaining your future husband The clue of
or wife was this. Take a clue of blue yarn and go to a blue yarn.
lime-kiln. Throw the clue into the kiln, but keep one end
of the thread in your hand and wind it on to another clue.
As you come near the end somebody or something will hold
the other end tight in the kiln. Then you call out, " Who
holds ? " giving the thread at the same time a gentle pull.
Some one or something will thereupon pull the other end
of the thread, and a voice will mention the name of your
future husband or wife.[3] Another way is this. Go to the

---

[1] Robert Burns, *Hallowe'en*, with
the poet's note ; Rev. Walter Gregor,
op. cit. p. 84 ; Miss E. J. Guthrie, *op.
cit.* p. 69 ; Rev. J. G. Campbell, *op.
cit.* p. 287.

[2] R. Burns, *l.c.* ; Rev. Walter
Gregor, *l.c.* ; Miss E. J. Guthrie, *op.*

cit. pp. 70 *sq.* ; Rev. J. G. Campbell,
op. cit. p. 286.

[3] R. Burns, *l.c.* ; Rev. W. Gregor,
l.c. ; Miss E. J. Guthrie, *op. cit.* p.
73 ; Rev. J. G. Campbell, *op. cit.* p.
285 ; A. Goodrich-Freer, "More
Folklore from the Hebrides," *Folk-lore*,
xiii. (1902) pp. 54 *sq.*

The winnowing basket.

barn alone and secretly. Be sure to open both doors and if possible take them off their hinges; for if the being who is about to appear should catch you in the barn and clap the doors to on you, he or she might do you a mischief. Having done this, take the sieve or winnowing-basket, which in Lowland Scotch is called a *wecht* or *waicht*, and go through the action of winnowing corn. Repeat it thrice, and at the third time the apparition of your future husband or wife will pass through the barn, entering at the windy door and passing out at the other.[1] Or this. Go to a southward running stream, where the lands of three lairds meet, or to a ford where the dead and living have crossed. Dip the left sleeve of your shirt in the water. Then go home, take off the shirt, hang it up before a fire to dry, and go to bed, taking care that the bed stands so that you can see your shirt hanging before the fire. Keep awake, and at midnight you will see the form of your future spouse come into the room and turn the other side of the sleeve to the fire to dry it.[2] A Highland form of divination at Hallowe'en is to take a shoe by the tip and throw it over the house, then observe the direction in which the toe points as it lies on the ground on the other side; for in that direction you are destined to go before long. If the shoe should fall sole uppermost, it is very unlucky for you.[3]

These ways of prying into the future are practised outside of the house; others are observed in the kitchen or the parlour before the cheerful blaze of the fire. Thus the white of eggs, dropped in a glass of pure water, indicates by certain marks how many children a person will have. The impatience and clamour of the children, eager to ascertain the exact number of their future progeny, often induced the housewife to perform this ceremony for them by daylight; and the kindly mother, standing with her face to the window, dropping the white of an egg into a crystal

The wet shirt.
The thrown shoe.
The white of eggs in water.

[1] R. Burns, *l.c.*; Rev. W. Gregor, *op. cit.* p. 85; Miss E. J. Guthrie, *op. cit.* p. 71; Rev. J. G. Campbell, *op. cit.* p. 285. According to the last of these writers, the winnowing had to be done in the devil's name.
[2] R. Burns, *l.c.*; Rev. W. Gregor, *l.c.*; Miss E. J. Guthrie, *op. cit.* p. 72; Rev. J. G. Campbell, *op. cit.* p. 286; A. Goodrich-Freer, "More Folklore from the Hebrides," *Folklore*, xiii. (1902) p. 54.
[3] Rev. J. G. Campbell, *op. cit.* p. 283.

glass of clean water, and surrounded by a group of children intently watching her proceedings, made up a pretty picture.[1] When the fun of the evening had fairly commenced, the names of eligible or likely matches were written on the chimney-piece, and the young man who wished to try his fortune was led up blindfolded to the list. Whatever name he put his finger on would prove that of his future wife.[2] Again, two nuts, representing a lad and a lass whose names were announced to the company, were put side by side in the fire. If they burned quietly together, the pair would be man and wife, and from the length of time they burned and the brightness of the flame the length and happiness of the married life of the two were augured. But if instead of burning together one of the nuts leaped away from the other, then there would be no marriage, and the blame would rest with the person whose nut had thus started away by itself.[3] Again, a dish of milk and meal (in Gaelic *fuarag*, in Lowland Scotch *crowdie*) or of beat potatoes was made and a ring was hidden in it. Spoons were served out to the company, who supped the contents of the dish hastily with them, and the one who got the ring would be the first to be married.[4] Again, apples and a silver sixpence were put in a tub of water ; the apples naturally floated on the top and the sixpence sank to the bottom. Whoever could lift an apple or the sixpence from the water with his mouth, without using his teeth, was counted very lucky and got the prize to himself.[5] Again, three plates or basins were placed on the hearth. One was filled with clean water, another with dirty water, and the third was empty. The enquirer was blindfolded, knelt in front of the hearth, and groped about till he put his finger in one of them. If he lighted on the plate with the clean water, he would wed a maid ;

The names on the chimney-piece.

The nuts in the fire.

The milk and meal.

The apples in the water.

The three plates.

---

[1] Rev. J. G. Campbell, *op. cit.* pp. 283 *sq.* ; A. Goodrich-Freer, *l.c.*

[2] Rev. J. G. Campbell, *op. cit.* p. 284.

[3] R. Burns, *l.c.* ; Rev. W. Gregor, *op. cit.* p. 85 ; Miss E. J. Guthrie, *op. cit.* p. 70 ; Rev. J. G. Campbell, *op. cit.* p. 284. Where nuts were not to be had, peas were substituted.

[4] Rev. J. G. Campbell, *op. cit.* p.

284.

[5] Rev. J. G. Campbell, *l.c.* According to my recollection of Hallowe'en customs observed in my boyhood at Helensburgh, in Dumbartonshire, another way was to stir the floating apples and then drop a fork on them as they bobbed about in the water. Success consisted in pinning one of the apples with the fork.

if on the plate with the dirty water, he would marry a widow ; and if on the empty plate, he would remain a bachelor. For a girl the answer of the oracle was analogous ; she would marry a bachelor, a widower, or nobody according to the plate into which she chanced to dip her finger. But to make sure, the operation had to be repeated thrice, the position of the plates being changed each time. If the enquirer put his or her finger into the same plate thrice or even twice, it was quite conclusive.[1]

The sliced apple.

These forms of divination in the house were practised by the company in a body ; but the following had to be performed by the person alone. You took an apple and stood with it in your hand in front of a looking-glass. Then you sliced the apple, stuck each slice on the point of the knife, and held it over your left shoulder, while you looked into the glass and combed your hair. The spectre of your future husband would then appear in the mirror stretching forth his hand to take the slices of the apple over your shoulder. Some say that the number of slices should be nine, that you should eat the first eight yourself, and only throw the ninth over your left shoulder for your husband ; also that at each slice you should say,

The white of egg in water.

"In the name of the Father and the Son."[2] Again, take an egg, prick it with a pin, and let the white drop into a wine-glass nearly full of water. Take some of this in your mouth and go out for a walk. The first name you hear called out aloud will be that of your future husband or wife. An old woman told a lady that she had tried this mode of divination in her youth, that the name of Archibald "came up as it were from the very ground," and that Archibald sure enough was the name of her husband.[3]

The salt cake or salt herring.

In South Uist and Eriskay, two of the outer Hebrides, a salt cake called *Bonnach Salainn* is eaten at Hallowe'en to induce dreams that will reveal the future. It is baked of

[1] R. Burns, *l.c.* ; Rev. W. Gregor, *op. cit.* pp. 85 *sq.* ; Miss E. J Guthrie, *op. cit.* pp. 72 *sq.* ; Rev. J. G. Campbell, *op. cit.* p. 287.

[2] R. Burns, *l.c.* ; Rev. W. Gregor, *op. cit.* p. 85 ; Miss E. J. Guthrie, *op. cit.* pp. 69 *sq.* ; Rev. J. G. Campbell, *op. cit.* p. 285. It is the last of these writers who gives what may be called the Trinitarian form of the divination.

[3] Miss E. J. Guthrie, *Old Scottish Customs* (London and Glasgow, 1885), pp. 74 *sq.*

common meal with a great deal of salt.   After eating it you
may not drink water nor utter a word, not even to say your
prayers.   A salt herring, eaten bones and all in three bites,
is equally efficacious, always provided that you drink no
water and hold your tongue.[1]

In the northern part of Wales it used to be customary
for every family to make a great bonfire called *Coel Coeth* on
Hallowe'en.   The fire was kindled on the most conspicuous
spot near the house; and when it had nearly gone out every one
threw into the ashes a white stone, which he had first marked.
Then having said their prayers round the fire, they went to
bed.   Next morning, as soon as they were up, they came to
search out the stones, and if any one of them was found to
be missing, they had a notion that the person who threw it
would die before he saw another Hallowe'en.[2]   A writer on
Wales at the beginning of the nineteenth century says
that "the autumnal fire is still kindled in North Wales,
being on the eve of the first day of November, and is
attended by many ceremonies; such as running through
the fire and smoke, each casting a stone into the fire, and all
running off at the conclusion to escape from the black short-
tailed sow; then supping upon parsnips, nuts, and apples;
catching up an apple suspended by a string with the mouth
alone, and the same by an apple in a tub of water: each
throwing a nut into the fire; and those that burn bright,
betoken prosperity to the owners through the following
year, but those that burn black and crackle, denote misfortune.   On the following morning the stones are searched
for in the fire, and if any be missing, they betide ill to those
who threw them in."[3]   According to Sir John Rhys, the
habit of celebrating Hallowe'en by lighting bonfires on the
hills is perhaps not yet extinct in Wales, and men still living

Marginal notes: Hallowe'en fires in Wales. Omens drawn from stones thrown into the fire.

[1] A. Goodrich-Freer, "More Folk-lore from the Hebrides," *Folk-lore*, xiii. (1902) p. 55.

[2] Pennant's manuscript, quoted by J. Brand, *Popular Antiquities of Great Britain* (London, 1882–1883), i. 389 *sq.*

[3] Sir Richard Colt Hoare, *The Itinerary of Archbishop Baldwin through Wales A.D. MCLXXXVIII. by Giraldus de Barri* (London, 1806), ii. 315; J. Brand, *Popular Antiquities*, i. 390. The passage quoted in the text occurs in one of Hoare's notes on the Itinerary. The dipping for apples, burning of nuts, and so forth, are mentioned also by Marie Trevelyan, *Folk-lore and Folk-stories of Wales* (London, 1909), pp. 253, 255.

can remember how the people who assisted at the bonfires would wait till the last spark was out and then would suddenly take to their heels, shouting at the top of their voices, " The cropped black sow seize the hindmost ! "   The saying, as Sir John Rhys justly remarks, implies that originally one of the company became a victim in dead earnest. Down to the present time the saying is current in Carnarvonshire, where allusions to the cutty black sow are still occasionally made to frighten children.[1]   We can now understand why in Lower Brittany every person throws a pebble into the midsummer bonfire.[2]   Doubtless there, as in Wales and the Highlands of Scotland,[3] omens of life and death have at one time or other been drawn from the position and state of the pebbles on the morning of All Saints' Day.   The custom, thus found among three separate branches of the Celtic stock, probably dates from a period before their dispersion, or at least from a time when alien races had not yet driven home the wedges of separation between them.

In Wales, as in Scotland, Hallowe'en was also the great season for forecasting the future in respect of love and marriage, and some of the forms of divination employed for this purpose resembled those which were in use among the Scotch peasantry.   Two girls, for example, would make a little ladder of yarn, without breaking it from the ball, and having done so they would throw it out of the window. Then one of the girls, holding the ball in her hand, would wind the yarn back, repeating a rhyme in Welsh.   This she did thrice, and as she wound the yarn she would see her future husband climbing up the little ladder.   Again, three bowls or basins were placed on a table.   One of them contained clean water, one dirty water, and one was empty. The girls of the household, and sometimes the boys too, then eagerly tried their fortunes.   They were blindfolded, led up to the table, and dipped their hands into a bowl.   If they happened to dip into the clean water, they would marry maidens or bachelors ; if into the dirty water, they would be widowers or widows ; if into the empty bowl, they would

Divination by stones in the ashes.

Divination as to love and marriage at Hallowe'en in Wales.

---

[1] (Sir) John Rhys, *Celtic Heathendom* (London and Edinburgh, 1888), pp. 515 *sq.*   As to the Hallowe'en bonfires in Wales compare J. C.

Davies, *Folk-lore of West and Mid-Wales* (Aberystwyth, 1911), p. 77.

[2] See above, p. 183.

[3] See above, p. 231.

live unmarried.   Again, if a girl, walking backwards, would
place a knife among the leeks on Hallowe'en, she would see
her future husband come and pick up the knife and throw
it into the middle of the garden.[1]

In Ireland the Hallowe'en bonfires would seem to have
died out, but the Hallowe'en divination has survived.
Writing towards the end of the eighteenth century, General
Vallancey tells us that on Hallowe'en or the vigil of Saman,
as he calls it, " the peasants in Ireland assemble with sticks
and clubs (the emblems of laceration) going from house to
house, collecting money, bread-cake, butter, cheese, eggs,
etc., etc., for the feast, repeating verses in honour of the
solemnity, demanding preparations for the festival, in the
name of St. Columb Kill, desiring them to lay aside the
fatted calf, and to bring forth the black sheep.   The good
women are employed in making the griddle cake and candles;
these last are sent from house to house in the vicinity, and
are lighted up on the (Saman) next day, before which they
pray, or are supposed to pray, for the departed souls of the
donor.   Every house abounds in the best viands they can afford:
apples and nuts are devoured in abundance : the nut-shells
are burnt, and from the ashes many strange things are foretold :
cabbages are torn up by the root : hemp seed is sown by the
maidens, and they believe, that if they look back, they will see
the apparition of the man intended for their future spouse :
they hang a smock before the fire, on the close of the feast,
and sit up all night, concealed in a corner of the room, convinced that his apparition will come down the chimney and
turn the smock : they throw a ball of yarn out of the window,
and wind it on the reel within, convinced, that if they repeat
the *Pater Noster* backwards, and look at the ball of yarn
without, they will then also see his *sith* or apparition :
they dip for apples in a tub of water, and endeavour to bring
one up in the mouth : they suspend a cord with a cross-
stick, with apples at one point, and candles lighted at the
other, and endeavour to catch the apple, while it is in a
circular motion, in the mouth.   These, and many other
superstitious ceremonies, the remains of Druidism, are

*Divination
at Hallow-
e'en in
Ireland.*

---

[1] Marie Trevelyan, *Folk-lore and Folk-stories of Wales* (London, 1909), pp.
254 *sq.*

observed on this holiday, which will never be eradicated, while the name of *Saman* is permitted to remain."[1]

In Queen's County, Ireland, down to the latter part of the nineteenth century children practised various of these rites of divination on Hallowe'en. Girls went out into the garden blindfold and pulled up cabbages: if the cabbage was well grown, the girl would have a handsome husband, but if it had a crooked stalk, the future spouse would be a stingy old man. Nuts, again, were placed in pairs on the bar of the fire, and from their behaviour omens were drawn of the fate in love and marriage of the couple whom they represented. Lead, also, was melted and allowed to drop into a tub of cold water, and from the shapes which it assumed in the water predictions were made to the children of their future destiny. Again, apples were bobbed for in a tub of water and brought up with the teeth; or a stick was hung from a hook with an apple at one end and a candle at the other, and the stick being made to revolve you made a bite at the apple and sometimes got a mouthful of candle instead.[2]

In County Leitrim, also, down to near the end of the nineteenth century various forms of divination were practised at Hallowe'en. Girls ascertained the character of their future husbands by the help of cabbages just as in Queen's County. Again, if a girl found a branch of a briar-thorn which had bent over and grown into the ground so as to form a loop, she would creep through the loop thrice late in the evening in the devil's name, then cut the briar and put it under her pillow, all without speaking a word. Then she would lay her head on the pillow and dream of the man she was to marry. Boys, also, would dream in like manner of love and marriage at Hallowe'en, if only they would gather ten leaves of ivy without speaking, throw away one, and put the other nine under their pillow. Again, divination was practised by means of a cake called *barm-breac*, in which a nut and a ring were baked. Whoever got the ring would be married first; whoever got the nut would marry a widow or a widower; but if the nut were an empty shell, he or she

---

[1] (General) Charles Vallancey, *Collectanea de Rebus Hibernicis*, iii. (Dublin, 1786), pp. 459-461.

[2] Miss A. Watson, quoted by A. C. Haddon, "A Batch of Irish Folk-lore," *Folk-lore*, iv. (1893) pp. 361 *sq.*

would remain unwed.   Again, a girl would take a clue of
worsted, go to a lime kiln in the gloaming, and throw the
clew into the kiln in the devil's name, while she held fast the
other end of the thread.   Then she would rewind the thread
and ask, " Who holds my clue ? " and the name of her future
husband would come up from the depth of the kiln.   Another
way was to take a rake, go to a rick and walk round it nine
times, saying, " I rake this rick in the devil's name."   At the
ninth time the wraith of your destined partner for life would
come and take the rake out of your hand.   Once more, before
the company separated for the night, they would rake the
ashes smooth on the hearth, and search them next morning
for tracks, from which they judged whether anybody should
come to the house, or leave it, or die in it before another
year was out.[1]   In County Roscommon, which borders on   Divination
County Leitrim, a cake is made in nearly every house on   at Hallow-
Hallowe'en, and a ring, a coin, a sloe, and a chip of wood   County
are put into it.   Whoever gets the coin will be rich ; who-   Ros-
ever gets the ring will be married first ; whoever gets the   common.
chip of wood, which stands for a coffin, will die first ; and
whoever gets the sloe will live longest, because the fairies
blight the sloes in the hedges on Hallowe'en, so that the
sloe in the cake will be the last of the year.   Again, on the
same mystic evening girls take nine grains of oats in their
mouths, and going out without speaking walk about till they
hear a man's name pronounced ; it will be the name of their
future husband.   In County Roscommon, too, on Hallowe'en
there is the usual dipping in water for apples or sixpences,
and the usual bites at a revolving apple and tallow candle.[2]

    In the Isle of Man also, another Celtic country, Hallow-   Hallowe'en
e'en was celebrated down to modern times by the kindling   fires in the
of fires, accompanied with all the usual ceremonies designed to
prevent the baneful influence of fairies and witches.   Bands
of young men perambulated the island by night, and at the
door of every dwelling-house they struck up a Manx rhyme,
beginning

           " *Noght oie howney hop-dy-naw,*"

---

[1] Leland L. Duncan, "Further
Notes from County Leitrim," *Folk-lore*,
v. (1894) pp. 195-197.

[2] H. J. Byrne, "All Hallows Eve
and other Festivals in Connaught,"
Folk-lore, xviii. (1907) pp. 437 *sq.*

that is to say, " This is Hollantide Eve." For Hollantide is the Manx way of expressing the old English *All hallowen tide*, that is, All Saints' Day, the first of November. But as the people reckon this festival according to the Old Style, Hollantide in the Isle of Man is our twelfth of November. The native Manx name for the day is *Sauin* or *Laa Houney*. Potatoes, parsnips and fish, pounded up together and mixed with butter, formed the proper evening meal (*mrastyr*) on

Divination at Hallowe'en in the Isle of Man. Hallowe'en in the Isle of Man.[1] Here, too, as in Scotland forms of divination are practised by some people on this important evening. For example, the housewife fills a thimble full of salt for each member of the family and each guest ; the contents of the thimblefuls are emptied out in as many neat little piles on a plate, and left there over night. Next morning the piles are examined, and if any of them has fallen down, he or she whom it represents will die within the year. Again, the women carefully sweep out the ashes from under the fireplace and flatten them down neatly on the open hearth. If they find next morning a footprint turned towards the door, it signifies a death in the family within the year ; but if the footprint is turned in the opposite direction, it bodes a marriage. Again, divination by eavesdropping is practised in the Isle of Man in much the same way as in Scotland. You go out with your mouth full of water and your hands full of salt and listen at a neighbour's door, and the first name you hear will be the name of your husband. Again, Manx maids bandage their eyes and grope about the room till they dip their hands in vessels full of clean or dirty water, and so on ; and from the thing they touch they draw corresponding omens. But some people in the Isle of Man observe these auguries, not on Hallowe'en or Hollantide Eve, as they call it, which was the old Manx New Year's Eve, but on the modern New Year's Eve, that is, on the thirty-first of December. The change no doubt marks a transition from the ancient to the modern mode of dating the beginning of the year.[2]

In Lancashire, also, some traces of the old Celtic celebra-

---

[1] Joseph Train, *Historical and Statistical Account of the Isle of Man* (Douglas, Isle of Man, 1845), ii. 123 ; (Sir) John Rhys, *Celtic Folk-lore, Welsh*

and *Manx* (Oxford, 1901), i. 315 *sqq.*
[2] (Sir) John Rhys, *Celtic Folk-lore, Welsh and Manx* (Oxford, 1901), i. 318-321.

tion of Hallowe'en have been reported in modern times. It is said that " fires are still lighted in Lancashire, on Hallowe'en, under the name of Beltains or Teanlas ; and even such cakes as the Jews are said to have made in honour of the Queen of Heaven, are yet to be found at this season amongst the inhabitants of the banks of the Ribble. . . . Both the fires and the cakes, however, are now connected with superstitious notions respecting Purgatory, etc."[1]   On Hallowe'en, too, the Lancashire maiden " strews the ashes which are to take the form of one or more letters of her lover's name ; she throws hemp-seed over her shoulder and timidly glances to see who follows her."[2]   Again, witches in Lancashire used to gather on Hallowe'en at the Malkin Tower, a ruined and desolate farm-house in the forest of Pendle.   They assembled for no good purpose ; but you could keep the infernal rout at bay by carrying a lighted candle about the fells from eleven to twelve o'clock at night.   The witches tried to blow out the candle, and if they succeeded, so much the worse for you ; but if the flame burned steadily till the clocks had struck midnight, you were safe.   Some people performed the ceremony by deputy ; and parties went about from house to house in the evening collecting candles, one for each inmate, and offering their services to *late* or *leet* the witches, as the phrase ran.   This custom was practised at Longridge Fell in the early part of the nineteenth century.[3]   In Northumberland on Hallowe'en omens of marriage were drawn from nuts thrown into the fire ; and the sports of ducking for apples and biting at a revolving apple and lighted candle were also practised on that evening.[4]   The equivalent of the Hallowe'en bonfires is reported also from France.   We are told that in the department of Deux-

Hallowe'en fires and divination in Lanca-shire.

Candles lighted to keep off the witches.

Divination at Hallowe'en in North-umberland.

Hallowe'en fires in France.

[1] John Harland and T. T. Wilkinson, *Lancashire Folk-lore* (Manchester and London, 1882), pp. 3 *sq.*

[2] J. Harland and T. T. Wilkinson, *op. cit.* p. 140.

[3] Annie Milner, in William Hone's *Year Book* (London, preface dated January, 1832), coll. 1276-1279 (letter dated June, 1831) ; R. T. Hampson,

Medii Aevi Kalendarium (London, 1841), i. 365 ; T. F. Thiselton Dyer, *British Popular Customs* (London, 1876), p. 395.

[4] *County Folk-lore*, vol. iv. *Northumberland*, collected by M. C. Balfour (London, 1904), p. 78.   Compare W. Henderson, *Notes on the Folk-lore of the Northern Counties of England* (London, 1879), pp. 96 *sq.*

Sèvres, which forms part of the old province of Poitou, young people used to assemble in the fields on All Saints' Day (the first of November) and kindle great fires of ferns, thorns, leaves, and stubble, at which they roasted chestnuts. They also danced round the fires and indulged in noisy pastimes.[1]

§ 7. The Midwinter Fires

A Mid-winter festival of fire.

If the heathen of ancient Europe celebrated, as we have good reason to believe, the season of Midsummer with a great festival of fire, of which the traces have survived in many places down to our own time, it is natural to suppose that they should have observed with similar rites the corresponding season of Midwinter; for Midsummer and Midwinter, or, in more technical language, the summer solstice and the winter solstice, are the two great turning-points in the sun's apparent course through the sky, and from the standpoint of primitive man nothing might seem more appropriate than to kindle fires on earth at the two moments when the fire and heat of the great luminary in heaven begin to wane or to wax. In this way the savage philosopher, to whose meditations on the nature of things we owe many ancient customs and ceremonies, might easily imagine that he helped the labouring sun to relight his dying lamp, or at all events to blow up the flame into a brighter blaze. Certain it is that the winter solstice, which the ancients erroneously assigned to the twenty-fifth of December, was celebrated in antiquity as the Birthday of the Sun, and that festal lights or fires were kindled on this joyful occasion.

Christmas the continuation of an old heathen festival of the sun.

Our Christmas festival is nothing but a continuation under a Christian name of this old solar festivity; for the ecclesiastical authorities saw fit, about the end of the third or the beginning of the fourth century, arbitrarily to transfer the nativity of Christ from the sixth of January to the twenty-fifth of December, for the purpose of diverting to their Lord the worship which the heathen had hitherto paid on that day to the sun.[2]

---

[1] Baron Dupin, in *Mémoires publiées par la Société Royale des Antiquaires de France*, iv. (1823) p. 108.

[2] The evidence for the solar origin of Christmas is given in *Adonis, Attis, Osiris*, Second Edition, pp. 254-256.

In modern Christendom the ancient fire-festival of the winter solstice appears to survive, or to have survived down to recent years, in the old custom of the Yule log, clog, or block, as it was variously called in England.[1] The custom was widespread in Europe, but seems to have flourished especially in England, France, and among the South Slavs ; at least the fullest accounts of the custom come from these quarters.   That the Yule log was only the winter counterpart of the Midsummer bonfire, kindled within doors instead of in the open air on account of the cold and inclement weather of the season, was pointed out long ago by our English antiquary John Brand ; [2] and the view is supported by the many quaint superstitions attaching to the Yule log, superstitions which have no apparent connexion with Christianity but carry their heathen origin plainly stamped upon them.   But while the two solstitial celebrations were both festivals of fire, the necessity or desirability of holding the winter celebration within doors lent it the character of a private or domestic festivity, which contrasts strongly with the publicity of the summer celebration, at which the people gathered on some open space or conspicuous height, kindled a huge bonfire in common, and danced and made merry round it together.

Among the Germans the custom of the Yule log is known to have been observed in the eleventh century ; for in the year 1184 the parish priest of Ahlen, in Münsterland, spoke of " bringing a tree to kindle the festal fire at the Lord's Nativity." [3]   Down to about the middle of the nineteenth century the old rite was kept up in some parts of central Germany, as we learn from an account of it given by a contemporary writer.   After mentioning the custom of

Marginal notes: The Yule log is the Midwinter counterpart of the Midsummer bonfire.

The Yule log in Germany.

---

[1] For the various names (Yu-batch, Yu-block, Yule-log, etc.) see Francis Grose, *Provincial Glossary*, New Edition (London, 1811), p. 141 ; Joseph Wright, *The English Dialect Dictionary* (London, 1898–1905), vi. 593, *s.v.* " Yule."

[2] " I am pretty confident that the Yule block will be found, in its first use, to have been only a counterpart of the Midsummer fires, made within doors because of the cold weather at

this winter solstice, as those in the hot season, at the summer one, are kindled in the open air " (John Brand, *Popular Antiquities of Great Britain*, London, 1882–1883, i. 471).   His opinion is approved by W. Mannhardt (*Der Baumkultus der Germanen und ihrer Nachbarstämme*, p. 236).

[3] " *Et arborem in nativitate domini ad festivum ignem suum adducendam esse dicebat* " (quoted by Jacob Grimm, *Deutsche Mythologie*,[4] i. 522).

feeding the cattle and shaking the fruit-trees on Christmas night, to make them bear fruit, he goes on as follows: "Other customs pointing back to the far-off times of heathendom may still be met with among the old-fashioned peasants of the mountain regions. Such is in the valleys of the Sieg and Lahn the practice of laying a new log as a foundation of the hearth. A heavy block of oak-wood, generally a stump grubbed up from the ground, is fitted either into the floor of the hearth, or into a niche made for the purpose in the wall under the hook on which the kettle hangs. When the fire on the hearth glows, this block of wood glows too, but it is so placed that it is hardly reduced to ashes within a year. When the new foundation is laid, the remains of the old block are carefully taken out, ground to powder, and strewed over the fields during the Twelve Nights. This, so people fancied, promotes the fruitfulness of the year's crops."[1] In some parts of the Eifel Mountains, to the west of Coblentz, a log of wood called the *Christbrand* used to be placed on the hearth on Christmas Eve; and the charred remains of it on Twelfth Night were put in the corn-bin to keep the mice from devouring the corn.[2] At Weidenhausen and Girkshausen, in Westphalia, the practice was to withdraw the Yule log (*Christbrand*) from the fire so soon as it was slightly charred; it was then kept carefully to be replaced on the fire whenever a thunder-storm broke, because the people believed that lightning would not strike a house in which the Yule log was smouldering.[3] In some villages near Berleburg in Westphalia the old custom was to tie up the Yule log in the last sheaf cut at harvest.[4] On Christmas Eve the peasantry of the Oberland, in Meiningen, a province of Central Germany, used to put a great block of wood called the *Christklotz* on the fire before they went to bed; it should burn all night, and the charred remains were believed to guard the house for the whole year against the risk of

[1] Montanus, *Die deutschen Volksfeste, Volksbräuche und deutscher Volksglaube* (Iserlohn, N.D.), p. 12. The Sieg and Lahn are two rivers of Central Germany, between Siegen and Marburg.

[2] J. H. Schmitz, *Sitten und Sagen,*

Lieder, Sprüchwörter und Räthsel des Eifler Volkes (Treves, 1856–1858), i. 4.

[3] Adalbert Kuhn, *Sagen, Gebräuche und Märchen aus Westfalen* (Leipsic, 1859), ii. § 319, pp. 103 *sq.*

[4] A. Kuhn, *op. cit.* ii. § 523, p. 187.

fire, burglary, and other misfortunes.[1]   The Yule log seems The Yule
log in
Switzer-
land. to be known only in the French-speaking parts of Switzerland, where it goes by the usual French name of *Bûche de Noël.*   In the Jura mountains of the canton of Bern, while the log is burning on the hearth the people sing a blessing over it as follows :—

> *" May the log burn !*
> *May all good come in !*
> *May the women have children*
> *And the sheep lambs !*
> *White bread for every one*
> *And the vat full of wine !"*

The embers of the Yule log were kept carefully, for they were believed to be a protection against lightning.[2]

" The Christmas fires, which were formerly lit everywhere The Yule
log in
Belgium. in the Low Countries, have fallen into disuse.   But in Flanders a great log of wood, called the *kersavondblok* and usually cut from the roots of a fir or a beech, is still put on the fire ; all the lights in the house are extinguished, and the whole family gathers round the log to spend part of the night in singing, in telling stories, especially about ghosts, were-wolves, and so on, and also in drinking gin.   At Grammont and in the neighbourhood of that town, where the Yule log is called *Kersmismot,* it is customary to set fire to the remainder of the gin at the moment when the log is reduced to ashes.   Elsewhere a piece of the log is kept and put under the bed to protect the house against thunder and lightning.   The charcoal of the log which burned during Christmas Night, if pounded up and mixed with water, is a cure for consumption.   In the country of Limburg the log burns several nights, and the pounded charcoal is kept as a preventive (so they say), of toothache." [3]

In several provinces of France, and particularly in The Yule
log in
France. Provence, the custom of the Yule log or *tréfoir,* as it was called in many places, was long observed.   A French

---

[1] August Witzschel, *Sagen, Sitten und Gebräuche aus Thüringen* (Vienna, 1878), p. 172.

[2] E. Hoffmann-Krayer, *Feste und Bräuche des Schweizervolkes* (Zurich,

1913), pp. 108 *sq.*

[3] Le Baron de Reinsberg-Düringsfeld, *Calendrier Belge* (Brussels, 1861–1862), ii. 326 *sq.* Compare J. W. Wolf, *Beiträge zur deutschen Mythologie* (Göttingen, 1852–1858), i. 117.

writer of the seventeenth century tells us that on Christmas Eve the log was prepared, and when the whole family had assembled in the kitchen or parlour of the house, they went and brought it in, walking in procession and singing Provençal verses to the following effect :—

> " *Let the log rejoice,*
> *To-morrow is the day of bread ;*
> *Let all good enter here ;*
> *Let the women bear children ;*
> *Let the she-goats bring forth kids ;*
> *Let the ewes drop lambs ;*
> *Let there be much wheat and flour,*
> *And the vat full of wine.*"

Then the log was blessed by the smallest and youngest child of the house, who poured a glass of wine over it saying, *In nomine patris,* etc. ; after which the log was set on the fire. The charcoal of the burnt wood was kept the whole year, and used as an ingredient in several remedies.[1]

French super-stitions as to the Yule log.   Amongst the superstitions denounced by the same writer is "the belief that a log called the *trefoir* or Christmas brand, which you put on the fire for the first time on Christmas Eve and continue to put on the fire for a little while every day till Twelfth Night, can, if kept under the bed, protect the house for a whole year from fire and thunder ; that it can prevent the inmates from having chilblains on their heels in winter ; that it can cure the cattle of many maladies ; that if a piece of it be steeped in the water which cows drink it helps them to calve ; and lastly that if the ashes of the log be strewn on the fields it can save the wheat from mildew."[2]

The Yule log at Marseilles and in Perigord.   In Marseilles the Yule log used to be a great block of oak, which went by the name of *calendeau* or *calignau* ; it was sprinkled with wine and oil, and the head of the house kindled it himself.[3]   "The Yule log plays a great part at the festival of the winter solstice in Perigord. The countryman thinks that it is best made of plum-tree, cherry, or oak, and

---

[1] J. B. Thiers, *Traité des Super-stitions*[5] (Paris, 1741), i. 302 *sq.* ; Eugène Cortet, *Essai sur les Fêtes Religieuses* (Paris, 1867), pp. 266 *sq*.

[2] J. B. Thiers, *Traité des Supersti-tions* (Paris, 1679), p. 323.

[3] Aubin-Louis Millin, *Voyage dans les Départemens du Midi de la France* (Paris, 1807–1811), iii. 336 *sq.* The fire so kindled was called *caco fuech.*

that the larger it is the better.   If it burns well, it is a good
omen, the blessing of heaven rests upon it.   The charcoal Virtues
ascribed to
and ashes, which are collected very carefully, are excellent the char-
for healing swollen glands ; the part of the trunk which has coal and
not been burnt in the fire is used by ploughmen to make the ashes of the
burnt log.
wedge (*técoin ou cale*) for their plough, because they allege that
it causes the seeds to thrive better; and the women keep pieces
of it till Twelfth Night for the sake of their chickens.   Nevertheless if you sit down on the log, you become subject to
boils, and to cure yourself of them you must pass nine times
under a bramble branch which happens to be rooted in the
ground at both ends.   The charcoal heals sheep of a disease
called the *goumon* ; and the ashes, carefully wrapt up in
white linen, preserve the whole household from accidents.
Some people think that they will have as many chickens as
there are sparks that fly out of the brands of the log when
they shake them ; and others place the extinct brands under
the bed to drive away vermin.   In Vienne, on Christmas
Eve, when supper is over, the master of the house has a
great log—the Christmas brand—brought in, and then,
surrounded by all the spectators gathered in profound
silence, he sprinkles salt and water on the log.   It is then
put on the fire to burn during the three festivals ; but they
carefully preserve a piece to be kindled every time that it
thunders." [1]   In Berry, a district of Central France, the Yule The Yule
log in
Berry.
log was called the *cosse de Nau*, the last word being an
abbreviation of the usual French word for Christmas (Noël).
It consisted of an enormous tree-trunk, so heavy that the
united strength of several men was needed to carry it in
and place it on the hearth, where it served to feed the fire
during the three days of the Christmas festivity.   Strictly
speaking, it should be the trunk of an old oak-tree which
had never been lopped and had been felled at midnight.   It

[1] Alfred de Nore, *Coutumes, Mythes
et Traditions des Provinces de France*
(Paris and Lyons, 1846), pp. 151 *sq.*
The three festivals during which the
Yule log is expected to burn are prob-
ably Christmas Day (December 25th),
St. Stephen's Day (December 26th),
and St. John the Evangelist's Day
(December 27th).   Compare J. L. M.

Noguès, *Les Mœurs d'autrefois en
Saintonge et en Aunis* (Saintes, 1891),
pp. 45-47.   According to the latter
writer, in Saintonge it was the mistress
of the house who blessed the Yule log,
sprinkling salt and holy water on it ;
in Poitou it was the eldest male who
officiated.   The log was called the
cosse de Nô.

was placed on the hearth at the moment when the tinkle of
the bell announced the elevation of the host at the midnight
mass ; and the head of the family, after sprinkling it with
holy water, set it on fire.   The remains of the log were
preserved till the same day next year.   They were kept
under the bed of the master of the house ; and whenever
thunder was heard, one of the family would take a piece of
the log and throw it on the fire, which was believed to guard
the family against lightning.   In the Middle Ages, we are
told, several fiefs were granted on condition that the vassal
should bring in person a Yule log every year for the hearth
of his liege lord.[1]

Similar customs and beliefs survived till recent years in
some of the remote country villages of the picturesque
district known as the Bocage of Normandy.   There it was
the grandfather or other oldest man of the family who
chose the Yule log in good time and had it ready for
Christmas Eve.   Then he placed it on the hearth at the
moment when the church bell began to ring for the evening service.   Kneeling reverently at the hearth with the
members of his family in a like attitude of devotion, the
old man recited three *Pater Nosters* and three *Aves*, and
invoked the blessing of heaven on the log and on the
cottage.   Then at the sound of the bell which proclaimed
the sacrament of the mass, or, if the church was too far
off to allow the tinkle of the bell to be heard, at the
moment when they judged that the priest was elevating
the host before the high altar, the patriarch sprinkled the
burning log with holy water, blessed it in the name of
the Father and of the Son and of the Holy Ghost, and
drew it out of the fire.   The charred log was then carefully kept till the following Christmas as a precious relic
which would guard the house against the levin bolt, evil
spirits, sorcerers, and every misfortune that might befall
in the course of the year.[2]   In the department of Orne

[1] Laisnel de Salle, *Croyances et
Légendes du Centre de la France* (Paris,
1875), i. 1-3.
[2] Jules Lecœur, *Esquisses du Bocage
Normand* (Condé-sur-Noireau, 1883–
1887), ii. 291.   The author speaks of
the custom as still practised in out-of-

the-way villages at the time when he
wrote.   The usage of preserving the
remains of the Yule-log (called *tréfouet*)
in Normandy is mentioned also by
Melle Amélie Bosquet, *La Normandie
Romanesque et Merveilleuse* (Paris and
Rouen, 1845), p. 294.

"the Yule-log is called *trefouet* ; holy water is poured on
it ; it should last the three days of the festival, and the
remains of it are kept to be put on the fire when it thunders.
This brand is a protection both against thunder and against
sorcerers."[1]   In Upper Brittany, also, the Yule log is thought
to be a safeguard against thunder and lightning.   It is
sprinkled with holy water on Christmas morning and allowed
to burn till evening.   If a piece of it is thrown into the
well, it will ensure a supply of good water.[2]

"In almost all the families of the Ardennes," we are
told, "at the present day they never fail to put the Yule
log on the fireplace, but formerly it was the object of a
superstitious worship which is now obsolete.   The charred
remains of it, placed under the pillow or under the house,
preserved the house from storms, and before it was burned
the Virgin used to come and sit on it, invisible, swaddling
the infant Jesus.   At Nouzon, twenty years ago, the
traditional log was brought into the kitchen on Christmas
Eve, and the grandmother, with a sprig of box in her hand,
sprinkled the log with holy water as soon as the clock
struck the first stroke of midnight.   As she did so she
chanted,

> ' *When Christmas comes,*
> *Every one should rejoice,*
> *For it is a New Covenant.*'

Following the grandmother and joining in the song, the
children and the rest of the family marched thrice round
the log, which was as fine a log as could be got."[3]   We
can now, perhaps, understand why in Perigord people
who sat on the Yule log suffered from boils,[4] and why in
Lorraine young folks used to be warned that if they sat
on it they would have the scab.[5]   The reason probably
was that the Virgin and child were supposed to be seated,

The Yule
log in the
Ardennes.

---

[1] A. de Nore, *Coutumes, Mythes, et
Traditions des Provinces de France*
(Paris and Lyons, 1846), p. 256.

[2] Paul Sébillot, *Coutumes populaires
de la Haute-Bretagne* (Paris, 1886),
pp. 217 *sq.*

[3] Albert   Meyrac,   *Traditions,
Coutumes, Légendes et Contes des*
Ardennes (Charleville, 1890), pp.
96 *sq.*

[4] See above, p. 251.

[5] Lerouze, in *Mémoires de l'Aca-
demie Celtique*, iii. (1809) p. 441,
quoted by J. Brand, *Popular Antiquities of Great Britain* (London,
1882–1883), i. 469 note.

invisible, upon the log and to resent the indignity of contact with mortal children.

On Christmas Eve the mountaineers of Rupt, in the Vosges, also never fail to put on the hearth the largest log which the hearth can hold ; they call it *la galeuche de Noë*, that is, the Yule log. Next morning they rake the ashes for any charred fragments and keep them as valuable talismans to guard them against the stroke of lightning. At Vagney and other places near it in the Vosges it used to be customary on the same evening to grease the hinges and the latches of the doors, that no harsh grating sound should break the slumbers of the infant Christ. In the Vosges Mountains, too, as indeed in many other places, cattle acquired the gift of speech on Christmas Eve and conversed with each other in the language of Christians. Their conversation was, indeed, most instructive ; for the future, it seems, had no secret worth mentioning for them. Yet few people cared to be caught eavesdropping at the byre ; wise folk contented themselves with setting a good store of fodder in the manger, then shut the door, and left the animals to their ruminations. A farmer of Vecoux once hid in a corner of the byre to overhear the edifying talk of the beasts. But it did him little good; for one ox said to another ox, " What shall we do to-morrow ? " and the other replied, " We shall carry our master to the churchyard." Sure enough the farmer died that very night and was buried next morning.[1] In Franche-Comté, the province of France to the west of the Jura mountains, if the Yule log is really to protect a house against thunder and lightning, it is essential that it should burn during the midnight mass, and that the flame should not go out before the divine service is concluded. Otherwise the log is quite useless for the purpose.[2] In Burgundy the log which is placed on the fire on Christmas Eve is called the *suche*. While it is burning, the father of the family, assisted by his wife and children, sings Christmas carols ; and when he has finished,

[1] L. F. Sauvé, *Le Folk-lore des Hautes-Vosges* (Paris, 1889), pp. 370 *sq.*

[2] Charles Beauquier, *Les Mois en Franche-Comté* (Paris, 1900), p. 183.

he tells the smallest children to go into a corner of the
room and pray God that the log may give them sweeties.
The prayer is invariably answered.[1]

In England the customs and beliefs concerning the The Yule
Yule log, clog, or block, as it was variously called, used log and the Yule
to be similar. On the night of Christmas Eve, says the candle in
antiquary John Brand, "our ancestors were wont to light England.
up candles of an uncommon size, called Christmas Candles,
and lay a log of wood upon the fire, called a Yule-clog or
Christmas-block, to illuminate the house, and, as it were, to
turn night into day. This custom is, in some measure, still
kept up in the North of England. In the buttery of St.
John's College, Oxford, an ancient candle-socket of stone still
remains ornamented with the figure of the Holy Lamb. It
was formerly used to burn the Christmas Candle in, on
the high table at supper, during the twelve nights of that
festival." [2]   "A tall mould candle, called a Yule candle,
is lighted and set on the table ; these candles are presented
by the chandlers and grocers to their customers. The
Yule-log is bought of the carpenters' lads. It would be
unlucky to light either of them before the time, or to stir
the fire or candle during the supper ; the candle must not
be snuffed, neither must any one stir from the table till
supper is ended. In these suppers it is considered unlucky
to have an odd number at table. A fragment of the log is
occasionally saved, and put under a bed, to remain till next
Christmas : it secures the house from fire ; a small piece of
it thrown into a fire occurring at the house of a neighbour,
will quell the raging flame. A piece of the candle should
likewise be kept to ensure good luck." [3]   In the seventeenth
century, as we learn from some verses of Herrick, the
English custom was to light the Yule log with a fragment
of its predecessor, which had been kept throughout the year
for the purpose ; where it was so kept, the fiend could do no
mischief.[4]   Indeed the practice of preserving a piece of the

[1] A. de Nore, *Coutumes, Mythes, et Traditions des Provinces de France* (Paris and Lyons, 1846), pp. 302 *sq.*

[2] John Brand, *Popular Antiquities of Great Britain* (London, 1882–1883), i. 467.

[3] J. Brand, *op. cit.* i. 455; *The Denham Tracts*, edited by Dr. James Hardy (London, 1892–1895), ii. 25 *sq.*

[4] Herrick, *Hesperides*, "Ceremonies for Christmasse" :

Yule-log of one year to light that of the next was observed by at least one family at Cheadle in Staffordshire down to the latter part of the nineteenth century.[1]

The Yule log in the North of England.

In the North of England farm-servants used to lay by a large knotty block of wood for the Christmas fire, and so long as the block lasted they were entitled by custom to ale at their meals. The log was as large as the hearth could hold.[2] At Belford, in Northumberland, "the lord of the manor sends round to every house, on the afternoon of Christmas Eve, the Yule Logs—four or five large logs—to be burnt on Christmas Eve and Day. This old custom has always, I am told, been kept up here."[3] The custom of burning the Yule log at Christmas used to be observed in Wensleydale and other parts of Yorkshire, and prudent housewives carefully preserved pieces of the log throughout the year. At Whitby the portions so kept were stowed away under the bed till next Christmas, when they were burnt with the new log; in the interval they were believed to protect the house from conflagration, and if one of them were thrown into the fire, it would quell a raging storm.[4] The practice and the belief were similar at Filey on the coast of Yorkshire, where besides the Yule log a tall Yule candle was lit on the same evening.[5] In the West Riding, while the log

The Yule-log in Yorkshire.

" Come, bring with a noise,
    My merrie merrie boyes,
The Christmas log to the firing; . . .
    With the last yeeres brand
    Light the new block."

And, again, in his verses, " Ceremonies for Candlemasse Day " :

" Kindle the Christmas brand, and then
    Till sunne-set let it burne;
Which quencht, then lay it up agen,
    Till Christmas next returne.
Part must be kept, wherewith to teend
    The Christmas log next yeare ;
And where 'tis safely kept, the fiend
    Can do no mischiefe there."

See The Works of Robert Herrick (Edinburgh, 1823), vol. ii. pp. 91, 124. From these latter verses it seems that the Yule log was replaced on the fire on Candlemas (the second of February).

[1] Miss C. S. Burne and Miss G. F. Jackson, Shropshire Folk-lore (London, 1883), p. 398 note [2]. See also below, pp. 257, 258, as to the Lincolnshire, Herefordshire, and Welsh practice.

[2] Francis Grose, Provincial Glossary, Second Edition (London, 1811), pp. 141 sq. ; T. F. Thiselton Dyer, British Popular Customs (London, 1876), p. 466.

[3] County Folk-lore, vol. iv. Northumberland, collected by M. C. Balfour and edited by Northcote W. Thomas (London, 1904), p. 79.

[4] County Folk-lore, vol. ii. North Riding of Yorkshire, York and the Ainsty, collected and edited by Mrs. Gutch (London, 1901), pp. 273, 274, 275 sq.

[5] County Folk-lore, vol. vi. East Riding of Yorkshire, collected and edited by Mrs. Gutch (London, 1912), pp. 23, 118, compare p. 114.

blazed cheerfully, the people quaffed their ale and sang,
"Yule! Yule! a pack of new cards and a Christmas
stool!"[1]   At Clee, in Lincolnshire, "when Christmas Eve The Yule
has come the Yule cake is duly cut and the Yule log lit, log in
Lincoln-
and I know of some even middle-class houses where the shire.
new log must always rest upon and be lighted by the
old one, a small portion of which has been carefully stored
away to preserve a continuity of light and heat."[2]   At the The Yule
village of Wootton Wawen in Warwickshire, down to 1759 log in War
wickshire,
at least, the Yule-block, as it was called, was drawn into the Shrop-
house by a horse on Christmas Eve "as a foundation for the shire, and
Hereford
fire on Christmas Day, and according to the superstition of shire.
those times for the twelve days following, as the said block was
not to be entirely reduc'd to ashes till that time had passed
by."[3]   As late as 1830, or thereabout, the scene of lighting the
hearth-fire on Christmas Eve, to continue burning throughout the Christmas season, might have been witnessed in the
secluded and beautiful hill-country of West Shropshire,
from Chirbury and Worthen to Pulverbatch and Pontesbury.
The Christmas brand or brund, as they called it, was a
great trunk of seasoned oak, holly, yew, or crab-tree, drawn
by horses to the farm-house door and thence rolled by
means of rollers and levers to the back of the wide open
hearth, where the fire was made up in front of it.   The
embers were raked up to it every night, and it was carefully
tended, that it might not go out during the whole Christmas
season.   All those days no light might be struck, given, or
borrowed.   Such was the custom at Worthen in the early
part of the nineteenth century.[4]   In Herefordshire the
Christmas feast "lasted for twelve days, and no work was

[1] John Aubrey, *Remaines of Gentilisme and Judaisme* (London, 1881),
p. 5.
[2] *County Folk-lore*, vol. v. *Lincolnshire*, collected by Mrs. Gutch and
Mabel Peacock (London, 1908), p.
219. Elsewhere in Lincolnshire the
Yule-log seems to have been called the
Yule-clog (*op. cit.* pp. 215, 216).
[3] Mrs. Samuel Chandler (Sarah
Whateley), quoted in *The Folk-lore
Journal*, i. (1883) pp. 351 *sq.*
[4] Miss C. S. Burne and Miss G. F.

Jackson, *Shropshire Folk-lore* (London,
1883), pp. 397 *sq.* One of the informants of these writers says (*op. cit.*
p. 399): "In 1845 I was at the
Vessons farmhouse, near the Eastbridge
Coppice (at the northern end of the
Stiperstones). The floor was of flags,
an unusual thing in this part. Observing a sort of roadway through the
kitchen, and the flags much broken, I
enquired what caused it, and was
told it was from the horses' hoofs
drawing in the 'Christmas Brund.'"

done.   All houses were, and are now, decorated with sprigs of holly and ivy, which must not be brought in until Christmas Eve.   A Yule log, as large as the open hearth could accommodate, was brought into the kitchen of each farmhouse, and smaller ones were used in the cottages. W—— P—— said he had seen a tree drawn into the kitchen at Kingstone Grange years ago by two cart horses ; when it had been consumed a small portion was carefully kept to be used for lighting next year's log.   ' Mother always kept it very carefully ; she said it was lucky, and kept the house from fire and from lightning.'   It seems to have been the general practice to light it on Christmas Eve." [1]   " In many parts of Wales it is still customary to keep part of the Yule-log until the following Christmas Eve ' for luck.'   It is then put into the fireplace and burnt, but before it is consumed the new log is put on, and thus ' the old fire and the new ' burn together.   In some families this is done from force of habit, and they cannot now tell why they do it ; but in the past the observance of this custom was to keep witches away, and doubtless was a survival of fire-worship." [2]

The Yule log in Wales.

The Yule log in Servia.

The cutting of the oak tree to form the Yule log.

But nowhere, apparently, in Europe is the old heathen ritual of the Yule log preserved to the present day more perfectly than in Servia.   At early dawn on Christmas Eve (*Badnyi Dan*) every peasant house sends two of its strongest young men to the nearest forest to cut down a young oak tree and bring it home.   There, after offering up a short prayer or crossing themselves thrice, they throw a handful of wheat on the chosen oak and greet it with the words, " Happy *Badnyi* day to you ! "   Then they cut it down, taking care that it shall fall towards the east at the moment when the sun's orb appears over the rim of the eastern horizon. Should the tree fall towards the west, it would be the worst possible omen for the house and its inmates in the ensuing year ; and it is also an evil omen if the tree should be caught and stopped in its fall by another tree.   It is im-

[1] Mrs. Ella Mary Leather, *The Folk-lore of Herefordshire* (Hereford and London, 1912), p. 109.   Compare Miss C. S. Burne, " Herefordshire Notes," *The Folk-lore Journal*, iv.   (1886) p. 167.

[2] Marie Trevelyan, *Folk-lore and Folk-stories of Wales* (London, 1909), p. 28.

portant to keep and carry home the first chip from the fallen oak. The trunk is sawn into two or three logs, one of them rather longer than the others. A flat, unleavened cake of the purest wheaten flour is brought out of the house and broken on the larger of the logs by a woman. The logs are left for the present to stand outside, leaning on one of the walls of the house. Each of them is called a Yule log (*badnyak*).

Meanwhile the children and young people go from house to house singing special songs called *Colleda* because of an old pagan divinity Colleda, who is invoked in every line. In one of them she is spoken of as "a beautiful little maid"; in another she is implored to make the cows yield milk abundantly. The day is spent in busy preparations. The women bake little cakes of a special sort in the shape of lambs, pigs, and chickens; the men make ready a pig for roasting, for in every Servian house roast pig is the principal dish at Christmas. A bundle of straw, tied with a rope, is brought into the courtyard and left to stand there near the Yule logs.

Prayers to Colleda.

At the moment when the sun is setting all the members of the family assemble in the central hall (the great family kitchen) of the principal house. The mother of the family (or the wife of the chief of the Zadrooga)[1] gives a pair of

The bring-ing in of the Yule log.

[1] " In earlier ages, and even so late as towards the middle of the nineteenth century, the Servian village organisa-tion and the Servian agriculture had yet another distinguishing feature. The dangers from wild beasts in old time, the want of security for life and pro-perty during the Turkish rule, or rather misrule, the natural difficulties of the agriculture, more especially the lack in agricultural labourers, induced the Servian peasants not to leave the parental house but to remain together on the family's property. In the same yard, within the same fence, one could see around the ancestral house a number of wooden huts which con-tained one or two rooms, and were used as sleeping places for the sons, nephews and grandsons and their wives. Men and women of three generations could be often seen living in that way together, and working together the land which was considered as common property of the whole family. This expanded family, remaining with all its branches together, and, so to say, under the same roof, working together, divid-ing the fruits of their joint labours to-gether, this family and an agricultural association in one, was called *Zadrooga* (The Association). This combination of family and agricultural association has morally, economically, socially, and politically rendered very important ser-vices to the Servians. The headman or chief (called *Stareshina*) of such family association is generally the oldest male member of the family. He is the administrator of the common property and director of work. He is the execu-tive chairman of the association. Gener-ally he does not give any order without having consulted all the grown-up male

woollen gloves to one of the young men, who goes out and presently returns carrying in his gloved hands the largest of the logs. The mother receives him at the threshold, throwing at him a handful of wheat, in which the first chip of the oak tree cut in the early morning for the Yule log has been kept all day. Entering the central hall with the Yule log the young man greets all present with the words : " Good evening, and may you have a happy Christmas ! " and they all answer in chorus, " May God and the happy and holy Christmas help thee ! " In some parts of Servia the chief of the family, holding a glass of red wine in his hand, greets the Yule log as if it were a living person, and drinks to its health. After that, another glass of red wine is poured on the log. Then the oldest male member of the family, assisted by the young man who brought in the log, places it on the burning fire so that the thicker end of the log protrudes for about a foot from the hearth. In some places this end is smeared with honey.

The ceremony with the straw.

Next the mother of the family brings in the bundle of straw which was left standing outside. All the young children arrange themselves behind her in a row. She then walks slowly round the hall and the adjoining rooms, throwing handfuls of straw on the floor and imitating the cackling of a hen, while all the children follow her peeping with their lips as if they were chickens cheeping and waddling after the mother bird. When the floor is well strewn with straw, the father or the eldest member of the family throws a few walnuts in every corner of the hall, pronouncing the words : " In the name of God the Father, and the Son, and the Holy Ghost, Amen ! " A large pot, or a small wooden box, filled with wheat is placed high in the east corner of the hall, and a tall candle of yellow wax is stuck in the middle of the wheat. Then the father of the family reverently lights the candle

The Yule candle.

members of the *Zadrooga* " (Chedo Mijatovich, *Servia and the Servians*, London, 1908, pp. 237 *sq.*). As to the house-communities of the South Slavs see further Og. M. Utiešenović, *Die Hauskommunionen der Südslaven* (Vienna, 1859) ; F. Demelić, *Le Droit Coutumier des Slaves Méridionaux* (Paris, 1876), pp. 23 *sqq.* ; F. S.

Krauss, *Sitte und Brauch der Süd-slaven* (Vienna, 1885), pp. 64 *sqq.* Since Servia, freed from Turkish oppression, has become a well-regulated European state, with laws borrowed from the codes of France and Germany, the old house-communities have been rapidly disappearing (Chedo Mijatovich, *op. cit.* p. 240).

and prays God to bless the family with health and happiness, the fields with a good harvest, the beehives with plenty of honey, the cattle and sheep with young, and the cows with abundant milk and rich cream. After that they all sit down to supper, squatting on the floor, for the use of chairs and tables is forbidden on this occasion.

By four o'clock next morning (Christmas Day) the whole village is astir ; indeed most people do not sleep at all that night. It is deemed most important to keep the Yule log burning brightly all night long. Very early, too, the pig is *The roast* laid on the fire to roast, and at the same moment one of the *pig.* family goes out into the yard and fires a pistol or gun ; and when the roast pig is removed from the fire the shot is repeated. Hence for several hours in the early morning of Christmas Day such a popping and banging of firearms goes on that a stranger might think a stubborn skirmish was in progress. Just before the sun rises a girl goes and draws *The draw-* water at the village spring or at the brook. Before she fills *ing of the* her vessels, she wishes the water a happy Christmas and *water.* throws a handful of wheat into it. The first cupfuls of water she brings home are used to bake a special Christmas cake (*chesnitsa*), of which all the members partake at dinner, and portions are kept for absent relatives. A small silver coin is baked in the cake, and he or she who gets it will be lucky during the year.

All the family gathered round the blazing Yule log now *The* anxiously expect the arrival of the special Christmas visiter, *Christmas* who bears the title of *polaznik*. He is usually a young boy *(polaznik).* of a friendly family. No other person, not even the priest or the mayor of the village, would be allowed to set foot in the house before the arrival of this important personage. Therefore he ought to come, and generally does come, very early in the morning. He carries a woollen glove full of wheat, and when the door is opened at his knock he throws handfuls of wheat on the family gathered round the hearth, greeting them with the words, " Christ is born ! " They all answer, " He is born indeed," and the hostess flings a hand-ful of wheat over the Christmas visiter, who moreover casts some of his wheat into the corners of the hall as well as upon the people. Then he walks straight to the hearth,

takes a shovel and strikes the burning log so that a cloud
of sparks flies up the chimney, while he says, " May you
have this year so many oxen, so many horses, so many
sheep, so many pigs, so many beehives full of honey, so
much good luck, prosperity, progress, and happiness ! "
Having uttered these good wishes, he embraces and kisses
his host. Then he turns again to the hearth, and after
crossing himself falls on his knees and kisses the projecting
part of the Yule log. On rising to his feet he places a coin
on the log as his gift. Meanwhile a low wooden chair has
been brought in by a woman, and the visiter is led to it to
take his seat. But just as he is about to do so, the chair is
jerked away from under him by a male member of the
family and he measures his length on the floor. By this
fall he is supposed to fix into the ground all the good
wishes which he has uttered that morning. The hostess
thereupon wraps him in a thick blanket, and he sits quietly
muffled in it for a few minutes ; the thick blanket in which
he is swathed is believed, on the principles of homoeopathic
magic, to ensure that the cows will give thick cream the
next year. While he sits thus enriching the milk of the
dairy, the lads who are to herd the sheep in the coming year
go to the hearth and kneeling down before it kiss each
other across the projecting end of the Yule log. By this
demonstration of affection they are thought to seal the
love of the ewes for their lambs.[1]

The
Yule log
among the
Servians of
Slavonia.

The ritual of the Yule log is observed in a similar
form by the Servians who inhabit the southern provinces
of Austria. Thus in Syrmia, a district of Slavonia which
borders on Servia, the head of the house sends out
one or two young men on Christmas Eve to cut the
Yule log in the nearest forest. On being brought in, the
log is not mixed with the ordinary fuel but placed by
itself, generally leaning against a fruit-tree till the evening
shadows begin to fall. When a man carries it into the
kitchen and lays it on the fire, the master of the house
throws corn over him, and the two greet each other solemnly,
the one saying, " Christ is born," and the other answering,
" He is born indeed." Later in the evening the master of

[1] Chedo Mijatovich, *Servia and the Servians* (London, 1908), pp. 98-105.

the house pours a glass of wine on the charred end of the log, whereupon one of the younger men takes the burnt piece of wood, carries it to the orchard, and sets it up against one of the fruit-trees. For this service he is rewarded by the master of the house with a piece of money. On Christmas Day, when the family is assembled at table, they expect the arrival of the special Christmas visiter (called *polazenik*), the only person who is allowed to enter the house that day. When he comes, he goes to the hearth, stirs the fire with the poker and says, " Christ is born. May the family enjoy all good luck and happiness in this year ! May the cattle increase in number like the sparks I have struck ! " As he says these words, the mistress of the house pours corn over him and leads him to the parlour, where he takes the place of honour beside the master of the house. He is treated with marked attention and respect. The family are at pains to entertain him ; they sing their best songs for his amusement, and after midnight a numerous band of men and maidens escorts him by torchlight, with songs and jubilation, to his own house.[1]

The Christmas visiter (*polazenik*).

Among the Servians of Dalmatia, Herzegovina, and Montenegro it is customary on Christmas Eve (*Badnyi Dan*) to fetch a great Yule log (*badnyak*), which serves as a symbol of family luck. It is generally cut from an evergreen oak, but sometimes from an olive-tree or a beech. At nightfall the master of the house himself brings in the log and lays it on the fire. Then he and all present bare their heads, sprinkle the log with wine, and make a cross on it. After that the master of the house says, " Welcome, O log ! May God keep you from mishap ! " So saying he strews peas, maize, raisins, and wheat on the log, praying for God's blessing on all members of the family living and dead, for heaven's blessing on their undertakings, and for domestic prosperity. In Montenegro they meet the log with a loaf of bread and a jug of wine, drink to it, and pour wine on it, whereupon the whole family drinks out of the same beaker. In Dalmatia and other places, for example in Rizano, the Yule logs are decked by young women with red silk, flowers,

The Yule log among the Servians of Dalmatia, Herzegovina, and Montenegro.

[1] Baron Rajacsich, *Das Leben, die Sitten und Gebräuche der im Kaiser-* *thume Oesterreich lebenden Südslaven* (Vienna, 1873), pp. 122-128.

laurel leaves, ribbons, and even gold wire ; and the lights near the doorposts are kindled when the log is brought into the house.   Among the Morlaks, as soon as the master of the house crosses the threshold with the Yule log, one of the family must sprinkle corn on him and say, " God bless you," to which he answers, " The same to you."   A piece of the log is kept till New Year's Day to kindle a light with or it is carried out to the fields to protect them from hail.   It is customary to invite before hand a Christmas visiter (*pola-žaynik*) and to admit no one else into the house on that day.   He comes early, carrying in his sleeves a quantity of corn which he throws into the house, saying, " Christ is born."   One of the household replies, " He is born indeed," and throws corn on the visiter.   Then the newcomer goes up to the hearth, pokes the fire and strikes the burning log with the poker so hard that sparks fly off in all directions. At each blow he says, " I wish the family as many cows, calves, sucking pigs, goats, and sheep, and as many strokes of good luck, as the sparks that now fly from the log." With these words he throws some small coins into the ashes.[1]   In Albania down to recent years it was a common custom to burn a Yule log at Christmas, and with it corn, maize, and beans ; moreover, wine and *rakia* were poured on the flames, and the ashes of the fire were scattered on the fields to make them fertile.[2]   The Huzuls, a Slavonic people of the Carpathians, kindle fire by the friction of wood on Christmas Eve (Old Style, the fifth of January) and keep it burning till Twelfth Night.[3]

It is remarkable how common the belief appears to have been that the remains of the Yule-log, if kept throughout the year, had power to protect the house against fire and especially against lightning.[4]   As the Yule log was

The Yule log in Albania.

Belief that the Yule log protects against fire and lightning.

[1] Baron Rajacsich, *Das Leben, die Sitten und Gebräuche der im Kaiserthume Oesterreich lebenden Südslaven* (Vienna, 1873), pp. 129-131. The Yule log (*badnyak*) is also known in Bulgaria, where the women place it on the hearth on Christmas Eve. See A. Strausz, *Die Bulgaren* (Leipsic, 1898), p. 361.

[2] M. Edith Durham, *High Albania* (London, 1909), p. 129.

[3] R. F. Kaindl, *Die Huzulen* (Vienna, 1894) p. 71.

[4] See above, pp. 248, 249, 250, 251, 252, 253, 254, 255, 256, 258. Similarly at Candlemas people lighted candles in the churches, then took them home and kept them, and thought that by lighting them at any time they could keep off thunder, storm, and tempest. See Barnabe Googe, *The Popish Kingdom* (reprinted London, 1880), p. 48 *verso*.

frequently of oak,[1] it seems possible that this belief may be
a relic of the old Aryan creed which associated the oak-
tree with the god of thunder.[2] Whether the curative and
fertilizing virtues ascribed to the ashes of the Yule log,
which are supposed to heal cattle as well as men, to enable
cows to calve, and to promote the fruitfulness of the earth,[3]
may not be derived from the same ancient source, is a
question which deserves to be considered.

Thus far we have regarded only the private or domestic
celebration of the fire-festival at midwinter. The public
celebration of such rites at that season of the year appears
to have been rare and exceptional in Central and Northern
Europe. However, some instances are on record. Thus at
Schweina, in Thuringia, down to the second half of the
nineteenth century, the young people used to kindle a great
bonfire on the Antonius Mountain every year on Christmas
Eve. Neither the civil nor the ecclesiastical authorities were
able to suppress the celebration ; nor could the cold, rain,
and snow of the season damp or chill the enthusiasm of the
celebrants. For some time before Christmas the young men
and boys were busy building a foundation for the bonfire on
the top of the mountain, where the oldest church of the
village used to stand. The foundation consisted of a pyra-
midal structure composed of stones, turf, and moss. When
Christmas Eve came round, a strong pole, with bundles of
brushwood tied to it, was erected on the pyramid. The
young folk also provided themselves with poles to which old
brooms or faggots of shavings were attached. These were
to serve as torches. When the evening grew dark and the
church bells rang to service, the troop of lads ascended the
mountain ; and soon from the top the glare of the bonfire
lit up the darkness, and the sound of a hymn broke the
stillness of night. In a circle round the great fire lesser
fires were kindled ; and last of all the lads ran about swinging their lighted torches, till these twinkling points of fire,
moving down the mountain-side, went out one by one in the
darkness. At midnight the bells rang out from the church

*Public
celebra-
tions of the
fire-festival
at Mid-
winter.*

*The bon-
fire on
Christmas
Eve at
Schweina
in
Thuringia.*

---

[1] See above, pp. 248, 250, 251,
257, 258, 263.

[2] See *The Magic Art and the*

Evolution of Kings, ii. 356 *sqq.*

[3] See above, pp. 248, 249, 250,
251, 264.

tower, mingled with the blast of horns and the sound of singing. Feasting and revelry were kept up throughout the night, and in the morning young and old went to early mass to be edified by hearing of the light eternal.[1]

Bonfires on Christmas Eve in Normandy.

In the Bocage of Normandy the peasants used to repair, often from a distance of miles, to the churches to hear the midnight mass on Christmas Eve. They marched in procession by torchlight, chanting Christmas carols, and the fitful illumination of the woods, the hedges, and the fields as they moved through the darkness, presented a succession of picturesque scenes. Mention is also made of bonfires kindled on the heights ; the custom is said to have been observed at Athis near Condé down to recent years.[2]

Bonfires on St. Thomas's Day in the Isle of Man.

In the Isle of Man, " on the twenty-first of December, a day dedicated to Saint Thomas, the people went to the mountains to catch deer and sheep for Christmas, and in the evenings always kindled a large fire on the top of every *fingan* or cliff. Hence, at the time of casting peats, every one laid aside a large one, saying, ' *Faaid mooar moayney son oie'l fingan* ' ; that is, ' a large turf for Fingan Eve.' "[3]   At

The "Burning of the Clavie" at Burghead on the last day of December.

Burghead, an ancient village on the southern shore of the Moray Firth, about nine miles from the town of Elgin, a festival of fire called " the Burning of the Clavie " has been celebrated from time immemorial on Hogmanay, the last day of December. A tar-barrel is sawn in two, one half of it is set on the top of a stout pole, and filled with tar and other combustibles. The half-barrel is fastened to the pole by means of a long nail, which is made for the purpose and furnished gratuitously by the village blacksmith. The nail must be knocked in with a stone ; the use of a hammer is forbidden. When the shades of evening have begun to fall, the Clavie, as it is called, is set on fire by means of a burning peat, which is always fetched from the same house ; it may not be kindled with a match. As soon as it is in a blaze, it is shouldered by a man, who proceeds to carry it at a run, flaring and dripping melted tar, round the old

[1] August Witzschel, *Sagen, Sitten und Gebräuche aus Thüringen* (Vienna, 1878), pp. 171 *sq.*

[2] Jules Lecœur, *Esquisses du Bocage Normand* (Condé-sur-Noireau, 1883–

1887), ii. 289 *sq.*

[3] Joseph Train, *Historical and Statistical Account of the Isle of Man* (Douglas, Isle of Man, 1845), ii. 124, referring to Cregeen's *Manx Dictionary*, p. 67.

boundaries of the village; the modern part of the town is not
included in the circuit.   Close at his heels follows a motley
crowd, cheering and shouting.   One bearer relieves another
as each wearies of his burden.   The first to shoulder the
Clavie, which is esteemed an honour, is usually a man who
has been lately married.   Should the bearer stumble or fall,
it is deemed a very ill omen for him and for the village.   In
bygone times it was thought necessary that one man should
carry it all round the village; hence the strongest man was
chosen for the purpose.   Moreover it was customary to carry
the burning Clavie round every fishing-boat and vessel in the
harbour; but this part of the ceremony was afterwards discontinued.   Finally, the blazing tar-barrel is borne to a small
hill called the Doorie, which rises near the northern end of
the promontory.   Here the pole is fixed into a socket in a
pillar of freestone, and fresh fuel is heaped upon the flames,
which flare up higher and brighter than ever.   Formerly the
Clavie was allowed to burn here the whole night, but now,
after blazing for about half an hour, it is lifted from the
socket and thrown down the western slope of the hill.   Then
the crowd rushes upon it, demolishes it, and scrambles for
the burning, smoking embers, which they carry home and
carefully preserve as charms to protect them against witchcraft and misfortune.[1]   The great antiquity of Burghead, The old
where this curious and no doubt ancient festival is still rampart at
annually observed, appears from the remains of a very re- Burghead.
markable rampart which formerly encircled the place.   It
consists of a mound of earth faced on both sides with a
solid wall of stone and strengthened internally by oak
beams and planks, the whole being laid on a foundation of
boulders.   The style of the rampart agrees in general with
Caesar's description of the mode in which the Gauls constructed their walls of earth, stone, and logs,[2] and it resembles
the ruins of Gallic fortifications which have been discovered

[1] R. Chambers, *The Book of Days*
(London and Edinburgh, 1886), ii.
789-791, quoting *The Banffshire
Journal*; Miss C. F. Gordon Cumming, *In the Hebrides* (London, 1883),
p. 226; Miss E. J. Guthrie, *Old
Scottish Customs* (London and Glasgow,
1885), pp. 223-225; Ch. Rogers,

Social Life in Scotland (Edinburgh,
1884–1886), iii. 244 *sq.*; *The Folk-lore
Journal*, vii. (1889) pp. 11-14, 46.
Miss Gordon Cumming and Miss
Guthrie say that the burning of the
Clavie took place upon Yule Night;
but this seems to be a mistake.

[2] Caesar, *De bello Gallico*, vii. 23.

in France, though it is said to surpass them in the strength and solidity of its structure. No similar walls appear to be known in Britain. A great part of this interesting prehistoric fortress was barbarously destroyed in the early part of the nineteenth century, much of it being tumbled into the sea and many of the stones used to build the harbour piers.[1]

Procession
with burn-
ing tar-
barrels on
Christmas
Eve (Old
Style) at
Lerwick.
In Lerwick, the capital of the Shetland Islands, "on Christmas Eve, the fourth of January,—for the old style is still observed—the children go *a guizing*, that is to say, they disguising themselves in the most fantastic and gaudy costumes, parade the streets, and infest the houses and shops, begging for the wherewithal to carry on their Christmas amusements. One o'clock on Yule morning having struck, the young men turn out in large numbers, dressed in the coarsest of garments, and, at the double-quick march, drag huge tar barrels through the town, shouting and cheering as they go, or blowing loud blasts with their 'louder horns.' The tar barrel simply consists of several—say from four to eight—tubs filled with tar and chips, placed on a platform of wood. It is dragged by means of a chain, to which scores of jubilant youths readily yoke themselves. They have recently been described by the worthy burgh officer of Lerwick as 'fiery chariots, the effect of which is truly grand and terrific.' In a Christmas morning the dark streets of Lerwick are generally lighted up by the bright glare, and its atmosphere blackened by the dense smoke of six or eight tar barrels in succession. On the appearance of daybreak, at six A.M., the morning revellers put off their coarse garments—well begrimed by this time—and in their turn become guizards. They assume every imaginable form of costume—those of

---

[1] Hugh W. Young, F.S.A. Scot., *Notes on the Ramparts of Burghead as revealed by recent Excavations* (Edinburgh, 1892), pp. 3 *sqq.*; *Notes on further Excavations at Burghead* (Edinburgh, 1893), pp. 7 *sqq.* These papers are reprinted from the *Proceedings of the Society of Antiquaries of Scotland*, vols. xxv., xxvii. Mr. Young concludes as follows : "It is proved that the fort at Burghead was raised by a people skilled in engineering ; who used square-headed nails, axes and chisels of iron ; who shot balista stones over 20 lbs. in weight ; and whose daily food was the *bos longifrons*. A people who made paved roads, and sunk artesian wells, and used Roman beads and pins. The riddle of Burghead should not now be very difficult to read " (*Notes on further Excavations at Burghead*, pp. 14 *sq.*). For a loan of Mr. Young's pamphlets I am indebted to the kindness of Sheriff-Substitute David J. Mackenzie of Kilmarnock.

soldiers, sailors, highlanders, Spanish chevaliers, etc. Thus disguised, they either go in pairs, as man and wife, or in larger groups, and proceed to call on their friends, to wish them the compliments of the season. Formerly, these adolescent guizards used to seat themselves in crates, and accompanied by fiddlers, were dragged through the town." [1]

The Persians used to celebrate a festival of fire called *Sada* or *Saza* at the winter solstice. On the longest night of the year they kindled bonfires everywhere, and kings and princes tied dry grass to the feet of birds and animals, set fire to the grass, and then let the birds and beasts fly or run blazing through the air or over the fields and mountains, so that the whole air and earth appeared to be on fire. [2]

Persian festival of fire at the winter solstice.

§ 8. *The Need-fire*

The fire-festivals hitherto described are all celebrated periodically at certain stated times of the year. But besides these regularly recurring celebrations the peasants in many parts of Europe have been wont from time immemorial to resort to a ritual of fire at irregular intervals in seasons of distress and calamity, above all when their cattle were attacked by epidemic disease. No account of the popular European fire-festivals would be complete without some notice of these remarkable rites, which have all the greater claim on our attention because they may perhaps be regarded as the source and origin of all the other fire-festivals; certainly they must date from a very remote antiquity. The general name by which they are known among the Teutonic peoples is need-fire. [3]

European festivals of fire in seasons of distress and calamity.

The need fire.

[1] Robert Cowie, M.A., M.D., *Shetland, Descriptive and Historical* (Aberdeen, 1871), pp. 127 *sq.*; *County Folk-lore*, vol. iii. *Orkney and Shetland Islands*, collected by G. F. Black and edited by Northcote W. Thomas (London, 1903), pp. 203 *sq.* A similar celebration, known as Up-helly-a', takes place at Lerwick on the 29th of January, twenty-four days after Old Christmas. See *The Scapegoat*, pp. 167-169. Perhaps the popular festival of Up-helly-a' has absorbed some of the features of the Christmas Eve celebration.

[2] Thomas Hyde, *Historia Religionis veterum Persarum* (Oxford, 1700), pp. 255-257.

[3] On the need-fire see Jacob Grimm, *Deutsche Mythologie*,⁴ i. 501 *sqq.* ; J. W. Wolf, *Beiträge zur deutschen Mythologie* (Göttingen and Leipsic, 1852–1857), i. 116 *sq.*, ii. 378 *sqq.* ; Adalbert Kuhn, *Die Herabkunft des Feuers und des Göttertranks* ² (Gütersloh, 1886), pp. 41 *sqq.* ; Walter K.

The history of the need-fire can be traced back to the early Middle Ages ; for in the reign of Pippin, King of the Franks, the practice of kindling need-fires was denounced as a heathen superstition by a synod of prelates and nobles held under the presidency of Boniface, Archbishop of Mainz.[1] Not long afterwards the custom was again forbidden, along with many more relics of expiring paganism, in an " Index of Superstitions and Heathenish Observances," which has been usually referred to the year 743 A.D., though some scholars assign it a later date under the reign of Charlemagne.[2]   In Germany the need-fires would seem to have been popular

down to the second half of the nineteenth century.   Thus in the year 1598, when a fatal cattle-plague was raging at Neustadt, near Marburg, a wise man of the name of Joh. Köhler induced the authorities of the town to adopt the following remedy.   A new waggon-wheel was taken and twirled round an axle, which had never been used before, until the friction elicited fire.   With this fire a bonfire was next kindled between the gates of the town, and all the cattle were driven through the smoke and flames.   Moreover, every householder had to rekindle the fire on his hearth by means of a light taken from the bonfire.   Strange to say, this salutary measure had no effect whatever in staying the

---

Kelly, *Curiosities of Indo-European Tradition and Folk - lore* (London, 1863), pp. 48 *sqq.* ; W. Mannhardt, *Der Baumkultus der Germanen und ihrer Nachbarstämme* (Berlin, 1875), pp. 518 *sqq.* ; Charles Elton, *Origins of English History* (London, 1882), pp. 293 *sqq.* ; Ulrich Jahn, *Die deutschen Opfergebräuche bei Ackerbau und Viehzucht* (Breslau, 1884), pp. 26 *sqq.* Grimm would derive the name *need*-fire (German, *niedfyr, nodfyr, nodfeur, nothfeur*) from *need* (German, *noth*), 'necessity,' so that the phrase need-fire would mean "a forced fire." This is the sense attached to it in Lindenbrog's glossary on the capitularies, quoted by Grimm, *op. cit.* i. p. 502 : "*Eum ergo ignem* nodfeur *et* nodfyr, *quasi necessarium ignem vocant.*" C. L. Rochholz would connect *need* with a verb *nieten* "to churn," so that need-fire would mean

" churned fire." See C. L. Rochholz, *Deutscher Glaube und Brauch* (Berlin, 1867), ii. 149 *sq.* This interpretation is confirmed by the name *ankenmilch bohren*, which is given to the need-fire in some parts of Switzerland. See E. Hoffmann - Krayer, " Fruchtbarkeitsriten im schweizerischen Volksbrauch," *Schweizerisches Archiv für Volkskunde*, xi. (1907) p. 245.

[1] " *Illos sacrilegos ignes, quos* niedfyr *vocant,*" quoted by J. Grimm, *Deutsche Mythologie*,[4] i. 502 ; R. Andree, *Braunschweiger Volkskunde* (Brunswick, 1896), p. 312.

[2] *Indiculus Superstitionum et Paganiarum*, No. XV., " De *igne fricato de ligno i.e.* nodfyr." A convenient edition of the *Indiculus* has been published with a commentary by H. A. Saupe (Leipsic, 1891). As to the date of the work, see the editor's introduction, pp. 4 *sq.*

cattle - plague, and seven years later the sapient Joh.
Köhler himself was burnt as a witch. The farmers, whose
pigs and cows had derived no benefit from the need-fire,
perhaps assisted as spectators at the burning, and, while they
shook their heads, agreed among themselves that it served
Joh. Köhler perfectly right.[1] According to a writer who
published his book about nine years afterwards, some of the
Germans, especially in the Wassgaw mountains, confidently
believed that a cattle-plague could be stayed by driving the
animals through a need-fire which had been kindled by the
violent friction of a pole on a quantity of dry oak wood ; but
it was a necessary condition of success that all fires in the
village should previously be extinguished with water, and any
householder who failed to put out his fire was heavily fined.[2]

The method of kindling the need-fire is described as
follows by a writer towards the end of the seventeenth
century : " When an evil plague has broken out among
the cattle, large and small, and the herds have thereby
suffered great ravages, the peasants resolve to light a
need-fire. On a day appointed there must be no single
flame in any house nor on any hearth. From every house
a quantity of straw and water and underwood must be
brought forth ; then a strong oaken pole is fixed firmly in
the earth, a hole is bored in it, and a wooden winch, well
smeared with pitch and tar, is inserted in the hole and
turned round forcibly till great heat and then fire is
generated. The fire so produced is caught in fuel and fed
with straw, heath, and underwood till it bursts out into a
regular need-fire, which must then be somewhat spread out
between walls or fences, and the cattle and horses driven
through it twice or thrice with sticks and whips. Others set
up two posts, each with a hole in it, and insert a winch,
along with old greasy rags, in the holes. Others use a thick
rope, collect nine kinds of wood, and keep them in violent
motion till fire leaps forth. Perhaps there may be other

Method of kindling the need-fire.

---

[1] Karl Lynker, *Deutsche Sagen una
Sitten in hessischen Gauen*[2] (Cassel
and Göttingen, 1860), pp. 252 *sq.*,
quoting a letter of the mayor (*Schult-
heiss*) of Neustadt to the mayor of
Marburg dated 12th December 1605.

[2] Bartholomäus Carrichter, *Der
Teutschen Speisskammer* (Strasburg,
1614), Fol. pag. 17 and 18, quoted
by C. L. Rochholz, *Deutscher Glaube
und Brauch* (Berlin, 1867), ii. 148
sq.

ways of generating or kindling this fire, but they are all directed simply at the cure of the cattle. After passing twice or thrice through the fire the cattle are driven to their stalls or to pasture, and the heap of wood that had been collected is destroyed, but in some places every householder must take with him a brand, extinguish it in a washing-tub or trough, and put it in the manger where the cattle are fed, where it must lie for some time. The poles that were used to make the need-fire, together with the wood that was employed as a winch, are sometimes burned with the rest of the fuel, sometimes carefully preserved after the cattle have been thrice driven through the flames."[1]

The mode of kindling the need-fire about Hildesheim.

Sometimes the need-fire was known as the "wild fire," to distinguish it no doubt from the tame fire produced by more ordinary methods. The following is Grimm's account of the mode of kindling it which prevailed in some parts of Central Germany, particularly about Hildesheim, down apparently to the first half of the nineteenth century: "In many places of Lower Saxony, especially among the mountains, the custom prevails of preparing the so-called ' wild fire' for the purpose of preventing cattle-plague ; and through it first the pigs, then the cows, and last of all the geese are driven. The proceedings on the occasion are as follows. The principal farmers and parishioners assemble, and notice is served to every inhabitant to extinguish entirely all fire in his house, so that not even a spark remains alight in the whole village. Then young and old repair to a road in a hollow, usually towards evening, the women carrying linen, and the men wood and tow. Two oaken poles are driven into the ground about a foot and a half from each other. Each pole has in the side facing the other a socket into which a cross-piece as thick as a man's arm is fitted. The sockets are stuffed with linen, and the cross-piece is rammed in as tight as possible, while the poles are bound together at the top by ropes. A rope is wound about the round, smooth cross-piece, and the free ends of the rope at both sides are gripped by several

---

[1] Joh. Reiskius, *Untersuchung des Notfeuers* (Frankfort and Leipsic, 1696), p. 51, quoted by J. Grimm, *Deutsche Mythologie,*[4] i. 502 *sq.* ; R. Andree, *Braunschweiger Volkskunde* (Brunswick, 1896), p. 313.

persons, who pull the cross-piece to and fro with the utmost rapidity, till through the friction the linen in the sockets takes fire. The sparks of the linen are immediately caught in tow or oakum and waved about in a circle until they burst into a bright glow, when straw is applied to it, and the flaming straw used to kindle the brushwood which has been stacked in piles in the hollow way. When this wood has blazed up and the fire has nearly died out again, the people hasten to the herds, which have been waiting in the background, and drive them forcibly, one after the other, through the glow. As soon as all the beasts are through, the young folk rush wildly at the ashes and cinders, sprinkling and blackening each other with them ; those who have been most sprinkled and blackened march in triumph behind the cattle into the village and do not wash themselves for a long time. If after long rubbing the linen should not catch fire, they guess that there is still fire somewhere in the village ; then a strict search is made from house to house, any fire that may be found is put out, and the householder is punished or upbraided. The ' wild fire' must be made by prolonged friction ; it may not be struck with flint and steel. Some villages do not prepare it yearly as a preventive of cattle-plague, but only kindle it when the disease has actually broken out." [1] In the Halberstadt district the ends of the rope which was used to make the cross-piece revolve in the sockets had to be pulled by two chaste young men. [2]

In the Mark down to the first half of the nineteenth century the practice was similar. We read that " in many parts of the Mark there still prevails on certain occasions the custom of kindling a need-fire, it happens particularly when a farmer has sick pigs. Two posts of dry wood are planted in the earth amid solemn silence before the sun rises, and round these posts hempen ropes are pulled to and fro till the wood kindles ; whereupon the fire is fed with dry leaves and twigs and the sick beasts are driven through it. In some places the fire is produced by the friction of an old cart-wheel." [3]

The mode of kindling the need-fire in the Mark.

[1] J. Grimm, *Deutsche Mythologie*,[4] i. 503 *sq.*

[2] J. Grimm, *op. cit.* i. 504.

[3] Adalbert Kuhn, *Märkische Sagen und Märchen* (Berlin, 1843), p. 369.

In Mecklenburg the need-fire used to be lighted by the friction of a rope wound about an oaken pole or by rubbing two boards against each other. Having been thus elicited, the flame was fed with wood of seven kinds. The practice was forbidden by Gustavus Adolphus, Duke of Mecklenburg, in 1682 ; but the prohibition apparently had little effect, for down to the end of the eighteenth century the custom was so common that the inhabitants even of large towns made no scruple of resorting to it. For example, in the month of July 1792 sickness broke out among the cattle belonging to the town of Sternberg ; some of the beasts died suddenly, and so the people resolved to drive all the survivors through a need-fire. On the tenth day of July the magistrates issued a proclamation announcing that next morning before sunrise a need-fire would be kindled for the behoof of all the cattle of the town, and warning all the in-habitants against lighting fires in their kitchens that evening. So next morning very early, about two o'clock, nearly the whole population was astir, and having assembled outside one of the gates of the town they helped to drive the timid cattle, not without much ado, through three separate need-fires ; after which they dispersed to their homes in the unalterable conviction that they had rescued the cattle from destruction. But to make assurance doubly sure they deemed it advisable to administer the rest of the ashes as a bolus to the animals. However, some people in Mecklenburg used to strew the ashes of the need-fire on fields for the purpose of protecting the crops against vermin. As late as June 1868 a traveller in Mecklenburg saw a couple of peasants sweating away at a rope, which they were pulling backwards and forwards so as to make a tarry roller revolve with great speed in the socket of an upright post. Asked what they were about, they vouchsafed no reply ; but an old woman who appeared on the scene from a neighbouring cottage was more communicative. In the fulness of her heart she confided to the stranger that her pigs were sick, that the two taciturn bumpkins were her sons, who were busy extracting a need-fire from the roller, and that, when they succeeded, the flame would be used to ignite a heap of rags and brushwood, through which the ailing swine would be driven. She further explained that the persons who kindle a need-fire should always be two brothers or at least bear the same Christian name.[1]

In the summer of 1828 there was much sickness among the pigs and the cows of Eddesse, a village near Meinersen, in the south of Hanover. When all ordinary measures to arrest the malady failed, the farmers met in solemn con- clave on the village green and determined that next morn- ing there should be a need-fire. Thereupon the head man of the village sent word from house to house that on the following day nobody should kindle a fire before sunrise, and that every- body should stand by ready to drive out the cattle. The same afternoon all the necessary preparations were made for giving effect to the decision of the collective wisdom. A narrow street was enclosed with planks, and the village carpenter set to work at the machinery for kindling the fire. He took two posts of oak wood, bored a hole about three inches deep and broad in each, and set the two poles up facing each other at a distance of about two feet. Then he fitted a roller of oak wood into the two holes of the posts, so that it formed a cross-piece between them. About two o'clock next morning every householder brought a bundle of straw and brushwood and laid it down across the street in a prescribed order. The sturdiest swains who could be found were chosen to make the need-fire. For this purpose a long hempen rope was wound twice round the oaken roller in the oaken posts : the pivots were well smeared with pitch and tar : a bundle of tow and other tinder was laid close at hand, and all was ready. The stalwart clodhoppers now seized the two ends of the rope and went to work with a will. Puffs of smoke soon issued from the sockets, but to the consternation of the bystanders not a spark of fire could be elicited. Some people openly declared their suspicion that some rascal had not put out the fire in his house, when suddenly the tinder burst into flame. The cloud passed away from all faces ; the fire was applied to the heaps of fuel, and when the flames had somewhat died down, the herds were forcibly driven through the fire, first the pigs,

The mode of kindling the need-fire in Hanover.

[1] Karl Bartsch, *Sagen, Märchen und Gebräuche aus Mecklenburg* (Vienna, 1879–1880), ii. 149-151.

next the cows, and last of all the horses. The herdsmen then drove the beasts to pasture, and persons whose faith in the efficacy of the need-fire was particularly robust carried home brands.[1]

The mode of kindling the need-fire in the Harz Mountains. Again, at a village near Quedlinburg, in the Harz Mountains, it was resolved to put a herd of sick swine through the need-fire. Hearing of this intention the Superintendent of Quedlinburg hurried to the spot and has described for us what he saw. The beadles went from house to house to see that there was no fire in any house ; for it is well known that should there be common fire burning in a house the need-fire will not kindle. The men made their rounds very early in the morning to make quite sure that all lights were out. At two o'clock a night-light was still burning in the parsonage, and this was of course a hindrance to the need-fire. The peasants knocked at the window and earnestly entreated that the night-light might be extinguished. But the parson's wife refused to put the light out ; it still glimmered at the window ; and in the darkness outside the angry rustics vowed that the parson's pigs should get no benefit of the need-fire. However, as good luck would have it, just as the morning broke, the night-light went out of itself, and the hopes of the people revived. From every house bundles of straw, tow, faggots and so forth were now carried to feed the bonfire. The noise and the cheerful bustle were such that you might have thought they were all hurrying to witness a public execution. Outside the village, between two garden walls, an oaken post had been driven into the ground and a hole bored through it. In the hole a wooden winch, smeared with tar, was inserted and made to revolve with such force and rapidity that fire and smoke in time issued from the socket. The collected fuel was then thrown upon the fire and soon a great blaze shot up. The pigs were now driven into the upper end of the street. As soon as they saw the fire, they turned tail, but the peasants drove them through with shrieks and shouts and lashes of whips. At the other end of the street there was another crowd waiting, who

---

[1] Carl und Theodor Colshorn, *Märchen und Sagen* (Hanover, 1854), pp. 234-236, from the description of an eye-witness.

chased the swine back through the fire a second time.
Then the other crowd repeated the manœuvre, and the herd
of swine was driven for the third time through the smoke
and flames. That was the end of the performance. Many
pigs were scorched so severely that they gave up the ghost.
The bonfire was broken up, and every householder took
home with him a brand, which he washed in the water-barrel
and laid for some time, as a treasure of great price, in the
manger from which the cattle were fed. But the parson's
wife had reason bitterly to repent her folly in refusing to
put out that night-light ; for not one of her pigs was driven
through the need-fire, so they died.[1]

In Brunswick, also, the need-fire is known to have been
repeatedly kindled during the nineteenth century. After
driving the pigs through the fire, which was kindled by the
friction of wood, some people took brands home, dipped
them in water, and then gave the water to the pigs to drink,
no doubt for the purpose of inoculating them still more
effectually with the precious virtue of the need-fire. In the
villages of the Drömling district everybody who bore a hand
in kindling the "wild fire" must have the same Christian
name ; otherwise they laboured in vain. The fire was produced by the friction of a rope round the beams of a door ;
and bread, corn, and old boots contributed their mites to
swell the blaze through which the pigs as usual were driven.
In one place, apparently not far from Wolfenbüttel, the need-
fire is said to have been kindled, contrary to custom, by the
smith striking a spark from the cold anvil.[2] At Ganders-
heim down to about the beginning of the nineteenth
century the need-fire was lit in the common way by causing
a cross-bar to revolve rapidly on its axis between two
upright posts. The rope which produced the revolution of
the bar had to be new, but it was if possible woven from
threads taken from a gallows-rope, with which people had
been hanged. While the need-fire was being kindled in this
fashion, every other fire in the town had to be put out ;

The mode of kindling the need-fire in Brunswick.

[1] Heinrich Pröhle, *Harzbilder,
Sitten und Gebräuche aus dem Harz-
gebirge* (Leipsic, 1855), pp. 74 *sq.* The
date of this need-fire is not given ;

probably it was about the middle of
the nineteenth century.

[2] R. Andree, *Braunschweiger Volkskunde* (Brunswick, 1896), pp. 313 *sq.*

search was made through the houses, and any fire discovered to be burning was extinguished.   If in spite of every precaution no flame could be elicited by the friction of the rope, the failure was set down to witchcraft ; but if the efforts were successful, a bonfire was lit with the new fire, and when the flames had died down, the sick swine were driven thrice through the glowing embers.[1]   On the lower Rhine the need-fire is said to have been kindled by the friction of oak-wood on fir-wood, all fires in the village having been previously extinguished.   The bonfires so kindled were composed of wood of nine different sorts ; there were three such bonfires, and the cattle were driven round them with great gravity and devotion.[2]

The mode of kindling the need-fire in Silesia and Bohemia.

In Silesia, also, need-fires were often employed for the purpose of curing a murrain or preventing its spread. While all other lights within the boundaries were extingished, the new fire was produced by the friction of nine kinds of wood, and the flame so obtained was used to kindle heaps of brushwood or straw to which every inhabitant had contributed.   Through these fires the cattle, both sick and sound, were driven in the confident expectation that thereby the sick would be healed and the sound saved from sickness.[3]   When plague breaks out among the herds at Dobischwald, in Austrian Silesia, a splinter of wood is chipped from the threshold of every house, the cattle are driven to a cross-road, and there a tree, growing at the boundary, is felled by a pair of twin brothers.   The wood of the tree and the splinters from the thresholds furnish the fuel of a bonfire, which is kindled by the rubbing of two pieces of wood together.   When the bonfire is ablaze, the horns of the cattle are pared and the parings thrown into the flames, after which the animals are driven through the fire.   This is believed to guard the herd against the plague.[4] The Germans of Western Bohemia resort to similar measures for staying a murrain.   You set up a post, bore a hole in it, and insert in the hole a stick, which you have first of all smeared

---

[1] R. Andree, *op. cit.* pp. 314 *sq.*

[2] Montanus, *Die deutschen Volksfeste, Volksbräuche und deutscher Volksglaube* (Iserlohn, N.D.), p. 127.

[3] Paul Drechsler, *Sitte, Brauch und*

Volksglaube in Schlesien (Leipsic, 1903–1906), ii. 204.

[4] Anton Peter, *Volksthümliches aus Österreichisch - Schlesien* (Troppau, 1865–1867), ii. 250.

with pitch and wrapt in inflammable stuffs. Then you wind a rope round the stick and give the two ends of the rope to two persons who must either be brothers or have the same baptismal name. They haul the rope backwards and forwards so as to make the tarred stick revolve rapidly, till the rope first smokes and then emits sparks. The sparks are used to kindle a bonfire, through which the cattle are driven in the usual way. And as usual no other fire may burn in the village while the need-fire is being kindled ; for otherwise the rope could not possibly be ignited.[1] In Upper Austria sick pigs are reported to have been driven through a need-fire about the beginning of the nineteenth century.[2]

The need-fire is still in use in some parts of Switzerland, but it seems to have degenerated into a children's game and to be employed rather for the dispersal of a mist than for the prevention or cure of cattle-plague. In some cantons it goes by the name of "mist-healing," while in others it is called "butter-churning." On a misty or rainy day a number of children will shut themselves up in a stable or byre and proceed to make fire for the purpose of improving the weather. The way in which they make it is this. A boy places a board against his breast, takes a peg pointed at both ends, and, setting one end of the peg against the board on his breast, presses the other end firmly against a second board, the surface of which has been flaked into a nap. A string is tied round the peg, and two other boys pull it to and fro, till through the rapid motion of the point of the peg a hole is burnt in the flaked board, to which tow or dry moss is then applied as a tinder. In this way fire and smoke are elicited, and with their appearance the children fancy that the mist will vanish.[3] We may conjecture that this method of dispersing a mist, which is now left to children, was formerly practised in all seriousness by grown men in Switzerland. It is thus that religious or magical rites dwindle away into the sports

The use of the need-fire in Switzerland.

[1] Alois John, *Sitte, Brauch und Volksglaube im deutschen Westböhmen* (Prague, 1905), p. 209.

[2] C. L. Rochholz, *Deutscher Glaube und Brauch* (Berlin, 1867), ii. 149.

[3] E. Hoffmann-Krayer, "Fruchtbarkeitsriten im schweizerischen Volksbrauch," *Schweizerisches Archiv für Volkskunde*, xi. (1907) pp. 244-246.

of children. In the canton of the Grisons there is still in common use an imprecation, "Mist, go away, or I'll heal you," which points to an old custom of burning up the fog with fire. A longer form of the curse lingers in the Vallée des Bagnes of the canton Valais. It runs thus : "Mist, mist, fly, fly, or St. Martin will come with a sheaf of straw to burn your guts, a great log of wood to smash your brow, and an iron chain to drag you to hell." [1]

The mode of kindling the need-fire in Sweden and Norway.
In Sweden the need-fire is called, from the mode of its production, either *vrid-eld*, "turned fire," or *gnid-eld*, "rubbed fire." Down to near the end of the eighteenth century the need-fire was kindled, as in Germany, by the violent rubbing of two pieces of wood against each other ; sometimes nine different kinds of wood were used for the purpose. The smoke of the fire was deemed salutary ; fruit-trees and nets were fumigated with it, in order that the trees might bear fruit and the nets catch fish. Cattle were also driven through the smoke.[2] In Sundal, a narrow Norwegian valley, shut in on both sides by precipitous mountains, there lived down to the second half of the nineteenth century an old man who was very superstitious. He set salmon-traps in the river Driva, which traverses the valley, and he caught

The need-fire as a protection against witchcraft.
many fish both in spring and autumn. When his fishing went wrong, he kindled *naueld* ("need-fire") or *gnideild* ("rubbed fire," "friction fire") to counteract the witchcraft, which he believed to be the cause of his bad luck. He set up two planks near each other, bored a hole in each, inserted a pointed rod in the holes, and twisted a long cord round the rod. Then he pulled the cord so as to make the rod revolve rapidly. Thus by reason of the friction he at last drew fire from the wood. That contented him, for "he believed that the witchery was thus rendered powerless, and that good luck in his fishing was now ensured." [3]

Slavonic peoples hold the need-fire in high esteem.

[1] E. Hoffmann-Krayer, *op. cit.* p. 246.

[2] J. Grimm, *Deutsche Mythologie*,[4] i. 505.

[3] "Old-time Survivals in remote Norwegiar. Dales," *Folk-lore*, xx. (1909) pp. 314, 322 *sq.* This record of Norwegian folk-lore is translated from a little work *Sundalen og Öksendalens Beskrivelse* written by Pastor Chr. Glükstad and published at Christiania "about twenty years ago."

They call it " living fire," and attribute to it a healing virtue.
The ascription of medicinal power to fire kindled by the
friction of wood is said to be especially characteristic of the
Slavs who inhabit the Carpathian Mountains and the Balkan
peninsula. The mode in which they produce the need-fire
differs somewhat in different places. Thus in the Schar
mountains of Servia the task is entrusted to a boy and girl
between eleven and fourteen years of age. They are led
into a perfectly dark room, and having stripped themselves
naked kindle the fire by rubbing two rollers of lime wood
against each other, till the friction produces sparks, which
are caught in tinder. The Serbs of Western Macedonia
drive two oaken posts into the ground, bore a round hole
in the upper end of each, insert a roller of lime wood in the
holes, and set it revolving rapidly by means of a cord, which
is looped round the roller and worked by a bow. Elsewhere
the roller is put in motion by two men, who hold each one
end of the cord and pull it backwards and forwards forcibly
between them. Bulgarian shepherds sometimes kindle the
need-fire by drawing a prism-shaped piece of lime wood to
and fro across the flat surface of a tree-stump in the forest.[1]
But in the neighbourhood of Küstendil, in Bulgaria, the
need-fire is kindled by the friction of two pieces of oak wood
and the cattle are driven through it.[2]

In many districts of Russia, also, " living fire " is made by
the friction of wood on St. John's Day, and the herds are
driven through it, and the people leap over it in the conviction
that their health is thereby assured ; when a cattle-plague is
raging, the fire is produced by rubbing two pieces of oak wood
against each other, and it is used to kindle the lamps before
the holy pictures and the censers in the churches.[3] Thus it
appears that in Russia the need-fire is kindled for the sake
of the cattle periodically as well as on special emergencies.
Similarly in Poland the peasants are said to kindle fires in

[1] Prof. Vl. Titelbach, " Das heilige Feuer bei den Balkanslaven," *Internationales Archiv für Ethnographie*, xiii. (1900) pp. 2 *sq.* We have seen (above, p. 220) that in Russia the need-fire is, or used to be, annually kindled on the eighteenth of August. As to the need-fire in Bulgaria see also below, pp. 284 *sq.*

[2] F. S. Krauss, " Altslavische Feuergewinnung," *Globus*, lix. (1891) p. 318, quoting P. Ljiebenov, *Baba Ega* (Trnovo, 1887), p. 44.

[3] F. S. Krauss, *op. cit.* p. 319, quoting *Wisla*, vol. iv. pp. 1, 244 *sqq.*

the village streets on St. Rochus's day and to drive the cattle thrice through them in order to protect the animals against the murrain. The fire is produced by rubbing a pole of poplar wood on a plank of poplar or fir wood and catching the sparks in tow. The embers are carried home to be used

The need-fire in Slavonia. as remedies in sickness.[1] As practised in Slavonia, the custom of the need-fire used to present some interesting features, which are best described in the words of an eye-witness :—" In the year 1833 I came for the first time as a young merchant to Slavonia ; it was to Gaj that I went, in the Požega district. The time was autumn, and it chanced that a cattle-plague was raging in the neighbourhood, which inflicted much loss on the people. The peasants believed that the plague was a woman, an evil spirit (*Kuga*), who was destroying the cattle ; so they sought to banish her. I had then occasion to observe the proceedings in the villages of Gaj, Kukunjevac, Brezina, and Brekinjska. Towards evening the whole population of the village was busy laying a ring of brushwood round the boundaries of the village. All fires were extinguished throughout the village. Then pairs of men in several places took pieces of wood, which had been specially prepared for the purpose, and rubbed them together till they emitted sparks. The sparks were allowed to fall on tinder and fanned into a flame, with which the dry brushwood was kindled. Thus the fire burned all round the village. The peasants persuaded themselves that thereupon *Kuga* must take her departure." [2]

The need-fire in Servia. This last account leaves no doubt as to the significance of the need-fire in the minds of Slavonian peasantry. They regard it simply as a barrier interposed between their cattle and the evil spirit, which prowls, like a hungry wolf, round the fold and can, like a wolf, be kept at bay by fire. The same interpretation of the need-fire comes out, hardly less clearly, in the account which another writer gives of a cere-mony witnessed by him at the village of Setonje, at the foot of the Homolje mountains in the great forest of Servia. An

---

[1] F. S. Krauss, *op. cit.* p. 318, quoting Oskar Kolberg, in *Mazowsze*, vol. iv. p. 138.

[2] F. S Krauss, " Slavische Feuer-

bohrer," *Globus*, lix. (1891) p. 140. The evidence quoted by Dr. Krauss is that of his father, who often told of his experience to his son.

epidemic was raging among the children, and the need-fire
was resorted to as a means of staying the plague. It was
produced by an old man and an old woman in the first of
the ways described above ; that is, they made it in the dark
by rubbing two sticks of lime wood against each other.
Before the healing virtue of the fire was applied to the inhabitants of the village, two old women performed the
following ceremony. Both bore the name of Stana, from the
verb *stati*, " to remain standing " ; for the ceremony could
not be successfully performed by persons of any other name.
One of them carried a copper kettle full of water, the other
an old house-lock with the key. Thus equipped they repaired
to a spot outside of the village, and there the old dame with
the kettle asked the old dame with the lock, " Whither
away ? " and the other answered her, " I came to shut the
village against ill-luck." With that she locked the lock and
threw it with the key into the kettle of water. Then they
marched thrice round the village, repeating the ceremony of
the lock and key at each round. Meantime all the villagers,
arrayed in their best clothes, were assembled in an open
place. All the fires in the houses had been previously extinguished. Two sturdy yokels now dug a tunnel through
a mound beside an oak tree ; the tunnel was just high enough
to let a man creep through it on all fours. Two fires, lit by
the need-fire, were now laid, one at each end of the tunnel ;
and the old woman with the kettle took her stand at
the entrance of the tunnel, while the one with the lock
posted herself at the exit. Facing the latter stood another
woman with a great pot of milk before her, and on the
other side was set a pot full of melted swine's fat. All
was now ready. The villagers thereupon crawled through
the tunnel on hands and knees, one behind the other. Each,
as he emerged from the tunnel, received a spoonful of milk
from the woman and looked at his face reflected in the pot
of melted swine's fat. Then another woman made a cross
with a piece of charcoal on his back. When all the inhabitants had thus crept through the tunnel and been doctored
at the other end, each took some glowing embers home with
him in a pot wherewith to rekindle the fire on the domestic
hearth. Lastly they put some of the charcoal in a vessel

of water and drank the mixture in order to be thereby magically protected against the epidemic.[1]

It would be superfluous to point out in detail how admirably these measures are calculated to arrest the ravages of disease ; but for the sake of those, if there are any, to whom the medicinal effect of crawling through a hole on hands and knees is not at once apparent, I shall merely say that the procedure in question is one of the most powerful specifics which the wit of man has devised for maladies of all sorts. Ample evidence of its application will be adduced in a later part of this work.[2]

The need-fire in Bulgaria. In Bulgaria the herds suffer much from the raids of certain blood-sucking vampyres called *Ustrels*. An *Ustrel* is the spirit of a Christian child who was born on a Saturday and died unfortunately before he could be baptized. On the ninth day after burial he grubs his way out of the grave and attacks the cattle at once, sucking their blood all night and returning at peep of dawn to the grave to rest from his labours. In ten days or so the copious draughts of blood which he has swallowed have so fortified his constitution that he can undertake longer journeys ; so when he falls in with great herds of cattle or flocks of sheep he returns no more to the grave for rest and refreshment at night, but takes up his quarters during the day either between the horns of a sturdy calf or ram or between the hind legs of a milch-cow. Beasts whose blood he has sucked die the same night. In any herd that he may fasten on he begins with the fattest animal and works his way down steadily through the leaner kine till not one single beast is left alive. The carcases of the victims swell up, and when the hide is stripped off you can always perceive the livid patch of flesh where the monster sucked the blood of the poor creature. In a single night he may, by working hard, kill five cows ; but he seldom exceeds that number. He can change his shape and weight very easily ; for example, when he is sitting by day between the horns of a ram, the animal scarcely feels his weight, but at night he will sometimes throw himself on an ox or a cow

---

[1] Prof. Vl. Titelbach, " Das heilige Feuer bei den Balkanslaven," *Internationales Archiv für Ethnographie,* xiii. (1900) p. 3.

[2] See below, vol. ii. pp. 168 *sqq.*

so heavily that the animal cannot stir, and lows so pitifully
that it would make your heart bleed to hear.   People who
were born on a Saturday can see these monsters, and they
have described them accurately, so that there can be no
doubt whatever about their existence.   It is, therefore, a
matter of great importance to the peasant to protect his
flocks and herds against the ravages of such dangerous
vampyres.   The way in which he does so is this.   On a Saturday morning before sunrise the village drummer gives the
signal to put out every fire in the village ; even smoking is
forbidden.   Next all the domestic animals, with the exception of fowls, geese, and ducks, are driven out into the open.
In front of the flocks and herds march two men, whose
names during the ceremony may not be mentioned in the
village.   They go into the wood, pick two dry branches, and
having stript themselves of their clothes they rub the two
branches together very hard till they catch fire ; then with
the fire so obtained they kindle two bonfires, one on each
side of a cross-road which is known to be frequented by
wolves.   After that the herd is driven between the two fires.
Coals from the bonfires are then taken back to the village
and used to rekindle the fires on the domestic hearths.   For
several days no one may go near the charred and blackened
remains of the bonfires at the cross-road.   The reason is that
the vampyre is lying there, having dropped from his seat between the cow's horns when the animals were driven between
the two fires.   So if any one were to pass by the spot during
these days, the monster would be sure to call him by name
and to follow him to the village ; whereas if he is left alone,
a wolf will come at midnight and strangle him, and in a few
days the herdsmen can see the ground soaked with his slimy
blood.   So that is the end of the vampyre.[1]   In this Bulgarian
custom, as in the Slavonian custom described above, the
conception of the need-fire as a barrier set up between the
cattle and a dangerous spirit is clearly worked out.   The
spirit rides the cow till he comes to the narrow pass between
the two fires, but the heat there is too much for him ;
he drops in a faint from the saddle, or rather from the
horns, and the now riderless animal escapes safe and sound

---

[1] Adolf Strausz, *Die Bulgaren* (Leipsic, 1898), pp. 194-199.

beyond the smoke and flame, leaving her persecutor prostrate on the ground on the further side of the blessed
barrier.

The need-
fire in
Bosnia and
Herze-
govina.

In Bosnia and Herzegovina there are some local differences in the mode of kindling the need-fire, or " living fire,"
as it is called. Thus at Jablanica both the uprights and the
roller or cross-piece, which by its revolution kindles the fire,
are made of cornel-tree wood ; whereas at Dolac, near Sara-
jevo, the uprights and the cross-piece or roller are all made
of lime wood. In Gacko, contrary to the usual custom, the
fire is made by striking a piece of iron on an anvil, till
sparks are given out, which are caught in tinder. The
" living fire " thus produced is employed for purposes of
healing. In particular, if any one suffers from wounds or
sores, ashes of the need-fire are sprinkled on the ailing part.
In Gacko it is also believed that if a pregnant woman wit-
nesses a conflagration, her child will either be born with a
red eruption on its skin or will contract the malady sooner
or later afterwards. The only remedy consists in ashes of
the need-fire, which are mixed with water and given to the
child to drink.[1]

The need-
fire in
England.

In England the earliest notice of the need-fire seems to
be contained in the Chronicle of Lanercost for the year
1268. The annalist tells with pious horror how, when an
epidemic was raging in that year among the cattle, " certain
beastly men, monks in garb but not in mind, taught the
idiots of their country to make fire by the friction of wood
and to set up an image of Priapus, whereby they thought to
succour the animals." [2] The use of the need-fire is particularly attested for the counties of Yorkshire and Northumber-

The need-
fire in
Yorkshire.

land. Thus in Yorkshire down to the middle of the
eighteenth century " the favourite remedy of the country

---

[1] *Wissenschaftliche Mittheilungen
aus Bosnien und der Hercegovina*,
redigirt von Moriz Hoernes, iii.
(Vienna, 1895) pp. 574 *sq.*

[2] " *Pro fidei divinae integritate ser-
vanda recolat lector quod, cum hoc anno
in Laodonia pestis grassaretur in
pecudes armenti, quam vocant usitate
Lungessouth, quidam bestiales, habitu
claustrales non animo, docebant idiotas*
*patriae ignem confrictione de lignis
educere et simulachrum Priapi statuere,
et per haec bestiis succurrere,*" quoted
by J. M. Kemble, *The Saxons in
England* (London, 1849), i. 358 *sq.* ;
A. Kuhn, *Die Herabkunft des Feuers
und des Göttertranks* [2] (Gütersloh,
1886), p. 43 ; Ulrich Jahn, *Die
deutschen Opfergebräuche bei Ackerbau
und Viehzucht* (Breslau, 1884) p. 31.

people, not only in the way of cure, but of prevention, was
an odd one ; it was to smoke the cattle almost to suffocation,
by kindling straw, litter, and other combustible matter about
them.   The effects of this mode of cure are not stated, but
the most singular part of it was that by which it was
reported to have been discovered.   An angel (says the
legend), descended into Yorkshire, and there set a large tree
on fire ; the strange appearance of which or else the savour
of the smoke, incited the cattle around (some of which were
infected) to draw near the miracle, when they all either
received an immediate cure or an absolute prevention of the
disorder.   It is not affirmed that the angel staid to speak to
anybody, but only that he left a *written* direction for the
neighbouring people to catch this supernatural fire, and to
communicate it from one to another with all possible speed
throughout the country ; and in case it should be extinguished and utterly lost, that then new fire, of equal virtue,
might be obtained, not by any common method, but by
rubbing two pieces of wood together till they ignited.   Upon
what foundation this story stood, is not exactly known, but
it put the farmers actually into a hurry of communicating
flame and smoke from one house to another with wonderful
speed, making it run like wildfire over the country." [1]   Again,
we read that " the father of the writer, who died in 1843, in
his seventy-ninth year, had a perfect remembrance of a great
number of persons, belonging to the upper and middle
classes of his native parish of Bowes, assembling on the
banks of the river Greta to work for need-fire.   A disease
among cattle, called the murrain, then prevailed to a very
great extent through that district of Yorkshire.   The cattle
were made to pass through the smoke raised by this
miraculous fire, and their cure was looked upon as certain,
and to neglect doing so was looked upon as wicked.   This
fire was produced by the violent and continued friction of
two dry pieces of wood until such time as it was thereby
obtained.   'To work as though one was working for need-

[1] W. G. M. Jones Barker, *The
Three Days of Wensleydale* (London,
1854), pp. 90 *sq.* ; *County Folk-lore*,
vol. ii., *North Riding of Yorkshire*,
York and the Ainsty, collected and
edited by Mrs. Gutch (London, 1901),
p. 181.

fire' is a common proverb in the North of England."[1]   At Ingleton, a small town nestling picturesquely at the foot of the high hill of Ingleborough in western Yorkshire, "within the last thirty years or so it was a common practice to kindle the so-called 'Need-fire' by rubbing two pieces of wood briskly together, and setting ablaze a large heap of sticks and brushwood, which were dispersed, and cattle then driven through the smoking brands.   This was thought to act as a charm against the spread or developement of the various ailments to which cattle are liable, and the farmers seem to have had great faith in it."[2]   Writing about the middle of the nineteenth century, Kemble tells us that the will-fire or need-fire had been used in Devonshire for the purpose of staying a murrain within the memory of man.[3]

The need-fire in Northumberland.

So in Northumberland, down to the first half of the nineteenth century, "when a contagious disease enters among cattle, the fires are extinguished in the adjacent villages.   Two pieces of dried wood are then rubbed together until fire be produced ; with this a quantity of straw is kindled, juniper is thrown into the flame, and the cattle are repeatedly driven through the smoke.   Part of the forced fire is sent to the neighbours, who again forward it to others, and, as great expedition is used, the fires may be seen blazing over a great extent of country in a very short space of time."[4]   "It is strange," says the antiquary William Henderson, writing about 1866, "to find the custom of lighting 'need-fires' on the occasion of epidemics among cattle still lingering among us, but so it is.   The vicar of Stamfordham writes thus

---

[1] *The Denham Tracts, a Collection of Folklore by Michael Aislabie Denham*, edited by Dr. James Hardy (London, 1892–1895), ii. 50.

[2] Harry Speight, *Tramps and Drives in the Craven Highlands* (London, 1895), p. 162. Compare, *id.*, *The Craven and North-West Yorkshire Highlands* (London, 1892), pp. 206 *sq.*

[3] J. M. Kemble, *The Saxons in England* (London, 1849), i. 361 note.

[4] E. Mackenzie, *An Historical, Topographical and Descriptive View of the County of Northumberland*, Second Edition (Newcastle, 1825), i. 218, quoted in *County Folk-lore*, vol.

iv. *Northumberland*, collected by M. C. Balfour (London, 1904), p. 45. Compare J. T. Brockett, *Glossary of North Country Words*, p. 147, quoted by Mrs. M. C. Balfour, *l.c.* : "*Need-fire* . . . an ignition produced by the friction of two pieces of dried wood. The vulgar opinion is, that an angel strikes a tree, and that the fire is thereby obtained. Need-fire, I am told, is still employed in the case of cattle infected with the murrain. They were formerly driven through the smoke of a fire made of straw, etc." The first edition of Brockett's *Glossary* was published in 1825.

respecting it : ' When the murrain broke out among the cattle about eighteen years ago, this fire was produced by rubbing two pieces of dry wood together, and was carried from place to place all through this district, as a charm against cattle taking the disease. Bonfires were kindled with it, and the cattle driven into the smoke, where they were left for some time. Many farmers hereabouts, I am informed, had the need-fire.' " [1]

In the earliest systematic account of the western islands of Scotland we read that " the inhabitants here did also make use of a fire called *Tin-egin, i.e.* a forced fire, or fire of necessity, which they used as an antidote against the plague or murrain in cattle ; and it was performed thus : all the fires in the parish were extinguished, and then eighty-one married men, being thought the necessary number for effecting this design, took two great planks of wood, and nine of them were employed by turns, who by their repeated efforts rubbed one of the planks against the other until the heat thereof produced fire ; and from this forced fire each family is supplied with new fire, which is no sooner kindled than a pot full of water is quickly set on it, and afterwards sprinkled upon the people infected with the plague, or upon the cattle that have the murrain. And this they all say they find successful by experience : it was practised in the main land, opposite to the south of Skie, within these thirty years." [2]

Martin's account of the need-fire in the Highlands of Scotland.

In the island of Mull, one of the largest of the Hebrides, the need-fire was kindled as late as 1767. " In consequence of a disease among the black cattle the people agreed to perform an incantation, though they esteemed it a wicked thing. They carried to the top of Carnmoor a wheel and nine spindles of oakwood. They extinguished every fire in

The need-fire in the island of Mull.

---

[1] W. Henderson, *Notes on the Folklore of the Northern Counties of England and the Borders* (London, 1879), pp. 167 *sq.* Compare *County Folklore*, vol. iv. *Northumberland*, collected by M. C. Balfour (London, 1904), p. 45. Stamfordham is in Northumberland. The vicar's testimony seems to have referred to the first half of the nineteenth century.

[2] M. Martin, " Description of the Western Islands of Scotland," in J. Pinkerton's *General Collection of Voyages and Travels*, iii. (London, 1809), p. 611. The second edition of Martin's book, which Pinkerton reprints, was published at London in 1716. For John Ramsay's account of the need-fire, see above, pp. 147 *sq.*

every house within sight of the hill; the wheel was then turned from east to west over the nine spindles long enough to produce fire by friction. If the fire were not produced before noon, the incantation lost its effect. They failed for several days running. They attributed this failure to the obstinacy of one householder, who would not let his fires be put out for what he considered so wrong a purpose. However, by bribing his servants they contrived to have them extinguished and on that morning raised their fire.

Sacrifice of a heifer. They then sacrificed a heifer, cutting in pieces and burning while yet alive, the diseased part. They then lighted their own hearths from the pile and ended by feasting on the remains. Words of incantation were repeated by an old man from Morven, who came over as master of the ceremonies, and who continued speaking all the time the fire was being raised. This man was living a beggar at Bellochroy. Asked to repeat the spell, he said, the sin of repeating it once had brought him to beggary, and that he dared not say those words again. The whole country believed him accursed." [1] From this account we see that in Mull the kindling of the need-fire as a remedy for cattle disease was accompanied by the sacrifice of one of the diseased animals; and though the two customs are for the most part mentioned separately by our authorities, we may surmise that they were often, perhaps usually, practised together for the purpose of checking the ravages of sickness in the herds.[2]

The need-fire in Caithness. In the county of Caithness, forming the extreme north-east corner of the mainland of Scotland, the practice of the need-fire survived down at least to about 1788. We read that "in those days, when the stock of any considerable farmer was seized with the murrain, he would send for one of the charm-doctors to superintend the raising of a *need-fire*. It was done by friction, thus; upon any small island, where the stream of a river or burn ran on each side, a circular booth was erected, of stone and turf, as it could be had, in

---

[1] J. Grimm, *Deutsche Mythologie*,[4] i. 506, referring to Miss Austin as his authority.

[2] As to the custom of sacrificing one of a plague-stricken herd or flock for the purpose of saving the rest, see below, pp. 300 *sqq.*

which a semicircular or highland couple of birch, or other hard wood, was set ; and, in short, a roof closed on it.   A straight pole was set up in the centre of this building, the upper end fixed by a wooden pin to the top of the couple, and the lower end in an oblong *trink* in the earth or floor ; and lastly, another pole was set across horizontally, having both ends tapered, one end of which was supported in a hole in the side of the perpendicular pole, and the other in a similar hole in the couple leg.   The horizontal stick was called the auger, having four short arms or levers fixed in its centre, to work it by ; the building having been thus finished, as many men as could be collected in the vicinity, (being divested of all kinds of metal in their clothes, etc.), would set to work with the said auger, two after two, constantly turning it round by the arms or levers, and others occasionally driving wedges of wood or stone behind the lower end of the upright pole, so as to press it the more on the end of the auger : by this constant friction and pressure, the ends of the auger would take fire, from which a fire would be instantly kindled, and thus the *needfire* would be accomplished.   The fire in the farmer's house, etc., was immediately quenched with water, a fire kindled from this needfire, both in the farm-houses and offices, and the cattle brought to feel the smoke of this new and sacred fire, which preserved them from the murrain." [1]

The last recorded case of the need-fire in Caithness happened in 1809 or 1810.   At Houstry, Dunbeath, a crofter named David Gunn had made for himself a kail-yard and in doing so had wilfully encroached on one of those prehistoric ruins called *brochs*, which the people of the neighbourhood believed to be a fairy habitation.   Soon afterwards a murrain broke out among the cattle of the district and carried off many beasts.   So the wise men put their heads together and resolved to light a *teine-eigin* or need-fire as the best way of stopping the plague.   They cut a branch from a tree in a neighbouring wood, stripped it of bark, and carried it to a small island in the Houstry Burn.   Every fire in the

The need fire in Caithness.

---

[1] John Jamieson, *Etymological Dictionary of the Scottish Language*, New Edition, revised by J. Longmuir and D. Donaldson, iii. (Paisley, 1880) pp. 349 *sq*., referring to " Agr. Surv. Caithn., pp. 200, 201."

district having been quenched, new fire was made by the friction of wood in the island, and from this sacred flame all the hearths of the houses were lit afresh. One of the sticks used in making the fire was preserved down to about the end of the nineteenth century ; apparently the mode of operation was the one known as the fire-drill : a pointed stick was twirled in a hole made in another stick till fire was elicited by the friction.[1]

Another account of the use of need-fire in the Highlands of Scotland runs as follows : " When, by the neglect of the prescribed safeguards [against witchcraft], the seeds of iniquity have taken root, and a person's means are decaying in consequence, the only alternative, in this case, is to resort to that grand remedy, the *Tein Econuch*, or ' Forlorn Fire,' which seldom fails of being productive of the best effects. The cure for witchcraft, called *Tein Econuch*, is wrought in the following manner:—A consultation being held by the unhappy sufferer and his friends as to the most advisable measures of effecting a cure, if this process is adopted, notice is privately communicated to all those householders who reside within the nearest of two running streams, to extinguish their lights and fires on some appointed morning. On its being ascertained that this notice has been duly observed, a spinning-wheel, or some other convenient instrument, calculated to produce fire by friction, is set to work with the most furious earnestness by the unfortunate sufferer, and all who wish well to his cause. Relieving each other by turns, they drive on with such persevering diligence, that at length the spindle of the wheel, ignited by excessive friction, emits ' forlorn fire ' in abundance, which, by the application of tow, or some other combustible material, is widely extended over the whole neighbourhood. Communicating the fire to the tow, the tow communicates it to a candle, the candle to a fir-torch, the torch to a cartful of peats, which the master of the ceremonies, with pious ejaculations for the success of the experiment, distributes to messengers, who will proceed with portions of it to the different houses within the said two running streams, to kindle the different fires. By the influence

Another account of the need-fire in the Highlands.

---

[1] R. C. Maclagan, "Sacred Fire,"   to the fire-drill see *The Magic Art and Folk-lore*, ix. (1898) pp. 280 *sq.* As   *the Evolution of Kings*, ii. 207 *sqq.*

of this operation, the machinations and spells of witchcraft are rendered null and void." [1]

In various parts of the Highlands of Scotland the need-fire was still kindled during the first half of the nineteenth century, as we learn from the following account :—

" *Tein-eigin*, neid-fire, need-fire, forced fire, fire produced by the friction of wood or iron against wood.

" The fire of purification was kindled from the neid-fire, while the domestic fire on the hearth was re-kindled from the purification fire on the knoll.   Among other names, the purification fire was called *Teine Bheuil*, fire of Beul, and *Teine mor Bheuil*, great fire of Beul.   The fire of Beul was divided into two fires between which people and cattle rushed australly for purposes of purification.   The ordeal was trying, as may be inferred from phrases still current. *Is teodha so na teine teodha Bheuil*, ' Hotter is this than the hot fire of Beul.'   Replying to his grandchild, an old man in Lewis said . . . ' Mary ! sonnie, it were worse for me to do that for thee than to go between the two great fires of Beul.'

" The neid-fire was resorted to in imminent or actual calamity upon the first day of the quarter, and to ensure success in great or important events.

" The writer conversed with several persons who saw the neid-fire made, and who joined in the ceremony.   As mentioned elsewhere, a woman in Arran said that her father, and the other men of the townland, made the neid-fire on the knoll on *La buidhe Bealltain*—Yellow Day of Beltane. They fed the fire from *cuaile mor conaidh caoin*—great bundles of sacred faggots brought to the knoll on Beltane Eve.   When the sacred fire became kindled, the people rushed home and brought their herds and drove them through and round the fire of purification, to sain them from the *bana bhuitseach mhor Nic Creafain Mac Creafain*— the great arch witch Mac Crauford, now Crawford.   That was in the second decade of this century.

" John Macphail, Middlequarter, North Uist, said that

Alexander Carmichael's account of the need-fire in the Highlands of Scotland during the nineteenth century.

The need fire in Arran.

[1] W. Grant Stewart, *The Popular Superstitions and Festive Amusements of the Highlanders of Scotland* (Edinburgh, 1823), pp. 214-216 ; Walter K. Kelly, *Curiosities of Indo - European Tradition and Folk-lore* (London, 1863), pp. 53 *sq.*

the last occasion on which the neid-fire was made in North
Uist was *bliadhna an t-sneachda bhuidhe*—the year of the
yellow snow— 1829 (?).　 The snow lay so deep and
remained so long on the ground, that it became yellow.
Some suggest that the snow was originally yellow, as snow
is occasionally red.　 This extraordinary continuance of
snow caused much want and suffering throughout the Isles.
The people of North Uist extinguished their own fires and
generated a purification fire at Sail Dharaich, Sollas.　 The
fire was produced from an oak log by rapidly boring with
an auger.　 This was accomplished by the exertions of *naoi
naoinear ciad ginealach mac*—the nine nines of first-begotten
sons.　 From the neid-fire produced on the knoll the people
of the parish obtained fire for their dwellings.　 Many cults
and ceremonies were observed on the occasion, cults and
ceremonies in which Pagan and Christian beliefs intermingled.
Sail Dharaich, Oak Log, obtained its name from the log of
oak for the neid-fire being there.　 A fragment of this log
riddled with auger holes marks a grave in *Cladh Sgealoir*,
the burying-ground of *Sgealoir*, in the neighbourhood.

 " Mr. Alexander Mackay, Edinburgh, a native of Reay,
Sutherland, says :—' My father was the skipper of a fishing
crew.　 Before beginning operations for the season, the crew
of the boat met at night in our house to settle accounts for
the past, and to plan operations for the new season.　 My
mother and the rest of us were sent to bed.　 I lay in the
kitchen, and was listening and watching, though they
thought I was asleep.　 After the men had settled their past
affairs and future plans, they put out the fire on the hearth,
not a spark being allowed to live.　 They then rubbed two
pieces of wood one against another so rapidly as to produce
fire, the men joining in one after the other, and working
with the utmost energy and never allowing the friction to
relax.　 From this friction-fire they rekindled the fire on the
hearth, from which all the men present carried away a
kindling to their own homes.　 Whether their success was
due to their skill, their industry, their perseverance, or to
the neid-fire, I do not know, but I know that they were
much the most successful crew in the place.　 They met on
Saturday, and went to church on Sunday like the good men

and the good Christians they were—a little of their Pagan faith mingling with their Christian belief. I have reason to believe that other crews in the place as well as my father's crew practised the neid-fire.'

" A man at Helmsdale, Sutherland, saw the *tein-eigin* made in his boyhood.

" The neid-fire was made in North Uist about the year 1829, in Arran about 1820, in Helmsdale about 1818, in Reay about 1830." [1]

From the foregoing account we learn that in Arran the annual Beltane fire was regularly made by the friction of wood, and that it was used to protect men and cattle against a great witch. When we remember that Beltane Eve or the Eve of May Day (Walpurgis Night) is the great witching time of the year throughout Europe, we may surmise that wherever bonfires have been ceremonially kindled on that day it has been done simply as a precaution against witchcraft; indeed this motive is expressly alleged not only in Scotland, but in Wales, the Isle of Man, and many parts of Central Europe.[2] It deserves, further, to be noticed that in North Uist the wood used to kindle the need-fire was oak, and that the nine times nine men by whose exertions the flame was elicited were all first-born sons. Apparently the first-born son of a family was thought to be endowed with more magical virtue than his younger brothers. Similarly in the Punjaub " the supernatural power ascribed to the first born is not due to his being unlucky, but the idea underlying the belief seems to be that being the first product of the parents, he inherits the spiritual powers (or magnetism) in a high degree. The success of such persons in stopping rain and hail and in stupefying snakes is proverbial. It is believed that a first child born with feet forward can cure backache by kicking the patient in the back, on a crossing." [3]

The Beltane fires a precaution against witchcraft.

[1] Alexander Carmichael, *Carmina Gadelica* (Edinburgh, 1900), ii. 340 *sq.*

[2] See above, pp. 154, 156, 157, 159 *sq.*

[3] *Census of India, 1911*, vol. xiv. *Punjab*, Part i. *Report*, by Pandit Harikishan Kaul (Lahore, 1912), p. 302. So in the north-east of Scotland " those who were born with their feet first possessed great power to heal all kinds of sprains, lumbago, and rheumatism, either by rubbing the affected part, or by trampling on it. The chief virtue lay in the feet. Those who came into the world in this fashion often

In the north-east of Aberdeenshire and the neighbourhood, when the cattle-disease known as the "quarter-ill" broke out, "the 'muckle wheel' was set in motion and turned till fire was produced. From this virgin flame fires were kindled in the byres. At the same time, if neighbours requested the favour, live coals were given them to kindle fires for the purification of their homesteads and turning off the disease. Fumigating the byres with juniper was a method adopted to ward off disease. Such a fire was called 'needfyre.' The kindling of it came under the censure of the Presbytery at times."[1]

In Perthshire the need-fire was kindled as a remedy for cattle-disease as late as 1826. "A wealthy old farmer,

---

exercised their power to their own profit." See Rev. Walter Gregor, *Notes on the Folk-lore of the North-East of Scotland* (London, 1881), pp. 45 *sq.*

[1] Rev. Walter Gregor, *Notes on the Folk-lore of the North-East of Scotland* (London, 1881), p. 186. The fumigation of the byres with juniper is a charm against witchcraft. See J. G. Campbell, *Witchcraft and Second Sight in the Highlands and Islands of Scotland* (Glasgow, 1902), p. 11. The "quarter-ill" is a disease of cattle, which affects the animals only in one limb or quarter. "A very gross superstition is observed by some people in Angus, as an antidote against this ill. A piece is cut out of the thigh of one of the cattle that has died of it. This they hang up within the chimney, in order to preserve the rest of the cattle from being infected. It is believed that as long as it hangs there, it will prevent the disease from approaching the place. It is therefore carefully preserved ; and in case of the family removing, transported to the new farm, as one of their valuable effects. It is handed down from one generation to another" (J. Jamieson, *Etymological Dictionary of the Scottish Language*, revised by J. Longmuir and D. Donaldson, iii. 575, *s.v.* "Quarter-ill"). See further Rev. W. Gregor, *op. cit.* pp. 186 *sq.* : "The fore-legs of one of the animals that had died

were cut off a little above the knee, and hung over the fire-place in the kitchen. It was thought sufficient by some if they were placed over the door of the byre, in the 'crap o' the wa'.' Sometimes the heart and part of the liver and lungs were cut out, and hung over the fire-place instead of the fore-feet. Boiling them was at times substituted for hanging them over the hearth." Compare W. Henderson, *Notes on the Folk-lore of the Northern Counties of England and the Borders* (London, 1879), p. 167 : "A curious aid to the rearing of cattle came lately to the knowledge of Mr. George Walker, a gentleman of the city of Durham. During an excursion of a few miles into the country, he observed a sort of rigging attached to the chimney of a farmhouse well known to him, and asked what it meant. The good wife told him that they had experienced great difficulty that year in rearing their calves ; the poor little creatures all died off, so they had taken the leg and thigh of one of the dead calves, and hung it in a chimney by a rope, since which they had not lost another calf." In the light of facts cited below (pp. 315 *sqq.*) we may conjecture that the intention of cutting off the legs or cutting out the heart, liver, and lungs of the animals and hanging them up or boiling them, is by means of homoeopathic magic to inflict corresponding injuries on the witch who cast the fatal spell on the cattle.

having lost several of his cattle by some disease very prevalent at present, and being able to account for it in no way so rationally as by witchcraft, had recourse to the following remedy, recommended to him by a weird sister in his neighbourhood, as an effectual protection from the attacks of the foul fiend. A few stones were piled together in the barnyard, and woodcoals having been laid thereon, the fuel was ignited by *will-fire*, that is fire obtained by friction ; the neighbours having been called in to witness the solemnity, the cattle were made to pass through the flames, in the order of their dignity and age, commencing with the horses and ending with the swine. The ceremony having been duly and decorously gone through, a neighbouring farmer observed to the enlightened owner of the herd, that he, along with his family, ought to have followed the example of the cattle, and the sacrifice to Baal would have been complete."[1]

In County Leitrim, Ireland, in order to prevent fever from spreading, "all the fires on the townland, and the two adjoining (one on each side), would be put out. Then the men of the three townlands would come to one house, and get two large blocks of wood. One would be set in the ground, and the other one, fitted with two handles, placed on the top of it. The men would then draw the upper block backwards and forwards over the lower until fire was produced by friction, and from this the fires would be lighted again. This would prevent the fever from spreading."[2]

The need-fire in Ireland.

Thus it appears that in many parts of Europe it has been customary to kindle fire by the friction of wood for the purpose of curing or preventing the spread of disease, particularly among cattle. The mode of striking a light by rubbing two dry sticks against each other is the one to which all over the world savages have most commonly resorted for the sake of providing themselves with fire ;[3] and we can scarcely doubt that the practice of kindling the need-fire in this primitive fashion is merely a survival from the time

The use of the need-fire a relic of a time when all fires were kindled by the friction of wood.

[1] *The Mirror*, 24th June, 1826, quoted by J. M. Kemble, *The Saxons in England* (London, 1849), i. 360 note[2].

[2] Leland L. Duncan, "Fairy Beliefs and other Folklore Notes from County Leitrim," *Folk-lore*, vii. (1896) pp. 181 *sq.*

[3] (Sir) Edward B. Tylor, *Researches into the Early History of Mankind*, Third Edition (London, 1878), pp. 237 *sqq.*; *The Magic Art and the Evolution of Kings*, ii. 207 *sqq.*

when our savage forefathers lit all their fires in that way.
Nothing is so conservative of old customs as religious or
magical ritual, which invests these relics of the past with
an atmosphere of mysterious virtue and sanctity.   To the
educated mind it seems obvious that a fire which a man
kindles with the sweat of his brow by laboriously rubbing one
stick against each other can possess neither more nor less
virtue than one which he has struck in a moment by the
friction of a lucifer match ; but to the ignorant and superstitious this truth is far from apparent, and accordingly they
take infinite pains to do in a roundabout way what they
might have done directly with the greatest ease, and what,
even when it is done, is of no use whatever for the purpose in
hand.   A vast proportion of the labour which mankind has
expended throughout the ages has been no better spent ; it
has been like the stone of Sisyphus eternally rolled up
hill only to revolve eternally down again, or like the water
poured for ever by the Danaids into broken pitchers which it
could never fill.

The belief
that the
need-fire
cannot
kindle if
any other
fire remains
alight in
the neigh-
bourhood.   The curious notion that the need-fire cannot kindle if
any other fire remains alight in the neighbourhood seems to
imply that fire is conceived as a unity which is broken up
into fractions and consequently weakened in exact proportion
to the number of places where it burns; hence in order to
obtain it at full strength you must light it only at a single
point, for then the flame will burst out with a concentrated
energy derived from the tributary fires which burned on all
the extinguished hearths of the country.   So in a modern city
if all the gas were turned off simultaneously at all the burners
but one, the flame would no doubt blaze at that one burner
with a fierceness such as no single burner could shew when
all are burning at the same time.   The analogy may help
us to understand the process of reasoning which leads the
peasantry to insist on the extinction of all common fires when
the need-fire is about to be kindled.   Perhaps, too, it may
partly explain that ceremonial extinction of all old fires
on other occasions which is often required by custom as a
preliminary to the lighting of a new and sacred fire.[1]   We

---

[1] For some examples of such extinc-
tions, see *The Magic Art and the*   *Evolution of Kings,* ii. 261 *sqq.,* 267
sq. ; *Spirits of the Corn and of the*

have seen that in the Highlands of Scotland all common fires were extinguished on the Eve of May-day as a preparation for kindling the Beltane bonfire by friction next morning;[1] and no doubt the reason for the extinction was the same as in the case of the need-fire. Indeed we may assume with a fair degree of probability that the need-fire was the parent of the periodic fire-festivals; at first invoked only at irregular intervals to cure certain evils as they occurred, the powerful virtue of fire was afterwards employed at regular intervals to prevent the occurrence of the same evils as well as to remedy such as had actually arisen.

The need-fire of Europe has its parallel in a ceremony which used to be observed by the Iroquois Indians of North America. "Formerly when an epidemic prevailed among the Iroquois despite the efforts to stay it, it was customary for the principal shaman to order the fires in every cabin to be extinguished and the ashes and cinders to be carefully removed; for it was believed that the pestilence was sent as a punishment for neglecting to rekindle 'new fire,' or because of the manner in which the fire then in use had been kindled. So, after all the fires were out, two suitable logs of slippery elm (*Ulmus fulva*) were provided for the new fire. One of the logs was from six to eight inches in diameter and from eight to ten feet long; the other was from ten to twelve inches in diameter and about ten feet long. About midway across the larger log a cuneiform notch or cut about six inches deep was made, and in the wedge-shaped notch punk was placed. The other log was drawn rapidly to and fro in the cut by four strong men chosen for the purpose until the punk was ignited by the friction thus produced. Before and during the progress of the work of igniting the fire the shaman votively sprinkled *tcar-hŭ'-ĕñ-wĕ*, 'real tobacco,' three several times into the cuneiform notch and offered earnest prayers to the Fire-god, beseeching him 'to aid, to bless, and

The need-fire among the Iroquois of North America.

Wild, i. 311, ii. 73 *sq.*; and above, pp. 124 *sq.*, 132-139. The reasons for extinguishing fires ceremonially appear to vary with the occasion. Sometimes the motive seems to be a fear of burning or at least singeing a ghost, who is hovering invisible in the air; sometimes it is apparently an idea that a fire is old and tired with burning so long, and that it must be relieved of the fatiguing duty by a young and vigorous flame.

[1] Above, pp. 147, 154. The same custom appears to have been observed in Ireland. See above, p. 158.

to redeem the people from their calamities.' The ignited punk was used to light a large bonfire, and then the head of every family was required to take home ' new fire ' to rekindle a fire in his or her fire-place." [1]

§ 9. *The Sacrifice of an Animal to stay a Cattle-Plague*

The burnt sacrifice of a calf in England and Wales.

Sometimes apparently in England as well as in Scotland the kindling of a need-fire was accompanied by the sacrifice of a calf. Thus in Northamptonshire, at some time during the first half of the nineteenth century, " Miss C—— and her cousin walking saw a fire in a field and a crowd round it. They said, ' What is the matter ? ' ' Killing a calf.' ' What for ? ' ' To stop the murrain.' They went away as quickly as possible. On speaking to the clergyman he made enquiries. The people did not like to talk of the affair, but it appeared that when there is a disease among the cows or the calves are born sickly, they sacrifice (*i.e.* kill and burn) one ' for good luck.' " [2]   It is not here said that the fire was a need-fire, of which indeed the two horrified ladies had probably never heard ; but the analogy of the parallel custom in Mull [3] renders it probable that in Northamptonshire also the fire was kindled by the friction of wood, and that the calf or some part of it was burnt in the fire. Certainly the practice of burning a single animal alive in order to save all the others would seem to have been not uncommon in England down to the nineteenth century. Thus a farmer in Cornwall about the year 1800, having lost many cattle by disease, and tried many remedies in vain, consulted with some of his neighbours and laying their heads together " they recalled to their recollections a tale, which tradition had handed down from remote antiquity, that the calamity would not cease until he had actually burned alive the finest calf which he had upon his farm ; but that, when this sacrifice was made, the murrain would afflict his cattle no more." Accordingly, on a day appointed they met, lighted a large fire, placed the best calf in it, and standing round the blazing

[1] J. N. B. Hewitt, " New Fire among the Iroquois," *The American Anthropologist*, ii. (1889) p. 319.

[2] J. Grimm, *Deutsche Mythologie*,[4] i. 507.

[3] See above, p. 290.

pile drove the animal with pitchforks back into the flames
whenever it attempted to escape. Thus the victim was
burned alive to save the rest of the cattle.[1] " There can be
no doubt but that a belief prevailed until a very recent
period, amongst the small farmers in the districts remote
from towns in Cornwall, that a living sacrifice appeased the
wrath of God. This sacrifice must be by fire ; and I have
heard it argued that the Bible gave them warranty for this
belief. . . . While correcting these sheets I am informed of
two recent instances of this superstition. One of them was
the sacrifice of a calf by a farmer near Portreath, for the
purpose of removing a disease which had long followed his
horses and his cows. The other was the burning of a living
lamb, to save, as the farmer said, ' his flocks from spells
which had been cast on 'em.' "[2] In a recent account of the
fire-festivals of Wales we read that " I have also heard my
grandfather and father say that in times gone by the people
would throw a calf in the fire when there was any disease
among the herds. The same would be done with a sheep
if there was anything the matter with a flock. I can remember myself seeing cattle being driven between two fires
to ' stop the disease spreading.' When in later times it was
not considered humane to drive the cattle between the fires, the
herdsmen were accustomed to force the animals over the wood
ashes to protect them against various ailments."[3]   Writing
about 1866, the antiquary W. Henderson says that a live ox
was burned near Haltwhistle in Northumberland "only twenty
years ago " to stop a murrain.[4] "About the year 1850 disease
broke out among the cattle of a small farm in the parish of
Resoliss, Black Isle, Ross-shire. The farmer prevailed on
his wife to undertake a journey to a wise woman of renown

Burnt
sacrifice of
a pig in
Scotland.

[1] William Hone, *Every-day Book*
(London, preface dated 1827), i. coll.
853 *sq.* (June 24th), quoting Hit-
chin's *History of Cornwall.*

[2] Hunt, *Romances and Drolls of the
West of England*, 1st series, p. 237,
quoted by W. Henderson, *Notes on the
Folk-lore of the Northern Counties of
England and the Borders* (London,
1879), p. 149. Compare J. G. Dalyell, *The Darker Superstitions of Scotland* (Edinburgh, 1834), p. 184 :

" Here also may be found a solution
of that recent expedient so ignorantly
practised in the neighbouring kingdom,
where one having lost many of his herd
by witchcraft, as he concluded, burnt
a living calf to break the spell and preserve the remainder."

[3] Marie Trevelyan, *Folk - lore ana
Folk-stories of Wales* (London, 1909),
p. 23.

[4] W. Henderson, *op. cit.* pp. 148
sq.

in Banffshire to ask a charm against the effects of the ' ill ee.' The long journey of upwards of fifty miles was performed by the good wife, and the charm was got. One chief thing ordered was to burn to death a pig, and sprinkle the ashes over the byre and other farm buildings. This order was carried out, except that the pig was killed before it was burned. A more terrible sacrifice was made at times. One of the diseased animals was rubbed over with tar, driven forth, set on fire, and allowed to run till it fell down and died."[1] " Living animals have been burnt alive in sacrifice within memory to avert the loss of other stock. The burial of three puppies ' brandise-wise ' in a field is supposed to rid it of weeds. Throughout the rural districts of Devon witchcraft is an article of current faith, and the toad is thrown into the flames as an emissary of the evil one."[2]

The calf is burnt in order to break a spell which has been cast on the herd.

But why, we may ask, should the burning alive of a calf or a sheep be supposed to save the rest of the herd or the flock from the murrain? According to one writer, as we have seen, the burnt sacrifice was thought to appease the wrath of God.[3] The idea of appeasing the wrath of a ferocious deity by burning an animal alive is probably no more than a theological gloss put on an old heathen rite ; it would hardly occur to the simple mind of an English bumpkin, who, though he may be stupid, is not naturally cruel and does not conceive of a divinity who takes delight in the contemplation of suffering. To his thinking God has little or nothing to do with the murrain, but witches, ill-wishers, and fairies have a great deal to do with it. The English farmer who burned one of his lambs alive said that he did it "to save his flocks from spells which had been cast on them " ; and the Scotch farmer who was bidden to burn a pig alive for a similar

<hr>

[1] Rev. Walter Gregor, *Notes on the Folk-lore of the North-East of Scotland* (London, 1881), p. 186.

[2] R. N. Worth, *History of Devonshire*, Second Edition (London, 1886), p. 339. The diabolical nature of the toad probably explains why people in Herefordshire think that if you wear a toad's heart concealed about your person you can steal to your heart's content without being found out. A suspected thief was overheard boasting, "They never catches *me* : and they never ooll neither. I allus wears a toad's heart round my neck, *I* does." See Mrs. Ella M. Leather, in *Folk-lore*, xxiv. (1913) p. 238.

[3] Above, p. 301.

purpose, but who had the humanity to kill the animal first, believed that this was a remedy for the "evil eye" which had been cast upon his beasts. Again, we read that "a farmer, who possessed broad acres, and who was in many respects a sensible man, was greatly annoyed to find that his cattle became diseased in the spring. Nothing could satisfy him but that they were bewitched, and he was resolved to find out the person who had cast the evil eye on his oxen. According to an anciently-prescribed rule, the farmer took one of his bullocks and bled it to death, catching all the blood on bundles of straw. The bloody straw was then piled into a heap, and set on fire. Burning with a vast quantity of smoke, the farmer expected to see the witch, either in reality or in shadow, amidst the smoke." [1] Such reasons express the real beliefs of the peasants. "Cattle, like human beings, were exposed to the influences of the evil eye, of forespeaking, and of the casting of evil. Witches and warlocks did the work of evil among their neighbours' cattle if their anger had been aroused in any way. The fairies often wrought injury amongst cattle. Every animal that died suddenly was killed by the dart of the fairies, or, in the language of the people, was 'shot-a-dead.' Flint arrows and spear-heads went by the name of 'faery dairts.' . . . When an animal died suddenly the canny woman of the district was sent for to search for the 'faery dairt,' and in due course she found one, to the great satisfaction of the owner of the dead animal." [2]

But how, we must still ask, can burning an animal alive break the spell that has been cast upon its fellows by a witch or a warlock? Some light is thrown on the question by the following account of measures which rustic wiseacres in Suffolk are said to have adopted as a remedy for witchcraft. "A woman I knew forty-three years had been employed by my predecessor to take care of his poultry. At the time I came to make her acquaintance she was a bedridden toothless crone, with chin and nose all but meeting. She did

Mode in which the burning of a bewitched animal is supposed to break the spell.

---

[1] Robert Hunt, *Popular Romances of the West of England*, Third Edition (London, 1881), p. 320. The writer does not say where this took place; probably it was in Cornwall or Devon-shire.

[2] Rev. Walter Gregor, *Notes on the Folk-lore of the North-East of Scotland* (London, 1881), p. 184.

not discourage in her neighbours the idea that she knew more than people ought to know, and had more power than others had.   Many years before I knew her it happened one spring that the ducks, which were a part of her charge, failed to lay eggs. . . . She at once took it for granted that the ducks had been bewitched.   This misbelief involved very shocking consequences, for it necessitated the idea that so diabolical an act could only be combated by diabolical cruelty.   And the most diabolical act of cruelty she could imagine was that of baking alive in a hot oven one of the ducks.   And that was what she did.   The sequence of thought in her mind was that the spell that had been laid on the ducks was that of preternaturally wicked wilfulness ; that this spell could only be broken through intensity of suffering, in this case death by burning ; that the intensity of suffering would break the spell in the one roasted to death ; and that the spell broken in one would be altogether broken, that is, in all the ducks. . . . Shocking, however, as was this method of exorcising the ducks, there was nothing in it original.   Just about a hundred years before, everyone in the town and neighbourhood of Ipswich had heard, and many had believed, that a witch had been burnt to death in her own house at Ipswich by the process of burning alive one of the sheep she had bewitched.   It was curious, but it was as convincing as curious, that the hands and feet of this witch were the only parts of her that had not been incinerated.   This, however, was satisfactorily explained by the fact that the four feet of the sheep, by which it had been suspended over the fire, had not been destroyed in the flames that had consumed its body." [1]   According to a slightly different account of the same tragic incident, the last of the " Ipswitch witches," one Grace Pett, " laid her hand heavily on a farmer's sheep, who, in order to punish her, fastened one of the sheep in the ground and burnt it, except the feet, which were under the earth.   The next morning Grace Pett was found burnt to a cinder, except her

---

[1] *County Folk-lore, Printed Extracts, No. 2, Suffolk,* collected and edited by the Lady Eveline Camilla Gurdon (London, 1893), pp. 190 *sq.*, quoting *Some Materials for the History of Wherstead* by F. Barham Zincke (Ipswich, 1887), p. 168.

feet.   Her fate is recorded in the *Philosophical Transactions*
as a case of spontaneous combustion." [1]

This last anecdote is instructive, if perhaps not strictly
authentic.   It shews that in burning alive one of a bewitched
flock or herd what you really do is to burn the witch, who
is either actually incarnate in the animal or perhaps more
probably stands in a relation of sympathy with it so close as
almost to amount to identity.   Hence if you burn the creature
to ashes, you utterly destroy the witch and thereby save the
whole of the rest of the flock or herd from her abominable
machinations; whereas if you only partially burn the animal,
allowing some parts of it to escape the flames, the witch is
only half-baked, and her power for mischief may be hardly,
if at all, impaired by the grilling.   We can now see that in such
matters half-measures are useless.   To kill the animal first
and burn it afterwards is a weak compromise, dictated no
doubt by a well-meant but utterly mistaken kindness ; it is
like shutting the stable-door when the steed is stolen, for
obviously by leaving the animal's, and therefore the witch's,
body nearly intact at the moment of death, it allows her soul
to escape and return safe and sound to her own human
body, which all the time is probably lying quietly at home
in bed.   And the same train of reasoning that justifies
the burning alive of bewitched animals justifies and indeed
requires the burning alive of the witches themselves ; it is
really the only way of destroying them, body and soul,
and therefore of thoroughly extirpating the whole infernal
crew.

In the Isle of Man the practice of burning cattle alive
in order to stop a murrain seems to have persisted down to
a time within living memory.   On this subject I will quote
the evidence collected by Sir John Rhys : " A respectable
farmer from Andreas told me that he was driving with his
wife to the neighbouring parish of Jurby some years ago,
and that on the way they beheld the carcase of a cow or an
ox burning in a field, with a woman engaged in stirring the
fire.   On reaching the village to which they were going,
they found that the burning beast belonged to a farmer

*In burning
the be-
witched
animal you
burn the
witch
herself.*

*Practice
of burning
cattle and
sheep as
sacrifices
in the Isle
of Man.*

[1] *County Folk-lore, Printed Ex-*   to Murray's *Handbook for Essex,*
tracts, No. 2, Suffolk, p. 191, referring   *Suffolk,* etc., p. 109.

whom they knew. They were further told it was no wonder that the said farmer had one of his cattle burnt, as several of them had recently died. Whether this was a case of sacrifice or not I cannot say. But let me give you another instance : a man whom I have already mentioned, saw at a farm nearer the centre of the island a live calf being burnt. The owner bears an English name, but his family has long been settled in Man. The farmer's explanation to my informant was that the calf was burnt to secure luck for the rest of the herd, some of which were threatening to die. My informant thought there was absolutely nothing the matter with them, except that they had too little to eat. Be that as it may, the one calf was sacrificed as a burnt-offering to secure luck for the rest of the cattle. Let me here also quote Mr. Moore's note in his *Manx Surnames*, p. 184, on the place name *Cabbal yn Oural Losht*, or the Chapel of the Burnt Sacrifice. ' This name,' he says, ' records a circumstance which took place in the nineteenth century, but which, it is to be hoped, was never customary in the Isle of Man. A farmer, who had lost a number of his sheep and cattle by murrain, burned a calf as a propitiatory offering to the Deity on this spot, where a chapel was afterwards built. Hence the name.' Particulars, I may say, of time, place, and person could be easily added to Mr. Moore's statement, excepting, perhaps as to the deity in question ; on that point I have never been informed, but Mr. Moore is probably right in the use of the capital *d*, as the sacrificer is, according to all accounts, a highly devout Christian. One more instance : an octogenarian woman, born in the parish of Bride, and now living at Kirk Andreas, saw, when she was a ' lump of a girl ' of ten or fifteen years of age, a live sheep being burnt in a field in the parish of Andreas, on May-day, whereby she meant the first of May reckoned according to the Old Style. She asserts very decidedly that it was *son oural*, ' as a sacrifice,' as she put it, and ' for an object to the public ' : those were her words when she expressed herself in English. Further, she made the statement that it was a custom to burn a sheep on old May-day for a sacrifice. I was fully alive to the interest of this evidence, and cross-examined her so far as

her age allows of it, and I find that she adheres to her
statement with all firmness." [1]

But Manxmen burn beasts when they are dead as well
as when they are alive; and their reasons for burning the
dead animals may help us to understand their reasons for
burning the living animals.   On this subject I will again
quote Sir John Rhys: "When a beast dies on a farm, of
course it dies, according to the old-fashioned view of things,
as I understand it, from the influence of the evil eye or the
interposition of a witch.   So if you want to know to whom
you are indebted for the loss of the beast, you have simply
to burn its carcase in the open air and watch who comes
first to the spot or who first passes by; that is the criminal
to be charged with the death of the animal, and he cannot
help coming there—such is the effect of the fire.   A Michael
woman, who is now about thirty, related to me how she
watched while the carcase of a bewitched colt was burning,
how she saw the witch coming, and how she remembers her
shrivelled face, with nose and chin in close proximity.
According to another native of Michael, a well-informed
middle-aged man, the animal in question was oftenest a calf,
and it was wont to be burnt whole, skin and all.   The object,
according to him, is invariably to bring the bewitcher on
the spot, and he always comes; but I am not clear what
happens to him when he appears.   My informant added,
however, that it was believed that, unless the bewitcher got
possession of the heart of the burning beast, he lost all his
power of bewitching." [2]

By burning a bewitched animal you compel the witch to appear.

---

[1] (Sir) John Rhys, "Manx Folk-
lore and Superstitions," *Folk-lore*, ii.
(1891) pp. 300-302; repeated in his
Celtic Folk-lore, Welsh and Manx
(Oxford, 1901), i. 306 *sq.* Sir John
Rhys does not doubt that the old
woman saw, as she said, a live sheep
being burnt on old May-day; but he
doubts whether it was done as a
sacrifice.   He adds: "I have failed
to find anybody else in Andreas or
Bride, or indeed in the whole island,
who will now confess to having ever
heard of the sheep sacrifice on old
May-day."   However, the evidence I
have adduced of a custom of burnt
sacrifice among English rustics tends
to confirm the old woman's statement,
that the burning of the live sheep
which she witnessed was not an act of
wanton cruelty but a sacrifice performed for the public good.

[2] (Sir) John Rhys, "Manx Folk-
lore and Superstitions," *Folk-lore*, ii.
(1891) pp. 299 *sq.*; *id., Celtic Folk-
lore, Welsh and Manx* (Oxford, 1901),
i. 304 *sq.*   We have seen that by
burning the blood of a bewitched
bullock a farmer expected to compel
the witch to appear.   See above,
p. 303.

Magic
sympathy
between
the witch
and the
bewitched
animal.

These statements shew that in the Isle of Man the sympathetic relation between the witch and his or her animal victim is believed to be so close that by burning the animal you compel the witch to appear. The original idea may have been that, by virtue of a magic sympathy which binds the two together, whatever harm you do to the animal is felt by the witch as if it were done to herself. That notion would fully explain why Manx people used also to burn bewitched animals alive ; in doing so they probably imagined that they were simultaneously burning the witch who had cast the spell on their cattle.

Parallel
belief in
magic
sympathy
between
the animal
shape of a
were-wolf
and his or
her ordin-
ary human
shape : by
wounding
the wolf
you simul-
taneously
wound the
man or
woman.

This explanation of the reason for burning a bewitched animal, dead or alive, is confirmed by the parallel belief concerning were-wolves. It is commonly supposed that certain men and women can transform themselves by magic art into wolves or other animals, but that any wound inflicted on such a transformed beast (a were-wolf or other were-animal) is simultaneously inflicted on the human body of the witch or warlock who had transformed herself or himself into the creature. This belief is widely diffused ; it meets us in Europe, Asia, and Africa. For example, Olaus Magnus tells us that in Livonia, not many years before he wrote, a noble lady had a dispute with her slave on the subject of were-wolves, she doubting whether there were any such things, and he maintaining that there were. To convince her he retired to a room, from which he soon appeared in the form of a wolf. Being chased by the dogs into the forest and brought to bay, the wolf defended himself fiercely, but lost an eye in the struggle. Next day the slave returned to his mistress in human form but with only one eye.[1] Again, it happened in the year 1588 that a gentleman in a village among the mountains of Auvergne, looking out of the window one evening, saw a friend of his going out to hunt. He begged him to bring him back some of his bag, and his friend said that he would. Well, he had not gone very far before he met a huge wolf. He fired and missed it, and the animal attacked him furiously, but he stood on his guard and with an adroit stroke of his

---

[1] Olaus Magnus, *Historia de Gentium Septentrionalium Conditionibus,* lib xviii. cap. 47, p. 713 (ed. Bâle, 1567).

hunting knife he cut off the right fore-paw of the brute, which thereupon fled away and he saw it no more. He returned to his friend, and drawing from his pouch the severed paw of the wolf he found to his horror that it was turned into a woman's hand with a golden ring on one of the fingers. His friend recognized the ring as that of his own wife and went to find her. She was sitting by the fire with her right arm under her apron. As she refused to draw it out, her husband confronted her with the hand and the ring on it. She at once confessed the truth, that it was she in the form of a were-wolf whom the hunter had wounded. Her confession was confirmed by applying the severed hand to the stump of her arm, for the two fitted exactly. The angry husband delivered up his wicked wife to justice ; she was tried and burnt as a witch.[1] It is said that a were-wolf, scouring the streets of Padua, was caught, and when they cut off his four paws he at once turned into a man, but with both his hands and feet amputated.[2] Again, in a farm of the French district of Beauce, there was once a herdsman who never slept at home. These nocturnal absences naturally attracted attention and set people talking. At the same time, by a curious coincidence, a wolf used to prowl round the farm every night and to excite the dogs in the farmyard to fury by thrusting his snout derisively through the cat's hole in the great gate. The farmer had his suspicions and he determined to watch. One night, when the herdsman went out as usual, his master followed him quietly till he came to a hut, where with his own eyes he saw the man put on a broad belt and at once turn into a wolf, which scoured away over the fields. The farmer smiled a sickly sort of smile and went back to the farm. There he took a stout stick and sat down at the cat's hole to wait. He had not long to wait. The dogs barked like mad, a wolf's snout shewed through the hole, down came the stick, out gushed the blood, and a voice was heard to say without the gate, " A good job too. I had still three years to run." Next day the herdsman appeared as usual,

[1] Collin de Plancy, *Dictionnaire Infernal* (Paris, 1825–1826), iii. 473 *sq.*, referring to Boguet.

[2] Collin de Plancy, *op. cit.* iii. 473.

but he had a scar on his brow, and he never went out again at night.[1]

In China also the faith in similar transformations is reflected in the following tale. A certain man in Sung-yang went into the mountains to gather fuel. Night fell and he was pursued by two tigers, but scrambled up a tree out of their reach. Then said the one tiger to the other tiger, " If we can find Chu-Tu-shi, we are sure to catch this man up the tree." So off went one of them to find Chu-Tu-shi, while the other kept watch at the foot of the tree. Soon after that another tiger, leaner and longer than the other two, appeared on the scene and made a grab at the man's coat. But fortunately the moon was shining, the man saw the paw, and with a stroke of his axe cut off one of its claws. The tigers roared and fled, one after the other, so the man climbed down the tree and went home. When he told his tale in the village, suspicion naturally fell on the said Chu-Tu-shi ; and next day some men went to see him in his house. They

---

[1] Felix Chapiseau, Le Folk-lore de la Beauce et du Perche (Paris, 1902), i. 239 sq. The same story is told in Upper Brittany. See Paul Sébillot, Traditions et Superstitions de la Haute-Bretagne (Paris, 1882), i. 292. It is a common belief that a man who has once been transformed into a were-wolf must remain a were-wolf for seven years unless blood is drawn from him in his animal shape, upon which he at once recovers his human form and is delivered from the bondage and misery of being a were-wolf. See F. Chapiseau, op. cit. i. 218-220 ; Amélie Bosquet, La Normandie Romanesque et Merveilleuse (Paris and Rouen, 1845), p. 233. On the belief in were-wolves in general, see W. Hertz, Der Werwolf (Stuttgart, 1862) ; J. Grimm, Deutsche Mythologie,[4] i. 915 sqq.; (Sir) Edward B. Tylor, Primitive Culture [2] (London, 1873), i. 308 sqq.; R. Andree, Ethnographische Parallelen und Vergleiche (Stuttgart, 1878), pp. 62-80. In North Germany it is believed that a man can turn himself into a wolf by girding himself with a strap made out of a wolf's hide. Some say that the strap must have nine, others say twelve, holes and a buckle ; and that according to the number of the hole through which the man inserts the tongue of the buckle will be the length of time of his transformation. For example, if he puts the tongue of the buckle through the first hole, he will be a wolf for one hour ; if he puts it through the second, he will be a wolf for two days ; and so on, up to the last hole, which entails a transformation for a full year. But by putting off the girdle the man can resume his human form. The time when were-wolves are most about is the period of the Twelve Nights between Christmas and Epiphany ; hence cautious German farmers will not remove the dung from the cattle-stalls at that season for fear of attracting the were-wolves to the cattle. See Adalbert Kuhn, Märkische Sagen und Märchen (Berlin, 1843), p. 375 ; Ulrich Jahn, Volkssagen aus Pommern und Rügen (Stettin, 1886), pp. 384, 386, Nos. 491, 495. Down to the time of Elizabeth it was reported that in the county of Tipperary certain men were annually turned into wolves. See W. Camden, Britain, translated into English by Philemon Holland (London, 1610), "Ireland," p. 83.

were told that they could not see him ; for he had been out the
night before and had hurt his hand, and he was now ill in
bed.   So they put two and two together and reported him
to the police.   The police arrived, surrounded the house, and
set fire to it ; but Chu-Tu-shi rose from his bed, turned into a
tiger, charged right through the police, and escaped, and to
this day nobody ever knew where he went to.[1]

The Toradjas of Central Celebes stand in very great fear
of were-wolves, that is of men and women, who have the
power of transforming their spirits into animals such as cats,
crocodiles, wild pigs, apes, deer, and buffaloes, which roam
about battening on human flesh, and especially on human
livers, while the men and women in their own proper human
form are sleeping quietly in their beds at home.   Among
them a man is either born a were-wolf or becomes one by
infection ; for mere contact with a were-wolf, or even with
anything that has been touched by his spittle, is quite
enough to turn the most innocent person into a were-wolf ;
nay even to lean your head against anything against which a
were-wolf has leaned his head suffices to do it.   The penalty
for being a were-wolf is death ; but the sentence is never passed
until the accused has had a fair trial and his guilt has been
clearly demonstrated by an ordeal, which consists in dipping
the middle finger into boiling resin.   If the finger is not
burnt, the man is no were-wolf ; but if it is burnt, a were-
wolf he most assuredly is, so they take him away to a quiet
spot and hack him to bits.   In cutting him up the executioners are naturally very careful not to be bespattered
with his blood, for if that were to happen they would of
course be turned into were-wolves themselves.   Further,
they place his severed head beside his hinder-quarters to
prevent his soul from coming to life again and pursuing
his depredations.   So great is the horror of were-wolves
among the Toradjas, and so great is their fear of contracting
the deadly taint by infection, that many persons have assured
a missionary that they would not spare their own child if
they knew him to be a were-wolf.[2]   Now these people,

*Were-
wolves
among the
Toradjas
of Central
Celebes.*

[1] J. J. M. de Groot, *The Religious
System of China*, v. (Leyden, 1907)
p. 548.
   [2] A. C. Kruijt, " De weerwolf bij
de Toradja's van Midden-Celebes,"
*Tijdschrift voor Indische Taal- Land-
en Volkenkunde*, xli. (1899) pp. 548-
551, 557-560.

whose faith in were-wolves is not a mere dying or dead superstition but a living, dreadful conviction, tell stories of were-wolves which conform to the type which we are examining. They say that once upon a time a were-wolf came in human shape under the house of a neighbour, while his real body lay asleep as usual at home, and calling out softly to the man's wife made an assignation with her to meet him in the tobacco-field next day. But the husband was lying awake and he heard it all, but he said nothing to anybody. Next day chanced to be a busy one in the village, for a roof had to be put on a new house and all the men were lending a hand with the work, and among them to be sure was the were-wolf himself, I mean to say his own human self ; there he was up on the roof working away as hard as anybody. But the woman went out to the tobacco-field, and behind went unseen her husband, slinking through the underwood. When they were come to the field, he saw the were-wolf make up to his wife, so out he rushed and struck at him with a stick. Quick as thought, the were-wolf turned himself into a leaf, but the man was as nimble, for he caught up the leaf, thrust it into the joint of bamboo, in which he kept his tobacco, and bunged it up tight. Then he walked back with his wife to the village, carrying the bamboo with the were-wolf in it. When they came to the village, the human body of the were-wolf was still on the roof, working away with the rest. The man put the bamboo in a fire. At that the human were-wolf looked down from the roof and said, " Don't do that." The man drew the bamboo from the fire, but a moment afterwards he put it in the fire again, and again the human were-wolf on the roof looked down and cried, " Don't do that." But this time the man kept the bamboo in the fire, and when it blazed up, down fell the human were-wolf from the roof as dead as a stone.[1] Again, the following story went round among the Toradjas not so very many years ago. The thing happened at Soemara, on the Gulf of Tomori. It was evening and some men sat chatting with a certain Hadji Mohammad. When it had grown dark, one of the men went out of the house for something or other. A little while afterwards one of the company

[1] A. C. Kruijt, *op. cit.* pp. 552 *sq.*

thought he saw a stag's antlers standing out sharp and clear against the bright evening sky. So Hadji Mohammad raised his gun and fired. A minute or two afterwards back comes the man who had gone out, and says he to Hadji Mohammad, "You shot at me and hit me. You must pay me a fine." They searched him but found no wound on him anywhere. Then they knew that he was a were-wolf who had turned himself into a stag and had healed the bullet-wound by licking it. However, the bullet had found its billet, for two days afterwards he was a dead man.[1]

In Sennar, a province of the Egyptian Sudan, the Hammeg and Fungi enjoy the reputation of being powerful magicians who can turn themselves into hyaenas and in that guise scour the country at night, howling and gorging themselves. But by day they are men again. It is very dangerous to shoot at such human hyaenas by night. On the Jebel Bela mountain a soldier once shot at a hyaena and hit it, but it dragged itself off, bleeding, in the darkness and escaped. Next morning he followed up the trail of blood and it led him straight to the hut of a man who was everywhere known for a wizard. Nothing of the hyaena was to be seen, but the man himself was laid up in the house with a fresh wound and died soon afterwards. And the soldier did not long survive him.[2] *Werewolves in the Egyptian Sudan*

But the classical example of these stories is an old Roman tale told by Petronius. It is put in the mouth of one Niceros. Late at night he left the town to visit a friend of his, a widow, who lived at a farm five miles down the road. He *The werewolf story in Petronius.*

---

[1] A. C. Kruijt, *op. cit.* pp. 553. For more evidence of the belief in were-wolves, or rather in were-animals of various sorts, particularly were-tigers, in the East Indies, see J. J. M. de Groot, "De Weertijger in onze Koloniën en op het oostaziatische Vasteland," *Bijdragen tot de Taal- Land- en Volkenkunde van Nederlandsch-Indië,* xlix. (1898) pp. 549-585 ; G. P. Rouffaer, "Matjan Gadoengan," *Bijdragen tot de Taal- Land- en Volkenkunde van Neder- landsch-Indië,* l. (1899) pp. 67-75 ; J. Knebel, "De Weertijger op Midden-

Java, den Javaan naverteld," *Tijd- schrift voor Indische Taal- Land- en Volkenkunde,* xli. (1899) pp. 568-587 ; L. M. F. Plate, "Bijdrage tot de kennis van de lykanthropie bij de Sasaksche bevolking in Oost-Lombok," *Tijdschrift voor Indische Taal- Land- en Volkenkunde,* liv. (1912) pp. 458- 469 ; G. A. Wilken, "Het animisme bij de volken van den Indischen Archi- pel," *Verspreide Geschriften* (The Hague, 1912), iii. 25-30.

[2] Ernst Marno, *Reisen im Gebiete des blauen und weissen Nil* (Vienna, 1874), pp. 239 *sq.*

was accompanied by a soldier, who lodged in the same house, a man of Herculean build. When they set out it was near dawn, but the moon shone as bright as day. Passing through the outskirts of the town, they came amongst the tombs, which lined the highroad for some distance. There the soldier made an excuse for retiring behind a monument, and Niceros sat down to wait for him, humming a tune and counting the tombstones to pass the time. In a little he looked round for his companion, and saw a sight which froze him with horror. The soldier had stripped off his clothes to the last rag and laid them at the side of the highway. Then he performed a certain ceremony over them, and immediately was changed into a wolf, and ran howling into the forest. When Niceros had recovered himself a little, he went to pick up the clothes, but found that they were turned to stone. More dead than alive, he drew his sword, and, striking at every shadow cast by the tombstones on the moonlit road, he tottered to his friend's house. He entered it like a ghost, to the surprise of the widow, who wondered to see him abroad so late. " If you had only been here a little ago," said she, " you might have been of some use. For a wolf came tearing into the yard, scaring the cattle and bleeding them like a butcher. But he did not get off so easily, for the servant speared him in the neck." After hearing these words, Niceros felt that he could not close an eye, so he hurried away home again. It was now broad daylight, but when he came to the place where the clothes had been turned to stone, he found only a pool of blood. He reached home, and there lay the soldier in bed like an ox in the shambles, and the doctor was bandaging his neck. " Then I knew," said Niceros, " that the man was a were-wolf, and never again could I break bread with him, no, not if you had killed me for it." [1]

---

[1] Petronius, *Sat.* 61 *sq.* (pp. 40 *sq.*, ed. Fr. Buecheler,[3] Berlin, 1882). The Latin word for a were-wolf (*versipellis*) is expressive : it means literally " skin-shifter," and is equally appropriate whatever the particular animal may be into which the wizard transforms himself. It is to be regretted that we have no such general term in English.

The bright moonlight which figures in some of these were-wolf stories is perhaps not a mere embellishment of the tale but has its own significance ; for in some places it is believed that the transformation of were-wolves into their bestial shape takes place particularly at full moon. See A. de Nore, *Coutumes, Mythes et Traditions*

These stories may help us to understand the custom of Witches like were-wolves can temporarily transform themselves into animals. burning a bewitched animal, which has been observed in our own country down to recent times, if indeed it is even now extinct. For a close parallel may be traced in some respects between witches and were-wolves. Like were-wolves, witches are commonly supposed to be able to transform themselves temporarily into animals for the purpose of playing their mischievous pranks ;[1] and like were-wolves they can in their animal disguise be compelled to unmask themselves to any one who succeeds in drawing their blood. In either case the animal-skin is conceived as a cloak thrown round the wicked enchanter ; and if you can only pierce the skin, whether by the stab of a knife or the shot of a gun, you so rend the disguise that the man or woman inside of it stands revealed in his or her true colours. Strictly speaking, the stab should be given on the brow or between the eyes in the case both of a witch and of a were-wolf ;[2] and it is vain to shoot at a were-wolf unless you have had the bullet blessed in a chapel

---

des Provinces de France (Paris and Lyons, 1846), pp. 99, 157 ; J. L. M. Noguès, *Les Mœurs d'autrefois en Saintonge et en Aunis* (Saintes, 1891), p. 141.

[1] J. G. Campbell, *Witchcraft and Second Sight in the Highlands and Islands of Scotland* (Glasgow, 1902), p. 6 : " In carrying out their un-hallowed cantrips, witches assumed various shapes. They became gulls, cormorants, ravens, rats, mice, black sheep, swelling waves, whales, and very frequently cats and hares." To this list of animals into which witches can turn themselves may be added horses, dogs, wolves, foxes, pigs, owls, magpies, wild geese, ducks, serpents, toads, lizards, flies, wasps, and butter-flies. See A. Wuttke, *Der deutsche Volksaberglaube*[2] (Berlin, 1869), p. 150 § 217; L. Strackerjan, *Aberglaube und Sagen aus dem Herzogthum Olden-burg* (Oldenburg, 1867), i. 327 § 220 ; Ulrich Jahn, *Hexenwesen und Zauberei in Pommern* (Breslau, 1886), p. 7. In his *Topography of Ireland* (chap. 19), a work completed in 1187 A.D., Giraldus Cambrensis records that " it has also been a frequent complaint, from old

times as well as in the present, that certain hags in Wales, as well as in Ireland and Scotland, changed themselves into the shape of hares, that, sucking teats under this counterfeit form, they might stealthily rob other people's milk." See *The Historical Works of Giraldus Cambrensis*, revised and edited by Thomas Wright (London, 1887), p. 83.

[2] *The Folk-lore Journal*, iv. (1886) p. 266 ; Collin de Plancy, *Diction-naire Infernal* (Paris, 1825–1826), iii. 475 ; J. L. M. Noguès, *Les Mœurs d'autrefois en Saintonge et en Aunis* (Saintes, 1891), p. 141. In Scotland the cut was known as " scoring above the breath." It consisted of two in-cisions made crosswise on the witch's forehead, and was " confided in all throughout Scotland as the most power-ful counter-charm." See Sir Walter Scott, *Letters on Demonology and Witchcraft* (London, 1884), p. 272 ; J. G. Dalyell, *The Darker Super-stitions of Scotland* (Edinburgh, 1834), pp. 531 *sq.* ; M. M. Banks, " Scoring a Witch above the Breath," *Folk-lore*, xxiii. (1912) p. 490.

of St. Hubert or happen to be carrying about you, without
knowing it, a four-leaved clover ; otherwise the bullet will
merely rebound from the were-wolf like water from a duck's
back.[1]   However, in Armenia they say that the were-wolf,
who in that country is usually a woman, can be killed neither
by shot nor by steel ; the only way of delivering the unhappy
woman from her bondage is to get hold of her wolf's skin
and burn it ; for that naturally prevents her from turning
into a wolf again.   But it is not easy to find the skin, for
she is cunning enough to hide it by day.[2]   So with witches,
it is not only useless but even dangerous to shoot at one of
them when she has turned herself into a hare ; if you do, the
gun may burst in your hand or the shot come back and kill
you.   The only way to make quite sure of hitting a witch-
animal is to put a silver sixpence or a silver button in your
gun.[3]   For example, it happened one evening that a native
of the island of Tiree was going home with a new gun, when
he saw a black sheep running towards him across the plain
of Reef.   Something about the creature excited his suspicion,
so he put a silver sixpence in his gun and fired at it.
Instantly the black sheep became a woman with a drugget
coat wrapt round her head.   The man knew her quite well,
for she was a witch who had often persecuted him before in
the shape of a cat.[4]

Wounds
inflicted on
an animal
into which
a witch has
trans-
formed
herself are
inflicted on
the witch
herself.

Again, the wounds inflicted on a witch-hare or a witch-cat
are to be seen on the witch herself, just as the wounds inflicted
on a were-wolf are to be seen on the man himself when he
has doffed the wolf's skin.   To take a few instances out of
a multitude, a young man in the island of Lismore was
out shooting.   When he was near Balnagown loch, he started

---

[1] J. L. M. Noguès, *l.c.* ; L. F.
Sauvé, *Le Folk-lore des Hautes-Vosges*
(Paris, 1889), p. 187.

[2] M. Abeghian, *Der armenische
Volksglaube* (Leipsic, 1899), p. 117.
The wolf-skin is supposed to fall down
from heaven and to return to heaven
after seven years, if the were-wolf has
not been delivered from her unhappy
state in the meantime by the burning
of the skin.

[3] J. G. Campbell, *Witchcraft and*

*Second Sight in the Highlands and
Islands of Scotland* (Glasgow, 1902),
p. 8 ; compare A. Wuttke, *Der deutsche
Volksaberglaube*[2] (Berlin, 1869), p. 150
§ 217.   Some think that the sixpence
should be crooked.   See Rev. W.
Gregor, *Notes on the Folk-lore of the
North-East of Scotland* (London, 1881),
pp. 71 *sq.*, 128 ; *County Folk-lore*,
vol. v. *Lincolnshire*, collected by Mrs.
Gutch and Mabel Peacock (London,
1908), p. 75.

[4] J. G. Campbell, *op. cit.* p. 30.

a hare and fired at it.   The animal gave an unearthly scream,
and then for the first time it occurred to him that there were
no real hares in Lismore.   He threw away his gun in terror
and fled home ; and next day he heard that a notorious
witch was laid up with a broken leg.   A man need be no
conjuror to guess how she came by that broken leg.[1]   Again,
at Thurso certain witches used to turn themselves into cats
and in that shape to torment an honest man.   One night he
lost patience, whipped out his broadsword, and put them to
flight.   As they were scurrying away he struck at them and
cut off a leg of one of the cats.   To his astonishment it was
a woman's leg, and next morning he found one of the witches
short of the corresponding limb.[2]   Glanvil tells a story of
" an old woman in Cambridge-shire, whose astral spirit,
coming into a man's house (as he was sitting alone at the
fire) in the shape of an huge cat, and setting her self before
the fire, not far from him, he stole a stroke at the back of it
with a fire-fork, and seemed to break the back of it, but it
scambled from him, and vanisht he knew not how.   But
such an old woman, a reputed witch, was found dead in her
bed that very night, with her back broken, as I have heard
some years ago credibly reported."[3]   In Yorkshire during the
latter half of the nineteenth century a parish clergyman was
told a circumstantial story of an old witch named Nanny,
who was hunted in the form of a hare for several miles over
the Westerdale moors and kept well away from the dogs,
till a black one joined the pack and succeeded in taking a
bit out of one of the hare's legs.   That was the end of the
chase, and immediately afterwards the sportsmen found old
Nanny laid up in bed with a sore leg.   On examining the
wounded limb they discovered that the hurt was precisely in
that part of it which in the hare had been bitten by the
black dog and, what was still more significant, the wound had
all the appearance of having been inflicted by a dog's teeth.
So they put two and two together.[4]   The same sort of thing

---

[1] J. G. Campbell, *op. cit.* p. 33.

[2] (Sir) Edward B. Tylor, *Primitive
Culture* [2] (London, 1873), i. 314.

[3] Joseph   Glanvil,   *Saducismus
Triumphatus or Full and Plain*

*Evidence concerning Witches and Ap-
paritions* (London, 1681), Part ii. p.
205.

[4] Rev. J. C. Atkinson, *Forty Years
in a Moorland Parish* (London, 1891),
pp. 82-84.

is often reported in Lincolnshire. "One night," said a servant from Kirton Lindsey, "my father and brother saw a cat in front of them. Father knew it was a witch, and took a stone and hammered it. Next day the witch had her face all tied up, and shortly afterwards died." Again, a Bardney bumpkin told how a witch in his neighbourhood could take all sorts of shapes. One night a man shot a hare, and when he went to the witch's house he found her plastering a wound just where he had shot the hare.[1] So in County Leitrim, in Ireland, they say that a hare pursued by dogs fled to a house near at hand, but just as it was bolting in at the door one of the dogs came up with it and nipped a piece out of its leg. The hunters entered the house and found no hare there but only an old woman, and her side was bleeding; so they knew what to think of her.[2]

Wounded witches in the Vosges. Again, in the Vosges Mountains a great big hare used to come out every evening to take the air at the foot of the Mont des Fourches. All the sportsmen of the neighbourhood tried their hands on that hare for a month, but not one of them could hit it. At last one marksman, more knowing than the rest, loaded his gun with some pellets of a consecrated wafer in addition to the usual pellets of lead. That did the trick. If puss was not killed outright, she was badly hurt, and limped away uttering shrieks and curses in a human voice. Later it transpired that she was no other than the witch of a neighbouring village who had the power of putting on the shape of any animal she pleased.[3] Again, a hunter of Travexin, in the Vosges, fired at a hare and almost shot away one of its hind legs. Nevertheless the creature contrived to escape into a cottage through the open door. Immediately a child's cries were heard to proceed from the cottage, and the hunter could distinguish these words, "Daddy, daddy, come quick! Poor mammy has her leg broken."[4]

Wounded witches in Swabia. In Swabia the witches are liable to accidents of the same sort when they go about their business in the form

[1] *County Folk-lore*, vol. v. *Lincolnshire*, collected by Mrs. Gutch and Mabel Peacock (London, 1908), pp. 79, 80.

[2] Leland L. Duncan, "Folk-lore Gleanings from County Leitrim," *Folk-lore*, iv. (1893) pp. 183 *sq.*

[3] L. F. Sauvé, *Le Folk-lore des Hautes-Vosges* (Paris, 1889), p. 176.

[4] L. F. Sauvé, *op. cit.* pp. 176 *sq.*

of animals. For example, there was a soldier who was betrothed to a young woman and used to visit her every evening when he was off duty. But one evening the girl told him that he must not come to the house on Friday nights, because it was never convenient to her to see him then. This roused his suspicion, and the very next Friday night he set out to go to his sweetheart's house. On the way a white cat ran up to him in the street and dogged his steps, and when the animal would not make off he drew his sword and slashed off one of its paws. On that the cat bolted. The soldier walked on, but when he came to his sweetheart's house he found her in bed, and when he asked her what was the matter, she gave a very confused reply. Noticing stains of blood on the bed, he drew down the coverlet and saw that the girl was weltering in her gore, for one of her feet was lopped off. "So that's what's the matter with you, you witch!" said he, and turned on his heel and left her, and within three days she was dead.[1] Again, a farmer in the neighbourhood of Wiesensteig frequently found in his stable a horse over and above the four horses he actually owned. He did not know what to make of it and mentioned the matter to the smith. The smith said quietly, "The next time you see a fifth horse in the stable, just you send for me." Well, it was not long before the strange horse was there again, and the farmer at once sent for the smith. He came bringing four horse-shoes with him, and said, "I'm sure the nag has no shoes; I'll shoe her for you." No sooner said than done. However, the smith overreached himself; for next day when his friend the farmer paid him a visit he found the smith's own wife prancing about with horse-shoes nailed on her hands and feet. But it was the last time she ever appeared in the shape of a horse.[2]

Once more, in Silesia they tell of a miller's apprentice, a sturdy and industrious young fellow, who set out on his travels. One day he came to a mill, and the miller told

The miller's wife and the two grey cats

[1] Ernst Meier, *Deutsche Sagen, Sitten und Gebräuche aus Schwaben* (Stuttgart, 1852), pp. 184 *sq.*, No. 203.
[2] E. Meier, *op. cit.* pp. 191 *sq.*,

No. 215. A similar story of the shoeing of a woman in the shape of a horse is reported from Silesia. See R. Kühnau, *Schlesische Sagen* (Berlin, 1910–1913), iii. pp. 27 *sq.*, No. 1380.

him that he wanted an apprentice but did not care to engage one, because hitherto all his apprentices had run away in the night, and when he came down in the morning the mill was at a stand. However, he liked the looks of the young chap and took him into his pay. But what the new apprentice heard about the mill and his predecessors was not encouraging ; so the first night when it was his duty to watch in the mill he took care to provide himself with an axe and a prayer-book, and while he kept one eye on the whirring, humming wheels he kept the other on the good book, which he read by the flickering light of a candle set on a table. So the hours at first passed quietly with nothing to disturb him but the monotonous drone and click of the machinery. But on the stroke of twelve, as he was still reading with the axe lying on the table within reach, the door opened and in came two grey cats mewing, an old one and a young one. They sat down opposite him, but it was easy to see that they did not like his wakefulness and the prayer-book and the axe. Suddenly the old cat reached out a paw and made a grab at the axe, but the young chap was too quick for her and held it fast. Then the young cat tried to do the same for the prayer-book, but the apprentice gripped it tight. Thus balked, the two cats set up such a squalling that the young fellow could hardly say his prayers. Just before one o'clock the younger cat sprang on the table and fetched a blow with her right paw at the candle to put it out. But the apprentice struck at her with his axe and sliced the paw off, whereupon the two cats vanished with a frightful screech. The apprentice wrapped the paw up in paper to shew it to his master. Very glad the miller was next morning when he came down and found the mill going and the young chap at his post. The apprentice told him what had happened in the night and gave him the parcel containing the cat's paw. But when the miller opened it, what was the astonishment of the two to find in it no cat's paw but a woman's hand ! At breakfast the miller's young wife did not as usual take her place at the table. She was ill in bed, and the doctor had to be called in to bind up her right arm, because in hewing wood, so they said, she had made a slip and cut off her own right hand. But the apprentice packed up his traps and turned his back on that mill before the sun had set.[1]

It would no doubt be easy to multiply instances, all equally well attested and authentic, of the transformation of witches into animals and of the damage which the women themselves have sustained through injuries inflicted on the animals.[2] But the foregoing evidence may suffice to establish the complete parallelism between witches and were-wolves in these respects. The analogy appears to confirm the view that the reason for burning a bewitched animal alive is a belief that the witch herself is in the animal, and that by burning it you either destroy the witch completely or at least unmask her and compel her to reassume her proper human shape, in which she is naturally far less potent for mischief than when she is careering about the country in the likeness of a cat, a hare, a horse, or what not. This principle is still indeed clearly recognized by people in Oldenburg, though, as might be expected, they do not now carry out the principle to its logical conclusion by burning the bewitched animal or person alive; instead they resort to a feeble and, it must be added, perfectly futile subterfuge dictated by a mistaken humanity or a fear of the police. "When anything living is bewitched in a house, for example, children or animals, they burn or boil the nobler inwards of animals, especially the hearts, but also the lungs or the liver. If animals have died, they take the inwards of one of them or of an animal of the same kind slaughtered for the purpose; but if that is not possible they take the inwards of a cock, by preference a black one. The

[1] R. Kühnau, *Schlesische Sagen* (Berlin, 1910–1913), iii. pp. 23 *sq.*, No. 1375. Compare *id.*, iii. pp. 28 *sq.*, No. 1381.

[2] See for example L. Strackerjan, *Aberglaube und Sagen aus dem Herzogthum Oldenburg* (Oldenburg, 1867), i. pp. 328, 329, 334, 339; W. von Schulenburg, *Wendische Volkssagen und Gebräuche aus dem Spreewald* (Leipsic, 1880), pp. 164, 165 *sq.*; H. Pröhle, *Harzsagen* (Leipsic, 1859), i. 100 *sq.* The belief in such things is said to be universal among the ignorant and superstitious in Germany. See A. Wuttke, *Der deutsche Volksaberglaube* [2]

(Berlin, 1869), p. 150, § 217. In Wales, also, "the possibility of injuring or marking the witch in her assumed shape so deeply that the bruise remained a mark on her in her natural form was a common belief" (J. Ceredig Davies, *Folk-lore of West and Mid-Wales*, Aberystwyth, 1911, p. 243). For Welsh stories of this sort, see J. Ceredig Davies, *l.c.*; Rev. Elias Owen, *Welsh Folk-lore* (Oswestry and Wrexham, N.D., preface dated 1896), pp. 228 *sq.*; M. Trevelyan, *Folk-lore and Folk-stories of Wales* (London, 1909), p. 214.

heart, lung, or liver is stuck all over with needles, or marked with a cross cut, or placed on the fire in a tightly closed vessel, strict silence being observed and doors and windows well shut. When the heart boils or is reduced to ashes, the witch must appear, for during the boiling she feels the burning pain. She either begs to be released or seeks to borrow something, for example, salt or a coal of fire, or she takes the lid off the pot, or tries to induce the person whose spell is on her to speak. They say, too, that a woman comes with a spinning-wheel. If it is a sheep that has died, you proceed in the same way with a tripe from its stomach and prick it with needles while it is on the boil. Instead of boiling it, some people nail the heart to the highest rafter of the house, or lay it on the edge of the hearth, in order that it may dry up, no doubt because the same thing happens to the witch. We may conjecture that other sympathetic means of destruction are employed against witchcraft. The following is expressly reported : the heart of a calf that has died is stuck all over with needles enclosed in a bag, and thrown into flowing water before sunset." [1]

There is the same reason for burning bewitched things.

And the same thing holds good also of inanimate objects on which a witch has cast her spell. In Wales they say that " if a thing is bewitched, burn it, and immediately afterwards the witch will come to borrow something of you. If you give what she asks, she will go free ; if you refuse it, she will burn, and a mark will be on her body the next day." [2] So, too, in Oldenburg, " the burning of things that are bewitched or that have been received from witches is another way of breaking the spell. It is often said that the burning should take place at a cross-road, and in several places cross-roads are shewn where the burning used to be performed. . . . As a rule, while the things are burning, the guilty witches appear, though not always in their own shape. At the burning of bewitched butter they often appear as cockchafers and can be killed with impunity. Victuals received from witches may be safely consumed if only you

---

[1] L. Strackerjan, *Aberglaube und Sagen aus dem Herzogthum Oldenburg* (Oldenburg, 1867), i. p. 361, § 239.

[2] Marie Trevelyan, *Folk - lore and Folk-stories of Wales* (London, 1909), p. 210.

first burn a portion of them."[1]   For example, a young man
in Oldenburg was wooing a girl, and she gave him two fine
apples as a gift.   Not feeling any appetite at the time, he
put the apples in his pocket, and when he came home he
laid them by in a chest.   Two or three days afterwards he
remembered the apples and went to the chest to fetch them.
But when he would have put his hand on them, what was
his horror to find in their stead two fat ugly toads in the
chest!   He hastened to a wise man and asked him what he
should do with the toads.   The man told him to boil the
toads alive, but while he was doing so he must be sure on no
account to lend anything out of the house.   Well, just as he
had the toads in a pot on the fire and the water began to
grow nicely warm, who should come to the door but the girl
who had given him the apples, and she wished to borrow
something ; but he refused to give her anything, rated her
as a witch, and drove her out of the house.   A little afterwards in came the girl's mother and begged with tears in her
eyes for something or other ; but he turned her out also.
The last word she said to him was that he should at least
spare her daughter's life ; but he paid no heed to her and
let the toads boil till they fell to bits.   Next day word came
that the girl was dead.[2]   Can any reasonable man doubt
that the witch herself was boiled alive in the person of the
toads ?

Moreover, just as a witch can assume the form of an
animal, so she can assume the form of some other human
being, and the likeness is sometimes so good that it is
difficult to detect the fraud.   However, by burning alive
the person whose shape the witch has put on, you force
the witch to disclose herself, just as by burning alive the
bewitched animal you in like manner oblige the witch to
appear.   This principle may perhaps be unknown to science,
falsely so called, but it is well understood in Ireland and has
been acted on within recent years.   In March 1895 a peasant
named Michael Cleary, residing at Ballyvadlea, a remote and
lonely district in the county of Tipperary, burned his wife

Similarly by burning alive a person whose form a witch has assumed, you compel the witch to disclose herself.

The burning alive of a supposed witch in Ireland in 1895.

[1] L. Strackerjan, *Aberglaube und Sagen aus dem Herzogthum Oldenburg* (Oldenburg, 1867), i. p. 358, § 238.

[2] L. Strackerjan, *op. cit.* i. p. 360, § 238e.

Bridget Cleary alive over a slow fire on the kitchen hearth in the presence of and with the active assistance of some neighbours, including the woman's own father and several of her cousins. They thought that she was not Bridget Cleary at all, but a witch, and that when they held her down on the fire she would vanish up the chimney; so they cried, while she was burning, " Away she goes ! Away she goes !" Even when she lay quite dead on the kitchen floor (for contrary to the general expectation she did not disappear up the chimney), her husband still believed that the woman lying there was a witch, and that his own dear wife had gone with the fairies to the old *rath* or fort on the hill of Kylena- granagh, where he would see her at night riding a grey horse and roped to the saddle, and that he would cut the ropes, and that she would stay with him ever afterwards. So he went with some friends to the fort night after night, taking a big table-knife with him to cut the ropes. But he never saw his wife again. He and the men who had held the woman on the fire were arrested and tried at Clonmel for wilful murder in July 1895 ; they were all found guilty of man- slaughter and sentenced to various terms of penal servitude and imprisonment ; the sentence passed on Michael Cleary was twenty years' penal servitude.[1]

Sometimes bewitched animals are buried alive instead of being burned.

However, our British peasants, it must be confessed, have not always acted up to the strict logical theory which seems to call for death by fire as the proper treatment both of bewitched animals and of witches. Sometimes, perhaps in moments of weakness, they have merely buried the bewitched animals alive instead of burning them. For example, in the year 1643, "many cattle having died, John Brughe and Neane Nikclerith, also one of the initiated, conjoined their mutual skill for the safety of the herd. The surviv- ing animals were drove past a tub of water containing two enchanted stones : and each was sprinkled from the liquid contents in its course. One, however, being unable to walk, 'was by force drawin out at the byre dure ;

---

[1] " The ' Witch-burning ' at Clon- mell," *Folk-lore*, vi. (1895) pp. 373- 384. The account there printed is based on the reports of the judicial proceedings before the magistrates and the judge, which were published in *The Irish Times* for March 26th, 27th, and 28th, April 2nd, 3rd, 6th, and 8th, and July 6th, 1895.

and the said Johnne with Nikclerith smelling the nois thereof said it wald not leive, caused ane hoill to be maid in Maw Greane, quhilk was put quick in the hole and maid all the rest of the cattell theireftir to go over that place : and in that devillische maner, be charmeing,' they were cured." [1]   Again, during the prevalence of a murrain about the year 1629, certain persons proposed to stay the plague with the help of a celebrated " cureing stane" of which the laird of Lee was the fortunate owner.   But from this they were dissuaded by one who " had sene bestiall curet be taking ane quik seik ox, and making ane deip pitt, and bureing him therin, and be calling the oxin and bestiall over that place."   Indeed Issobell Young, the mother of these persons, had herself endeavoured to check the progress of the distemper by taking " ane quik ox with ane catt, and ane grit quantitie of salt," and proceeding " to burie the ox and catt quik with the salt, in ane deip hoill in the grund, as ane sacrifice to the devill, that the rest of the guidis might be fred of the seiknes or diseases." [2]   Writing towards the end of the eighteenth century, John Ramsay of Ochtertyre tells us that " the violent death even of a brute is in some cases held to be of great avail.   There is a disease called the *black spauld*, which sometimes rages like a pestilence among black cattle, the symptoms of which are a mortification in the legs and a corruption of the mass of blood.   Among the other engines of superstition that are directed against this fatal malady, the first cow seized with it is commonly buried alive, and the other cattle are forced to pass backwards and forwards over the pit.   At other times the heart is taken out of the beast alive, and then the carcass is buried.   It is remarkable that the leg affected is cut off, and hung up in some part of the house or byre, where it remains suspended, notwithstanding the seeming danger of infection. There is hardly a house in Mull where these may not be seen.   This practice seems to have taken its rise antecedent to Christianity, as it reminds us of the pagan custom of

---

[1] John Graham Dalyell, *The Darker Superstitions of Scotland* (Edinburgh, 1834), p. 185. In this passage " quick" is used in the old sense of " living," as in the phrase " the qᵘick and the dead."

Nois is " nose," *hoill* is " hole," *quhilk* (*whilk*) is " which," and *be* is " by."

[2] J. G. Dalyell, *op. cit.* p. 186. *Bestiall* = animals ; *seik* = sick ; *calling* = driving ; *guidis* = cattle.

hanging up offerings in their temples. In Breadalbane, when a cow is observed to have symptoms of madness, there is recourse had to a peculiar process. They tie the legs of the mad creature, and throw her into a pit dug at the door of the fold. After covering the hole with earth, a large fire is kindled upon it ; and the rest of the cattle are driven out, and forced to pass through the fire one by one." [1]   In this latter custom we may suspect that the fire kindled on the grave of the buried cow was originally made by the friction of wood, in other words, that it was a need-fire. Again, writing in the year 1862, Sir Arthur Mitchell tells us that " for the cure of the murrain in cattle, one of the herd is still sacrificed for the good of the whole. This is done by burying it alive. I am assured that within the last ten years such a barbarism occurred in the county of Moray." [2]

Calves killed and buried to save the rest of the herd.   Sometimes, however, the animal has not even been buried alive, it has been merely killed and then buried. In this emasculated form the sacrifice, we may say with confidence, is absolutely useless for the purpose of stopping a murrain. Nevertheless, it has been tried. Thus in Lincolnshire, " when the cattle plague was so prevalent in 1866, there was, I believe, not a single cowshed in Marshland but had its wicken cross over the door ; and other charms more powerful than this were in some cases resorted to. I never heard of the use of the needfire in the Marsh, though it was, I believe, used on the wolds not many miles off. But I knew of at least one case in which a calf was killed and solemnly buried feet pointing upwards at the threshold of the cowshed. When our garth-man told me of this, I pointed out to him that the charm had failed, for the disease had not spared that shed. But he promptly replied, ' Yis, but owd Edwards were a soight too cliver ; he were that mean he slew nobbutt a wankling cauf as were bound to deny anny road ; if he had nobbutt tekken his best cauf it wud hev worked reight enuff ; 'tain't

<hr>

[1] John Ramsay, of Ochtertyre, *Scotland and Scotsmen in the Eighteenth Century*, edited by Alexander Allardyce (Edinburgh and London, 1888), ii. 446 *sq.* As to the custom of cutting off the leg of a diseased animal and hanging it up in the house, see above,

p. 296, note [1].

[2] (Sir) Arthur Mitchell, A.M., M.D., *On Various Superstitions in the North-West Highlands and Islands of Scotland* (Edinburgh, 1862), p. 12 (reprinted from the *Proceedings of the Society of Antiquaries of Scotland*, vol. iv.).

in reason that owd skrat 'ud be hanselled wi' wankling draffle.' " [1]

[1] *County Folk-lore*, vol. v. *Lincolnshire*, collected by Mrs. Gutch and Mabel Peacock (London, 1908), p. 75, quoting Rev. R. M. Heanley, " The Vikings : traces of their Folklore in Marshland," a paper read before the Viking Club, London, and printed in its *Saga-Book*, vol. iii. Part i. Jan. 1902. The wicken-tree is the mountain-ash or rowan tree, which is a very efficient, or at all events a very popular protective against witchcraft. See *County Folk-lore*, vol. v. *Lincolnshire*, pp. 26 *sq.*, 98 *sq.* ; Mabel Peacock, " The Folklore of Lincolnshire," *Folklore*, xii. (1901) p. 175 ; J. G. Campbell, *Witchcraft and Second Sight in the Highlands and Islands of Scotland* (Glasgow, 1902), pp. 11 *sq.* ; Rev. Walter Gregor, *Notes on the Folk-lore of the North-East of Scotland* (London, 1881), p. 188. See further *The Scapegoat*, pp. 266 *sq.*

CHAPTER V

THE INTERPRETATION OF THE FIRE-FESTIVALS

§ 1. *On the Fire-festivals in general*

General resemblance of the European fire-festivals to each other.

THE foregoing survey of the popular fire-festivals of Europe suggests some general observations. In the first place we can hardly help being struck by the resemblance which the ceremonies bear to each other, at whatever time of the year and in whatever part of Europe they are celebrated. The custom of kindling great bonfires, leaping over them, and driving cattle through or round them would seem to have been practically universal throughout Europe, and the same may be said of the processions or races with blazing torches round fields, orchards, pastures, or cattle-stalls. Less widespread are the customs of hurling lighted discs into the air [1] and trundling a burning wheel down hill ; [2] for to judge by the evidence which I have collected these modes of distributing the beneficial influence of the fire have been confined in the main to Central Europe. The ceremonial of the Yule log is distinguished from that of the other fire-festivals by the privacy and domesticity which characterize it ; but, as we have already seen, this distinction may well be due simply to the rough weather of midwinter, which is apt not only to render a public assembly in the open air disagreeable, but also at any moment to defeat the object of the assembly by extinguishing the all-important fire under a downpour of rain or a fall of snow. Apart from these local or seasonal differences, the general resemblance between

[1] Above, pp. 116 *sq.*, 119, 143, 141, 143, 161, 162 *sq.*, 163 *sq.*, 166, 165, 166, 168 *sq.*, 172.   173, 191, 201.
[2] Above, pp. 116, 117 *sq.*, 119,

the fire-festivals at all times of the year and in all places is tolerably close.   And as the ceremonies themselves resemble each other, so do the benefits which the people expect to reap from them.   Whether applied in the form of bonfires blazing at fixed points, or of torches carried about from place to place, or of embers and ashes taken from the smouldering heap of fuel, the fire is believed to promote the growth of the crops and the welfare of man and beast, either positively by stimulating them, or negatively by averting the dangers and calamities which threaten them from such causes as thunder and lightning, conflagration, blight, mildew, vermin, sterility, disease, and not least of all witchcraft.

But we naturally ask, How did it come about that benefits so great and manifold were supposed to be attained by means so simple?   In what way did people imagine that they could procure so many goods or avoid so many ills by the application of fire and smoke, of embers and ashes?   In short, what theory underlay and prompted the practice of these customs?   For that the institution of the festivals was the outcome of a definite train of reasoning may be taken for granted ; the view that primitive man acted first and invented his reasons to suit his actions afterwards, is not borne out by what we know of his nearest living representatives, the savage and the peasant.   Two different explanations of the fire-festivals have been given by modern enquirers.   On the one hand it has been held that they are sun-charms or magical ceremonies intended, on the principle of imitative magic, to ensure a needful supply of sunshine for men, animals, and plants by kindling fires which mimic on earth the great source of light and heat in the sky.   This was the view of Wilhelm Mannhardt.[1]   It may be called the solar theory.   On the other hand it has been maintained that the ceremonial fires have no necessary reference to the sun but are simply purificatory in intention, being designed to burn up and destroy all harmful influences, whether these are conceived in a personal form as witches, demons, and monsters, or in an impersonal form as a sort of pervading taint or corruption of the air.   This is the view of Dr.

Two explanations suggested of the fire-festivals. According to W. Mannhardt, they are charms to secure a supply of sunshine ; according to Dr. E. Westermarck they are purificatory, being intended to burn and destroy all harmful influences.

[1] W. Mannhardt, *Der Baumkultus der Germanen und ihrer Nachbarstämme* (Berlin, 1875), pp. 521 *sqq.*

Edward Westermarck [1] and apparently of Professor Eugen Mogk.[2] It may be called the purificatory theory. Obviously the two theories postulate two very different conceptions of the fire which plays the principal part in the rites. On the one view, the fire, like sunshine in our latitude, is a genial creative power which fosters the growth of plants and the development of all that makes for health and happiness ; on the other view, the fire is a fierce destructive power which blasts and consumes all the noxious elements, whether spiritual or material, that menace the life of men, of animals, and of plants. According to the one theory the fire is a stimulant, according to the other it is a disinfectant ; on the one view its virtue is positive, on the other it is negative.

The two explanations are perhaps not mutually exclusive.

Yet the two explanations, different as they are in the character which they attribute to the fire, are perhaps not wholly irreconcilable. If we assume that the fires kindled at these festivals were primarily intended to imitate the sun's light and heat, may we not regard the purificatory and disinfecting qualities, which popular opinion certainly appears to have ascribed to them, as attributes derived directly from the purificatory and disinfecting qualities of sunshine ? In this way we might conclude that, while the imitation of sunshine in these ceremonies was primary and original, the purification attributed to them was secondary and derivative. Such a conclusion, occupying an intermediate position between the two opposing theories and recognizing an element of truth in both of them, was adopted by me in earlier editions of this work ; [3] but in the meantime Dr. Wester-

[1] E. Westermarck, "Midsummer Customs in Morocco," *Folk-lore,* xvi. (1905) pp. 44 *sqq.* ; *id., The Origin and Development of the Moral Ideas* (London, 1906–1908), i. 56 ; *id., Ceremonies and Beliefs connected with Agriculture, certain Dates of the Solar Year, and the Weather in Morocco* (Helsingfors, 1913), pp. 93-102.

[2] E. Mogk, "Sitten und Gebräuche im Kreislauf des Jahres," in R. Wuttke's *Sächsische Volkskunde* [2] (Dresden, 1901), pp. 310 *sq.*

[3] *The Golden Bough,* Second Edition (London, 1900), iii. 312 : "The custom of leaping over the fire

and driving cattle through it may be intended, on the one hand, to secure for man and beast a share of the vital energy of the sun, and, on the other hand, to purge them of all evil influences ; for to the primitive mind fire is the most powerful of all purificatory agents"; and again, *id.* iii. 314 : "It is quite possible that in these customs the idea of the quickening power of fire may be combined with the conception of it as a purgative agent for the expulsion or destruction of evil beings, such as witches and the vermin that destroy the fruits of the earth. Certainly the fires are often inter-

marck has argued powerfully in favour of the purificatory theory alone, and I am bound to say that his arguments carry great weight, and that on a fuller review of the facts the balance of evidence seems to me to incline decidedly in his favour.   However, the case is not so clear as to justify us in dismissing the solar theory without discussion, and accordingly I propose to adduce the considerations which tell for it before proceeding to notice those which tell against it.   A theory which had the support of so learned and sagacious an investigator as W. Mannhardt is entitled to a respectful hearing.

§ 2. *The Solar Theory of the Fire-festivals*

In an earlier part of this work we saw that savages resort to charms for making sunshine,[1] and it would be no wonder if primitive man in Europe did the same.   Indeed, when we consider the cold and cloudy climate of Europe during a great part of the year, we shall find it natural that sun-charms should have played a much more prominent part among the superstitious practices of European peoples than among those of savages who live nearer the equator and who consequently are apt to get in the course of nature more sunshine than they want.   This view of the festivals may be supported by various arguments drawn partly from their dates, partly from the nature of the rites, and partly from the influence which they are believed to exert upon the weather and on vegetation.

Theory that the fire-festivals are charms to ensure a supply of sunshine.

First, in regard to the dates of the festivals it can be no mere accident that two of the most important and widely spread of the festivals are timed to coincide more or less exactly with the summer and winter solstices, that is, with the two turning-points in the sun's apparent course in the sky when he reaches respectively his highest and his lowest elevation at noon.   Indeed with respect to the midwinter celebration of Christmas we are not left to conjecture; we

Coincidence of two of the festivals with the solstices.

preted in the latter way by the persons who light them ; and this purgative use of the element comes out very prominently, as we have seen, in the general expulsion of demons from towns and villages.   But in the present class of cases this aspect of fire may be secondary, if indeed it is more than a later misinterpretation of the custom."

[1] *The Magic Art and the Evolution of Kings*, i. 311 *sqq.*

know from the express testimony of the ancients that it was instituted by the church to supersede an old heathen festival of the birth of the sun,[1] which was apparently conceived to be born again on the shortest day of the year, after which his light and heat were seen to grow till they attained their full maturity at midsummer. Therefore it is no very far-fetched conjecture to suppose that the Yule log, which figures so prominently in the popular celebration of Christmas, was originally designed to help the labouring sun of midwinter to rekindle his seemingly expiring light.

Attempt of the Bush-men to warm up the fire of Sirius in midwinter by kindling sticks.

The idea that by lighting a log on earth you can rekindle a fire in heaven or fan it into a brighter blaze, naturally seems to us absurd; but to the savage mind it wears a different aspect, and the institution of the great fire-festivals which we are considering probably dates from a time when Europe was still sunk in savagery or at most in barbarism. Now it can be shewn that in order to increase the celestial source of heat at midwinter savages resort to a practice analogous to that of our Yule log, if the kindling of the Yule log was originally a magical rite intended to rekindle the sun. In the southern hemisphere, where the order of the seasons is the reverse of ours, the rising of Sirius or the Dog Star in July marks the season of the greatest cold instead of, as with us, the greatest heat; and just as the civilized ancients ascribed the torrid heat of midsummer to that brilliant star,[2] so the modern savage of South Africa attributes to it the piercing cold of midwinter and seeks to mitigate its rigour by warming up the chilly star with the genial heat of the sun. How he does so may be best described in his own words as follows :—[3]

---

[1] See *Adonis, Attis, Osiris,* Second Edition, pp. 254 *sqq.*

[2] Manilius, *Astronom.* v. 206 *sqq.* :

"*Cum vero in vastos surget Nemeaeus hiatus,*
Exoriturque Canis, latratque Canicula flammas
Et rabit igne suo geminatque incendia solis,
Qua subdente facem terris radiosque movente," etc.

Pliny, *Naturalis Historia,* xviii. 269 *sq.* : "*Exoritur dein post triduum fere*

ubique confessum inter omnes sidus ingens quod canis ortum vocamus, sole partem primam leonis ingresso. Hoc fit post solstitium XXIII. die. Sentiunt id maria et terrae, multae vero et ferae, ut suis locis diximus. Neque est minor ei veneratio quam descriptis in deos stellis, accenditque solem et magnam aestus obtinet causam."

[3] *Specimens of Bushman Folklore,* collected by the late W. H. I. Bleek, Ph.D., and L. C. Lloyd (London, 1911), pp. 339, 341. In quoting the

" The Bushmen perceive Canopus, they say to a child :
' Give me yonder piece of wood, that I may put the end of
it in the fire, that I may point it burning towards grandmother, for grandmother carries Bushman rice ; grandmother
shall make a little warmth for us ; for she coldly comes out ;
the sun [1] shall warm grandmother's eye for us.'   Sirius comes
out ; the people call out to one another : ' Sirius comes
yonder ;' they say to one another : ' Ye must burn a stick for
us towards Sirius.'   They say to one another : ' Who was it
who saw Sirius ? '   One man says to the other : ' Our brother
saw Sirius.'   The other man says to him : ' I saw Sirius.'
The other man says to him : ' I wish thee to burn a stick
for us towards Sirius ; that the sun may shining come out
for us ; that Sirius may not coldly come out.'   The other
man (the one who saw Sirius) says to his son : ' Bring me
the small piece of wood yonder, that I may put the end
of it in the fire, that I may burn it towards grandmother ;
that grandmother may ascend the sky, like the other one,
Canopus.'   The child brings him the piece of wood, he (the
father) holds the end of it in the fire.   He points it burning
towards Sirius ; he says that Sirius shall twinkle like
Canopus.   He sings ; he sings about Canopus, he sings
about Sirius ; he points to them with fire,[2] that they may
twinkle like each other.   He throws fire at them.   He
covers himself up entirely (including his head) in his kaross
and lies down.   He arises, he sits down ; while he does not
again lie down ; because he feels that he has worked, putting
Sirius into the sun's warmth ; so that Sirius may warmly
come out.   The women go out early to seek for Bushman
rice ; they walk, sunning their shoulder blades." [3]   What the
Bushmen thus do to temper the cold of midwinter in the
southern hemisphere by blowing up the celestial fires may
have been done by our rude forefathers at the corresponding
season in the northern hemisphere.

---

passage I have omitted the brackets
which the editors print for the purpose
of indicating the words which are
implied, but not expressed, in the
original Bushman text.

[1] " The sun is a little warm, when
this star appears in winter " (Editors of

Specimens of Bushman Folklore).

[2] " With the stick that he had held
in the fire, moving it up and down
quickly " (Editors).

[3] " They take one arm out of the
kaross, thereby exposing one shoulder
blade to the sun " (Editors).

The burn-
'ng wheels
and discs
of the fire-
festivals
may be
direct
imitations
of the sun.

Not only the date of some of the festivals but the manner of their celebration suggests a conscious imitation of the sun. The custom of rolling a burning wheel down a hill, which is often observed at these ceremonies, might well pass for an imitation of the sun's course in the sky, and the imitation would be especially appropriate on Midsummer Day when the sun's annual declension begins. Indeed the custom has been thus interpreted by some of those who have recorded it.[1] Not less graphic, it may be said, is the mimicry of his apparent revolution by swinging a burning tar-barrel round a pole.[2] Again, the common practice of throwing fiery discs, sometimes expressly said to be shaped like suns, into the air at the festivals may well be a piece of imitative magic. In these, as in so many cases, the magic force may be supposed to take effect through mimicry or sympathy : by imitating the desired result you actually produce it : by counterfeiting the sun's progress through the heavens you really help the luminary to pursue his celestial journey with punctuality and despatch. The name " fire of heaven," by which the midsummer fire is sometimes popularly known,[3] clearly implies a consciousness of a connexion between the earthly and the heavenly flame.

The wheel
sometimes
used to
kindle the
fire by
friction

Again, the manner in which the fire appears to have been originally kindled on these occasions has been alleged in support of the view that it was intended to be a mock-sun. As some scholars have perceived, it is highly probable

---

[1] See above, pp. 161, 162 sq. On the wheel as an emblem of the sun, see J. Grimm, Deutsche Mythologie,[4] ii. 585 ; A. Kuhn, Die Herabkunft des Feuers und des Göttertranks [2] (Gütersloh, 1886), pp. 45 sqq. ; H. Gaidoz, " Le dieu gaulois du soleil et le symbolisme de la roue," Revue Archéologique, iii. Série, iv. (1884) pp. 14 sqq. ; William Simpson, The Buddhist Praying Wheel (London, 1896), pp. 87 sqq. It is a popular Armenian idea that " the body of the sun has the shape of the wheel of a water-mill ; it revolves and moves forward. As drops of water sputter from the mill-wheel, so sunbeams shoot out from the spokes of the sun-wheel " (M. Abeghian, Der armenische Volks-

glaube, Leipsic, 1899, p. 41). In the old Mexican picture-books the usual representation of the sun is " a wheel, often brilliant with many colours, the rays of which are so many blood-stained tongues, by means of which the Sun receives his nourishment " (E. J. Payne, History of the New World called America, Oxford, 1892, i. 521).

[2] Above, p. 169.

[3] Ernst Meier, Deutsche Sagen, Sitten und Gebräuche aus Schwaben (Stuttgart, 1852), p. 225 ; F. Panzer, Beitrag zur deutschen Mythologie (Munich, 1848–1855), ii. 240 ; Anton Birlinger, Volksthümliches aus Schwaben (Freiburg im Breisgau, 1861–1862), ii. 57, 97 ; W. Mannhardt, Baumkultus, p. 510.

that at the periodic festivals in former times fire was may also be an imitation of the sun
universally obtained by the friction of two pieces of wood.[1]
We have seen that it is still so procured in some places both
at the Easter and the midsummer festivals, and that it is
expressly said to have been formerly so procured at the
Beltane celebration both in Scotland and Wales.[2] But what
makes it nearly certain that this was once the invariable
mode of kindling the fire at these periodic festivals is the
analogy of the need-fire, which has almost always been
produced by the friction of wood, and sometimes by the
revolution of a wheel. It is a plausible conjecture that the
wheel employed for this purpose represents the sun,[3] and if
the fires at the regularly recurring celebrations were formerly
produced in the same way, it might be regarded as a confirmation of the view that they were originally sun-charms.
In point of fact there is, as Kuhn has indicated,[4] some
evidence to shew that the midsummer fire was originally
thus produced. We have seen that many Hungarian swineherds make fire on Midsummer Eve by rotating a wheel
round a wooden axle wrapt in hemp, and that they drive
their pigs through the fire thus made.[5] At Obermedlingen,
in Swabia, the 'fire of heaven,' as it was called, was made
on St. Vitus's Day (the fifteenth of June) by igniting a cart-
wheel, which, smeared with pitch and plaited with straw,
was fastened on a pole twelve feet high, the top of the pole
being inserted in the nave of the wheel. This fire was

---

[1] Compare J. Grimm, *Deutsche
Mythologie*,[4] i. 521 ; J. W. Wolf,
Beiträge zur deutschen Mythologie
(Göttingen und Leipsic, 1852–1857),
ii. 389 ; Adalbert Kuhn, *Die Herab-
kunft des Feuers und des Göttertranks*[2]
(Gütersloh, 1886), pp. 41 *sq.*, 47 ;
W. Mannhardt, *Baumkultus*, p. 521.
Lindenbrog in his Glossary on the
Capitularies (quoted by J. Grimm,
Deutsche Mythologie,[4] i. 502) expressly
says : "The rustics in many parts of
Germany, particularly on the festival of
St. John the Baptist, wrench a stake
from a fence, wind a rope round it,
and pull it to and fro till it catches
fire. This fire they carefully feed with
straw and dry sticks and scatter the
ashes over the vegetable gardens,
foolishly and superstitiously imagining
that in this way the caterpillar can be
kept off. They call such a fire *nodfeur*
or *nodfyr*, that is to say need-fire."

[2] Above, pp. 144 *sq.*, 147 *sq.*, 155,
169 *sq.*, 175, 177, 179.

[3] J. Grimm, *Deutsche Mythologie*,[4]
i. 509 ; J. W. Wolf, *Beiträge zur
deutschen Mythologie*, i. 117 ; A. Kuhn,
Die Herabkunft des Feuers,[2] pp. 47 *sq.* ;
W. Mannhardt, *Baumkultus*, p. 521 ;
W. E. Kelly, *Curiosities of Indo-
European Tradition and Folk-lore*
(London, 1863), p. 49.

[4] A. Kuhn, *Die Herabkunft des
Feuers und des Göttertranks*[2] (Gütersloh, 1886), p. 47.

[5] Above, p. 179.

made on the summit of a mountain, and as the flame ascended, the people uttered a set form of words, with eyes and arms directed heavenward.[1]   Here the fixing of a wheel on a pole and igniting it suggests that originally the fire was produced, as in the case of the need-fire, by the revolution of a wheel.   The day on which the ceremony takes place (the fifteenth of June) is near midsummer ; and we have seen that in Masuren fire is, or used to be, actually made on Midsummer Day by turning a wheel rapidly about an oaken pole,[2] though it is not said that the new fire so obtained is used to light a bonfire.   However, we must bear in mind that in all such cases the use of a wheel may be merely a mechanical device to facilitate the operation of fire-making by increasing the friction ; it need not have any symbolical significance.

The influence which the fires are supposed to exert on the weather and vegetation may be thought to be due to an increase of solar heat produced by the fires.

Further, the influence which these fires, whether periodic or occasional, are supposed to exert on the weather and vegetation may be cited in support of the view that they are sun-charms, since the effects ascribed to them resemble those of sunshine.   Thus, the French belief that in a rainy June the lighting of the midsummer bonfires will cause the rain to cease[3] appears to assume that they can disperse the dark clouds and make the sun to break out in radiant glory, drying the wet earth and dripping trees.   Similarly the use of the need-fire by Swiss children on foggy days for the purpose of clearing away the mist[4] may very naturally be interpreted as a sun-charm.   Again, we have seen that in the Vosges Mountains the people believe that the midsummer fires help to preserve the fruits of the earth and ensure good crops.[5]   In Sweden the warmth or cold of the coming season is inferred from the direction in which the flames of the May Day bonfire are blown ; if they blow to the south, it will be warm, if to the north, cold.[6]   No doubt at present the direction of the flames is regarded merely as an augury of the weather, not as a mode of influencing it. But we may be pretty sure that this is one of the cases in which magic has dwindled into divination.   So in the Eifel

---

[1] F. Panzer, *Beitrag zur deutschen Mythologie* (Munich, 1848–1855), ii. 240, § 443.

[2] Above, p. 177.

[3] Above, pp. 187 *sq.*

[4] Above, pp. 279 *sq.*

[5] Above, p. 188.

[6] Above, p. 159.

Mountains, when the smoke blows towards the corn-fields, this is an omen that the harvest will be abundant.[1] But the older view may have been not merely that the smoke and flames prognosticated, but that they actually produced an abundant harvest, the heat of the flames acting like sunshine on the corn. Perhaps it was with this view that people in the Isle of Man lit fires to windward of their fields in order that the smoke might blow over them.[2] So in South Africa, about the month of April, the Matabeles light huge fires to the windward of their gardens, "their idea being that the smoke, by passing over the crops, will assist the ripening of them."[3] Among the Zulus also "medicine is burned on a fire placed to windward of the garden, the fumigation which the plants in consequence receive being held to improve the crop."[4] Again, the idea of our European peasants that the corn will grow well as far as the blaze of the bonfire is visible,[5] may be interpreted as a remnant of the belief in the quickening and fertilizing power of the bonfires. The same belief, it may be argued, reappears in the notion that embers taken from the bonfires and inserted in the fields will promote the growth of the crops,[6] and it may be thought to underlie the customs of sowing flax-seed in the direction in which the flames blow,[7] of mixing the ashes of the bonfire with the seed-corn at sowing,[8] of scattering the ashes by themselves over the field to fertilize it,[9] and of incorporating a piece of the Yule log in the plough to make the seeds thrive.[10] The opinion that the flax or hemp will grow as high as the flames rise or the people leap over them [11] belongs clearly to the same class of ideas. Again, at Konz, on the banks of the Moselle, if the blazing wheel which was trundled down the hillside reached the river without being extinguished, this was hailed as a proof that the

[1] Above, p. 116.

[2] Above, p. 201.

[3] L. Decle, *Three Years in Savage Africa* (London, 1898), pp. 160 *sq.*

[4] Rev. J. Shooter, *The Kafirs of Natal and the Zulu Country* (London, 1857), p. 18.

[5] Above, pp. 140, 142.

[6] Above, pp. 119, 165, 166, 173, 203.

[7] Above, p. 140.

[8] Above, p. 121.

[9] Above, pp. 141, 170, 190, 203, 248, 250, 264.

[10] Above, p. 251.

[11] Above, pp. 119, 165, 166, 168, 173, 174.

vintage would be abundant. So firmly was this belief held that the successful performance of the ceremony entitled the villagers to levy a tax upon the owners of the neighbouring vineyards.[1] Here the unextinguished wheel might be taken to represent an unclouded sun, which in turn would portend an abundant vintage. So the waggon-load of white wine which the villagers received from the vineyards round about might pass for a payment for the sunshine which they had procured for the grapes. Similarly we saw that in the Vale of Glamorgan a blazing wheel used to be trundled down hill on Midsummer Day, and that if the fire were extinguished before the wheel reached the foot of the hill, the people expected a bad harvest; whereas if the wheel kept alight all the way down and continued to blaze for a long time, the farmers looked forward to heavy crops that summer.[2] Here, again, it is natural to suppose that the rustic mind traced a direct connexion between the fire of the wheel and the fire of the sun, on which the crops are dependent.

The effect which the bonfires are supposed to have in fertilizing cattle and women may also be attributed to an increase of solar heat produced by the fires.

But in popular belief the quickening and fertilizing influence of the bonfires is not limited to the vegetable world; it extends also to animals. This plainly appears from the Irish custom of driving barren cattle through the midsummer fires,[3] from the French belief that the Yule-log steeped in water helps cows to calve,[4] from the French and Servian notion that there will be as many chickens, calves, lambs, and kids as there are sparks struck out of the Yule log,[5] from the French custom of putting the ashes of the bonfires in the fowls' nests to make the hens lay eggs,[6] and from the German practice of mixing the ashes of the bonfires with the drink of cattle in order to make the animals thrive.[7] Further, there are clear indications that even human fecundity is supposed to be promoted by the genial heat of the fires. In Morocco the people think that childless couples can obtain offspring by leaping over the midsummer bonfire.[8] It is an Irish belief that a girl who jumps thrice over the midsummer bonfire will soon marry and become the mother

1 Above, pp. 118, 163 *sq.*
2 Above, p. 201.
3 Above, p. 203.
4 Above, p. 250.

5 Above, pp. 251, 262, 263, 264.
6 Above, p. 112.
7 Above, p. 141.
8 Above, p. 214.

of many children ;[1] in Flanders women leap over the Mid-summer fires to ensure an easy delivery ;[2] and in various parts of France they think that if a girl dances round nine fires she will be sure to marry within the year.[3] On the other hand, in Lechrain people say that if a young man and woman, leaping over the midsummer fire together, escape unsmirched, the young woman will not become a mother within twelve months :[4] the flames have not touched and fertilized her. In parts of Switzerland and France the lighting of the Yule log is accompanied by a prayer that the women may bear children, the she-goats bring forth kids, and the ewes drop lambs.[5] The rule observed in some places that the bonfires should be kindled by the person who was last married[6] seems to belong to the same class of ideas, whether it be that such a person is sup-posed to receive from, or to impart to, the fire a generative and fertilizing influence. The common practice of lovers leaping over the fires hand in hand may very well have originated in a notion that thereby their marriage would be blessed with offspring ; and the like motive would explain the custom which obliges couples married within the year to dance to the light of torches.[7] And the scenes of profligacy which appear to have marked the midsummer celebration among the Esthonians,[8] as they once marked the celebration of May Day among ourselves, may have sprung, not from the mere license of holiday-makers, but from a crude notion that such orgies were justified, if not required, by some mysterious bond which linked the life of man to the courses of the heavens at this turning-point of the year.

At the festivals which we are considering the custom of kindling bonfires is commonly associated with a custom of carrying lighted torches about the fields, the orchards, the pastures, the flocks and the herds; and we can hardly doubt that the two customs are only two different ways of attain-ing the same object, namely, the benefits which are believed to flow from the fire, whether it be stationary or portable.

The custom of carrying lighted torches about the country at the festivals may be explained

---

[1] Above, p. 204.
[2] Above, p. 194.
[3] Above, pp. 185, 189; compare p. 174.
[4] Above, p. 166.

[5] Above, pp. 249, 250.
[6] Above, pp. 107, 109, 111, 119; compare pp. 116, 192, 193.
[7] Above, p. 115.
[8] Above, p. 180.

as an
attempt to
diffuse the
sun's heat.

Accordingly if we accept the solar theory of the bonfires, we seem bound to apply it also to the torches; we must suppose that the practice of marching or running with blazing torches about the country is simply a means of diffusing far and wide the genial influence of the sunshine, of which these flickering flames are a feeble imitation. In favour of this view it may be said that sometimes the torches are carried about the fields for the express purpose of fertilizing them,[1] and for the same purpose live coals from the bonfires are sometimes placed in the fields "to prevent blight."[2] On the Eve of Twelfth Day in Normandy men, women, and children run wildly through the fields and orchards with lighted torches, which they wave about the branches and dash against the trunks of the fruit-trees for the sake of burning the moss and driving away the moles and field mice. "They believe that the ceremony fulfils the double object of exorcizing the vermin whose multiplication would be a real calamity, and of imparting fecundity to the trees, the fields, and even the cattle"; and they imagine that the more the ceremony is prolonged, the greater will be the crop of fruit next autumn.[3] In Bohemia they say that the corn will grow as high as they fling the blazing besoms into the air.[4] Nor are such notions confined to Europe. In Corea, a few days before the New Year festival, the eunuchs of the palace swing burning torches, chanting invocations the while, and this is supposed to ensure bountiful crops for the next season.[5] The custom of trundling a burning wheel

---

[1] Above, pp. 113, 142, 170, 233. The torches of Demeter, which figure so largely in her myth and on her monuments, are perhaps to be explained by this custom. See *Spirits of the Corn and of the Wild*, i. 57. W. Mannhardt thought (*Baumkultus*, p. 536) that the torches in the modern European customs are imitations of lightning. At some of their ceremonies the Indians of North-West America imitate lightning by means of pitch-wood torches which are flashed through the roof of the house. See J. G. Swan, quoted by Franz Boas, "The Social Organization and the Secret Societies of the Kwakiutl Indians," *Report of the United States*

National Museum for 1895 (Washington, 1897), p. 639.

[2] Above, p. 203.

[3] Amélie Bosquet, *La Normandie Romanesque et Merveilleuse* (Paris and Rouen, 1845), pp. 295 *sq.*; Jules Lecœur, *Esquisses du Bocage Normand* (Condé-sur-Noireau, 1883–1887), ii. 126-129. See *The Scapegoat*, pp. 316 *sq.*

[4] Br. Jelínek, "Materialen zur Vorgeschichte und Volkskunde Böhmens," *Mittheilungen der anthropolog. Gesellschaft in Wien*, xxi. (1891) p. 13 note.

[5] Mrs. Bishop, *Korea and her Neighbours* (London, 1898), ii. 56 *sq.*

over the fields, which used to be observed in Poitou for the express purpose of fertilizing them,[1] may be thought to embody the same idea in a still more graphic form ; since in this way the mock-sun itself, not merely its light and heat represented by torches, is made actually to pass over the ground which is to receive its quickening and kindly influence.   Once more, the custom of carrying lighted brands round cattle[2] is plainly equivalent to driving the animals through the bonfire ; and if the bonfire is a sun-charm, the torches must be so also.

§ 3. *The Purificatory Theory of the Fire-festivals*

Thus far we have considered what may be said for the theory that at the European fire-festivals the fire is kindled as a charm to ensure an abundant supply of sunshine for man and beast, for corn and fruits.   It remains to consider what may be said against this theory and in favour of the view that in these rites fire is employed not as a creative but as a cleansing agent, which purifies men, animals, and plants by burning up and consuming the noxious elements, whether material or spiritual, which menace all living things with disease and death.

Theory that the fires at the festivals are purifica-tory, being intended to burn up all harmful things.

First, then, it is to be observed that the people who practise the fire-customs appear never to allege the solar theory in explanation of them, while on the contrary they do frequently and emphatically put forward the purificatory theory.   This is a strong argument in favour of the puri-ficatory and against the solar theory ; for the popular ex-planation of a popular custom is never to be rejected except for grave cause.   And in the present case there seems to be no adequate reason for rejecting it.   The conception of fire as a destructive agent, which can be turned to account for the consumption of evil things, is so simple and obvious that it could hardly escape the minds even of the rude peasantry with whom these festivals originated.   On the other hand the conception of fire as an emanation of the sun, or at all events as linked to it by a bond of physical sympathy, is far less simple and obvious ; and though the

The puri-ficatory or destructive effect of the fires is often alleged by the people who light them.

---

[1] Above, pp. 190 *sq*.   [2] Above, pp. 178, 205, 206.

use of fire as a charm to produce sunshine appears to be undeniable,[1] nevertheless in attempting to explain popular customs we should never have recourse to a more recondite idea when a simpler one lies to hand and is supported by the explicit testimony of the people themselves. Now in the case of the fire-festivals the destructive aspect of fire is one upon which the people dwell again and again ; and it is highly significant that the great evil against which the fire is directed appears to be witchcraft. Again and again we are told that the fires are intended to burn or repel the witches ;[2] and the intention is sometimes graphically expressed by burning an effigy of a witch in the fire.[3] Hence, when we remember the great hold which the dread of witchcraft has had on the popular European mind in all ages, we may suspect that the primary intention of all these fire-festivals was simply to destroy or at all events get rid of the witches, who were regarded as the causes of nearly all the misfortunes and calamities that befall men, their cattle, and their crops.[4]

The great evil against which the fire at the festivals is directed appears to be witchcraft.

[1] See *The Magic Art and the Evolution of Kings*, i. 311 *sqq.*

[2] Above, pp. 108, 109, 116, 118 *sq.*, 121, 148, 154, 156, 157, 159, 160, 170, 171, 174, 175, 176, 180, 183, 185, 188, 232 *sq.*, 245, 252, 253, 280, 292, 293, 295, 297. For more evidence of the use of fire to burn or expel witches on certain days of the year, see *The Scapegoat*, pp. 158 *sqq.* Less often the fires are thought to burn or repel evil spirits and vampyres. See above, pp. 146, 170, 172, 202, 252, 282, 285. Sometimes the purpose of the fires is to drive away dragons (above, pp. 161, 195).

[3] Above, pp. 107, 116, 118 *sq.*, 159.

[4] " In short, of all the ills incident to the life of man, none are so formidable as witchcraft, before the combined influence of which, to use the language of an honest man who had himself severely suffered from its effects, the great laird of Grant himself could not stand them if they should fairly yoke upon him " (W. Grant Stewart, *The Popular Superstitions and Festive Amusements of the Highlanders of Scotland*, Edinburgh, 1823, pp. 202 *sq.*). " Every misfortune and calamity that took place in the parish, such as ill-health, the death of friends, the loss of stock, and the failure of crops ; yea to such a length did they carry their superstition, that even the inclemency of the seasons, were attributed to the influence of certain old women who were supposed to be in league, and had dealings with the Devil. These the common people thought had the power and too often the inclination to injure their property, and torment their persons " (*County Folk-lore*, vol. v. *Lincolnshire*, collected by Mrs. Gutch and Mabel Peacock, London, 1908, p. 76). " The county of Salop is no exception to the rule of superstition. The late vicar of a parish on the Clee Hills, startled to find that his parishioners still believed in witchcraft, once proposed to preach a sermon against it, but he was dissuaded from doing so by the parish schoolmaster, who assured him that the belief was so deeply rooted in the people's minds that he would be more likely to alienate them from the Church than to weaken their

This suspicion is confirmed when we examine the evils for which the bonfires and torches were supposed to provide a remedy. Foremost, perhaps, among these evils we may reckon the diseases of cattle ; and of all the ills that witches are believed to work there is probably none which is so constantly insisted on as the harm they do to the herds, particularly by stealing the milk from the cows.[1] Now it is significant that the need-fire, which may perhaps be regarded as the parent of the periodic fire-festivals, is kindled above all as a remedy for a murrain or other disease of cattle ; and the circumstance suggests, what on general grounds seems probable, that the custom of kindling the need-fire goes back to a time when the ancestors of the European peoples subsisted chiefly on the products of their herds, and when agriculture as yet played a subordinate part in their lives. Witches and wolves are the two great foes still dreaded by the herdsman in many parts of Europe ;[2] and we need not wonder that he should resort to fire as a powerful means of

Amongst the evils for which the fire-festivals are deemed remedies the foremost is cattle-disease, and cattle-disease is often supposed to be an effect of witchcraft.

---

faith in witchcraft" (Miss C. F. Burne and Miss G. F. Jackson, *Shropshire Folk-lore*, London, 1883, p. 145). "Wherever a man or any living creature falls sick, or a misfortune of any kind happens, without any natural cause being discoverable or rather lying on the surface, there in all probability witchcraft is at work. The sudden stiffness in the small of the back, which few people can account for at the time, is therefore called a 'witch-shot' and is really ascribed to witchcraft" (L. Strackerjan, *Aberglaube und Sagen aus dem Herzogthum Oldenburg*, Oldenburg, 1867, i. p. 298, § 209). What Sir Walter Scott said less than a hundred years ago is probably still true : "The remains of the superstition sometimes occur ; there can be no doubt that the vulgar are still addicted to the custom of scoring above the breath (as it is termed), and other counter-spells, evincing that the belief in witchcraft is only asleep, and might in remote corners be again awakened to deeds of blood" (*Letters on Demonology and Witchcraft*, London, 1884, p. 272). Compare L. Strackerjan, *op. cit.* i. p.

340, § 221 : "The great power, the malicious wickedness of the witches, cause them to be feared and hated by everybody. The hatred goes so far that still at the present day you may hear it said right out that it is a pity burning has gone out of fashion, for the evil crew deserve nothing else. Perhaps the hatred might find vent yet more openly, if the fear were not so great."

[1] For some evidence, see *The Magic Art and the Evolution of Kings*, ii. 52-55, 330 *sqq*. It is a popular belief, universally diffused in Germany, that cattle-plagues are caused by witches (A. Wuttke, *Der deutsche Volksaberglaube*,[2] Berlin, 1869, p. 149 § 216). The Scotch Highlanders thought that a witch could destroy the whole of a farmer's live stock by hiding a small bag, stuffed with charms, in a cleft of the stable or byre (W. Grant Stewart, *The Popular Superstitions and Festive Amusements of the Highlanders of Scotland*, Edinburgh, 1823, pp. 201 *sq.*).

[2] *The Magic Art and the Evolution of Kings*, ii. 330 *sqq*.

banning them both.   Among Slavonic peoples it appears that
the foes whom the need-fire is designed to combat are not so
much living witches as vampyres and other evil spirits,[1] and
the ceremony, as we saw, aims rather at repelling these
baleful beings than at actually consuming them in the
flames.   But for our present purpose these distinctions are
immaterial.   The important thing to observe is that among
the Slavs the need-fire, which is probably the original of all
the ceremonial fires now under consideration, is not a sun-
charm, but clearly and unmistakably nothing but a means of
protecting man and beast against the attacks of maleficent
creatures, whom the peasant thinks to burn or scare by the
heat of the fire, just as he might burn or scare wild animals.

Again, the
bonfires are
thought to
avert hail,
thunder,
lightning,
and other
maladies,
all of
which are
attributed
to the
maleficent
arts of
witches.

Again, the bonfires are often supposed to protect the
fields against hail[2] and the homestead against thunder and
lightning.[3]   But both hail and thunderstorms are frequently
thought to be caused by witches;[4] hence the fire which
bans the witches necessarily serves at the same time as a
talisman against hail, thunder, and lightning.   Further,
brands taken from the bonfires are commonly kept in
the houses to guard them against conflagration;[5] and
though this may perhaps be done on the principle of
homoeopathic magic, one fire being thought to act as a
preventive of another, it is also possible that the intention
may be to keep witch-incendiaries at bay.   Again, people
leap over the bonfires as a preventive of colic,[6] and look
at the flames steadily in order to preserve their eyes in
good health;[7] and both colic and sore eyes are in Germany,
and probably elsewhere, set down to the machinations of
witches.[8]   Once more, to leap over the Midsummer fires or

---

[1] Above, pp. 282, 284 *sq.*

[2] Above, pp. 118, 121, 144, 145, 176.

[3] Above, pp. 121, 122, 124, 140 *sq.*, 145, 146, 174, 176, 183, 184, 187, 188, 190, 191, 192, 249, 250, 252, 253, 254, 258.

[4] J. Grimm, *Deutsch Mythologie*,[4] ii. 908 *sqq.*; J. V. Grohmann, *Aberglauben und Gebräuche aus Böhmen und Mähren* (Prague and Leipsic, 1864), p. 32 § 182) ; A. Wuttke, *Der deutsche Volksaberglaube*[2] (Berlin, 1869), pp. 149 *sq.*, § 216; J. Ceredig Davies,

Folk-lore of West and Mid-Wales (Aberystwyth, 1911), p. 230; Alois John, *Sitte, Brauch und Volksglaube im deutschen Westböhmen* (Prague, 1905), p. 202.

[5] Above, pp. 108, 121, 140, 146, 165, 183, 188, 196, 250, 255, 256, 258.

[6] Above, pp. 107, 195 *sq.*

[7] Above, pp. 162, 163, 166, 171, 174.

[8] A. Wuttke, *Der deutsche Volksaberglaube*[2] (Berlin, 1869), p. 351, § 395.

to circumambulate them is thought to prevent a person from feeling pains in his back at reaping ;[1] and in Germany such pains are called "witch-shots" and ascribed to witchcraft.[2]

But if the bonfires and torches of the fire-festivals are to be regarded primarily as weapons directed against witches and wizards, it becomes probable that the same explanation applies not only to the flaming discs which are hurled into the air, but also to the burning wheels which are rolled down hill on these occasions; discs and wheels, we may suppose, are alike intended to burn the witches who hover invisible in the air or haunt unseen the fields, the orchards, and the vineyards on the hillside.[3] Certainly witches are constantly thought to ride through the air on broomsticks or other equally convenient vehicles ; and if they do so, how can you get at them so effectually as by hurling lighted missiles, whether discs, torches, or besoms, after them as they flit past overhead in the gloom ?   The South Slavonian peasant believes that witches ride in the dark hail-clouds ; so he shoots at the clouds to bring down the hags, while he curses them, saying, "Curse, curse Herodias, thy mother is a heathen, damned of God and fettered through the Redeemer's blood." Also he brings out a pot of glowing charcoal on which he has thrown holy oil, laurel leaves, and wormwood to make a smoke. The fumes are supposed to ascend to the clouds and stupefy the witches, so that they tumble down to earth. And in order that they may not fall soft, but may hurt themselves very much, the yokel hastily brings out a chair and tilts it bottom up so that the witch in falling may break her legs on the legs of the chair. Worse than that, he cruelly lays scythes, bill-hooks and other formidable weapons edge upwards so as to cut and mangle

---

[1] Above, pp. 165, 168, 189, compare 190.

[2] A. Wuttke, *Der deutsche Volksaberglaube*[2] (Berlin, 1869), p. 351, § 395 ; L. Strackerjan, *Aberglaube und Sagen aus dem Herzogthum Oldenburg* (Oldenburg, 1867), i. p. 298, § 209. See above, p. 343 note.

[3] In the Ammerland, a district of Oldenburg, you may sometimes see an old cart-wheel fixed over the principal door or on the gable of a house ; it serves as a charm against witchcraft and is especially intended to protect the cattle as they are driven out and in. See L. Strackerjan, *Aberglaube und Sagen aus dem Herzogthum Oldenburg* (Oldenburg, 1867), i. p. 357, § 236. Can this use of a wheel as a talisman against witchcraft be derived from the practice of rolling fiery wheels down hill for a similar purpose ?

the poor wretches when they drop plump upon them from the clouds.[1]

On this view the fertility supposed to follow the application of fire in the form of bonfires, torches, discs, rolling wheels, and so forth, is not conceived as resulting directly from an increase of solar heat which the fire has magically generated ; it is merely an indirect result obtained by freeing the reproductive powers of plants and animals from the fatal obstruction of witchcraft. And what is true of the reproduction of plants and animals may hold good also of the fertility of the human sexes. We have seen that the bonfires are supposed to promote marriage and to procure offspring for childless couples. This happy effect need not flow directly from any quickening or fertilizing energy in the fire ; it may follow indirectly from the power of the fire to remove those obstacles which the spells of witches and wizards notoriously present to the union of man and wife.[2]

On the whole, then, the theory of the purificatory virtue of the ceremonial fires appears more probable and more in accordance with the evidence than the opposing theory of their connexion with the sun. But Europe is not the only part of the world where ceremonies of this sort have been performed ; elsewhere the passage through the flames or smoke or over the glowing embers of a bonfire, which is the central feature of most of the rites, has been employed as a cure or a preventive of various ills. We have seen that the midsummer ritual of fire in Morocco is practically identical with that of our European peasantry ; and customs more or less similar have been observed by many races in various parts of the world. A consideration of some of them may help us to decide between the conflicting claims of the two rival theories, which explain the ceremonies as sun-charms or purifications respectively.

[1] F. S. Krauss, *Volksglaube und religiöser Brauch der Südslaven* (Münster i. W., 1890), pp. 118 *sq.*

[2] In German such spells are called *Nestelknüpfen* ; in French, *nouer l'aiguilette.* See J. Grimm, *Deutsche Mythologie,*[4] ii. 897, 983 ; A. Wuttke, *Der deutsche Volksaberglaube*[2] (Berlin, 1869), p. 252 § 396 ; E. Doutté, *Magie et Religion dans l'Afrique du Nord* (Algiers, 1908), pp. 87 *sq.*, 294 *sqq.* ; J. L. M. Noguès, *Les Mœurs d'autrefois en Saintonge et en Aunis* (Saintes, 1891), pp. 171 *sq.*